ALEXANDER KASTALSKY: HIS LIFE AND MUSIC

Alexander Kastalsky:
his Life and Music

SVETLANA ZVEREVA
State Institute for the Study of the Arts, Moscow

Translated by STUART CAMPBELL
University of Glasgow

ASHGATE

Published by   Ashgate Publishing Company
Ashgate Publishing Limited   Suite 420
Gower House   101 Cherry Street
Croft Road   Burlington, VT 05401-4405
Aldershot   USA
Hampshire GU11 3HR
England

The photograph on the dust jacket is from the collection of Russian Music Publishing, Moscow. Reproduced by permission.

Ashgate website: http//www.ashgate.com

British Library Cataloguing in Publication Data
Zvereva, Svetlana
    Alexander Kastalsky : his life and music
    1.Kastalsky, Alexander - Criticism and interpretation
    I.Title
    780.9'2

Library of Congress Cataloging-in-Publication Data
Zvereva, S. G. (Svetlana Georgievna)
    [Aleksandr Kastal'skii. English]
    Alexander Kastalsky : his life and music / Svetlana Zvereva.
        p. cm.
    Translation and 2nd version of S.G. Zvereva's Aleksandr Kastal'skii, including results of the author's research conducted since the original 1999 publication.
    Includes bibliographical references (p.) and index.
    ISBN 0-7546-0975-8 (alk. paper)
    1. Kastal§'kiæ, Aleksandr Dmitrievich, 1856-1926. 2. Church musicians--Russia--Biography. 3. Music--Russia--History and criticism. I. Title.

ML410.K1897 Z9413 2003
781.71'19'0092--dc21   2002034249

ISBN 0 7546 0975 8

Printed and bound in Great Britain by MPG Books Ltd, Bodmin, Cornwall

Contents

List of Plates

These can be found between pages 138–139

1 Archpriest D.I. Kastalsky, the composer's father. Moscow, second half of the 1870s

2 O.S. Kastalskaya, the composer's mother. Moscow, 1860s

3 Sasha Kastalsky (Alexander) with his sister Katya. Moscow, first half of the 1860s

4 A.D. Kastalsky with his wife Natalia. Late 1880s or early 1890s

5 Teachers at the Synodal School
Seated: D.I. Kokorin (1), A.V. Preobrazhensky (2), S.V. Smolensky (3), A.K. Smirnov (4), V.S. Orlov (6)
Standing: D.G. Grigoryev (2), A.D. Kastalsky (4), Yu.A. Lazarev (6)
Moscow, late 1890s

6 A.D. Kastalsky. Moscow, early 1900s

7 A performance of Kastalsky's *Play of the Furnace* by the Synodal Choir in the hall of the Synodal School. Moscow, 10 April 1909

8 A.D. Kastalsky, F.P. Stepanov, N.M. Danilin in the Augusteo concert hall. Rome, 1911

9 A.D. Kastalsky and the teacher N.N. Belkin (to the left of Kastalsky) with third-year students of the Moscow People's Choir Academy. Moscow, 1923

Preface

For many Russian composers of all generations, the ambience of the Russian Orthodox Church was an inalienable part of the environment where they lived and worked. Whether the church touched them spiritually or intellectually or not, it was always present in the background. Colourfully bedecked clergy processed; gloriously polychrome buildings glowed with icons, their designs conceived (and possibly executed) centuries ago; the odours of incense, candlewax and oil; the glorious sound of Russian voices in music alternating majesty with contemplation; and a bustle of purposeful activity around each worshipper while something timeless, of more solemn import, proceeded at a pace of its own in the sanctuary. To those sensitive to the experience, these elements formed an overwhelming amalgam of sights, sounds and smells, as they still are today. And even at those periods when the actual musical language parted company with the notions current in secular music of what was good, or with the ideals of what seemed, to the minds of serious people, appropriate to the worship of Almighty God, the grandeur inherent in the manner of performance kept the amalgam largely intact. Even without the impressive facade presented by imposing ritual, for many centuries the ideas and ideals clustered around the theology of the Orthodox Church were inseparable from those associated with the Russian state in its successive forms, and with the philosophical and social thought propounded by Russia's thinkers, writers and other artists. In Muscovy, as in imperial Russia, church and state were never separated.

For a long period in the twentieth century, however, this link was deliberately attenuated. The church, that essential constituent of the Russian background which, according to national tradition, should have been inescapable, was denied, with determined and brutal efforts made to eradicate it. In the post-Soviet era, with the opening or re-opening of many Russian Orthodox places of worship, and with clergymen once again conspicuous among the community, Orthodoxy seems to have recovered a great part of its former place in the life of the nation. The aesthetic aspect of this spiritual revival is shown in the emergence of more choirs singing sacred music, in both the church and the concert hall; demand for sheet music increased rapidly, and in new economic circumstances supply rose in response to demand.

It is possible to discern anew, without caveats and compromise, and discuss again this significant component even of Russian secular art and to acknowledge the interlocking of the sacred and secular within it. The perspective of art scholars has adjusted to a more natural, better balanced view of their subject, a view which may now be expressed with no hindrance save the financial constraints of the world of publishing. Curiosity about the repertories that flourished before also grew, and stimulated the market for books on church music; this growth goes hand in hand, of course, with a burgeoning of publications about every aspect of religious faith, with a natural concentration on the dominant indigenous form of Christianity.

An important series of volumes under the title 'Russian Sacred Music in Documents and Materials' began publication in Moscow in 1998 (see bibliography under 1998 and 2002 for particulars); there was by then no need to disguise music for the church as 'monuments of choral art' or 'masterpieces of Russian music of the Middle Ages'. This series opened with a focus on an important current in Russian church music of the turn of the nineteenth and twentieth centuries, a current which flowed in parallel with other simultaneous currents in the arts in Russia, as well as resembling developments elsewhere in certain points. The New Direction taken by the Moscow Synodal School of Church Music sought to retain (and where possible regain) what was precious in the oldest music of Russian Orthodoxy through the study of manuscript sources, to cultivate its features and virtues in new composition, and to create a church style sharing many of the musical features of Russian folk music being defined for the first time by their contemporaries; these features had been sensed in the nineteenth century, but had not been systematically recorded and codified until almost the arrival of the twentieth. Exploring modes rather than keys; exploiting the melodic variants which proliferated in Russian folksong practice; using heterophony (the simultaneous presence of more than one version of essentially the same melody); developing sonorities idiomatic to choral music; searching out fresh ideas for musical structure with roots in the groundplans of church music or the patterns of folk music rather than in the tonal basis of the sonata principle and its kindred in the tradition of European art music – these were some of the ideas cultivated by the composers of the New Direction.

The musical results, whether new compositions or old music studied and restored to use, met the criteria of being Russian in origin, founded on tradition, and sounding suitable for use in divine worship. Students of nineteenth-century church music will find some familiar elements in this outlook. Perhaps the most obvious is that of seeking artistic salvation in the present by appealing to the past. For many nineteenth-century artists and scholars, history conferred a welcome authority on their work. By recovering the integrity of the ancient, purity could be restored in the contemporary. Combining the scholarly examination of old sources with putting them back into practical use brings to mind the work on Gregorian chant carried out by several generations of Benedictines at Solesmes from 1833; like them, Stepan Smolensky and his successors in Russian musical palaeography wished to see the cause advanced by the publication of old sources in facsimiles and editions. The idea of a church style distinct from that of the concert hall or the opera house brings to mind many traditions in the church music of that time, from the Oxford movement initiated in the 1830s to the ideals of the École Niedermeyer in Paris as reformulated in 1853, or the Cecilian movement in German-speaking Roman Catholicism of the century's final decades. A variety of composers and styles were put forward as ideal embodiments of an austere and sacred tone suitable for worship, with Palestrina's champions the most numerous and diverse. The first collected edition of his compositions was published between 1862 and 1903, closely comparable in date with the *Gesamtausgaben* of Bach and Handel which demonstrated a related concern with recovering (in the interests of scholarship, performance and education) the art of great artists of earlier times. Universalism, for some represented by the golden age when Latin was the only language of worship in western Christianity, contended with local or national allegiances, for instance in Carl von Winterfeld's extraordinary promotion of the mainly forgotten Johannes Eccard as the composer of church music ideal for Lutherans, or Anglican support for John Marbeck, who had similarly been largely overlooked for several centuries.

Perhaps the closest approximation to the Moscow Synodal School is to be found in the Schola Cantorum, which opened its doors in Paris in 1894. Both schools provided a broad, rounded education in music which did not shy away from thorough study of academic musical subjects; neither was a mere craft school for church musicians, though both redressed a certain neglect of church music in rival institutions. Both championed reform in the music of their respective liturgical traditions, expecting to discover a road to a better future via the past. Both cultivated the music of earlier composers (Rameau and Monteverdi besides the expected Palestrina and Victoria in the case of the Schola Cantorum). And most intriguingly of all, both schools had a foot in the camp of ethnography: Charles Bordes collected and published Basque music at the behest of the Ministry of Education and drew on that experience in his own compositions; Vincent d'Indy used themes from his family region of the Ardèche in his works; and many of the New Direction's composers exploited features assimilated from Russian folk usage. Another example which shows developments in parallel might be the *English Hymnal* first published in 1906, with its emphases on plainsong, on the one hand, and folk melodies, on the other, and its compilers' desire to offer an alternative to the worldly values of excessive sentimentality or jovial muscularity found in the music of some Victorian hymns. The details of these apparent congruences remain to be explored, and there are, no doubt, areas of significant divergence. It is tempting to find contemporary points of similarity across boundaries of language, religious practice and tradition, though it can prove confusing.

The Russian composers had the benefit of a first-rate choir to perform their works; the Synodal Choir existed in the closest relationship to the Synodal School. A leading figure in both organizations was Alexander Kastalsky. He is the subject of this book, which is in fact the second to appear in the series mentioned above, though not so numbered; the book has arisen to a great extent out of the primary sources assembled for other volumes in the enterprise. The largest part of Kastalsky's energies as a composer, and the prime of his life, were devoted to composition for the church. Along with Smolensky the scholar, Kastalsky, as composer, folklorist and *animateur*, was the most compelling incarnation of the aims and ideals of the Synodal School. After 1917, it was a case of salvaging as much as possible from nearly 40 years of work, and Kastalsky earned his living in fields of composition other than church music. For many years, it was difficult to take an interest in his earlier works, and the later compositions with distinctly Soviet topics cast a pall over the earlier ones. His sacred works have not before been the object of detailed study, and nor has his career been presented as a whole until now.

Besides showing Kastalsky himself, his compositions and other activities in a new light, the book also sets him in the context of his time. And seen in that light, we find that Kastalsky not only had a great deal in common with contemporary Russian composers but in fact forged some of the ideas we hear in the works of composers more familiar to us.

For instance, Rachmaninoff's All-Night Vigil was composed in 1915 in memory of the founder of the modern Synodal School and progenitor of the concepts of the New Direction, Stepan Smolensky. His composition was performed for the first time by the Synodal Choir, and – besides being a central masterpiece of Russian music – embodies the musical ideas pioneered by Alexander Kastalsky (in its use of old chants, its modal bias, and its original choral textures and polyphony inspired by Russian folksong); Rachmaninoff had in fact approached Kastalsky for advice before entering the field of Kastalsky's recognized expertise. It does not detract from Rachmaninoff's supreme achievement to be aware that he was absorbing and taking further an idiom substantially developed by someone before him.

Likewise, we know the works which Stravinsky composed from about 1915 where he drew on features of Russian folk music but treated them in ways dissimilar to those of his mentors in the Belayev circle in St Petersburg. Leaving to one side *Renard*, and *The Soldier's Tale*, there is another central masterpiece of Russian music – *The Wedding* (*Svadebka*, known as *Les Noces*). It incorporates a multiplicity of melodic ideas associated with the Russian peasant wedding, but does so in a way which points to a highly imaginative compositional mind. Pedals and ostinati abound, and heterophony runs amok in a way in reality inconceivable in folk music but present there in embryo – in other words, within the conceptual framework of folkore. In that case, too, we find that Kastalsky entertained similar ideas before Stravinsky. Informed and inspired by the discoveries about folksong made by fellow-members of the Music Ethnography Commission, Kastalsky too made use of the essence of folk ideas, taking the potential within those ideas further than the people themselves did, in the series of works which he called 'restorations' (here translated as 'reconstructions'). The later Stravinsky was a repentant *quondam* Russian folklorist himself intent on making himself out to be a composer in the European mainstream. He advertised his unease by handling the term 'ethnographic' with protective gloves in *Chroniques de ma vie* (first published in 1935) ('this nationalistic, ethnographical aesthetic', referring to the 'Mighty Handful', p. 97; see also p. 106), or when in 1959 he chose richly resonant words ('aboriginal', 'fabrication') to claim that the borrowing of folk melodies in *Pribautki*, *Four Russian Peasant Choruses*, *Four Russian Songs* and *Berceuses du chat* was minimal: 'If any of these pieces *sounds* like aboriginal folk music, it may be because my powers of fabrication were able to tap some unconscious "folk" memory. In each case, however, the syllables and words of the songs dictated the music' ('Some musical questions' in *Memories and Commentaries*, p. 98). It could be that Kastalsky was in Stravinsky's mind (and sights) when he wrote that Tchaikovsky 'had no need to engage in archaeological research in order to present the age of Louis XIV' in his open letter about *The Sleeping Beauty* published in *The Times* on 18 October 1921.

On the one hand, Kastalsky continued the tradition of the 'Mighty Handful'. He was intimately acquainted with Russian folklore and church music, and found there productive ideas for fresh compositions. Most of his subjects were Russian, and a patriotic note sounds frequently in his correspondence. His sensitivity to the music of the nation to which he belonged, and care for its well-being, were observed by Rimsky-Korsakov (see Chapter 8). Kastalsky was one of the few composers mentioned with approval during the deliberations of the Congress of the Union of Composers in 1948, when Tikhon Khrennikov declared: 'Of course the pre-revolutionary era bequeathed to us not only the alien traditions of decadence, but also a number of healthy phenomena which were based on the firm foundations of the musical classics. Let me mention the names of Glazunov, Taneyev, Lyadov, Grechaninov, Ippolitov-Ivanov, Glière and Kastalsky. I should also mention Rachmaninoff who was actively at work at that time...' (T.N. Khrennikov: *Tridtsat' let sovetskoy muzïki i zadachi sovetskikh kompozitorov* (Thirty years of Soviet music and the tasks of Soviet composers). *In Pervïy vsesoynznïy s'yezd sovetskikh kompozitovov* (First All-Union Congress of Soviet Composers). Stenographic report, Moscow, 1948, p. 27).

On the other hand, Kastalsky had links too with more advanced tendencies in music. He was not the only composer of the early twentieth century to be intrigued by novel fusions of speaking and singing (note the 'melodeclamation' used in *V.I. Leninu. U groba*); Russian colleagues in that line included Rebikov and Gnesin in songs, while Shostakovich used simple choral declaiming at the very end of his second symphony, on a revolutionary subject). We find Kastalsky writing music for the theatre, and thinking about composing for the new medium of cinema. There is evidence of his involvement in a scheme to create a ballet on a theme from Orthodox worship. While he himself declared his instinctive affinity with composers who experimented rather than those who continued much as before, statements from later in his life suggest a strong disenchantment with those developments in music which took it far into realms of abstract experimentation, distant from tonal systems.

For some, Kastalsky was a singer of 'Cherubic Hymns', while for others he was the arranger of the 'official' version of the *Internationale*. Pigeonholing him was always difficult. This book provides explanations of these contradictory manifestations of his work and traces the threads that link them together. That task is not easily accomplished when its subject's life story is peopled by the protagonists of such antithetical aims as Pobedonostsev and Lunacharsky, Balakirev and Davidenko. A strand that runs through the life (and the book) is that in Russia, both before and after 1917, music was a field in which, for good or ill, the state took an interest.

This book, describing the career of a fascinating musician, fills an important gap in our knowledge of a rich and diverse phase of Russian musical history.

Stuart Campbell

From the Translator

Besides the over-riding aim of providing a version faithful to the author's original text, the translator has tried here to make the main part of the text read as freely and naturally as possible in English. The story of Kastalsky's life and work is absorbing in itself, and can only gain by being read without any need to surmount hurdles placed in its way by too literal adherence to Russian style or too strict an adherence to a system of transliteration which can sometimes be intimidating. It is hoped that ease in reading the prose parts of the book has been sensibly complemented by rigour in presenting information essential to the scholar: the footnotes, Bibliography, List of Kastalsky's Published Compositions, List of Published Writings and Interviews, Glossary of Terms and Index of Names conform to the system of transliteration used in *The New Grove Dictionary of Music and Musicians*, second edition, 29 volumes (London 2001). Likewise, when titles of compositions are mentioned, in the main text the English translation is given first, followed by the transliteration; in the scholarly apparatus, on the other hand, that order is reversed.

In the main text, for instance, the reader will encounter the familiar forms 'Rachmaninoff' and 'Prokofiev', whereas elsewhere they will appear as 'Rakhmaninov' and 'Prokof'yev'. Where the author might originally have written 'S.I. Taneyev', the reader will find 'Sergey Taneyev' – though the composer's middle initial and the patronymic for which it stands (Ivanovich) may be retrieved, along with other information about him, from the Index of Names. The Russian practice of mentioning people by their first name and patronymic has in most cases been sacrificed to fluency for the reader of this English version, though two principal categories of exception have been allowed. The names of Alexander Kastalsky and Stepan Smolensky occur very frequently, and, for the sake of diversity and to retain some flavour, they are sometimes referred to as Alexander Dmitriyevich and Stepan Vasilyevich respectively. Letter salutations shed light on the relationship between the correspondents, so they have not been adjusted; the majority are in the formal mode – e.g., Kastalsky writes 'Dear Boris Vladimirovich' when communicating with Asafyev. Reproducing the symbols for Russian soft and hard signs tells the reader in English little, while the reader of Russian knows they are there anyway; thus, whereas in the main text 'Nikolsky' is mentioned, in the systematic part he appears as Nikol'sky. Similarly, whereas 'Aleksandr' needs to be read attentively, 'Alexander' (as found in the main text) is immediately more acceptable to the eye. On the other hand, 'Nikolay' bears only a slight aural resemblance to 'Nicholas', and the former has been preferred – except that the last Russian emperor appears as Nicholas II.

There are times when a Russian concept cannot be matched readily with one in English. On several such occasions I have provided the original Russian word, so that at least those with a knowledge of Russian will understand the particular nuance, though I have tried to keep the text as little cluttered in that way as possible.

There are, however, a few terms which need to be discussed here. The oldest chestnut among them is *narod*, which means 'folk' (a 'folksong' is a *narodnaya pesnya*), 'people' (Lunacharsky, the 'People's Commissar for Education', was *Narodnïy komissar prosveshcheniya*), and 'nation' (his tsarist predecessors were 'Ministers for the Education of the Nation', *Ministrï Narodnogo prosveshcheniya*); it can also mean 'popular'. The word *narod* bundles together a range of closely related meanings, without any strain being apparent, where a user of English in translating it would have to choose one from among a number of options. The choice can be difficult – no more so than in translating the title of Chapter 4, where the reader should keep in mind that 'nation' (the word eventually selected) stands also for 'folk' and 'people'.

The full title of the institution with which Kastalsky was most closely associated was the Moscow Synodal School of Church Music. In Russian it is *Moskovskoye sinodalnoye uchilishche tserkovnogo peniya*. The last two words match what most readers of English would immediately understand as 'church music', though the final Russian word in fact denotes 'singing' rather than the more wide-ranging 'music'. But since the music used in the worship of the Russian Orthodox Church is exclusively vocal, I have normally chosen to use an expression which sounds natural in English ('church music') in preference to the awkward 'church singing'. English does not offer a term which refers specifically to a 'church choirmaster'. Russian has *regent* which means exactly that. I have been pedantic in retaining the distinction between a 'church choirmaster' (*regent*), someone who knows not only about choirmastering but also about the contents and structure of church services and what musical approach there is suitable when, and a 'choirmaster' (*khormeyster*) in a theatre, for example, who may have other specialist knowledge but not necessarily in the ecclesiastical area.

In Russian usage the word *Liturgiya* (Liturgy) refers to one type of church service – the Eucharist. In using 'Liturgy' and 'liturgical' I have adhered to that practice. When the English word 'liturgical' might have been employed in its wider meaning of 'relating to a service of worship', I have preferred to paraphrase it along just those lines.

Kastalsky applied the word *restavratsiya* ('restoration') to several of his compositions. Because these were experiments in re-creating something which existed in earlier times, often with more invention than pre-existing material, it seemed more honest to translate the term as 'reconstruction' rather than 'restoration'.

The generic Russian term which describes a large part of Kastalsky's output is *khorï*. This means literally 'choruses'. In order to avoid giving rise to too many irrelevant associations when that word is used nowadays in a church context, I have exercised some ingenuity to find appropriate variants without introducing 'anthem', 'canticle' or 'motet', which have other but equally misleading connotations.

The term *deystvo* occurs in the title of a work which Kastalsky called *Peshchnoye deystvo* which I have translated as 'Play of the Furnace'. An alternative translation would be 'Miracle Play of the Three Youths in the Burning, Fiery Furnace'. An Old Testament subject acted out in church is involved.

Where single dates are given for the period up to 1918, they refer to the Julian calendar in use in Russia at the time; they may be converted to the Gregorian calendar used in the west (and in Russia from 1918) by adding 12 days in the nineteenth century and 13 in the twentieth. In a handful of cases (mainly concerning events which took place outside Russia) the dates are given according to both calendars.

The author has taken advantage of the opportunity afforded by this second version of her book to make some changes in the text. In matters of fact, this edition supersedes the Russian one because it incorporates information brought to light through research conducted after publication. Author and translator have tried to make the text as easily comprehensible for readers as they can, by means of adding to the text here and there explanations of points which would not need to be clarified for Russian readers, and by outlining in the Glossary of Terms the most frequently occurring words likely to be problematic. This version differs from the one published in Moscow in having music examples, an annotated Index of Names, a Bibliography, and a list of Kastalsky's published writings about music (to complement the list of his published compositions).

As a writer of letters, Kastalsky had a wonderfully informal style in which colloquialisms, allusions and knowing silences (understandable by the recipient) grace a sentence structure which frequently goes off in surprising directions. The extensive quotations from this source help to bring the man alive. The translator's task was to reflect the correspondent's idiom and convey as far as possible what he meant to say – not to straighten out the thought processes spontaneously at work in his mind or tidy up his grammar.

The Library of the University of Glasgow, with its rich holdings of Russian materials, has provided answers to many queries; I am particularly indebted to the Music Librarian, Ms Morag Mackie, for her ready help. *Monuments of Russian Sacred Music*, whose editor-in-chief is Vladimir Morosan, contain admirable and easily available scores, and, moreover, translations and explanations of the music they publish; these volumes have proved invaluable sources of information.

The translation has been improved immeasurably as a result of the careful comparison of the Russian text with the English draft by the Revd. Andre Papkov of the Holy Trinity Monastery, Jordanville, New York. His particular contribution has involved providing appropriate equivalents in English for specialized Russian ecclesiastical terminology. But he also has a very good line in matching Kastalsky's often informal or earthy expressions to close English equivalents. The help of Fr. Andre's wife, Natalie, is also gratefully acknowledged. Fr. Alexander Williams, priest of the Orthodox Community of St Nicholas, Dunblane, Scotland, has also materially improved the text. Surviving errors and infelicities are, alas, the reponsibility of the translator. Thanks are also due to the following: Aleksey Naumov for his help in compiling the Index of Names; Gregor Trinkaus-Randall for providing information about his grandfather Ivan T. Gorokhoff; Dr. Denis Brearley for help with the bibliography; Russian Music Publishing in Moscow for setting the music examples.

List of Abbreviations

ChOIDR: *Chteniya v Obshchestve istorii i drevnostey rossiyskikh* (Readings at the Society for Russian History and Antiquities), scholarly publication, St Petersburg

GIMN: *Gosudarstvennïy institut muzïkal'noy nauki* (State Institute for Musical Science), Moscow

GTsMMK: *Gosudarstvennïy tsentral'nïy muzey muzïkal'noy kul'turï imeni M.I. Glinki* (State Central Museum of Musical Culture named after M.I. Glinka), archive, Moscow

MEC: = Music Ethnography Commission: *Muzïkal'no-etnograficheskaya komissiya pri Etnograficheskom otdele Obshchestva lyubiteley yestestvoznaniya, antropologii i etnografii, sostoyavshego pri Moskovskom universitete* (Commission for Music Ethnography in the Ethnography Section of the Society of Lovers of the Natural Sciences, Anthropology and Ethnography attached to the University of Moscow)

MUZO: *Muzïkal'nïy otdel* (Music Department) [of the People's Commissariat for Education]

RGADA: *Rossiyskiy gosudarstvennïy arkhiv drevnikh aktov* (Russian State Archive of Ancient Documents), Moscow

RGALI: *Rossiyskiy gosudarstvennïy arkhiv literaturï i iskusstva* (Russian State Archive for Literature and Art), Moscow

RGB: *Rossiyskaya gosudarstvennaya biblioteka* (Russian State Library), Moscow

RGIA: *Rossiyskiy gosudarstvennïy istoricheskiy arkhiv* (Russian State Historical Archive), St Petersburg

RMG: *Russkaya muzïkal'naya gazeta* ('Russian Musical Gazette'), music periodical

RNB: *Rossiyskaya natsional'naya biblioteka* (Russian National Library), St Petersburg

RUSAM = Russian Sacred Music [in Documents and Materials]: *Russkaya dukhovnaya muzïka v dokumentakh i materialakh*, series of publications

SovM: *Sovetskaya muzïka* ('Soviet Music'), music periodical

TsIAM: *Tsentral'nïy istoricheskiy arkhiv Moskvï* (Central Historical Archive of Moscow)

Chapter 1

The Kastalsky Family

'A person can't live without roots. That means particular people, a certain town, a specific country... If you were born in Moscow, and especially if at least three generations before you were born and lived their lives there, then you will inevitably look around you in a special way', – thus wrote Natalia Kastalskaya, daughter of the famous composer of church music Alexander Kastalsky, in her memoirs.[1] She knew every detail of her family tree thanks to an inherited family chronicle which her grandfather, the Moscow archpriest Dmitry Ivanovich Kastalsky, had written for the edification of his descendants, providing the manuscript with his own watercolour drawings. These *Notes* were handed over to a publisher where they disappeared; when pieced together again, the history of this Moscow family appears neither very extensive nor very old. It goes back to the end of the eighteenth century, to the time when the composer's grandfather Ivan Yegorovich Danilovsky was alive and serving as a junior deacon in the church at the village of Kuskovo on the outskirts of Moscow.

Ivan Danilovsky was very knowledgeable about the ancient art of painting Russian icons, and evidently possessed exceptional artistic gifts – he painted icons and compiled and drew Paschal tables. One of his icons was even accepted by the Cathedral of the Dormition in the Kremlin in Moscow. According to family tradition, it was precisely because of Ivan Danilovsky's talent for icon-painting that he was ordained a deacon at the Church of the Presentation of the Blessed Virgin in Dmitrov, and it was in the vicinity of Dmitrov that he was eventually buried.

None of Ivan Danilovsky's five sons retained their father's surname. The eldest, Pyotr Orlovsky, was a civil servant in the Moscow office of the imperial court; the second, Ioann Dmitrevsky, became a priest at the Moscow Church of St Dmitry of Thessalonika; the third, Platon Afinsky, was the archpriest of the church of the Reserve Palace by the Red Gates; finally, the fourth and fifth sons Dmitry and Mikhail entered the Bethany Theological Seminary and at the insistence of the rector chose for themselves the surname Kastalsky. On graduating from the seminary Mikhail was ordained and became deacon at the Church of the Saviour on

Carriage Row in Moscow. Dmitry showed himself to be a brilliant student, and with the blessing of Filaret (Drozdov), the Metropolitan of Moscow, entered Moscow Theological Academy in 1840. On completing his studies in 1844, Dmitry obtained the post of teacher of Patristics and Greek at the newly opened senior section of the Kazan Theological Academy. Upon completion of his master's dissertation on the subject 'Domestic Use of the Bible by the Early Christians' in 1845, Kastalsky obtained the degree of Master of Theology and in 1848 returned to Moscow where he remained as a professor at the Moscow Theological Seminary until 1853. Besides Patristics, he taught Logic, Psychology, Latin and German there. Dmitry Kastalsky continued with his study of theology: from the end of the 1840s his articles and sermons appeared regularly in the 'Muscovite' (*Moskvityanin*), 'Edifying Reading' (*Dushepoleznoye chteniye*), 'Sunday Talks' (*Voskresnïye Besedï*) and the 'Moscow Church Bulletin' (*Moskovskiye tserkovnïye vedomosti*).

In 1851 Dmitry Kastalsky married the daughter of the priest of the Kazan Church in Sushchevo, Olga Semyonovna Gruzova, a former pupil of the Alexandrovsky Institute, who had a decent command of the piano and who when times were hard for the family earned money by giving music lessons. One may conclude that during their early years of marriage the young couple were by no means prosperous from the reminiscences of Natalia Kastalskaya, who read in her grandfather's *Notes* a story of how in 1853 he lost his wallet containing ten silver roubles – that was his entire seminary earnings – and without his wife's lessons the family would have been in a tight spot. But even when he had a professor's salary, time and again Dmitry Kastalsky would trail his family around, as it expanded year by year, to live in turn with his father-in-law and his brother, since his own livelihood was insufficient.

Olga Kastalskaya was a quiet, God-fearing woman. As Natalia remembered her,

> Grandmother (my father's mother) had been educated at a boarding school and was a pianist. (To be sure, I never heard for myself how she played the piano – perhaps in old age she considered playing a sin.) She was inordinately kind. I remember her vividly, many years later, after grandfather's death, as a little old lady in a black widow's dress and a black headsquare with sparkling blue eyes, pink cheeks and trembling fingers. In his *Notes* grandfather called her strictly 'Olga' or 'my Olga', never anything else. They had nine children.[2]

Later on, when already a widow, Olga Kastalskaya quite often stayed in the home of her favourite son Alexander. Singers in the Synodal Choir used to recall how after services in the Cathedral of the Dormition in the

Kremlin where Kastalsky was the choirmaster you could often see him processing hand in hand with a little old lady dressed in black. Olga was a very devout woman; she tried to attend a church service every day and made pilgrimages to remote monasteries. In spite of the boarding-school education she had received in her youth, she was a profoundly straightforward, down-to-earth, rustic (*narodnïy*) type of Russian woman, whose language and train of thought Alexander Dmitriyevich with his innate gift for parody imitated in one of his letters to a friend:

> Haven't been to my mother's [to wish her a happy Christmas] yet (probably she'll be thinking: what a rascal and a scoundrel I've given birth to – she probably doesn't swear using 'son of a bitch'), and a composer of church music too! He's written a troparion and kontakion 'God is with us' ('*S nami Bog*'), the rotter! And the Christmas *heirmoi* 'When Augustus reigned alone' (*Avgustu yedinonachal'stvuyushchu*) and lots more – but when it comes to wishing his mum a happy Christmas, it's always tomorrow or the next day... That's what children are like nowadays, and he gets called 'director', and keeps company with fine gentlemen from St Petersburg. [...] Damn it, he's not got a father now, or he'd show you how you ought to respect your parents, and he'd pay no attention to that grey sponge-thing that grows on your chin...[3]

By this time archpriest Dmitry Kastalsky had long been dead: he died on 26 December 1892, and had been well known as a priest in Moscow. His pastoral service began not long before the birth of his son Alexander. After settling down to married life, Dmitry Kastalsky decided at the beginning of the 1850s to become a priest: in 1851 he was ordained by Metropolitan Filaret as priest of the Church of St Nicholas at the Moscow Theological Seminary, and two years later was transferred to the Church of St Mary at the Trade School, where Kastalsky had to teach scripture. He taught scripture at the same time in many Moscow educational institutions as well as the homes of the nobility and the merchant class. The result of his activities in this field was a handbook entitled 'The Divine Service' (*O bogosluzhenii*) (Moscow, 1874) which ran to several reprintings and contains an explanation of the church services as well as information about the music-books for worship and the hymns. In 1868 the Trade School was reorganized as the Imperial Higher Technical School, for which Kastalsky developed courses in Christian morals and Russian church history.

The next landmark in Father Dmitry's biography was his appointment in 1874 to the Church of St Peter and St Paul on Novaya Basmannaya Street, and three years later he was elevated to the rank of archpriest and transferred to become senior priest at the Kazan Cathedral on Red Square. By this time Dmitry Kastalsky had acquired wide and deserved renown as a preacher, and was valued highly by Metropolitan Filaret, his spiritual mentor. He also took part in the life of the diocese, becoming in 1871 one of the organizers of a school of icon-painting for children of the clergy, and from 1873 he participated most actively in the establishment of the Filaret School for Women in Moscow, which he headed for 16 years.

Alexander Dmitriyevich was born on 16/28 November 1856 and was the family's fourth child. He was named in honour of the saint–prince Alexander Nevsky, though there was nothing at all militant about his personality and, in his mother's words, he was 'an angel incarnate'. Alexander Dmitriyevich stood out from his brothers and sisters not just in personality; he later became the only representative among them of an artistic profession, greatly disappointing his father who shared the view held by many contemporaries that music was something frivolous and insecure. He compared Alexander, not without bitterness, with his brothers:

> My son Vsevolod works as an engineer in the Moscow city administration; my son Vladimir is a draughtsman at the Technical School; my son Nikolay is building a bridge at the Simonov Monastery. Alexander, I believe, ... gives music lessons.[4]

Natalia Kastalskaya left more detailed recollections of her father's brothers:

> My father had five brothers and they were all very different. The oldest, Vsevolod, with his head of dark curly hair and his little silvery, squared-off beard, was a strict parent and an engineer. A system of sewerage was introduced in Moscow for the first time using his plans. We were afraid of him. He spoke little, but in categorical terms... Then there was Uncle Nikolya, who in his youth had been a 'nihilist' and was a modest soul, with a wife who had been a member of the 'People's Will' organization; but when she died of consumption, Uncle Nikolya (who was also an engineer) embarked on ventures which without fail went bust (we children hadn't the foggiest idea what sort of ventures they were) and he became completely different – he was cheerful, wore a red tie and was always borrowing money from his humble relatives (in the hope of success) without ever paying it back, and on one of his trips, at the age of about sixty, he died – believe it or not, in ... Honolulu. [...] The third was Vladimir, or, as he called himself, Varim, who to my childhood memory seemed like an old man from a painting by Rembrandt. He was deaf and dumb. In childhood his wetnurse had given him 'dewdrops' to make him sleep – and insufficient attention had been paid. He learned to speak, but he spoke after his own fashion. [...] Papa, the fourth son, stood apart from his brothers and seemed to me to be 'not of this world'; nor was he very keen on achieving things in the way of physical construction. His range of interests was

independent of family and work. In his youth he called himself the 'dreamer', with a certain amount of resentment.[5]

After Alexander, the Kastalskys had five more children, only four of whom reached adulthood – Yekaterina, Sergey, Anna and Semyon. Alexander Dmitriyevich formed a great friendship with his sister Katya, although the subjects which engaged her were very distant from him: in 1887 Katya left for Switzerland and became an ophthalmologist. 'In my recollection', Natalia Kastalskaya recalled,

> Aunt Katya was slim, dark in complexion and beautiful; she wore a Russian cloth blouse, kept her hair short like a man's, carried in her side-pocket a watch with charms (presents from her colleagues), and when we were small we would never leave her in peace as we ran our fingers over the charms. She died at the age of 35 from typhus as a result of a heart defect.[6]

Alexander Dmitriyevich was by then a well-known composer of religious music, and dedicated his choral work 'Blessed are they whom Thou hast chosen' (*Blazheni yazhe izbral*) to her.

In childhood Alexander showed no particular inclination towards music and received no serious musical education; like other members of the Kastalsky family, he was drawn more to the natural sciences. The composer recalled:

> My father, the well-known Moscow archpriest Dmitry Kastalsky, discerned no special bent for music in me and therefore sent me to the Second Moscow *Gimnaziya* where I was an indifferent pupil. But my mother, a lively pianist who in her youth had also sung in and conducted the chapel choir at her boarding school, probably detected a certain gift for music in me and tried to teach me the piano and made me sing romances by Varlamov and Gurilyov as well as other songs. One of my many uncles was a great lover of folksongs and I was among the people he enlightened on the subject. Add to that visiting church services where a choir was singing (I can remember the beginning of a sacred concerto for Easter where the basses began with 'Today all living things rejoice' (*Dnes' usyaka plot' veselitsya...*)) and the pealing of bells, – and that is the sum total of my musical impressions and artistic education between the ages of 8 and 18. I can remember sawing away at something on a cheap violin and piping on a fife; I liked playing on a comb with a piece of paper stretched over it (under the guidance of the uncle I mentioned), and I would invariably pick something out on the piano by ear at family parties. I tried composition too (exactly what I don't remember), and I gleaned essential theoretical information from some old encyclopedia of my father's. But these activities were merely by the way: I was really keen on chemistry and reading books on

agriculture, and when I left the *Gimnaziya* intended to enter the Petrovskaya Academy of Agriculture.[7]

Kastalsky's childhood was spent in a large patriarchal family where there were never less than 20 people at table: on ordinary days they would eat cabbage soup and porridge, and on feast-days a kind of pie (*kulebyaka*) would be added... Summer was spent with Olga's parents at Sushchevo, or sometimes at the estate of Maksino near Moscow which was made available by her distant relative Yekaterina Protopopova – the mother-in-law of the composer Borodin. The archpriest loved it when the young people sang and danced. And therefore the family would often sing folksongs in chorus and arrange dances where Alexander Dmitriyevich would 'bash out' all kinds of polkas and waltzes for the company's enjoyment. The family often undertook pilgrimages on foot – usually to the Trinity-Sergiyev Monastery. The procession was accompanied by carts on which provisions and the small children were carried.

In spite of his 'angelic' character, Alexander Kastalsky seems to have caused his educated parent much grief, since his studies were not attended by any great success. He could not master the *Gimnaziya* course and was taken out of the eighth class (at the age of 17 or 18) by his father. It is hard to say what his fate would have been had not chance brought to the Kastalskys' home the Moscow Conservatoire teacher P.T. Konev, who at one of the family parties heard the luckless *Gimnaziya*-pupil improvizing on the piano. Konev began inviting Alexander to his house where he played him compositions by Beethoven, Schumann and Chopin and made him improvize preludes on the piano and eventually persuaded him to enter the Conservatoire.

'I can't say I was enormously enthusiastic about music when I entered the Moscow Conservatoire (1876)', the composer reminisced.

> My talents went more or less unnoticed by everyone except Konev, and I progressed rather slowly through the course, coping with the theoretical side only with difficulty; nor was I against dodging lessons on occasion (I had to walk to the Conservatoire and it was a long way, sometimes twice in the one day). The family got fed up with my piano exercises. I remember that one summer my grand piano was moved into a summer-house in the garden; the weather was very hot and as I did my exercises I would pour water over my neck to cool down. I studied theory at the Conservatoire with Tchaikovsky (one year), Gubert and Taneyev. I played timpani in the student orchestra, and once got a row from an irritated Nikolay Rubinstein for not counting rests carefully.[8]

After he became a teacher himself, Kastalsky confessed to his pupils that he had even skipped several lessons with Tchaikovsky who, as he thought, taught his subject in a dry and uninteresting manner. Kastalsky loved his lessons with Taneyev, however, and attended them punctiliously, having set himself the aim of becoming a virtuoso contrapuntist. The incident recalled in his reminiscences of throwing water over his collar while working on his piano-playing is also connected with Taneyev; as the latter sent Kastalsky away for the summer one year, he told him to come back a real pianist in the autumn. Working up to 14 hours a day, the pupil really did make a serious improvement in his piano technique over the summer, but he injured his hands and suffered pains all his life.

It is difficult to say how successful Kastalsky was with theoretical subjects. He considered that he had made more headway through independent study than by his Conservatoire exercises. He attended symphony concerts and rehearsals for them, and spent his meagre earnings from lessons buying scores of the works being performed. He paid particular attention to Glinka's *Ruslan and Lyudmila*, Borodin's symphonies, Rimsky-Korsakov's symphonic picture *Sadko*, and also the collections of Russian folksongs made by Balakirev and Melgunov. 'I was not specially drawn to the classics', Kastalsky admitted.

> I can remember from this period a good performance of Tchaikovsky's Liturgy by Sakharov's choir, which, given my attraction at that time to the Borodin-Musorgsky-Korsakov-Balakirev direction, made not the slightest impression on me. Generally speaking, I was a complete ignoramus about church music, although I was sensitive to the effects possible in choral sonority.[9]

His studies at the Conservatoire were short-lived. They came to an end when he applied to the Director to leave on account of family circumstances in November 1878. The real reasons for his action remain unclear. The possibility that the causes lay in disagreements with his father, who was dissatisfied with his son's choice of profession, cannot be excluded. As a matter of fact, private lessons in piano and music theory as well as working with student and amateur choirs and orchestras became for a time the main means of Alexander Dmitriyevich's livelihood. But besides his son's 'frivolous' profession, archpriest Kastalsky was disturbed by a further consideration: Alexander Dmitriyevich had become enamoured of Natalia, the daughter of the priest Lavrenty Pavlovsky, their late neighbour in Sushchevo. There were several reasons for parental concern. One of them was that Alexander Dmitriyevich's older brother Vsevolod was married to Natalia's older sister, and in the thinking of that time the marriage of a second couple came up against popular prejudice. Besides, even though Natalia was a priest's daughter, she was not noted for great religiosity – as often happened with children of the clergy. Moreover, at the end of the 1870s and the beginning of the 1880s the friendship between Alexander and Natalia offered no serious prospects, insofar as both were without means and lacked resources for family life. As a domestic tutor by education, Natalia earned small sums of money teaching French and German.

Meanwhile Alexander Dmitriyevich began his military service: from July until December 1881 he was a 'volunteer' in the Prince Karl of Prussia Grenadiers' Artillery brigade stationed in the Spassky barracks in the Kremlin. There the future composer studied 'the action of field weapons and service in the artillery'.[10] On returning from the army, Alexander Dmitriyevich decided to try his luck in the town of Kozlov where he intended to organize a chorus and orchestra of workers from the railway workshops, and also to accustom the people of Kozlov to serious music. This trip to a town in the remote provinces undoubtedly had as its aim not only to make some money: the young musician wanted to earn through energetic activity 'even the slightest calmness of spirit, the very tiniest confidence in my cause and my usefulness...'[11]

Alexander Dmitriyevich outlined the details of his life in Kozlov to Natalia: he reported on the pains he took to obtain instruments and the efforts he made to teach his pupils to play them – among them someone who had chosen the trumpet purely because it gleamed; he described the rehearsals of a quartet drawn from the local intelligentsia who could not produce a single note in tune; and he gave an account of his success in educating himself. As he himself put it, he did all the following: 'crammed Cramer', scraped at the cello and amused himself with the 'tiny fiddle'; in addition he analysed compositions by Glinka, Tchaikovsky, Dargomïzhsky, Rimsky-Korsakov, Schumann and other composers, and read scholarly books about Russian history. Kastalsky asked Natalia to send him music, 'little verses' for songs and biographies of musicians and composers so that he could learn from 'great and small'; he asked her to translate articles about music from foreign journals as well. Consequently not only articles were translated but also two major works by Adolf Bernhard Marx and Ludwig Bussler[12] on the theory and aesthetics of music.

Kastalsky subsequently destroyed his early experiments as a composer, unfortunately. We know from letters of the period that at the beginning of the 1880s Alexander Dmitriyevich worked on an opera *Mtsïri*, songs, piano miniatures and marches for orchestra; he even 'gave some thought' to a symphony. The composer admitted that his obstinate muse kept drawing him towards the Russian style against his will. On 26 January 1883 he wrote to Natalia:

> I got down to them [Bach chorales] once again thanks to my marches, which, blast them, never take the form I want and are always veering to one side, which though it's often very interesting is nonetheless not what I want. So that instead of a 'workers' march it turns out a kind of epic-naive march for some ancient Slavonic prince, or else a march at once triumphal and a bit crude, also in the Russian spirit, which thank goodness is not bad (in my opinion but still not what I want)...[13]

As a genuine pupil of Taneyev, who in his time had wrestled with the problem of creating a method of arranging ancient Russian church chants, Kastalsky also conceived the idea of giving himself some practice in that line: 'I am thinking about getting down to the *Obikhod*', he wrote to Natalia on 2 May 1883. 'I believe you can find enough in the way of characteristic melodies and all that strict, austere Great-Russian material there. I've got something in common with Musorgsky in that respect; he too was very keen on melodies and themes of that kind'.[14]

In the summer of 1884 the Kozlov workshops were closed and Alexander Dmitriyevich returned to his native Moscow where he was again busy with teaching. In the same year he approached the Moscow Assembly of Noble Deputies with a request that he be enrolled among the nobility (*dvoryanstvo*), something sought by the whole family after Father Dmitry had been awarded the Order of St Vladimir (fourth class) in 1880.[15] Alexander Dmitriyevich's petition was granted, and a note appeared in Kastalsky's record of employment at the Office of the Synod, saying that he was a hereditary nobleman.[16] Alexander Dmitriyevich never again raised the matter of his noble status, more than once emphasizing that his origins were in the 'nobility of the belfry', that is, the clergy.

Meanwhile, in 1886 the composer turned thirty. On 22 August of that year the priest of the church of the Grenadier Regiment, where Alexander Dmitriyevich had at one time served, entered in his register a record of the conclusion of a marriage between 'artilleryman' Kastalsky and the spinster Pavlovskaya.[17] This form of words was apparently explained by the young people's reluctance to draw the attention of colleagues and acquaintances of archpriest Kastalsky to their marriage.

The union of Alexander and Natalia proved an uncommonly successful one. As their daughter Natalia recalled:

> The relationship between my father and my mother was unique of its kind. I never encountered any other like it. Papa was for my mother the alpha and the

omega – she called him 'the most handsome of men!' Working on his libretto, translating foreign articles, writing texts and going into musical minutiae were all Mama's prerogatives. Mother was educated and clever like a man – she was a 'walking encyclopedia', and kept a book beside her even while she was eating. Looking after the house came last. [...] But now and then Mother would meet a decisive rebuff from Father, because she was a rationalist and a 'Voltairean' as we teased her, and the 'impractical' flights of my father's imagination struck her as stubbornness. [...] When my parents were together they were always young and cheerful (and so it continued into old age): they joked, they laughed – about work matters too, by the way, and they understood one another by the merest hint. This love lasted until death.[18]

In truth, it was a rare composition or article by Kastalsky which had not passed through his wife's hands, as she fulfilled the roles of adviser, editor, secretary, copyist and translator in one. Alexander Dmitriyevich originally intended to include in one of his autobiographical works a fragment relating how his whole household together helped him prepare the score of his opera *Klara Milich* for its première in the Zimin Theatre:

One cleaned up a section in the orchestral parts so that something essential could be inserted, someone else wrote in what was needed, a third person glued in an extra piece of paper – the work went on day in, day out. Then when it was ready we all carried the material to the theatre for the rehearsals. On one occasion the string holding a pile of orchestral parts together broke, and we were almost involved in a serious accident in the street.[19]

It often happened that the Kastalsky family operated with all hands on deck like this. The massive 'Requiem for Fallen Brothers' (*Bratskoye pominoveniye*), which exists in several versions, caused a special amount of bother, and Natalia had to recopy it many times besides preparing the foreign-language texts. And Natalia Kastalskaya's name appeared on the title-page of a work by her husband only once, when in 1911 the Kastalskys jointly wrote the text for the jubilee cantata for the 25th anniversary of the reform of the Moscow Synodal School of Church Music 'Verse about Russian Church Music' (*Stikh o tserkovnom russkom penii*).

Natalia Kastalskaya had a further responsibility far removed from art: she was concerned with selling those of her husband's compositions which he had had printed at his own expense.

The Kastalskys had two children – a daughter Natalia and a son Alexander, who were brought up in a spirit of freedom and democracy. Generally speaking, the family's whole style, as their daughter Natalia recalled, was 'typical of the intelligentsia who were not of noble birth (*raznochintsï*) – without prejudices or artificial manners'. Alexander

Dmitriyevich proved an excellent father – he would play with the children at sand castles, with wooden blocks, he built a 'farmyard' where a herd of wooden animals brought from Sergiyev Posad were kept, and he sang children's songs. When the children were older he would travel about Moscow with them, pointing out everything that was full of colour or typically Muscovite on the city's streets. (Subsequently a 'Symphony of the Moscow Streets' composed by Kastalsky was even published in the Proceedings of the Music Ethnography Commission (*Trudï Muzïkal'no-etnograficheskoy komissii*).[20])

When rare moments of leisure came along, Alexander Dmitriyevich found recreation in drawing. 'He absorbed the work of his contemporary Vrubel avidly, but also honoured Vasnetsov', as his daughter Natalia recalled.

> The landscapes of old Moscow by Apollinary Vasnetsov were greatly to his liking. The Impressionists astounded him by their 'freedom of pictorial breath' and freshness of vision. He also liked our 'Impressionists' – Byalïnitsky-Birulya with his pale-blue mists and spring water and Grabar with his 'Hoar-frost'. And most of all – Levitan, the foremost poet of Russia's Nature. And he was a 'dauber' himself, as he put it. He experienced van Gogh keenly, and drew his 'The Night Café' from memory using a small notebook. But Papa could not restrain himself, and in the foreground drew two figures who were either tramps or Dutch sailors.[21]

People who knew Kastalsky well remembered that he really loved to improvize, even while copying the works of other artists. For instance, in his copy of the familiar painting 'On the terrace' by Grabar, the composer depicted himself. But the matter was not limited to reproducing the works of others. Alexander Dmitriyevich drew his friends and acquaintances and in the summer he drew landscapes from life.[22] Kastalsky put himself to the test of drawing in the modern style, and earned the praise of the famous artist Georgy Yakulov for one experiment of that kind. Alexander Dmitriyevich's other passion was travelling. He was particularly attracted to the Crimea and the Caucasus, which he visited in both winter and summer, often pottering along the shore on a bicycle.

Kastalsky's children grew up to be neither musicians nor artists, but they became his like-minded helpers. His son Alexander – a prominent engineer in Soviet times – copied out Alexander Dmitriyevich's scores and helped him with orchestration; moreover, he edited and in 1960 published fragments of his unfinished composition 'Scenes from Peasant Merrymaking in Rus' (*Kartinï narodnïkh prazdnovaniy na Rusi*). His daughter Natalia was involved when she was young in 'plastic ballet' (a species of modern dance), and in the 1930s and 1940s worked as a proofreader in the foreign dictionaries section of the 'Encyclopedia' publishing-house.

Natalia was born on 19 October 1887. The following day another important event occurred in her father's life: he was taken on as an employee by the Moscow Synodal School of Church Music. Kastalsky's entire subsequent fate was to be connected with that educational institution.

Notes

1. N.A. Kastal'skaya: *Vospominaniya* (Recollections). GTsMMK, fond 12, no. 932, p.1.
2. *Ibid.*, pp. 2-2v.
3. Letter from A.D. Kastal'sky to Kh.N. Grozdov of 26 December 1915. GTsMMK, fond 370, no. 536, p. 12.
4. N.A. Kastal'skaya: *Vospominaniya*, p. 6v.
5. *Ibid.*, pp. 3-4.
6. *Ibid.*, p. 10.
7. A.D. Kastal'sky: *O moyey muzïkal'noy kar'yere i moi mïsli o tserkovnoy muzïke* (My career in music and my thoughts about church music), in *RUSAM*, vol. 1, p. 229.
8. *Ibid.*, pp. 229-230.
9. *Ibid.*, p. 230.
10. *Svidetel'stvo o vïpolnenii voinskoy povinnosti* (Certification that obligation of military service has been discharged). GTsMMK, fond 12, no. 929.
11. N. Kastal'skaya: *Nemnogoye ob ottse* (A little about my father), in *A.D. Kastal'sky. Stat'i. Vospominaniya. Materialï* (A.D. Kastalsky. Articles. Reminiscences. Materials). Moscow, 1960, p. 103.
12. In the late nineteenth century several theoretical works by the celebrated German theorist Bussler were translated into Russian by S.I. Taneyev and N.D. Kashkin and used as textbooks in music education institutions, in particular the Moscow Conservatoire and the Synodal School of Church Music.
13. N. Kastal'skaya: *Nemnogoye ob ottse*, in *A.D. Kastal'sky. Stat'i. Vospominaniya. Materialï*, p. 102.
14. *Ibid.*, p. 103.
15. *Delo Moskovskogo dvoryanskogo deputatskogo sobraniya o vnesenii v rodoslovnuyu knigu protoiyereya D.I. Kastal'skogo s semeystvom* (The case of the Moscow Assembly of Noble Deputies and entering the name of archpriest D.I. Kastal'sky and his family in the Book of Genealogy). TsIAM, fond 4, opis' 10, no. 915.
16. *Svidetel'stvo Moskovskogo deputatskogo sobraniya* (Certificate issued by the Moscow Assembly of Noble Deputies). GTsMMK, fond 12, nos. 932, 933.
17. *Svidetel'stvo o vïpolnenii voinskoy povinnosti* (Certification that obligation of military service has been discharged). GTsMMK, fond 12, no. 929.
18. N. Kastal'skaya: *Nemnogoye ob ottse*, in *A.D. Kastal'sky. Stat'i. Vospominaniya. Materialï*, p. 100.
19. A.D. Kastal'sky: *Iz vospominaniy o poslednikh godakh (Fragment chernovika stat'i)*, (From my reminiscences of recent years (Fragment from the draft of an article)). GTsMMK, fond 12, no. 191, p. 1. The composer dedicated his opera *Klara Milich* to his wife, N.L. Kastal'skaya.

20. *Iz zapisey A.D. Kastal'skogo* (From A.D. Kastal'sky's transcriptions): a) The cry of a blind beggar; b) Blind people's song; c) Excerpt from the Street Symphony, created at various times on the corner of Great and Middle Kislovka [Streets] in Moscow, in spring 1910), in *Trudï Muzïkal'no-etnograficheskoy komissii* (Proceedings of the Music Ethnography Commission), vol. 2. Moscow, 1911.

21. N.A. Kastal'skaya: *Vospominaniya*, p. 3.

22. The archive bearing Kastal'sky's name in GTsMMK contains two specimens of his work: *Monakh v lodke* (Monk in a boat) (canvas, oil) and *Pogrudnïy portret V.I. Rebikova v profil'* (Portrait of V.I. Rebikov in profile) (pencil, paper). GTsMMK, fond 12, nos. 990, 991.

Chapter 2

The Origins of Reform

Rumours of a decision to change the former four-year School for boy-choristers at the Synodal Choir into a secondary special choral educational institution had begun to circulate in Moscow in 1885, causing Moscow's musical brethren considerable puzzlement. 'Talk of a proposed Synodal Kapella with music classes attached to it on the model of the Court Kapella is going round Moscow', the Moscow music critic Semyon Kruglikov informed Rimsky-Korsakov in St Petersburg. 'The other day I even had a conversation with one of the teachers at our school, one Voydenov, in the course of which he told me the same thing in secret, about the reforms along precisely these lines being planned at the Synodal Choir, and went on to express a desire to join the staff there as a teacher and advised me to petition for the same thing through Balakirev'.[1] Kruglikov's colleague at Pyotr Shostakovsky's School of Music and Drama, Vasily Voydenov, whom he mentioned in his letter, was evidently not aware that Kruglikov's St Petersburg friends Balakirev and Rimsky-Korsakov were already looking after him, pulling strings on his behalf at the Synod to make him inspector (chief disciplinarian) of the Synodal School.

As a matter of fact, a precedent for the transformation of the Synodal School was to be found in the Court Kapella, where the two composers had been working since 1883. Rimsky-Korsakov described the people responsible for the reform at the Kapella in his *Chronicle of My Musical Life*.

Running ahead of our story, we can say that almost exactly the same group of people were behind the experiment which it was intended to carry out in Moscow. 'The changes which came about on Alexander III's accession affected even the Court Kapella, the director of which was Bakhmetev', wrote Rimsky-Korsakov.

The latter was given retirement. The Kapella's status and staffing were worked out afresh. Count Sergey Sheremetev (who did not have even an amateur's knowledge of music) was made head (*nachal'nik*) of the Kapella. That position appeared to require merely honorary representation of the Kapella, while the real work was placed in the hands of the manager (*upravlyayushchiy*) of the

Kapella and his assistant. Sheremetev chose Balakirev as manager, and Balakirev chose me as his assistant. The secret thread woven through this unexpected appointment lay in the hands of Terty Filippov, who was then a former state controller, and Pobedonostsev, the *Ober-Prokuror* [of the Holy Synod]. Balakirev, Filippov and Count Sheremetev were people linked by their religiosity, Orthodoxy and remnants of Slavophilism. In their wake came Sabler and Pobedonostsev, Samarin and, perhaps, Katkov – long-standing buttresses of Autocracy and Orthodoxy. Music as such did not play a significant role in Balakirev's appointment; the thread nonetheless led to him, a truly remarkable musician. And Balakirev, thinking he was on shaky ground as a theorist and teacher, chose as his assistant me, who had been engrossed in theoretical and teaching activities at the Conservatoire. I was appointed assistant manager of the Court Kapella in February 1883.[2]

To what extent Sergey Sheremetev, Terty Filippov, Yury Samarin and Mikhail Katkov were privy to the idea of reforming the Synodal School remains to be clarified; the other persons named by Rimsky-Korsakov (to whom Sergey Rachinsky, the outstanding educator, should be added) were to some extent connected with the transformations in the School after 1885. In Rimsky-Korsakov's opinion, it was none other than Balakirev who suggested to Pobedonostsev the idea of continuing the St Petersburg experiment in Moscow.[3] It is possible that Rimsky-Korsakov was mistaken and the idea occurred first not to Balakirev but to Rachinsky, who was closer both to Moscow and to Pobedonostsev. One way or another, the latter took the initiative in 1885 and appointed Andrey Shishkov as the new manager of the Moscow Synodal Printing Office to prepare the reform. As far as the two famous composers and Rachinsky are concerned, they put forward different candidates for the director's chair: the men from St Petersburg proposed Kruglikov, and Rachinsky suggested Stepan Smolensky.

In March 1885 Rimsky-Korsakov and Balakirev sent Kruglikov letters advising him not to refuse the offer which he would shortly receive from Shishkov. Rimsky-Korsakov not only recommended that he accept but also promised all possible help: Kruglikov was invited to St Petersburg to find out how things were organized at the Kapella, and the composer himself promised 'to call on him in Moscow to help'. By the onset of summer, however, no such offer had been received. The reason was simple: Shishkov had not been heeding the composers' advice, and on 18 April 1885 Nikolay Dobrovolsky was appointed inspector of the School, a responsibility which was later changed into the directorship; Dobrovolsky emerged from the Synodal Choir milieu, where he was a boy singer to start with and later a teacher.

In the summer of 1885, however, a meeting between Shishkov and Kruglikov took place nonetheless, and apparently as a result the latter was entrusted with the task of compiling syllabuses in musical subjects for the Synodal School. Kruglikov naturally turned to Rimsky-Korsakov for advice and in June 1885 received a detailed answer from him.[4] By October the music syllabuses were ready and were sent for examination to the selfsame manager of the Kapella and his assistant. Rimsky-Korsakov's answer was as follows:

> I have read your syllabus for the Synodal Choir's music classes, which is now with Balakirev, and at his request I have made some observations about it. I have also read Razumovsky's staveless hogwash (that is, your syllabus for teaching church chant). I consider it a capital error in your programme that you distribute it in accordance with the eight classes of the ordinary school. Education in music has nothing in common with learning at school, and cannot be conducted in parallel with it. Surely you would not put into the same class a pupil making good progress in music and one who was weak in the other school subjects?[5]

It thus became clear that Kruglikov did not share Rimsky-Korsakov's convictions about studying the normal school subjects and music at different times and giving priority to the latter: unlike the Kapella, the Synodal School at that time obviously thought of itself as a religious educational institution with a more profound study of the disciplines of church singing and music. As regards the more specific contents of Kruglikov's syllabuses, they are unknown; the 1885 syllabuses most likely remained only on paper, since when Smolensky became director in 1889 he found no such plans or syllabuses, and subsequently emphasized repeatedly that he had had to start everything from scratch.[6]

Neither did Kruglikov become director of the Synodal School during the 1880s. It cannot be excluded that this was partly a consequence of the weak position in the Synodal administration of his protectors at the Kapella. For the reforming activities of Rimsky-Korsakov and Balakirev had produced results not anticipated by the Synod: the Kapella had essentially been converted into a secular institution for musical education, and began to produce excellent orchestral musicians at the same time as education in church singing fell into decline.

History thus shows that neither Balakirev nor Rimsky-Korsakov, guided though they were by a sincere desire to bring about improvement in church music in Russia, played any significant part in the reforms at the Synodal School. Their colleagues from the Moscow Conservatoire Pyotr Tchaikovsky, Konstantin Albrekht, Nikolay Gubert, Dimitry Razumovsky and Sergey Taneyev enjoyed far more success in this respect; if they were not involved in the choice of the School's director, which at the end of the day was made in Synod quarters, they participated enthusiastically in the appointment of the new choirmaster for the Synodal Choir. He was Vasily Orlov, a graduate of the Moscow Conservatoire and a former pupil in Tchaikovsky's theory class.

Tchaikovsky sought the appointment of his talented pupil through both Pobedonostsev and Shishkov. His letter to Shishkov testifies to Tchaikovsky's fervent interest in the cause of improving church music:

> The importance which you attach to my opinion about such a significant matter makes me glad in the highest degree, as I feel most strongly about the flourishing of our church music... We are living through an extremely important era in Russian church music. From the end of the eighteenth century, as a result of unfavourable historical conditions, it constantly deviated from its true path in favour of an Italian-Catholic style and, in spite of the fact that in Russia, thanks to music books published by the Holy Synod, we have preserved in all their authenticity the ancient original melodies, it has lost its initial character and its organic connection with its whole environment and the overall system of Orthodox worship. [...] But circumstances have changed.
>
> At the present time, when, as I know, the Emperor himself is warmly sympathetic to the renaissance of church music, when Russian composers are not discouraged from devoting their abilities and efforts to their native church, when, on the contrary, they are encouraged to do so and when the number of people who understand the real demands of music for Orthodox worship increases daily – at such a time it is extremely important that the pre-eminent church choir of a capital city should be headed by someone whose attitude to the matter is not that of a routine craftsman but is authoritative, recognizing the sacred nature of the mission imposed upon him. Such a person must first and foremost possess a solid musical education; then he needs experience in the technique of his art, and finally, he must be up to coping with present-day demands in the field of church music...'[7]

Tchaikovsky had no reason to blush for his pupil later on; after several years' work with the Synodal Choir Orlov became a wonderful master of his craft, and the choir he directed won a reputation as one of the finest choirs in the world. Tchaikovsky followed Orlov's successes attentively – he attended his concerts and rehearsals and went to services in the Cathedral of the Dormition where the Synodal Choir sang (the composer usually stood near the right rear column of the church, on the right-hand side of it), and went to the School for exams. When Tchaikovsky died, the Synodal Choir conducted by Orlov honoured the composer's memory on the 3rd, 9th, 12th and 40th day after his death as well as six months afterwards by performing his Liturgy with the Communion verse added 'Blessed are they whom Thou hast chosen' *(Blazheni yazhe izbral)*, and thereafter sang these works annually on the day of Tchaikovsky's death (25 October) in the Church of the Great Ascension.

The attention which the composer paid to the School was always a matter of pride there, and his autographs were kept in glass cases in the foyer of the School like relics. The composer's autograph manuscripts of the choral pieces 'The Christ-child had a garden' *(Bïl u Khrista mladentsa sad)* and 'Our Father' *(Otche nash)*, and also Tchaikovsky's letter recommending Orlov as choirmaster, were placed there. The location of the letter of recommendation written by the composer for another pupil of his, Alexander Kastalsky, is unfortunately not known. Its contents are also unknown: most likely its patronage was rather formal in character, since Kastalsky was not one of Tchaikovsky's best pupils and was not noted for any particular gifts during his student years. Nothing in the 1880s presaged his future successes. Kastalsky was a humble and unnoticed teacher and, because he did not have a diploma, an inexpensive one. In the last resort that was the reason why, out of all the many musicians in Moscow, the choice fell on him.

In 1886 Orlov, the Synodal Choir's new choirmaster, asked the former inspector of the Moscow Conservatoire Albrekht to recommend an inexpensive piano teacher for the newly-opened educational establishment. It is possible that it was Albrekht, who had maintained contact with Kastalsky during his Kozlov saga and helped him organize an orchestra, who advised him to turn his attention to Kastalsky. It cannot be excluded, however, that Orlov himself showed concern for Alexander Dmitriyevich, his fellow-student at the Moscow Conservatoire. Be that as it may, in 1887 Kastalsky started teaching at the Synodal School. Tchaikovsky would probably have been astounded to find out that he had prepared the path into this institution for someone who would eventually solve a problem with which both Tchaikovsky and other composers had struggled.

Notes

1. N. Rimsky-Korsakov: *Polnoye sobraniye sochineniy* (Complete collection of works), *Literaturnïye proizvedeniya i perepiska* (Literary works and correspondence). Moscow, 1981, vol. 8a, p. 148.
2. N.A. Rimsky-Korsakov: *Letopis' moyey muzïkal'noy zhizni* (Chronicle of my musical life), Moscow, 1955, p. 151.
3. N. Rimsky-Korsakov: *Literaturnïye proizvedeniya i perepiska,* vol. 8a, p. 149.
4. *Ibid.,* pp. 149-150.
5. *Ibid.,* p. 154.

6. There is a possibility that S.N. Kruglikov's work can be judged on the basis of a document, preserved in the archive of the Moscow Synodal Office, dating from 1886 and containing a schedule of subjects taught at the Synodal School, a schedule of staff, the provisional rules for running the institution and also an explanatory note outlining an extended conception of a future reformed Synodal School. The explanatory note is signed by A.N. Shishkov, though the style of the document bears witness to the involvement in its writing of someone with a literary gift. RGADA, fond 1183, opis' 9, part 1, no. 46, 1886. Cf. *RUSAM*, vol. 2, book 1, pp. 310-321.

7. V.M. Metallov: *Sinodal'noye uchilishche tserkovnogo peniya v yego proshlom i nastoyashchem* (The Synodal School of Church Music in its past and present), in *RUSAM*, vol. 2, book 1, pp. 166-167.

Chapter 3

In Search of a 'Russian Style'

During the nineteenth century Russian religious music evolved as a sequence of experiments intended to strengthen the 'church' features and sense of national identity in the idiom of sacred music. The experiments moved in various directions, with each rejecting the ideas of its predecessors.[1] Thus, the 'German' direction which was brought into being by order of the state during the era of Nicholas I and took its cue from the Protestant chorale, was the antithesis of the 'Italian' direction, which referred to concerto-like compositions from the end of the eighteenth century and the beginning of the nineteenth century. After a time, though, the 'German' direction too found opponents. A vivid example of this rational and logical rejection is the research of Taneyev, who stood for the reorientation of Russian religious music away from Protestant and towards Catholic polyphonic models.

Let us look at the correspondence between Tchaikovsky and Taneyev in 1881. The first composer was writing an All-Night Vigil at that time, while the second was analysing the course of development of west European church music.[2] 'You ask about my Vigil', Tchaikovsky wrote to Taneyev on 5 August 1881.

> As ever, in this case I'm obeying my instincts more than following any particular way of thinking or preconceived theories. I've treated the melodies from the *Obikhod* and *Irmologion* very freely, somewhat in the manner of Bortnyansky, that is, I've not been in the least ashamed of forcing them into a specific rhythm, have sometimes changed them or been unfaithful to them and in some places I've completely abandoned them, giving free rein to my own invention. There is no or almost no element of counterpoint. The melody is always in the upper voice... [...] Write down for me, dear Seryozha, your thoughts about arrangements from the *Obikhod*.[3]

Five days later Taneyev sent a substantial answer to his former teacher where he set down the results of his theoretical investigations:

I shall tell you briefly my ideas about arrangements from the *Obikhod*. Catholic and Protestant music each represent something finished and complete. By examining more closely what composers from each tradition have done and how they have carried the development of a musical style to its logical conclusion, we can learn what we ought to do in our church music. Gregorian chant is the foundation of Catholic church music, as the chorale is the foundation of Protestant church music. On these foundations the Catholic and Protestant churches have erected magnificent edifices, whereas we have erected nothing whatsoever on our church melodies. What did western composers do with their melodies, and in what forms can a church melody be expressed in music? The most elementary way of arranging a melody is what might be called 'harmonic'. It is a simple harmonization; the melody is entrusted to one voice, the other voices accompany it, and the words are uttered by all the voices simultaneously.   Examples of such arrangements in the strict style are psalmodies, and in Protestant music harmonized chorales (for instance, those which conclude every Bach cantata).   If we look at our Russian Orthodox church music, we see that here such elementary arrangements are already in existence: they are the work of Bortnyansky, Turchaninov and Potulov. This represents, so to speak, the first stage of art (not from the historical point of view but from the musical); it offers little scope for artistic creativity, and is of little musical interest; it is nonetheless impossible to do without this form. Every time the text of a prayer is a long one (which happens in Russian Orthodoxy at every turn), we have to use this form. Only in those cases when the text of an individual melody is short can we have recourse to another kind of arrangement, where true art, richness and endless diversity of forms with scope for artistic thought begin. Contrapuntal arrangement of the melodies is involved here.

I shall dwell a little longer on what Catholic composers did in this area, for it is closer to our music than Protestant works intended to have organ accompaniment and including much that is unsuitable for unaccompanied choir.   Gregorian melodies are moreover far closer to ours than chorale melodies with their separate lines and pauses at the end of each, and so on. One can say that there is no real difference between Gregorian melodies and ours. [...]

In the final analysis the position can be reduced to the following: our church music is at the first stage of development. Ahead of it lies an endless realm of rich forms. As it enters this realm, our music, like west European music, can reach the highest stage of development and in the future work out an appropriate style for itself.[4]

It appears that Tchaikovsky was not greatly in sympathy with Taneyev's revelations and was at a loss to understand how it was possible to apply the very same method to two identical chants, as Taneyev saw them, the *znamenny* and the Gregorian, and produce different styles. Tchaikovsky did not share the theoretical approach of seeking the philosopher's stone which would allow the 'dead' heritage of the Russian Middle Ages to be brought to life, believing instead that at some future time 'a powerful and original talent' would be born who would point the path to independence. 'Creative geniuses never intellectualize about it', he replied to Taneyev. 'They seek beauty, and what sort it is, whether it is an original kind or borrowed from somewhere else, becomes clear later on...'.[5]

Fate decreed that neither Tchaikovsky nor Taneyev were to find this path.[6] Rimsky-Korsakov came much closer to solving the problem: in spite of his attachment to the Palestrina orientation, in a series of arrangements of monophonic chants he succeeded in obtaining a new, hitherto unknown quality.[7] What the Muscovite Tchaikovsky missed did not escape the notice of Rimsky-Korsakov from St Petersburg when he came to Moscow for the consecration of the Church of Christ the Saviour. With his Moscow friend Kruglikov, who had a thorough appreciation of the church service, the composer visited several ancient monasteries and was deeply impressed by the singing of the monks, which reflected an archaic beauty. Soon he had written some choral pieces where an image of a long-lost world was recreated by the hand of a great master. The devices Rimsky-Korsakov employed to depict it were well known from the secular compositions of the 'Mighty Handful' – from their operatic choruses of the Russian people and arrangements of folksongs. They included doubling the parts on many layers, parallelisms, devices from *podgolosochnaya* polyphony, responsorial and antiphonal singing, crescendo by means of texture and so on. 'In all the earlier literature', wrote Antonin Preobrazhensky, the scholar of Russian musical antiquities,

> there is no instance when a church melody, let alone one using the melody of an ancient chant taken from the church books, has been presented in the form of a choral song, with an initial introductory phrase *(zapev)* to each verse, variously in one, two or three parts. [...] In all the earlier literature we shall not find a single instance where the harmonizer has been so bold as to renounce harmony even temporarily in order to introduce the true chant melody in parallel octaves in two or three voices accompanied only by thirds or sixths – that is, as is done on the *kliros* when chants sung only by the clergy are performed.[8]

The master succeeded in undermining ideas which had held sway for centuries about the incompatibility of folk and church art and providing a model of how they could be combined in an artistic manner. As Preobrazhensky himself remarked, however, for all his extremely high assessment of Rimsky-Korsakov's innovation and in spite of the vividness of the artistic result, the composer's works do not reach beyond the framework of expert stylizations and do not qualify as a new style. The majority of scholars share Preobrazhensky's point of view, in particular Vasily Metallov, Stepan Smolensky, Alexander Nikolsky, Johann von Gardner, etc. A smaller number of voices (Nikolay Kompaneysky and a few others) have sometimes been heard pronouncing the composer the father of the new national direction.

Without entering this discussion, let us note only that Rimsky-Korsakov's extremely interesting insights did not win the fame or appreciation they deserved during his lifetime because they were published only in 1913, i.e. after the composer's death, when the subject of a new church style had long since lost its topicality. While the composer was alive only three of his innovative choral items enjoyed any popularity: 'Behold, the Bridegroom comes' (*Se zhenikh*), 'Thy bridal chamber' (*Chertog Tvoy*) and 'We hymn Thee' (*Tebe poyem*) – compositions which while without doubt vivid, did not shake belief in the strict style of harmony and polyphony propagated by the majority. Rimsky-Korsakov's discoveries were not understood even by Balakirev, his closest colleague in the 'Mighty Handful'.

Incidentally, during the 1880s, Kastalsky's first attempts at religious music were not appreciated either; he submitted them to a competition announced by the Moscow Society of Lovers of Church Music.[9] It is difficult to evaluate the quality of the young composer's first works. The only thing obvious from his reminiscences is that these compositions did not accord with the prevailing opinion that Russian chants should be treated contrapuntally after the western fashion. In fact the Society's jury for the competition, made up of Tchaikovsky, Taneyev, Arensky, Gubert and Kashkin, were guided in their assessments of the works submitted by the following criteria: they took a negative view of arrangements where the melody was doubled in thirds by adding one or two voices (the so-called 'monastery' style of harmonization), and of settings made according to the rules of academic harmony in the harmonic modes (i.e. using raised 7th degree) (known as the 'German' style); they looked with favour on arrangements corresponding to the strict style of harmony. As a result, in 1885 the first prize was unanimously awarded to the St Petersburg composer P.R. Veykhental, whose settings of church chants were very close to the experiments that Taneyev had been carrying out in those years. The possibility cannot be excluded that, had Rimsky-Korsakov submitted his *Heirmoi* in the archaic folk-church manner to this panel's judgement, they too would have been rejected.

In 1887 the Society published a unique collection of chant arrangements containing the best specimens (from the compilers' standpoint), the work of

P.R. Veykhental, Alexander Poluektov, Vladimir Kashperov and Vasily Komarov. The foreword to the collection is of interest where it states that the composers of the works presented sought:

> to come near the performance of the church chants in natural harmony, the way they undoubtedly were in ancient times but which was not written down then and was lost in practice for many reasons. [...] Weak vestiges of this singing in natural harmony can be heard in the choral performance of old sacristans and monks who have not gone through the modern school of church singing, in the style of peasants joining in the singing with the village clergy, in the singing of Old Believers when they sing without sheet music and therefore do not strictly observe the unison they intend; the fact that these are only weak vestiges becomes evident if you compare them with the rich and varied polyphony of folksongs and spiritual verses.[10]

In fact, however, the hopes of the collection's compilers were justified only in the settings by Komarov, the melodic fabric of which was reminiscent of folk heterophony. The other works in the collection maintain a style which, in the opinion of the same Komarov, 'contained very little that was Russian'.

Organizing competitions to find the best works was only one of the forms which the Society's activities took; founded in 1880, the Society had a very marked influence on church music life in Moscow over the first decade of its existence. Perhaps its most interesting and valuable initiative was to record the contemporary oral tradition of singing in the parish churches of the Moscow diocese. The idea of undertaking work of this kind, which the Society continued to do over a period of about 25 years, arose under the influence of the then new field of ethnography. It is no coincidence that the first to take part in it was the celebrated folklorist Yuly Melgunov, who was helped by Society members Komarov and Kashperov. In 1882 the same group recorded the melodies used in the Cathedral of the Dormition in the Moscow Kremlin as sung by the priest Pyotr Vinogradov. The Society's work cast doubt on the then current opinion that the pure, canonical tradition of church singing, uncorrupted by the influence of secular music, could be found only in the ancient manuscripts using 'hook' notation. The compilers of the Annual Cycle of Hymns (*Godovoy krug pesnopeniy*) assumed that it was the living tradition transcribed from the voices of experts that should be the object of study, and not a dead bookish inheritance. The 'folk' style of harmonizing church chants actually arose from the performing style of non-professional church singers drawn from among ordinary people, placing the key to creating national counterpoint into professional composers' hands.

We know that Rimsky-Korsakov was interested in the Society's activities and asked Kruglikov to get in touch with the members; one must presume that he also knew of the principles upheld by several members of the Society concerning arrangeents of Russian monody, which correspond surprisingly closely to his experimental choral pieces of 1883-84. Be that as it may, the composer, with his heightened feeling for national colour, found new ways of expressing what had been hanging in the Moscow air for a number of years. In the sacred compositions of the majority of his contemporaries, however, such ideas were realized using old means, and, what is more, the disparity between the challenges brought forward by the age and how they were met passed practically unnoticed.

The 1880s were thus a time when ideas ran ahead of the development of the language of music. All the preconditions for assimilating the heritage of church music were present, however, insofar as the musical folklore melodically akin to church chants had already been absorbed by composers of secular music. New forms in art were dictated by the age itself, where the 'Russian style' of Victor Vasnetsov reigned. The entry of sacred music upon a period of 'nationalism' was also not far off: the arrival of the 1880s – usually associated in Soviet historiography with the 'political reaction' which followed the assassination of Emperor Alexander II but linked in pre-revolutionary historiography with the strengthening of Russia's international prestige, the significant extension of her territories and the stabilization of the internal political situation – marked the beginning of a new era in the art of church music.

Notes

1. Readers wishing to learn more about the assimilation of ancient chants in Russian church music in the nineteenth century are referred to the following:
    A.V. Preobrazhensky: *Kul'tovaya muzïka v Rossii* (Religious music in Russia). Petrograd, 1924. German translation: Antonij V. Preobrazhenskij: *Die Kirchenmusik in Rußland. Von den Anfängen bis zum Anbruch des 20. Jahrhunderts*; ed. Andreas Wehrmeyer, translated by Ernst Kuhn and Andreas Wehrmeyer. Berlin, 1999.
    I.A. Gardner: *Bogosluzhebnoye peniye russkoy pravoslavnoy tserkvi. Istoriya* (The worship music of the Russian Orthodox Church. History), vol. 2. Jordanville, New York, 1982; published by the Monastery of the Holy Trinity.
    N.Yu. Plotnikova: *Mnogogolosnïye formï obrabotki drevnikh rospevov v russkoy dukhovnoy muzïke XIX-nachala XX vekov* (Polyphonic forms of setting ancient chants in Russian sacred music of the nineteenth and early twentieth centuries). Diss., Moscow State Conservatoire, 1996.
    N.S. Gulyanitskaya: *Russkoye 'garmonicheskoye peniye' (XIX vek)* (Russian 'harmonic singing' (nineteenth century)). Moscow, 1995.

Ditto: *Poetika muzïkal'noy kompozitsii. Teoreticheskiye aspektï russkoy dukhovnoy muzïki XX veka* (The poetics of musical composition. Theoretical aspects of Russian sacred music in the twentieth century). Moscow, 2002.

Istoriya russkoy muzïki v 10-ti tomakh (History of Russian Music in ten volumes), vols. 3-10a. Moscow, 1985-1998.

RUSAM, vol. 3.

2. From 1875 to 1879 Taneyev wrote contrapuntal exercises where Russian folksongs and chants from the *Obikhod* were used as *cantus firmi*. Between 1879 and 1890 he wrote 15 sacred hymns (variants included), 10 of which are contrapuntal settings. The composer himself described two ways of arranging chants contrapuntally: 1) the given part is placed in one voice in long notes while the other parts perform imitations which may be similar, but need not be, to the given melody; 2) the given part is broken up into separate phrases, with each of the phrases being imitated. See the edition: S.I. Taneyev: *Dukhovnaya muzïka* (Sacred Music), ed. N.Yu. Plotnikova. Moscow, 1999.

3. Letter of 5 August 1881 from Tchaikovsky to Taneyev. *P.I. Chaykovsky. S.I. Taneyev. Pis'ma* (Letters). Moscow, 1951, pp. 72-73.

4. Letter of 10 August 1881 from Taneyev to Tchaikovsky. *Ibid.*, pp. 74-76.

5. Letter of 23-25 August 1881 from Tchaikovsky to Taneyev. *Ibid.*, p. 76.

6. Cf. these publications of Tchaikovsky's sacred compositions accompanied by extended research articles: P.I. Chaykovsky: *Polnoye sobraniye sochineniy* (Complete Works), vol. 63. Moscow, 1990; Peter Tchaikovsky: *The Complete Sacred Choral Works*, in series *Monuments of Russian Sacred Music*, editor-in chief Vladimir Morosan, series II, vols. 1-3, Musica Russica, 1996.

7. The fullest information at present available about the sacred compositions of Rimsky-Korsakov is to be found in: M.P. Rakhmanova: *Nikolay Andreyevich Rimsky-Korsakov*. Moscow, 1995. See also the edition: Nikolai Rimsky-Korsakov: *The Complete Sacred Choral Works*, with introduction by Marina Rakhmanova, in series *Monuments of Russian Sacred Music*, editor-in-chief Vladimir Morosan, series III, Musica Russica, 1999.

8. A.V. Preobrazhensky: *Kul'tovaya muzïka v Rossii*, p. 109.

9. Cf. the detailed account of the activities of this Moscow organization as well as the publication of works by several of its members in vol. 3 of *RUSAM*.

10. V.M. Metallov: *Pyotr Dmitriyevich Samarin v yego sluzhenii delu tserkovnogo peniya* (Pyotr Dmitriyevich Samarin in his service to the cause of church music). Sergiyev Posad, 1917, p. 6.

Chapter 4

The Nation – a Powerful Force

Old institutions, old traditions, old customs – are a matter of great moment. A nation cherishes them like the ark of the covenant of their ancestors. But how often has history seen, and how often do we see now, that national (*narodnïye*) governments by no means cherish them, considering them old baggage, to be got rid of as soon as possible. They revile them pitilessly, they hasten to recast them in new forms and expect that a new spirit will immediately be instilled in the new forms.[1]

So wrote a man who devoted all his spiritual powers and all of his powerful intellect to preserving Russian traditions. Like many of his contemporaries, he considered that a land in the grip of terror and unrest could be saved neither by liberalizing her laws nor by borrowing experience from elsewhere, but only by the nation's own moral powers, by its religious traditions and ideals. The name of this man, which has never vanished from the printed page in over a century now, was Konstantin Petrovich Pobedonostsev.

Pobedonostsev came to the idea of the spiritual and moral saving of his fatherland by the same route as Dostoyevsky whom he deeply honoured. This route lay through Russian Orthodox places of worship, where both men were destined to experience the throbbing spiritual pulse of the multimillion-strong Russian nation.

Anyone Russian in soul and tradition understands what God's house means, what the church means to a Russian. It is not enough to be devout yourself, to sense and respect the demands of religious feeling; it is not enough to comprehend what the church means to the Russian nation and to love the church as your own, almost as part of you. You have to live the nation's life, you have to be at one in prayer with the nation, at one with those assembled in church, to feel yourself as one with the beating of the nation's heart, imbued with a common exultation, a common word and song. For this reason there are many who know the church only from domestic chapels where a select public gathers, who lack genuine understanding of their church or of its true aesthetic flavour, and at times look indifferently or perversely on what in the church's custom or service is particularly precious to the faithful and represents a pearl of eccesiastical beauty in their understanding.[2]

The grandson of a priest in the Zvenigorod diocese and the son of a Moscow University professor, Pobedonostsev was a profoundly devout believer in the 'old Muscovite' mould who held in honour the old statutory church services, preferring a quiet, poorly-attended service in a village church or a remote monastery to services for the élite. Fate decreed, however, that the talented law professor of Moscow University, author of fundamental works about the history of law, should for the greater part of his life worship in St Petersburg's court churches. In 1861 he received a proposal to teach jurisprudence to the young grand dukes and moved to St Petersburg. In 1880 came Pobedonostsev's appointment to the post of the state's principal ideologue – as *Ober-Prokuror* of the Holy Synod. The murder of Alexander II by members of the 'People's Will' in 1881 marked the start of the reign of his son, Grand Duke Alexander Alexandrovich, who fully shared the ideas of his recent teacher and now faithful and experienced aide. In this way, the drawing-up of a state policy based on the nation's traditional values became a reality in the Russia of the 1880s. What are the values under discussion? Here is what the scholar of the Middle Ages Stepan Smolensky had to say.

> In the reasoning of people who might be simple but were nonetheless filled with faith and power, I often heard very strong and unexaggerated notes, the same ones which could be heard in the pulses of national movements when the movement was called forth by the impotence of the previous administration and was on the point of overcoming some destructive calamity. Besides their amusing generalizations and notions concerning the future, these homespun politicians from the other side of the Moscow River (*Zamoskvorechye*) and the Taganka were in essence completely right, and their animated enthusiasm reminded me vividly of the stupendous impressions which I myself experienced during Alexander III's bows to the people from the Red Wing of the palace adjoining the Cathedral of the Dormition and during the coronation of Nicholas II.[3] I remember beginning to feel a thrill of elation during this conversation just as much as I did when I could see the bells in the Ivanov bell-tower ringing and could not hear their peals because of the astounding, indescribable 'Hurrah' of hundreds of thousands of the people...
>
> It was precisely this power, concealed, immense, by many unsuspected, perfectly healthy and independent, looking condescendingly at all the decay and lies of our administration, our culture – precisely this power, staring me in the face so unexpectedly and obviously, which struck my mind so forcefully. Its existence and incomparable strength were verified to my mind from an angle which I had not expected. I believed in this power, coming to an acknowledgement of its existence with the aid of generalizations from history,

and I could see it in reality and sense its boundless strength. The calm pulses of this power throb before our very eyes. What else is it but serving the motherland when a lone priest or monk conducts morning service in some remote hermitage, alone but for a psalmodist-cum-watchman in a completely empty church? I remember one Matins of that kind at which I found myself unexpectedly in a blizzard on a dark night. Who is this Rachinsky, who buried himself in his love for the world and his motherland? Who is that Moscow moneybags, for example, that eccentric, Solodovnikov, at the moment when his heart opens up and he remembers that he is a Russian? How precious to me were my involuntary tears when moments of the sweetest love for my native land came upon me! How expressive were those quiet but majestic movements of the nation which have been kept intact until now by hundreds and thousands – like the 'solemn greeting' of the icon in Kazan carried on 26 June from the Sedmiyezernaya hermitage,[4] or like the unending lines of pilgrims on their way to the Sergiyev monastery, or to Kiev, or to Solovki? Who was it, for instance, who saved Bulgaria, Serbia or our 'Holy Russia' in the cruel years of 1612 or 1812[5] if not faith – that same blind, unreasoning, ritual, worshipping faith against which all the horrors of the Turks, the Tatars, the Poles and the French, all the terrors of our 350-year yoke and our 500-year southern yoke crumbled?

I find it difficult to define in words and to name even approximately this power which so enlivens and invigorates the capacities of the nation, developing its endurance and long-suffering; can I deny in it the presence of that which sobers the nation and saves it in time of misfortune? For me, this is beyond question, it ennobles and heals me, and I look calmly on the future of my motherland, believing in the good sense of this power of a higher order. [...] What an immense, incalculable power is in the tsar's hands with this historically strengthened love of the nation for autocracy, despite the disgust of the selfsame nation at the embezzling and callous officialdom which has ensnared the country! I think that the tsar himself does not know how firm and strong he is in the massive love of the nation.[6]

The incorporation of such a long quotation may perhaps be forgiven, for the thoughts and feelings expressed in it are very important in understanding the state of mind of many of the creators and performers of church music within the New Direction, inasmuch as the quotation was written by the man who was its principal thinker. The 'pulses of the nation' which gave Smolensky strength in his difficult battle to create a great and original Russian culture, may be heard in the works of the composers of the school to the development of which he was able to lend impetus.

The three 'ideals of the Russian land' – 'faith', 'nation' and 'tsar' delineated in Smolensky's pronouncement were at the basis not only of the personal creed which he disseminated among his pupils and colleagues, but also at the root of the state's ideological conception. It was not western civilization but the simple Russian Orthodox soul and its moral foundations which were to save a country which, in the opinion of the statesmen who affirmed this idea, was sliding down into an abyss of social cataclysms. However, this brittle 'main value' receptive to everything good as well as bad needed to be defended most of all. The nation needed to be defended both from itself and from 'champions of enlightenment' who propagated rebellion and atheism. It seems that one should regard the tendency to teach currents of Christianity in education which arose at this time as precisely a reaction against the results of *narodnik* enlightenment. Let us say at once that the new ideas in teaching at the end of the nineteenth century were not a simple restoration of old ones – like authoritarian ideas. They were the fruit of a new age: after going through a centrifugal phase in its history and being disappointed by the results, society turned instead to the nation's historical experience.

The same kind of ideas were also discussed at a state level and underlay the reforms in education undertaken during the first years of Alexander III's rule, which aimed to make elementary schools into church schools to be created within church parishes under the control of the Synod. The model for organizing church parish schools was once more derived from the ideas of the peasants themselves about what their children should be taught. Pobedonostsev supposed:

> As the people understand things, a school teaches reading, writing and counting, but, indissolubly linked with that, it also teaches pupils to know God, to love and fear him, to love the Fatherland, and to respect one's parents. That is the sum total of knowledge, abilities and feelings which in combination form a person's conscience and give him the moral strength necessary to preserve his balance in life and endure the struggle with the evil inducements of nature and the evil promptings and temptations of thought.[7]

The creation of a network of church parish schools was the life's work of the *Ober-Prokuror*, and he was extremely successful in it. Suffice it to say that at the beginning of his service to the state in 1880 there were 237 such schools in Russia with 13,035 pupils, whereas at the end of it, in 1905, there were 43,696 schools with 1,782,883 pupils. The actual model for the school and the teaching concept applied in it were worked out by Pobedonostsev's close friend and colleague from the University of Moscow, the famous botanist and scientist Sergey Rachinsky. At the peak of his career Rachinsky gave up his professorial chair and moved to his ancestral estate of Tatevo in the Smolensk province, where using his own means he organized a hospital, a Society for Sobriety and five schools for peasant children. Right up to his death in 1901, Rachinsky was in charge of the venture he had begun, which had consequences of outstanding importance. This educational wave reached even Kazan, where the orientalist Nikolay Ilminsky and his relative Smolensky, a graduate of the Law and Arts faculties of Kazan University, began their assiduous working lives in the 1870s at the Seminary for Teachers of non-Russian minorities.

Sharing Rachinsky's convictions in full, Smolensky concentrated his efforts on teaching church music. In the 1870s when Smolensky started work in the seminary, methods of teaching this subject had hardly been developed. The young teacher, with his faith in the immense moral, educational and spiritual effect of church music, decided to fill this gap. To find out how matters stood in this field, he visited not only the Court Kapella and the Moscow Conservatoire where the first department of church music in Russia headed by Dimitry Razumovsky had recently been opened, but also travelled to Germany. The result of his efforts was the exemplary class in church music at the Kazan Teachers' Seminary, its fine choir and the textbook based on the numerical method 'Course in Church Choral Music' (*Kurs khorovogo tserkovnogo peniya*) which ran to several editions. The most important outcome of the broadening of Smolensky's powerful and versatile mind in the realm of church music was, however, his brilliant research in the field of church music archaeology which placed his name immediately after that of the famous scholar Razumovsky, whose acquaintance he had made in 1876 in Moscow, and which served Smolensky as a spur to his study of ancient Russian music. On returning to Kazan after meeting Razumovsky, who had accused him of being ignorant of the 'hook' notation, Smolensky immersed himself in investigating old forms of notation, and quickly became convinced of the fruitful influence of antiquity on the future development of the art.

At the same time Smolensky's teaching experience, enriched by his knowledge and lively feeling for tradition, gradually became more widely known; pupils from other peasant schools began to make their way to the Kazan Teachers' Seminary to study church music, in particular from the schools of Rachinsky with whom Smolensky began an intensive correspondence. He also visited Rachinsky's Tatevo school which made an indelible impression on him.

What were the ideals proclaimed by the new school of the 1880s? Let us examine the legacy of Rachinsky, who was one of its liveliest representatives. In his opinion, a school cannot be just a place where arithmetic and grammar are taught, but first and foremost it must be a school of instruction in Christianity and good morals in the Christian life under the direction of the Church. It is precisely Holy Scripture, the Church-Slavonic language and church art which constitute the miracle-working force which ennobles the souls of children who are unusually responsive to the beauty of the church which has been close to them since childhood; moreover, through church reading and music they enter the world of the present-day Russian language, literature and classical music in the most organic way. As Rachinsky wrote in his 'Notes on Village Schools' published in 1883:

> The educational influence of public reading in church is immense. Good church reading presupposes a complete understanding of what is being read; that is, from a formal point of view assimilating a system of complex and bold constructions, and from an inner point of view – an entire world of lofty poetry and profound theological thought. We need only recall the colossal contents of the readings from the Old Testament, the Epistles and canons of Holy Week. I turn to the judgement of people who are not believers but are sincere and know what I am talking about. The person who has sensed and understood this, who by his reading has brought to the consciousness of illiterate listeners even a tenth part of all these weighty contents – can his intellectual and artistic growth be denied? Can it be doubted that everything of permanent and true value offered by our secular literature will be accessible to him in both content and form?[8]

Rachinsky was especially enraptured by the musicality of peasant children who studied church music with unusual willingness, the 'pedagogical' value of which Rachinsky demonstrated to the 'unbelieving' community in the same work, provoking a huge resonance:

> Is there any need to insist on the incomparable beauty of our ancient church melodies to people who possess even a suspicion of sensitivity to music? Is there any need to remind the reader who is even slightly familiar with our church service of its inexhaustible variety? To someone engrossed in this world of austere grandeur with its profound illumination of all the movements of the human spirit, to such a person all the highest musical arts are accessible; to such a person both Bach and Palestrina as well as Mozart's brightest inspirations and Beethoven's and Glinka's most mystical feats of daring are understandable.[9]

Nature seemed to Rachinsky the crown of God's creation. As a remarkable natural scientist, he devoted a great deal of time to walks with his pupils, during which he not only made the children familiar with the laws of nature but also showed them the beauty and perfection of the world. Rachinsky strove to convey to his pupils his own instinctive vision of divine beauty in things both great and small, in nature and art, in the popular and the professional, in the secular and the sacred, in the Russian and the western. A folk spinning-wheel or a little horse on a wooden peasant cottage he saw as just as much a fine creation of the spirit as the melodic patterning in Russian chants which, in their turn, stood on the same level as the masterpieces of world musical culture.

Such a worldview was characteristic of many contemporaries and friends of Rachinsky; their writings demonstrate a new aesthetic which elevates the folk and the ecclesiastical to a single spiritual origin and proclaims the equality of all the loftiest manifestations of the human spirit regardless of when they arose or of their national origin. In the light of this aesthetic, Russian folk and ecclesiastical art was reclassified into the category of the 'loftiest' arts, to which the professional arts were assigned in accordance with post-Enlightenment tradition. Accordingly, new ways of looking at them also arose.

Let us look at the dry syllabus for the teaching of church music in the seminaries which Smolensky prepared in the 1880s on Pobedonostsev's instructions where it is said that the most important aspect for pupils studying church music is not assimilating it in theory or practice but grasping its artistic element. Glancing through the works of Pobedonostsev himself, we read the following panegyric to the beauty of Russian church music:

> Russian church music, like folksong, pours forth in a broad, free stream from the breast of the people, and the freer it is, the more fully it speaks to the heart. The melodies in Russia are the same as those of the Greeks, but the Russian people sing them differently because they have invested their whole soul in them. [...] How broadly and freely a festal heirmos pours forth from a Russian breast, with what solemn poetry is a dogmatik sung forth, a sticheron combined with a kanonarkh, what joyous animation permeates the canon for Easter or Christ's Nativity![10]

The artistic feeling, the hyperbole of emotion and meaning in these statements bore witness to the coming of age of the era of Orthodox Romanticism, idealizing Ancient Rus as the unpolluted source of the nation's spirit. Let us recall, if nothing more, the novels of Melnikov-Pechersky, which took the place of *narodnik* literature denouncing the church and poeticized the patriarchal life of the Russian Old Believers, the religious works of Victor Vasnetsov, associated by contemporaries with the work of Andrey Rublyov, or the scholarly works of Smolensky tinged with their romantic hymning of antiquity.

Beneath these new currents, the theme of searching for ways to save the huge country rang out loudly. It seems that it was exactly this sense of impending doom that forced people to listen more intently to 'the pulses of the nation' and helped give rise to the new 'Russian idea' based on the nation's religious experience, which coloured ideology and politics, literature and philosophy, art and teaching.

As regards the three heroes of this chapter – Pobedonostsev, Smolensky and Rachinsky, they did a great deal to promote that 'Russian renaissance' which Russia experienced on the eve of her catastrophe. And fate dealt kindly with them, for none of them was destined to find out how the battle for a great and distinctive Russia came to an end.

Notes

1. K.P. Pobedonostsev: *Dukhovnaya zhizn'* (The Spiritual Life), in his *Velikaya lozh' nashego vremeni* (The great lie of our time). Moscow, 1993, p. 321.
2. K.P. Pobedonostsev: *Tserkov'* (The church). *Ibid.,* p. 261.
3. The 'great entrance' of the sovereign and his suite from the Granovitaya Palace in the Kremlin to the Cathedral of the Dormition through the Red Wing, and the tsar's bow to the ground before his people were one of the most important parts of the coronation ceremony.
4. The icon of the Mother of God Hodigitria (the Pathfinder) was housed in the Sedmiyezernaya hermitage, founded in the seventeenth century not far from Kazan. A procession with the cross took place every year in its honour from the hermitage to the city of Kazan which attracted thousands of the faithful from every corner of Russia.
5. The author of the quotation was thinking about the Russo-Turkish war of 1877-78, ending in a Russian victory which furthered the freeing of the peoples of the Balkan peninsula from Turkish domination, the Polish intervention at the beginning of the seventeenth century which came to an end in 1612 with the liberation of Moscow by a Russian militia, the expulsion of the occupiers and the crowning of the new Romanov dynasty, and also the Patriotic War of 1812 against the French.
6. S.V. Smolensky: *Sinodal'nïy khor i uchilishche tserkovnogo peniya* (The Synodal Choir and School of Church Music), in *RUSAM*, vol. 1, pp. 76-77. Cf. *RUSAM*, vol. 4, containing S.V. Smolensky's reminiscences.
7. K.P. Pobedonostsev: *Narodnoye prosveshcheniye* (The enlightenment of the people), in his *Velikaya lozh' nashego vremeni*, pp. 138-139.
8. S.A. Rachinsky: *Zametki o sel'skikh shkolakh* (Remarks about village schools). St Petersburg, 1883, p. 96.
9. *Ibid.*, p. 97.
10. K.P. Pobedonostsev: *Tserkov'* in his *Velikaya lozh' nashego vremeni*, p. 263.

Chapter 5

'Moscow will come into its own!'

At the turn of the nineteenth and twentieth centuries a situation which had arisen almost three centuries earlier was repeated: a time when ecclesiastical art was taking wing most brilliantly coincided with a climax in Russian statehood and national self-consciousness. A further historical precedent was also repeated: the ancient capital again became the centre of a 'Russian renaissance'. The resurrection of the idea of the great Third Rome was no coincidence, inasmuch as Moscow was one of the fundamental symbols of the new religious and romantic world-view permeated by recollections of history. Stepan Smolensky became a Muscovite in 1889 and wrote:

> The love I felt before for my own native 'city of white stone' was joined by a new, conscious, and even firmer feeling of reverence for the heart of the Russian land. I read everything I could lay my hands on about Moscow, and fell even more passionately in love with her; systematically viewing the city and studying the architecture of Moscow from the Krutitsky Gate and the Simonov Monastery to the Vagankovo Cemetery and Kuntsevo, from the Donskoy monastery to the Novodevichy, from the Sparrow Hills to Sokolniki and Cherkizovo, fostered within me an acute ability to imagine the past as I stood on a spot where great events had taken place. Therefore a shiver went up my spine every time I walked across Red Square, drawing for myself scenes with Ivan the Terrible, the Time of Troubles and Peter I; for that reason I must have gone round or been inside the church of Vasily the Blessed about a hundred times, and I consider it one of the outstanding works created by Russians which gave me the greatest enlightenment about the theorems of our rhythm, both for the resemblance and the sum total as well as for a work of separate sections and also as a general model or plan of a whole composition; for that reason such architectural wonders as the western wall of the Kremlin with its Trinity tower are so dear to me; for that reason I developed an ability to 'read' fenestrations, capitals, the antiquity of the Cathedral of the Dormition, the charm of technique in an ancient manuscript and its chant, the distinctive profile even of the Okhotny Row, Balchug, the still unenlightened area beyond the Moscow river (*Zamoskvorechye*) and the ancient Rogozhsky cemetery. [...] It might seem ridiculous, giving steam and electricity their due, but the people

of the distant past were incomparably, unimaginably simpler, cleverer, more
direct and had more common sense, and – the main thing – were more honest,
religious and sincere than those of the present, and, moreover, far more
energetic and far more enterprising. It is for that reason that I set such great
store by the archaism which has escaped destruction – the intimately Russian
culture of the Old Believers, which is probably all that remains with us as a
healthy and devoutly Russian seed for future Russian antiquity.[1]

Having taken a back seat in Russian history for almost two centuries,
the ancient capital had preserved its powerful impulse as had been sensed
by the creators of the 'New Russian Style' in art,[2] which Igor Grabar called
in jest the 'new Moscow edition of Ancient Rus'.

The birth of the 'New Russian Style' goes back to 1882. On the estate
of Abramtsevo just outside Moscow an artistic colony had been established
with the aim of reviving folk handicrafts on a professional basis. The
construction there of a small church to a plan by Victor Vasnetsov was
completed in that year. The striving to convey the inner content of ancient
Russian icon-painting and the national system of belief are also
characteristic of the paintings of this artist, who in 1884 embarked on
decorating the interior of the Cathedral of St Vladimir in Kiev. The critic
P.N. Ge wrote about these frescoes and icons subsequently:

There are both ancient Russian and Byzantine features here; there is also a
portion borrowed from the Pre-Raphaelites; there is also, I believe, in several
figures on the gates of heaven an element borrowed from Michelangelo; but the
most important thing, which is the distinguishing feature of his work, is the
purely national spirit which breathes from his work, as from some descriptions
of lives of the saints.[3]

After the Cathedral of St Vladimir came work on the icons for the
iconostasis of the Cathedral of St Alexander Nevsky in Sofia, sketches for
the mosaic of the Church of the Saviour (*Spas na Krovi*)[4] in St Petersburg,
icons for the Russian church in Darmstadt and other commissions.

The 'New Russian Style', in which Victor Vasnetsov was followed by
his brother Apollinary, Nesterov, Vrubel, Roerich, Shchusev, Shekhtel,
Pokrovsky and other artists and architects, superseded the art of the
Itinerants, whose creativity had exhausted itself. The emergence of this
artistic trend in the Russian art of the 1880s was received by
contemporaries as a breath of fresh air bursting into an atmosphere of
intellectual stagnation. The critic V.L. Kign-Dedlov, who did not miss a
single exhibition at this time, confessed that he was tired of Russian
pictures:

The Itinerants had already done their job and made their careers, and turned into an exclusive circle; they were frozen in their naturalist traditions and had become boring. The academic exhibitions showed even more petrified old professors or else immature young people, among whom there were several timid, emerging talents. Naturalism had outlived itself. As you set out for an exhibition, you knew in advance what you were going to see: two or three 'peasants', and what's more the peasant would be as ugly as a stone carving of a Scythian fertility goddess, but oppressed and suffering; a hero from the intelligentsia, rickety in frame, but still protesting; a couple of historical subjects which could never abandon 'choosing a bride', with the candidates for bride all depicted with the one kind of face like Crimean apples 'according to the Russian taste', and episodes from the administrative-cum-management activities of Tsar Ivan, someone being flogged and someone else strangled; occasionally you would come upon something 'Christian' in subject – the catacombs, or martyrs of rare composure in the circus; and then the landscape held sway, monotonous, dull, each one just like the next, unable to go further beyond St Petersburg than Kolpino station on the Nicholas I railway line. Russian painting became depressed and lost all zest. And then, after all that tedium, I happened to find myself in the Cathedral of St Vladimir... Freedom and vitality were in the air, and I sensed that freedom and vitality as well as the courage of the artist who had risked his career by swimming against the prevailing tide.[5]

At the beginning of the twentieth century when it was proposed to Vasnetsov that he head the newly organized workshop for religious painting at the St Petersburg Academy of the Arts, he suggested instead that it should be founded in Moscow as an ancient city and a capital full of ancient monuments. The artist himself moved to Moscow in 1878. At almost the same time, Repin, Polenov and Surikov also moved to the 'original capital'. In 1893 Repin wrote that

it is now becoming ever clearer that Moscow will preside over Russia once again. In all areas of Russian life Moscow is manifesting herself on a gigantic scale, in a way unattainable by our fatherland's other cultural centres. They are obliged merely to imitate her, and on a more modest scale. Yes – Moscow will come into its own![6]

In the 1880s and 1890s many composers, performers and musical scholars who were open to Russia's 'heart' moved to Moscow. Among them were Arensky, Ippolitov-Ivanov, Safonov, Preobrazhensky, Metallov and Smolensky. At the beginning of the 1890s even Rimsky-Korsakov considered moving to Moscow, disappointed with the St Petersburg followers of the 'Mighty Handful'; he wrote to his friend Kruglikov:

Dear Semyon Nikolayevich,

I am certain that this letter will come as a surprise to you. I ask you to keep its contents entirely secret for the time being. [...] 2) At the St Petersburg Conservatoire things are going to the dogs: one can't imagine such slumber, such inertia and hopelessness. 3) The group of St Petersburg musicians (the former 'Mighty Handful') is embarking on some new phase which is alien to me. 4) In general, I feel the need for some kind of renewal, in a different air, in less foggy and gloomy winter days. I think that in different surroundings I'd come back to life, and perhaps start composing and so on again. You know I like Moscow, and I like it not just for its meat-pies (*rastegai*) but because life there is somehow more energetic and younger. To you Muscovites it looks the other way round; but we Petersburgers really can see more clearly, because we know our tired and wilted St Petersburg. This is not my opinion only; Moscow makes the same impression on other people too – Repin, for example. My wish would be: to leave my job at the Kapella, resettle in Moscow (in one of the little lanes), and take up a position as a professor at the Moscow Conservatoire, which I'd probably suit. I don't know what Safonov is like as a person, but as an organizer he is extremely energetic, and the results at the Moscow Conservatoire and at the Musical Society are far better, livelier and fresher than in St Petersburg. [...] I want to become a Muscovite in my old age; that's all there is to it![7]

The composer's dream did not come to pass, although it was thanks to Moscow, where some of his operas which went unacknowledged in St Petersburg were staged during the 1880s at Savva Mamontov's Private Opera and then in the Bolshoy Theatre, that Rimsky-Korsakov was able to overcome his crisis and start on a fruitful new stage in his compositions, one which gave the world many masterpieces. They include the opera *The Legend of the Invisible City of Kitezh* – a superb incarnation of the Orthodox romantic idea. In the 1880s, however, the time for this idea to bear fruit in great accomplishments had not yet come. Russian music, having bathed in the genius of Tchaikovsky and gone into raptures over the talents of Taneyev and Glazunov, was only beginning to absorb the religious-romantic ideals born of the new age. The fabled and beautiful Third Rome became one of them, and its image gave a creative impulse to an entire direction in Russian art at the turn of the century.

Notes

1. Stepan Vasil'yevich Smolensky: *Vospominaniya* (Reminiscences), in *RUSAM* vol. 4, pp. 273-274.
2. A number of books by art-historians are devoted to the 'New Russian Style', in particular the following work by Ye.I. Kirichenko, variously published as follows: *The*

Russian Style. London, 1991; *Zwischen Byzanz und Moskau. Der nationale Stil in der russischen Kunst.* Munich, 1991; *Russian Design and the Fine Arts, 1750-1917.* New York, 1991; *Russkiy stil'. Poiski vïrazheniya samobïtnosti. Narodnost' i natsional'nost'. Traditsii drevnerusskogo i narodnogo iskusstva v russkom iskusstve XVIII – nachala XX veka* (The Russian style. Quests for expressing distinctiveness. National identity and nationality. The traditions of ancient-Russian and folk art in Russian art from the eighteenth to the early twentieth century). Moscow, 1997

3. P.N. Ge: *Kharakternçye techeniya sovremennoy russkoy zhivopisi* (Characteristic trends in contemporary Russian painting), in *Zhizn'* (Life), book 1, 1899, p. 163.

4. The Church of the Resurrection of Christ ('The Saviour on the Blood', *Spas na krovi*) was built between 1882 and 1907 on the site of the assassination of Emperor Alexander II in 1881.

5. Cited from A.I. Uspensky: *Viktor Mikhaylovich Vasnetsov.* Moscow, 1906, pp. 82-84.

6. I.Ye. Repin and P.M. Tret'yakov: *Perepiska* (Correspondence). Moscow and Leningrad, 1946, p. 163.

7. N. Rimsky-Korsakov: *Polnoye sobraniye sochineniy* (Complete collection of works), *Literaturnïye proizvedeniya i perepiska* (Literary works and correspondence), vol. 8a, p. 209.

Chapter 6

History Stretching Back into the Past

While visiting Moscow on business in 1889, Smolensky received two proposals simultaneously which tied him fast to that city. Two people called on him in his room at the Moscow Grand Hotel on the very same day: Shishkov, the manager of the Moscow Synodal Printing Office, offered Smolensky the job of director of the Synodal School; and then Taneyev, the director of the Moscow Conservatoire, informed him that on his deathbed archpriest Razumovsky had given his blessing to Smolensky, the scholar from Kazan, heading the Department of Church Music at the Conservatoire. Three years earlier Smolensky had rejected Shishkov's offer, but this time he accepted. 'Without my own firm belief in the correctness of a path which I had fully thought through and chosen for myself, Nikolay Ilminsky's approbation from Kazan, the approval of my new but already tried and tested friend from Tatevo – Sergey Rachinsky, and through him my straightforward relationship unconnected with work directly with Konstantin Pobedonostsev – without those factors I should not have resolved to undertake this work with energy', Smolensky recalled later.[1]

The burden which the scholar was now shouldering was no easy one: he was required not just to create a professional institution providing education in choral music for the church but also to improve the singing of the Synodal Choir which was bound up with the School in the closest possible way. The responsibility was immense, since the choir in question was the oldest and best-known Russian church choir whose history was very familiar to Smolensky thanks to Razumovsky's researches.[2]

During the medieval period the future Synodal Choir was the choir of the Russian church's primate. After Rus's adoption of Christianity in the tenth century, the Russian church was one of the metropolitanates in the patriarchate of Constantinople. The seat of the Russian primate, the metropolitan, was Kiev, the capital city of the state. No information about the existence of a church choir in the service of the Kiev metropolitan has been found, but one may suppose, by analogy with the organization of other seats of the higher clergy in the Byzantine church, that singers were included among the staff of the first Orthodox metropolitans (who were Greeks) to arrive in Kiev. At the beginning of the fourteenth century Vladimir on the Klyazma became the permanent place of residence of the metropolitans of Kiev, and Moscow from the 1330s. During the second half of the fourteenth century and the first half of the fifteenth century the majority of Orthodox states, Byzantium included, were conquered by the Ottoman Turks. The Grand Principality of Moscow, which had united the Russian lands under its control, remained the only independent Orthodox power, a factor which promoted the formation of the concept of Russia's divinely-ordained destiny as the successor of Byzantium and custodian of the 'true faith'. The same concept was also reflected in the doctrine of Moscow as the 'Third Rome'. In the spirit of this idea, the Grand Prince of Moscow took the title 'tsar', that is, emperor. After the conquest of Constantinople by the Turks in 1453, the status of the Russian church changed as well: first, the metropolitanate of Moscow (rather than Kiev) was proclaimed, and in 1589 the patriarchate of Moscow was established.

Late fifteenth-century Moscow greeted her guests with a luxurious feast of architecture. By that time, Russian and Italian craftsmen had finished building the Moscow Kremlin and many of the cathedrals inside it – those of the Dormition, the Archangel Michael, and the Annunciation, as well as the tsar's Terem Palace and the Ascension and Chudov monasteries. The first extant references to choirs of singing clerks in the service of the metropolitan of Moscow and the grand prince of Moscow date from precisely this time, the second half of the fifteenth century. The music of the singing clerks of the grand prince and the metropolitan was woven into the fairytale-like symphony of the Kremlin's palaces, great houses and churches, and became an inalienable part of the magnificent façade which 'Muscovy' presented to the world. The austere *znamenny* chant, the majestic *putevoy* chant, the ornate *demestvo* and the festal *strochnoye* polyphony rang out during church services and various religious processions, coronations, tsar's weddings, the translations of prelates' relics, meetings with foreign ambassadors and so on. Services in the Cathedral of the Dormition in the Kremlin, the state's main cathedral church, were distinguished by the highest degree of splendour and solemnity.

The period of the Muscovite state was a time when, once the legacy of Byzantium had been assimilated, the art of church music flourished. Russian composers (*mastera peniya*) not only created an independent musical language but also invented ways of writing it down: they devised various forms of Russian notation based on Byzantine neumes. Documentary sources from the late sixteenth and seventeenth centuries confirm that the two leading choirs – the singing clerks of the sovereign and of the patriarch (formerly known as those of the grand prince and the metropolitan respectively) – were involved in many of the most important developments in the field of church music.[3] At the end of the seventeenth century, after a radical reform of the Russian church which occurred in the middle of that century and gave rise to a schism within the church, *partesnoye* polyphony along western lines surged into Russia, and the choirs of the tsar and the patriarch were among the first Russian choirs to master the new kind of singing and its stave notation.

The Synodal era of the Russian church coincides with the history of the Russian Empire (from the eighteenth century to the beginning of the twentieth century). It began with the gradual abolition of the patriarchate and the creation in 1721 of the Most Holy Synod, as head of which a layman was appointed – the *Ober-Prokuror*. The Patriarch's Singing Clerks came under the jurisdiction of the Synod, and they began to be known as the Synodal Choir, continuing as before to sing at services in the Cathedral of the Dormition in Moscow, which in the eighteenth century became a provincial town. The transfer of the Russian capital to St Petersburg in the eighteenth century and the move there of the Sovereign's Singing Clerks (thereafter the Court Kapella) marked the separation of the fates of two choirs which had formerly been closely linked with one another. While the Court Kapella provided the music for worship in the emperors' palaces and was subjected to the court's changing fashions and tastes, the Synodal Choir had to support the ancient singing traditions of the Cathedral of the Dormition, which enjoyed the special status of a 'peculiar ecclesiastical preserve' (*zapovednik*). The Synodal Choir subsisted on meagre subsidies and fell into decline during the eighteenth century but managed to achieve some improvement in its quality of singing only towards the end of the nineteenth century, during whose course several valiant attempts to recover its former glory were made. This process was greatly encouraged by the special ecclesiastical atmosphere of Moscow during the metropolitanate of Filaret (Drozdov), an enlightened spiritual leader, writer and scholar, who championed the cause of restoring and strengthening the old, in both spirit and letter, in contemporary church music, and regarded as worthless the arrangements of the ancient chants sent to him for his verdict by the director of the Court Kapella, Aleksey Lvov.

A school for young singers attached to the Synodal Choir was also established in the nineteenth century, though from time immemorial training had been given within the choir to new recruits. During the middle ages it had been guild-like in character: the younger singing clerks (the subtleties of singing and received payment in money and kind from the treasury in return. There were also special 'tutors' from the patriarch's choir who taught the under-clerks the 'roles' of characters in the liturgical drama the 'Play of the Furnace' (*Peshchnoye deystvo*) performed annually in the Cathedral of the Dormition before Christ's Nativity.

The age at which choristers first entered the Metropolitan's Choir, later the Patriarch's, can only be guessed at. The way medieval choirs were organized was different from the present-day one. A choir in those times was divided not into parts, each made up of singers with one particular compass and timbre, but into 'squads' (*stanitsï*) organized hierarchically: the most experienced masters sang in the senior squads, while young, less highly qualified singers sang in the junior ones. In the era of early *strochnoye* polyphony (in the sixteenth and seventeenth centuries) such a squad included representatives of all the singing 'parts' (lines/*stroki*) – *putniki* (the singers of the main melody), *vershniki* (who sang the top line), *nizhniki* (the singers of the lowest line) and *demestvenniki* (who sang any fourth part). Specialization in one 'line' or another was determined not by register or timbre but by knowledge of the different melodies in which each 'line' of a polyphonic score was laid out. Because the repertoire of the principal choirs in Moscow was very complex, however, it may be supposed that young people accepted into them had already received training in church music.

The earliest known reference to the age of a singing clerk from one of the younger squads, who was nine years of age, was discovered in a source of Russian origin from the end of the seventeenth century, that is from the time when the choir was already singing *partesnïye* compositions. In the eighteenth century one can speak with certainty of the existence of a group of children in the choir, comprising four people in 1763, and 12 in 1772. At the beginning of the nineteenth century the question of educating the young singers in the Synodal Choir arose in connection with the universal organization of state schools of the European type; as it was put in a letter of 1818 from the synodal choristers to the Minister of Religious Affairs and Education, Prince A.N. Golitsïn, someone who had been in the choir between the ages of 10 and 19 and learned singing 'had learned absolutely nothing else, not even how to write properly'. The reply to this letter was a decree from Avgustin, the Archbishop of Moscow, that the young choristers were required to study at parish and county schools, attending school at times when they were not singing. Teaching them music was the responsibility of the choirmaster of the Synodal Choir. Because of the frequency of rehearsals and services, however, the children had no time to attend school; it was therefore decided to teach general educational and church subjects in the School itself, with the task entrusted to a special instructor.

In 1857 the new statute of the Synodal Choir, which presupposed that there should be not 12 boys but 26, was ratified. At long last, in 1866, the school for boy singers attached to the choir, comprising four basic classes and one preparatory one, received official status as an independent educational establishment.

Subsequent years were marked by the dogged battle to improve the School waged for almost three decades by its inspector Ivan Berdnikov. He succeeded in extending the School's accommodation, raising the teachers' salaries, increasing the number of staff posts, and over a period of time even introducing the post of teacher of music theory, to which the Moscow Conservatoire teacher Nikolay Kashkin was appointed in 1870.

In 1881 the School's administration – obviously with an eye to the new state policy with regard to church music – petitioned Pobedonostsev about new regulations and staffing for the School. The turn of the Synodal School came, however, only five years later when in 1886 it was transformed into a secondary eight-year educational institution for church music, made up of three departments: a lower one (for classes 1-4, for teaching young choristers), a middle one (classes 5-6, to train assistant church choirmasters) and a higher one (classes 7-8, to train church choirmasters and teachers of singing). Other features of the School changed accordingly: instead of ten school subjects, it was planned to introduce 19; instead of 30 child choristers, it was proposed to select 65. The establishment of the Synodal Choir was also increased: instead of 30 boys there were meant to be 50, and instead of 24 adult singers, 30.

A Supervisory Council was established for the Choir and the School to 'superintend advance in the field of church music and direct the Synodal Choir towards success in the spirit of ancient Orthodox church music'; its first members were Tchaikovsky, Razumovsky and Gubert and the Council later included very many Moscow musicians – Safonov, Arensky, Taneyev, Kruglikov, Kashkin, Vasilenko, Ippolitov-Ivanov and others.

The range of general educational subjects studied in the junior choristers' department (for ages 7 – 11 approximately) corresponded to the course at a diocesan pre-seminary religious school; the middle and senior choirmasters' classes studied in accordance with a simplified syllabus of the religious seminaries. The range of general educational subjects accordingly hinged on changes in the syllabuses of religious educational institutions. It was the syllabuses of the music courses which were the area of priority for the directors of the School.

The period when the School was undergoing reform (1886-1917) was marked by intensive work. Over the course of 30 years we can observe four directors of the School in direct succession to one another, four brilliantly gifted people – Smolensky, Orlov, Kruglikov and Kastalsky – who felt their way ahead by trial and error, constructing in the end, however, a higher school of church music such as had in fact never before been seen in Russia, combining features of a conservatoire, a religious seminary, and a centre for academic research.

Notes

1. S.V. Smolensky: *Sinodal'nïy khor i uchilishche tserkovnogo peniya* (The Synodal Choir and School of Church Music), in *RUSAM*, vol. 1, pp. 59-60.
2. The author has in mind the following well-known work by D.V. Razumovsky: *Patriarshiye pevchiye d'yaki i podd'yaki* (The Patriarch's singing clerks and sub-clerks), in *Drevnosti. Arkheologicheskiy vestnik, izdavayemïy Moskovskim arkheologicheskim obshchestvom* (Antiquities. Archaeological herald, published by the Moscow Archaeology Society), vol. 1, Moscow, 1867-68, pp. 241-253. *Ibid.*, in *RUSAM*, vol. 2, book 1, pp. 24-43.
3. For church music in this period, see: Johann von Gardner: *Russian Church Singing. Vol. 2: History from the Origin to the Mid-Seventeenth Century*. Translated and edited by Vladimir Morosan, Crestwood, New York, 2000; S.G. Zvereva: *Der Kirchengesang in Rußland vom Ende 15. bis zur Anfang des 17. Jahrhunderts*, in *Grazer musikwissenschaftliche Arbeiten*, vol. 10: *Altrußische Musik*. Graz, 1993, pp. 71-84.

Chapter 7

Smolensky's Reforms

'I found the Synodal School and Choir in a very mixed state', Smolensky later recalled.

> The School was in utter confusion both educationally and as regards discipline; the Choir was comparatively well co-ordinated, sang well in tune and with a good sound, but was at the same time profoundly ignorant of the rudiments of music and of repertoire, and profoundly undisciplined in the way they earned money on the side (by discreetly singing in other choirs) and in the complete breakdown of discipline in the singers' behaviour. The poverty of the Choir and the School was absolutely complete in all respects without exception. Absolutely nowhere at all was there good order.[1]

The picture Smolensky painted of the morals of the inhabitants of the building on Bolshaya Nikitskaya Street is horrifying. Suffice it to say that the School's recent benefactor, its inspector Berdnikov, made his exit from School life in 1880 not because he died a natural death but as a result of injuries sustained in a beating-up administered by some of his pupils and adult singers one night. Adults and children alike were coarse, ignorant and lazy; fights and foul language were the norm.

The new director set about his task with a will, using all his temperament and eloquence, exhorting those susceptible of re-education and dismissing the refractory. All from greatest to least had to study. For the adults, special courses were introduced where singers received an education in music in accordance with the Synodal School's syllabus of musical subjects. The most capable of those completing these courses were then permitted to work as church choirmasters and teachers of church music. The School's teachers were sent to the Conservatoire to raise their qualifications. Smolensky took even the choirmaster Orlov in hand:

> Vasily Orlov was extraordinarily sensitive to the choir's sonority and balance, but generally speaking he was poorly educated and as a musician poorly read. His quite superb abilities as a conductor and his diligence developed during my time in charge. I never once allowed myself to give him directions,

remembering the saying that 'to teach a scholar is only to harm him', and while I respected the freedom of everyone in his work, I did once, though, in a friendly chat outline his aspiration (which I had divined) to broaden his musical education. The diploma of free artist (in bassoon) was not enough to satisfy Orlov as an outstanding practising choirmaster. I suggested arranging for him to study counterpoint in the strict style with Taneyev, justifying the suggestion by my desire to see Orlov as a teacher of counterpoint at the Synodal School. These lessons, broken off unexpectedly at the Conservatoire, nevertheless continued privately and led to Orlov's emergence as both an outstanding contrapuntist and a first-class choirmaster, for as soon as the course was finished I immediately got the Synodal Choir singing Palestrina, Lassus and Josquin des Pres, Mozart, Bach and Beethoven, after which it became child's play for them, now musically educated and real artists, the best choir of any that I have ever heard, to perform our Russian sacred music. Orlov worked fully twelve years with the utmost zeal, sincerity and with the greatest skill, and it is not surprising therefore if given his talents and knowledge he developed into a superlative choirmaster.[2]

Alexander Dmitriyevich Kastalsky was also taken up by Smolensky. To persuade the indecisive Kastalsky, however, who seemed to have little faith in himself, to get a move on, Smolensky had to use far more energy and cunning:

I found Alexander Kastalsky as teacher of piano-playing at the Synodal School, teaching his class in the most ill-starred conditions. It did not take long to size up this highly intelligent, educated and gentle man, who was extremely independent in his judgments and extremely assiduous in his work. Kastalsky's talent seemed to me beyond question, even if it was not great; but his knowledge was simply immense. Kastalsky is a great lover of painting and he loves flowers and reading. His wife Natalia is very intelligent and educated; they are both very honest and kind people. In their first years of married life they were very badly off, even poor. In his youth Kastalsky had for some reason not seen his education through to the end. For instance, he studied at the *gimnaziya* until the eighth class and then left without completing the course; then at the Conservatoire he had reached the second year of free composition and again left, becoming an army bandmaster in the county town of Kozlov.

I launched my attack on Kastalsky as follows. After sacking the perfectly unbearable Sokolov, a downright lazybones and scoundrel, as assistant choirmaster in the Synodal Choir, I contrived to have the very lovable 'Kuzka' (that was his nickname as the Conservatoire favourite) appointed 'extra administrative official of the Moscow Synod Office, delegated for duties as assistant choirmaster of the Synodal Choir'. This long title was needed to give Kastalsky the right to work, since he had never completed any course anywhere and could not occupy the position of assistant choirmaster without the essential status for it. Gaining better material security (and an official flat) by this means

Kastalsky's spirits rose and gave me the chance to take the attack further. I began to whisper into Kastalsky's ear that he was being looked at askance in St Petersburg as someone without the diploma of a free artist, and that my negotiations with Safonov and Taneyev showed the real possibility of Kastalsky sitting the Moscow Conservatoire final examination in composition. My lying to Kastalsky and frightening him went on for two years, as did Kastalsky's being drawn ever more into our small School world.   Alas, Kastalsky proved to be a very poor choirmaster, more suited to activities in the classroom and the study than to directing a choir energetically.   Then I put a little more pressure on him, demanding that he complete the course and advocating that he defend me at least against the charge of having chosen the wrong person.[3]

In the summer of 1893 Alexander Dmitriyevich nonetheless found the strength within himself to sit the Moscow Conservatoire examination for the title of free artist. For that he had to undergo tests in all subjects and write an examination cantata. Smolensky followed the venture with a sinking feeling, doubting at the bottom of his heart that there would be a successful outcome. This view was shared by Taneyev, who conducted the examinations.   A pleasant surprise lay in store, however, for both Smolensky and Taneyev. 'Taneyev confessed to me on the day of the composition examination', Smolensky noted in his diary,

> that he had hitherto looked upon this examination as a useless enterprise embarked on only because of my influence, but later completely changed his opinion of Kastalsky, greatly for the better, after his examinations in fugue and after 'Balthasar's Feast', which was regarded within the walls of the Conservatoire as something perfectly respectable. The diploma of free artist was awarded unanimously and to the complete satisfaction of all the members of the Artistic Board. The 'Feast' was composed over a period of three weeks and I heard it for myself at the exam and was amazed at the depth of my colleague's knowledge.[4]

Passing the examination really was of great importance to Kastalsky's career since he not only obtained the rights and status to which the holder of the diploma was entitled but also, being a teacher with a diploma, he was able later to teach the most varied subjects – the theory of music, harmony, *solfeggio*, church music, folk music, counterpoint and fugue.

Smolensky also drew Kastalsky into a further venture initiated shortly after his arrival at the Synodal School. On moving to Moscow, Stepan Vasilyevich was compelled to abandon his work on the church music manuscripts of the Solovetsky monastery, which were housed at the Theological Academy in Kazan. Deprived of the necessary materials, he decided to assemble in Moscow a library of ancient music manuscripts in order to be able to continue his work, and with the help of bishops he knew he 'stripped' the monasteries and churches of the Moscow, Arkhangelsk, Vologda, Olonets, Vladimir, Yaroslavl, Tula, Poltava and other dioceses for that purpose. Smolensky's 'emissaries' in the persons of staff-members of the Synodal School travelled to many corners of Russia to collect the manuscripts, on occasion bringing valuable rarities back with them. Kastalsky too was enlisted to collect and work on the manuscripts. As a result, when Smolensky left for St Petersburg in 1901, the Synodal School's 'little stone room' contained around 2,000 manuscripts and represented a source of pride to the director, who conducted studies in the palaeography of church music with students in the senior classes of the School's Manuscript Department.

Smolensky gathered in from the whole of Russia not just primary sources but also specialists, inviting to teaching posts at the School Antonin Preobrazhensky, a teacher from the Bakhmut public school and graduate of the Kazan Theological Academy, and Vasily Metallov, a priest from the Saratov diocese; at that time they were novice researchers, but they were to become later the authors of classic works on the music of the Middle Ages.

Smolensky's reforms moved simultaneously in several directions. One of them was the repertoire of the Synodal Choir, which horrified the director, an *intelligent* reared on highly artistic classic models.

> I decided first of all to make the Synodal Choir forget all the rubbish they knew and loved and which they taught others to love, then to teach them ancient melodies to the extent needed for them to be simply enchanted by the melodies' innate Russian beauty, and eventually to improve the technique and artistic level of the Synodal Choir through general musical education and by familiarizing them with models of genuine mastery and true inspiration. Orlov was of course initiated into all the details of this plan; he himself took part in working it out and most of all in bringing it to fruition.[5]

As a result, the Choir's repertoire was subjected to the strictest artistic censorship. In the category of 'Italian stuff' (*ital'yanshchina*), by which was meant the concerto compositions of Sarti, Bortnyansky, etc., only the least bravura and most artistic examples were kept; arrangements of the late chants so beloved by the public – the 'Ipatyev', 'Simonov' chants and suchlike – were learned with a maximum of grace and with the 'Russian colouring' in them emphasized. Smolensky probably understood that with repertoire of that kind it was unlikely that his choir could substantially raise its standard of performance, and so with Taneyev's advice it was decided on educational grounds to learn a number of choral masterpieces including compositions by the Netherlands contrapuntal school, Bach's Mass in B minor and Beethoven's in C major, and the Requiems of Mozart and Schumann. The works learned as study material were sometimes also performed for the public. Thus on 15 March 1891 Mozart's Requiem was heard at a symphonic assembly of the Russian Musical Society, rousing great interest in the Synodal Choir. The conductor of the concert, Safonov, director of the Moscow Conservatoire, sent a letter of thanks to Pobedonostsev in St Petersburg:

> Please allow me to express my heartfelt gratitude to you for the permission given to the Choir of the Synodal School to take part in the performance of Mozart's Requiem at the symphonic assembly on 15 March this year. This Choir's participation lent the performance of that immortal work a special charm. The superb selection of voices in the Synodal Choir and the ideal preparation made my difficult task a great deal easier. I may say without exaggeration that Moscow will not soon forget that performance of the Requiem with such rich vocal resources.[6]

The study of masterpieces of western music raised the intellectual level of the Synodal Choir extraordinarily; they now began to sing 'intelligently' and evolved a superlative technique. The beginning of this perfection, as Smolensky noted, can be dated to the winter of 1893-94. Along with the Tretyakov Gallery and the Bolshoy Theatre, the Synodal Choir became one of Moscow's principal attractions. Its concerts and the services for which it sang in the Cathedral of the Dormition were regarded as major events. The Synodal Choir's Historical Concerts in 1895 conducted by Orlov found the most powerful resonance with the public; they showed the development of Russian sacred music beginning with antiquity and ending with contemporary experiments. The series of programmes compiled by Smolensky proved to listeners the idea of the inevitability of the arrival of 'nationalism' in church music, and displayed the new currents in the work of the Choir and the School. Concerts in St Petersburg continued the series of triumphs, as did the first tour abroad three years later to Vienna, thanks to which the Synodal Choir won fame as one of the best in the world. Astounded listeners encountered for the first time not only old sacred music but also works by the young 'national' school.

And lastly, Smolensky's activities took one further direction which in many respects defined the Synodal Choir's growth in skill: the reform in teaching there. As has been said already, what Stepan Vasilyevich inherited was problematic. When he arrived at the School, four classes of pupils existed, but their level of knowledge was extremely low. At the age of fifteen the children knew neither multiplication tables nor the elementary rules of orthography. Things were no better when it came to their knowledge of the theory of music. 'The best pupil in the school, Aleksey Petrov', recalled Smolensky, 'refused to play an A major scale on the violin for me, saying that he did not know what he called the sharps and flats (*diyezov i bémulov*)...'[7]

On arriving at the School Smolensky began by developing new syllabuses. Over the course of the twelve years of his directorship these syllabuses were refined and adjusted, although Stepan Vasilyevich's basic aim remained immutable:

> The syllabus for training future choirmasters consisted in general terms of giving young people the very best general education and at the same time imparting such a stock of musical knowledge as would easily enable a young person who had completed the Synodal School course to become an excellent practical choirmaster or teacher of singing in a school. [...] Every school prepares a person for life, without any chance or indeed necessity of making him prematurely into a specialist of some kind, but with the obligation to inform the pupil of everything instructive and helpful, so that from school emerges a person with a lucid mind, able to reason for himself, in whatever direction he might apply his private abilities and individual inclinations. For that reason there is no school which produces ready-made doctors, local magistrates, engineers, technicians and so on. And thus from among doctors who have received a general education in medicine, there emerge oculists, surgeons, general physicians as well as specialists in the nerves, the ear, the throat and other diseases. It is the same with advocates, judicial investigators, *Prokurors* and judges. It is the same with church choirmasters, teachers of singing, teachers of the theory of church music, the history of church music and so on. Only a preliminary education that is as broad as possible can create a master of his art, because the power of great skill lies exactly not in being a mere craftsman but in having a broad view of the subject. It is understandable that this education must be adapted to the future field of specialty, but nothing is to be gained by taking time away for too intensified practical studies in the years when a person's mind is more disposed to absorbing knowledge, and there is no need to lose sight of this knowledge since acquiring it later in the school years is almost unattainable or at least entirely inconvenient and harmful, and the time for it has already been lost.[8]

Smolensky saw the ultimate objective of the transformation he effected in the Synodal School as being the creation not of a religious school with a bias towards producing choirmasters, and not a secular conservatoire with a bias towards church music (the model of the Court Kapella), but a kind of academy of church music, a graduate of which would be as broadly and harmoniously developed as possible in both music and scholarship. The personality of the director himself can undoubtedly be seen in this conception – a person with a fine classical university education as well as the outlook of that group in the Russian intelligentsia to which he belonged.

It remains only to say something about the concrete implementation of Smolensky's ideas in the School's syllabuses. Thus, Smolensky supposed that education in the junior department preparing singers for church choirs ought to be relatively complete in itself. For that reason, the boy choristers' department was envisaged as a choirmasters' department in miniature: along with essential subjects studied in every year at the School such as *solfeggio*, church music, piano and violin, courses in harmony, polyphony and musical forms specially devised for children were taught there, with the subjects then studied again more thoroughly in the choirmasters' department. The younger pupils played in the orchestra as well. As an amateur violinist who had played in a string quartet in Kazan, Smolensky gave every possible encouragement to instrumental music. The well-known teacher Anatoly Erarsky was invited to organize a children's symphony orchestra in the School, and he constructed equivalents for certain instruments not taught at the School: woodwind were replaced by little organs, and the role of the brass was taken by diatonic trumpets made to order. An orchestra like this could consequently play works by Lyadov, Arensky, Tchaikovsky and Taneyev scored for children's orchestra by Erarsky himself. The composers whose works were performed, Tchaikovsky particularly, were enraptured by this venture.

The idea of Russification also found a place in the School; it was embodied mainly in the lectures on the history of church music in the choirmasters' department. This course, distinguished by its fundamental character and high degree of professionalism, was based on the latest achievements of scholarship in church music archaeology. As a result, graduates knew the history of church music throughout the Christian world, had a good idea of the notation used for music in various denominations, had some skill in working with Russian church music manuscripts and had deciphered monuments of *znamenny* chant. In the teaching of *solfeggio* the idea of Russification took the form of a special course devised by Kastalsky and Vasily Tyutyunnik based on specimens of Russian church melodies, Russian art music and folksongs.

One must note, however, that in the School syllabuses published in 1897, in courses where the repertoire of church music was studied (such as Reading Choral Scores at the Piano or Simultaneous Playing of Choral Scores by String Quartets), that it was not only compositions by composers of the young national direction that were absent but even choral music by such classics as Tchaikovsky, Taneyev, Balakirev and Rimsky-Korsakov. On the other hand, Bortnyansky, Berezovsky, Sarti, Davïdov, Turchaninov,

Lvov, Lomakin, Lvovsky and Arkhangelsky were represented in abundance.[9]

As we analyse the sources linked to Smolensky's reforms in teaching, we can see that he stood for the equal rights of scholarly and musical subjects, the secular and the ecclesiastical, the Russian and the western. This stance is obvious in a letter from Smolensky to the future composer Alexander Nikolsky – at the time a graduate of the Penza Theological Seminary, who had asked him to outline how the School course differed from a conservatoire course. Smolensky replied:

> Our theoretical course is different from the conservatoire course in that when we deal with the fields of higher musical scholarship we have a quite different basis for our exercises in composition, which are not instrumental but vocal. As our whole basis is not in the least non-Russian, and is primarily linked to the church with a bias towards Russian antiquity, we have developed a special syllabus for ourselves where, while we have taken everything sensible and necessary from foreign practice, we study things that are our own, both old and new, working as our strength permits to the glory of God. All this is in answer to your question: what conservatoire course in composition can one enter after graduating from ours? In my opinion, one ought not to go on to any of them.[10]

The idea of the harmonious development of pupils, who in Smolensky's time began performing *znamenny* chant and compositions by Bach and Palestrina alongside harmonizations from the *Obikhod* and compositions by the 'classics' of church music, arose in Pobedonostsev's circle. In point of fact Smolensky succeeded in realizing in practice what the people concerned with education close to him had only dreamt about. The brilliant results of this idea became evident to all, though something else besides became clear: the majority of representatives of church circles as well as simple believers, who proved to include even many of Smolensky's associates in the reforms, did not share such ideas and were not yet ready to accept such liberalism in a church-music institution. In consequence Smolensky appeared to verge on being a free-thinker and he stood accused of many sins at once – from restoring Old Believer faith in the Synodal Church to conservatoire westernism. 'Remember that you are no more than the simplest of church singers', Sabler once exclaimed in a harsh tone of voice. 'We don't need historical concerts, or new trends, or learned publications! We need good singers in the Cathedral of the Dormition!'[11]

That observation made by Vladimir Sabler, the Vice-*Prokuror* of the Synod, corresponded in full with the official conclusion reached in a review of the Synodal School conducted in late 1900 and early 1901 by Pyotr Nechayev, a member of the Synod's Education Committee:

Smolensky, with his good knowledge of church music, and also his love for it and for music generally, would be an extremely useful person for the School if only he possessed in addition the requisite administrative tact, adopted a more attentive attitude towards the inner side of School life, and did not muddle up the School's tasks by introducing into the pupils' studies certain musical demands more appropriate to a conservatoire than to a strictly church-music School.[12]

In 1901 Smolensky left Moscow on being appointed director of the Court Kapella, and moved to St Petersburg. He followed events at the Synodal School after his departure attentively, and received detailed reports from like-minded people who remained in Moscow. The picture outlined in their letters was a cheerless one: truth to tell, a movement to make the School a craft school for choirmasters had begun. The time to turn the School into an academy had not yet arrived. It would be another ten years before society came round to the idea of the need for changes, a process helped to no little extent by the establishment of a new national school of composers of sacred music born in the wake of Smolensky's reforms.

Notes

1. S.V. Smolensky: *Sinodal'nïy khor i uchilishche tserkovnogo peniya* (The Synodal Choir and School of Church Music), in *RUSAM*, vol. 1, p. 43.
2. *Ibid.*, pp. 51-52.
3. *Ibid.*, p. 88.
4. S.V. Smolensky: *Pervïy dnevnik* (First diary). RGIA, fond 1119, opis' 1, no. 3, p. 76v.
5. S.V. Smolensky: *Sinodal'nïy khor i uchilishche tserkovnogo peniya*, in *RUSAM*, vol. 1, p. 86.
6. V.M. Metallov: *Sinodal'noye uchilishche tserkovnogo peniya v yego proshlom i nastoyashchem* (The Synodal School of Church Music in its past and present), Moscow, 1911, p. 55. *Ibid.*, in *RUSAM*, vol. 2, book 1, p. 132.
7. S.V. Smolensky: *Sinodal'nïy khor i uchilishche tserkovnogo peniya*, in *RUSAM*, vol. 1, p. 46.
8. *Ibid.*, pp. 52-53.
9. *Programmï predmetov, prepodavayemïkh v Sinodal'nom uchilishche tserkovnogo peniya* (Syllabuses for the subjects taught at the Synodal School of Church Music). Moscow, 1897, pp. 129-130.
10. Aleksandr Vasil'yevich Nikol'sky, in *RUSAM*, vol. 1, pp. 388-389.
11. S.V. Smolensky: *Sinodal'nïy khor i uchilishche tserkovnogo peniya*, in *RUSAM*, vol. 1, pp. 87 and 95.
12. V.M. Metallov: *Sinodal'noye uchilishche tserkovnogo peniya v yego proshlom i nastoyashchem*, pp. 80-81. *Ibid.*, in *RUSAM*, vol. 2, book 1, p. 149.

Chapter 8

'New Antiquity'

Smolensky's working day at the Synodal School often began long before his pupils formed up for morning prayer. Early in the morning Stepan Vasilyevich would arrive from his director's flat on the ground floor of the School and go into his 'little stone room' and busy himself with the manuscript treasures he had collected which were to render a great service to future toilers in the field of church music. Even while he was still in Kazan working with the manuscripts from the Solovetsky monastery, Smolensky came to believe that it was precisely these ancient folios covered with mysterious signs (*znamenami*) which would show church music composers the way out of their imprisonment in 'Europeanism'.

Smolensky was not the only person counting on the saving power of the Russian legacy, however; let us remember archpriest Razumovsky, to whom Tchaikovsky, Rimsky-Korsakov and Taneyev turned as to an oracle. But Razumovsky's faith in the 'hook' notation lacked that Romantic aureole, that poetic fervour typical of Smolensky's 'creed' as he served as a 'missionary' among his Synodal and conservatoire 'flock'. Nature had conferred brilliant talents as a speaker and writer on the scholar, and thanks to that, all his areas of activity – whether writing works of scholarship, letters, diaries, reminiscences or giving lectures – were distinguished by what we call a 'divine spark'. Stepan Vasilyevich had a gift for gathering round him people who, once they had fallen under the spell of his speaking, began to see the world through his eyes and serve his ideals. As his colleague Allemanov wrote to Smolensky,

> You love church music, and ancient Russian church music particularly, so much, you demonstrate its fascination with so much warmth, that it seems that even if it were not worth the paper it was written on, you could fall in love with it while listening to you. You are just like a reformer inspired in the highest degree by the ideals of his religion. And it is no wonder that people like you compel others to subscribe to their faith, to see things through their eyes.[1]

It was, of course, his pupils at the Synodal School and the Moscow Conservatoire who were converted to Smolensky's 'faith' in the first place.

As Alexander Nikolsky, who heard Stepan Vasilyevich's lectures in session 1894-95, recalled,

> Pictures, images and characters from a period long past, as they were outlined by Stepan Vasilyevich, were able to attract our full attention and sympathy, and there grew up at the same time a love for the artistic creation which expressed that period in details which eluded words. [...] It became clear to everyone that the soul of the nation is hidden in our church music; that it is not simply a set of melodies which our age has left far behind; it is not simply an inheritance of mere 'curiosity' value to the historian; it is not a relic which has lost its significance and its application to vital needs. No, indeed! The whole corpus of *znamenny* chants is an epic poem from the soul of the nation, a tablet containing its thoughts, the feelings and high-flown desires of that nation, and moreover of a distinctive nation, profound in its own way, exceedingly gifted, though also undeveloped.
>
> Stepan Vasilyevich went on to show that all these features are by no means obsolete, have by no means disappeared – on the contrary, being hitherto unused, they have preserved all their vitality and are able to provide the most luxuriant shoots, if only they can be sown and cherished as they ought. As you listened to him speaking with the breath of the most profound and fully considered conviction, you came willy-nilly to believe that all of this is a great truth. And a resolve was born in the innermost part of your soul to contribute your mite in the future to the cause of reviving the precious legacy of Russian melodic creativity. There was also the thought that this creativity could not be understood without history; minute theoretical analysis is insufficient for that, for it is dry and one-sided, though the main thing is that it lacks the living nerve, the key to which is in the hands of history alone.[2]

Russian antiquity became something near and dear to Smolensky's listeners; they felt its breath and relived events of long ago as part of their own fate. The vanished world resurrected in Smolensky's accounts appeared in all the fullness of its colours and sounds.

Smolensky's advocacy was the more persuasive as Nature had endowed him not only with a gift for preaching but also with a kind heart. The residents of the Synodal School were his family, and he was in their company from morning till night, joining in and associating with them and binding them together in every possible way. The boy singers replaced children of their own for the childless Smolenskys; they continued watching over and educating the growing Mishas, Pashas and Sashas even after they had grown up and in many cases become famous. The School's teachers and their families were regarded as relatives, any of whom could approach the director at any time with their troubles and problems – Stepan Vasilyevich's wife Anna Ilinichna would be seated in state by the big samovar from morning on, treating all the colleagues and pupils who called on her husband to tea, asking them about their affairs and supporting them with a kind word and advice.

As Kastalsky reminisced, one of the principal qualities of the always energetic and lively Smolensky was his ability to galvanize people. On settling in Moscow, he found himself at the centre of the movement to create a national church style and became one of its most active participants. However, like the members of the Moscow Society for Church Music, the scholar had only general ideas as to what that style should be like. The main one was the idea of a 'new antiquity', that is, the reconstruction of the ancient in the modern. Smolensky supposed that, as far as technical devices were concerned, they would have to be worked out by studying the laws of construction of folksong and church chants. In his opinion, certain discoveries in contemporary folklore studies were already pointing the way towards new approaches to the treatment of monody.

Which discoveries did Smolensky have in mind? We may assume that the first scholarly publications of folksongs did not escape his notice; they appeared in the late 1870s and 1880s and, besides arranging and publishing the songs, set themselves the aim of investigating the laws of the language of folk music. The following publications were of outstanding importance: Yuly Melgunov: 'Russian Songs, written down directly from the voice of the people, with explanations' (*Russkiye pesni, neposredstvenno s golosa naroda zapisannïye i s ob'yasneniyami*) (Part I, Moscow, 1879 and Part II, St Petersburg, 1885); Nikolay Palchikov: 'Peasant songs recorded in the village of Nikolayevka, Menzelin district of the Ufa province' (*Krest'yanskiye pesni, zapisannïye v sele Nikolayevke Menzelinskogo uyezda, Ufimskoy gubernii*) (St Petersburg, 1888); and Nikolay Lopatin and Vasily Prokunin: 'Russian lyrical folksongs' (*Russkiye narodnïye liricheskiye pesni*) (Moscow, 1889). These publications not only reproduced transcriptions of folk polyphony for the first time and reached conclusions about their *podgoloski*-polyphonic character and the principle of variants as the basis of the polyphonic fabric, but also offered a new approach to the compositional treatment of folksongs. Thus, in Prokunin's words, 'a song's mode and harmony should be deduced from the *podgoloski* transcribed from the choir'.[3]

Smolensky had been following the achievements of scholarship in that field and was probably among the first to try to project them on to the treatment of church chants, the more so as the idea of treating them contrapuntally in the strict style was aesthetically alien to him: he considered the results of such arrangements to be not in accordance with the national spirit, and to him the latter criterion was fundamental. (It was for that reason that the approval or disapproval of particular arrangements by worshippers drawn from the common people, especially Old Believers, was so important to him.) Smolensky's own sacred music compositions, however, were not notable for any new approach to the church chants. The few works which he composed for the church – 'Blessed be the Name of the Lord, from this time forth and for evermore' (*Budi Imya Gospodne*), 'Praise the Name of the Lord' (*Khvalite Imya Gospodne*), the Litanies (*Yektenii*), the 'Memorial service on themes from ancient chants' and others – were widely disseminated among church choirs and continue to be so, though they were not marked by any particular innovations. Written with genuine warmth, they expressed their composer's religious feeling in the ordinary musical language of his time. Not considering himself a composer, Stepan Vasilyevich honestly confessed that he 'does not dare give any examples, so as not to make a laughing-stock by my third-rateness of something I hold dear' and that 'the demands made on the new direction are not yet clear even to the people who love church music most of all'.[4] He realized only instinctively that the route to attaining a new quality lay through saturating musicians as deeply as possible in the sounds and images of antiquity, through an intellectual and emotional assimilation of the past, through intimacy with it. And the scholar placed his hopes in this matter not on fully-formed mature composers but rather on his pupils, who from their early years had been seeing the world through his eyes.

Least of all did Smolensky expect a Messiah to emerge from the ranks of professional composers of secular music, supposing that even the works of Rimsky-Korsakov were a long way away from a true Russian style.

> How would those gentlemen, particularly Rimsky-Korsakov, have composed if they had delved even slightly into that marvellous world of illumination represented by the serene, epic, lofty melodies, similar to the most wonderfully luxuriant ornamentation of our epic tales (*bïlinï*) and fairy tales (*skazki*) in their verbal texts! My words are too feeble to express the degree of my astonishment and the breadth of my idea, and the world of these melodies is truly immense. I am exasperated with the crude experiments in rhythm which simply testify to ignorance of Russian speech as it is matched to a melody, all these ugly 11/4 time-signatures and so on without a shred of calm naturalness. [...] There is no need to go to the length of becoming a precentor, but why should the composers not take a glance at the byways I indicated if only out of condescending curiosity?[5]

Stepan Vasilyevich apparently attempted to convert even Rimsky-Korsakov to his faith, though the latter's attitude towards the archaeological researches of medievalists was distinctly cool. The scholar had no success on that front at all. He was able to obtain far greater results from his Moscow colleagues, amongst whom a cult of Ancient Rus flared up as a result of Smolensky's preaching. Thanks to Stepan Vasilyevich's inquisitive mind and his liking for experiments, the technical devices needed for new treatments were gradually revealed too.

The starting-point was that in the very first months of his life in Moscow Smolensky tried to choose a repertoire for Sunday and feast-day worship for the Synodal Choir which was more stylish and corresponded better with the spirit and appointments of the Cathedral of the Dormition.

> Apart from a lack of clarity for me personally in certain parts of my attitude towards the art of ancient chant, which I knew only from books and to a certain extent from the Old Believers' practice (though soundly) and definitely intended to cultivate in the Cathedral of the Dormition, I embarked with the very greatest caution on converting to my own faith people with no desire to learn, who looked upon everything from the point of view of money and even then in an extremely stupid way, who stood up with extreme obstinacy for their viewpoint, one going back no further than the beginning of the nineteenth century. The 'new antiquity' had to be introduced very discreetly, cautiously and so gradually that neither singers nor priests nor the public would notice the shift to a different manner of singing. Naturally, the 'new antiquity' had first to win over the singers, and that first winning-over was the most difficult, especially among the boys.[6]

Despite the fact that the atmosphere in the Cathedral of the Dormition was very propitious for such experiments, changing the repertoire of a large choir was a bold step. Smolensky understood that pure unison singing at Sunday and feast-day services was a graft which would not take, and would provoke only irritation. He therefore decided to resort to cunning and gradually introduce new contents into the accustomed forms. The way music was practised in the Cathedral of the Dormition soon suggested to him a method by which it was possible to change the tastes of singers, clergy and worshippers without doing any great violence.

> During my very first weeks of working in Moscow I had occasion to get to know a series of perfectly ridiculous compositions of Muscovite manufacture. The latter circumstance, truth to tell, greatly concerned me, since I found myself entirely uninformed about that area of compositions, and it was the favourite cycle of the people in Moscow. I set myself the task of going through that whole literature with Orlov (of course, selected from the so-called 'working' compositions, that is, those beloved above all others and most often performed), and was amazed by their extremely ungrammatical layout. At the same time I started thinking about the question: why do people like these things so much? The undoubted simplicity, good sonority and good melodic quality of many of the compositions convinced me that this set of works represented exactly that middle road which I had to choose between Italian sweetness and

virtuosity on the one hand and *znamenny* and other ancient chants on the other; when I heard the 'ravaged' Cherubic Hymn (*Kheruvimskaya*) (that is, the one composed for the day of the October procession with the cross and sung annually thereafter in memory of the ravaging of Moscow by Napoleon's forces in 1812) my eyes were opened for the first time, in conjunction with other considerations, to the possibility of not trying to be too clever but making use of almost everything that was to hand, but simply giving it an artistic form. Drawing the 'ravaged', 'Ipatyev', 'Old Simonov' and all the other chant arrangements together with the harmonic and contrapuntal devices of Glinka, Musorgsky, Rimsky-Korsakov and the chance of being one's own Russian artistic self, bringing new and rational means to bear on old and already beloved materials – that is the path which I pointed out to Orlov, who, to the good fortune of myself, himself and the Synodal Choir, understood the idea correctly at once. I remember how Orlov's eyes sparkled when I put side by side for him individual sections of the melodies of the so-called Alexander Nevsky 'Mercy of peace' (*Milost' mira*) with the [folk]songs *Vdol' po matushke po Volge* and *Matushka, chto vo pole pïl'no*. After that conversation we decided to busy ourselves putting several of the best melodies of that kind into order and perform them undeviatingly on Sundays instead of compositions by Bortnyansky.[7]

The semi-folklore arrangements of recent melodies with whose aid Smolensky decided to introduce the 'new antiquity' to the musical part of the church service were extremely uncomplicated in their language: the basic melody appeared in the upper voice doubled in thirds while the bass supported them, moving among the notes of the basic triads. The chants whose authorship had been lost were, however, as greatly loved by worshippers as the icons 'Searcher of the lost', 'Assuage my sorrow', etc. which emerged in the same century and were in accord with popular religious feeling. As far as we can understand from Smolensky's memoirs, it was decided to choose the arrangements of the highest quality artistically and perform them with good taste, emphasizing their 'Russian notes'. It cannot be excluded that 'Russian notes' meant embellishing such arrangements with *podgoloski* on the model of the 'drawn-out' folksong.

The public noticed the 'new current' and adopted an extremely sympathetic attitude towards it, which inspired the participants in the experiment to take the next step. Smolensky wrote:

We agreed among ourselves, without asking the administration or taking advice from the priests (as in the choice of repertoire the Synodal singers were subordinate, however strange it might seem, to the senior priest of the cathedral and the priest on duty), to sing our own music and make our début with the eleven Gospel stichera arranged by A.G. Poluektov. We began to sing these stichera of the 'great' chant, that is with all the *fitï* and *litsa*, instead of communion verses. The harmonization was feeble, of course, as Poluektov was not a brilliant talent, for all that his work was distinguished by diligence and speed, but the basic melody was nevertheless maintained with perfect accuracy and harmonized far better than by Lvov.[8]

Despite the fact that, to begin with, the specimens of 'new antiquity' were not marked by any great artistic virtues, Smolensky's experiment in crossing folk and church arrangements of recent melodies, folksongs and medieval chants was spectacularly successful, as he became convinced when talking to some Old Believers visiting the Cathedral.

It seems that the new arrangements appealed not only to Old Believers but also to Pobedonostsev when he came to Moscow. Smolensky gave a colourful description of his meeting with the *Ober-Prokuror* and his impressions of the performance of the *znamenny* chant in St Petersburg and Moscow.

'Ah, these hooks! Ah, oh-ho-ho this *znamenny* chant, grieved the very lovable Konstantin Pobedonostsev. – They start off: u-u-u-u-u-u endlessly, then they have to say some word, and it's uuu-uuu-uuu again! How obstinate these people are ([Smolensky:] he means me)! It's the "specialists", the "experts", I've got Solovyov back there in Petersburg – who's bored me completely with his *fitï*; and Sabler is as obstinate as an old mule, he doesn't understand a thing and can't read music but is always saying "Wonderful! Superb!" And then someone sings to him: uuu-uuu... – But can you tell me yourself what it's like? I can understand, for instance, Turchaninov or Lvov's heirmoi in the fifth tone – that moves me, I've been hearing it since I was a child and I'm used to praying with it... No, don't sing any of that stuff when I'm here...

This conversation took place before the eucharist on one of the days of Easter in the Slavyansky Bazar Hotel. I remembered that we were talking about "Thou hast been robed in light" (*Tebe odeyushchagosya*) where at the word *uvï* ["alas"] the "uuuuuu..." which Pobedonostsev so greatly disliked really is long drawn out. As he made his way to the Cathedral he did not suspect that I would deliberately indicate that during the communion verse precisely the "Thou hast been robed in light" appointed for that day in the regulations should be sung, which the Synodal Choir performed delightfully, animatedly and with especially powerful expression. Pobedonostsev went into raptures about it and, turning to me, said: "And that was really good! You draw the 'uuu' out, but it's not dull, even though it's *znamenny* chant"'.[9]

Who was it who embellished these traditional Moscow arrangements and composed the new ones? Besides the Synodal School teacher Poluektov, Orlov the choirmaster too most likely lent a hand, he by that time having become with Taneyev's guidance an excellent contrapuntist. It is possible that in addition arrangements by other composers active in the

Moscow Society of Lovers of Church Music were also performed at these services – Komarov, Veykhental and Kashperov. (The structure of these services can be judged to some extent from the lithographed *Obikhod* of the Synodal Choir, a copy of which was presented to graduates on completing the School course.[10])

In 1896 works by another composer appeared among the Synodal Choir's sheet music – they were written by the Choir's assistant choirmaster Kastalsky, who by then had served his apprenticeship under Orlov for five years. Kastalsky had carried out all his duties as choirmaster conscientiously not only in preparing repertoire for worship but also teaching the choir the whole of the educational programme, which comprised a number of universal masterpieces and an anthology of Russian sacred music. On one occasion, when they were preparing for a service in the Cathedral, Orlov and Kastalsky decided to perform melodies from Serbian chants at it. As he compared the arrangement with the original in the *Obikhod*, however, Kastalsky found the arrangement unsatisfactory and on Orlov's advice made a new version. Kastalsky recalled:

> My harmonization, and indeed the 'It is meet' (*Dostoyno*) melody itself, struck me as quite compelling, and I was prompted to make an arrangement of 'Mercy of peace' (*Milost' mira*) as set out in the Serbian collection in a significantly more modest way. Although these harmonizations of mine appealed to everyone and are still in use by church choirs even now, I didn't attach the slightest artistic value to them. But success with them disposed me to take a closer look at the *Obikhod* melodies. My next, more valuable work was an experiment in arranging for choir (not harmonizations) several *znamenny* consistent, recurring melodic cells (*popevki*), which I combined in a single whole – 'Open to us the doors of compassion' (*Miloserdiya dveri*). In this regard I recollect that Stepan Smolensky, at that time director of the Synodal School, took a great interest in the progress of my work and kept asking me about the melodic cells I had taken for this piece.[11]

Smolensky not only began taking an interest in the new arrangements but thought most highly of them, writing in his 'Diary': 'Generally speaking, Alexander Kastalsky has begun composing straightaway and in a very powerful manner. What will come of this is hard to predict, but his scores are undoubtedly better than those of all present-day composers, even of the prominent ones among them'.[12] Stepan Vasilyevich also praised Kastalsky in materials he presented to Nikolay Findeyzen in 1898 for an article about the Synodal School, where he wrote: 'Kastalsky is a free artist of the Moscow Conservatoire (as a theorist) and the assistant choirmaster; he has begun composing only now, after many years of studying the ancient melodies. His style is Russian, entirely original and altogether good. He is an excellent, widely-read musician'.[13] Thanks to this publication, not just Moscow, where his choral music could be heard, but also the whole of Russia came to know of the new composer.

On 5 November 1898 another event which significantly influenced Kastalsky's subsequent fame took place: Pobedonostsev visited the Synodal School, and the choir organized a 'house concert' of compositions by Kastalsky for him. Smolensky noted in his 'Diary' that Alexander Dmitriyevich ought to note this 'day of unanimous recognition as one of the foremost composers in our field as a happy day in his life'.[14]

Kastalsky's works provoked universal interest, moving the composer to make further experiments, which proved to be entirely original and artistically convincing. The press very quickly started to speak about 'Kastalsky's direction' as having found a new path for Orthodox church music. There were also critics, however, who considered that the secret of the compositions' success lay not so much in themselves as in how they were performed by the Synodal Choir.

The majority of Kastalsky's new sacred compositions were indeed intended for the needs of the Cathedral of the Dormition. Reproduced lithographically according to the number of music desks for the Synodal Choir, his works began their life on the *kliros* long before they were published. Their first interpreter was the highly gifted Orlov, whose attitude to everything written by the composer was enthusiastic and sensitive. (Kastalsky's works later had the good fortune to be in the hands of two other remarkable choirmasters – Nikolay Danilin and Nikolay Golovanov.) As Kastalsky wrote in an autobiographical article:

> Almost everything I wrote for choir was performed by Vasily Orlov with a painstakingness which left nothing to be desired. He and I decided to introduce the singing of special melodies (variants of the basic melodies of the church 8-tone system, *na podoben*) into the services. Kastalsky would sit down to write stichera, sometimes, for speed, in lithographic ink; at the next rehearsal the stichera would be run through with the choir and at the service they would be sung by both sides of the *kliros*, without them leaving their places. When we were relaxing together we used to joke that my works went immediately from my desk to being sung by the Synodal Choir.[15]

Kastalsky paid close attention to interpretative peculiarities of his works in performance and inserted necessary amendments into his scores. Thus appeared new versions of his choral works, consolidated later into newly-copied lithographs or even published in typographically set music. And of course many amendments were brought into Kastalsky's scores by concert practice, which at that time was very intensive. The composer's works were performed most often at the Synodal Choir's concerts. But as the composer's fame grew, they were introduced into the repertoires of other choirs as well. The composer demanded the utmost of himself and constantly returned to his old works, trying to improve them or adapt them to particular situations. In this connection, almost every sacred work by Kastalsky exists in several versions, which is another feature of his legacy.

Thus Kastalsky's choral music was intended for practical performance and in many respects was subordinated to its requirements. In a certain sense a master's choral legacy is indeed inseparable from performers: the Synodal Choir and the composer represented a single creative phenomenon going back to common roots in the age-old traditions of Moscow church life. As the priest and composer Mikhail Lisitsïn who visited Moscow in 1906 asked in one his articles,

> What is the Synodal Choir? It is the very embodiment of Moscow and her Cathedral of the Dormition. It grew out of the singing of the priests of the Cathedral of the Dormition and represents its cultural continuation. Go to a service in the Cathedral of the Dormition on an ordinary day and you will be transported back to the seventeenth century. You will hear unison singing, adorned with *podgoloski* and chords thrown in at random, like sparks. [...] The Synodal Choir's way of singing has its roots there. The compositions of its leading light Alexander Kastalsky have developed out of this grain. Where in fact does all this crying-out of individual chords in the Synodal Choir's singing come from? What is the origin of these leaping chords in Mr Kastalsky's music? [...] They are all derived from the *podgolosok* chords used in unison singing. Kastalsky's manner of harmonization is a *podgolosok* one; in places Muscovite fecklessness, as in the picturesque ornament of the church of Saint Basil [on Red Square]. Like clusters of sparks, the sounds of his music sometimes rush about in a disordered way in all directions, but this affords its own beauty, its own unity.[16]

The work of Kastalsky and the composers who followed him reinterprets ancient traditions, and it influenced the performing manner of the Synodal Choir, which was based on the typically Russian art of flowing melismatic melody and transmitting the emotional palette of folksong-creativity – sincere, heartfelt, free from saccharine sentimentality and mannerism. During the Synodal Choir's foreign tours critics in Rome, Florence, Vienna and Dresden were staggered by the singers' wonderful *bel canto*, not suspecting that it was the fruit not just of Italian training but was formed from the basic material on which the Choir's repertoire rested: the infinitely long, vigorous and plastic melodic lines of the ancient chants.

Smolensky encouraged and inspired Kastalsky in every way to do further work, trying to acquaint him more intimately with Russian musical antiquity and furnishing him with ancient *Obikhod* melodies. It seems, though, that right to the very end he failed to understand Kastalsky's discovery of the new musical language to which he had himself led the composer and which was recognized and appreciated by many of his contemporaries, including Rimsky-Korsakov who was not exactly generous with praise, who imparted to Glazunov his opinion of Kastalsky: 'While Alexander Dmitriyevich is alive – so is Russian music. He is a master of Russian part-writing and will develop his ability to the level of supreme skill'.[17]

While acknowledging that Kastalsky possessed an unquestionable but very modest talent, Smolensky was personally very attached to the composer, maintained friendly relations with him until the end of his days and gave support and encouragement to his work as a composer; he regarded him, however, first and foremost as a scholar and archaeographer, his successor in the matter of studying musical antiquities. After he had become director of the Kapella, Stepan Vasilyevich recalled the first years of Kastalsky's career as a composer, and at that stage looked thus on what had taken place:

> At last the very sweet Kuzka got down to work, passed his exam brilliantly and wrote 'Open to us the doors of compassion' (*Miloserdiya dveri*) and his experiments in harmonizing Serbian chant. It was only the latter which saved Kastalsky from the attempts of Sh 2 [the *Prokuror* of the Moscow Synod Office Aleksey Shirinsky-Shikhmatov] to remove him from office, in spite of all my efforts to protect him. Sh 2 simply could not understand the significance of Kastalsky's experiments and continued to regard him as a quite useless assistant choirmaster. Only the Synodal Choir's magnificent performances of these compositions and the entirely serious newspaper reviews of them finally made Sh 2 understand and he let Kastalsky alone. Left thus in peace Kastalsky spread his wings, grew strong and moved along his true road, that is not as a composer but as a scholar and archaeologist, where a brilliant future undoubtedly lies ahead.[18]

It is obvious that Smolensky, unlike some contemporaries, did not see his Kuzka as a Messiah.

Notes

1. Letter from D.V. Allemanov to S.V. Smolensky of 27 December 1901. RGIA, fond 1119, opis' 1, no. 117.
2. A.V. Nikol'sky: *S.V. Smolensky i yego posledneye uchitel'stvo* (S.V. Smolensky and his last teaching experience), in *RUSAM*, vol. 1, p. 163.

3. Cited from the article of T. Shentalinskaya: *Voprosï variantnosti russkoy narodnoy pesni v otechestvennoy muzïkal'noy fol'kloristike dorevolyutsionnogo perioda* (Questions of the principles of variants in Russian folksong in Russian folklore studies of the prerevolutionary period). In *Iz istorii russkoy i sovetskoy muzïki* (From the history of Russian and Soviet music), issue no. 3. Moscow, 1978, p. 13.
4. S.V. Smolensky: *Vnimaniyu tserkovnïkh regentov i lyubiteley tserkovnogo peniya. (Nabroski stat'i)* (For the attention of church choirmasters and lovers of church music. (Drafts for an article). RNB, fond 816, opis' 3, no. 2625, p. 4.
5. Letter from S.V. Smolensky to N.F. Findeyzen of 10 August 1898. RNB, fond 816, opis' 3, no. 2676, p. 46v.
6. S.V. Smolensky: *Sinodal'nïy khor i uchilishche tserkovnogo peniya* (The Synodal Choir and School of Church Music), in *RUSAM*, vol. 1, p. 64.
7. *Ibid.*, p. 83.
8. *Ibid.*, p. 84.
9. *Ibid.*, p. 85.
10. *Sbornik pesnopeniy liturgii. [Steklograf Sinodal'nogo khora]* (Collection of hymns for the liturgy. [Lithographed by the Synodal Choir]. GTsMMK, N.S. Golovanov flat-museum, no. 1047.
11. A.D. Kastal'sky: *O moyey muzïkal'noy kar'yere i moi mïsli o tserkovnoy muzïke* (My musical career and my thoughts about church music), in *RUSAM*, vol. 1, p. 231.
12. S.V. Smolensky: *Pervïy dnevnik* (First diary). RGIA, fond 1119, opis' 1, no. 3.
13. Letter from S.V. Smolensky to N.F. Findeyzen of 3 November 1897. RNB, fond 816, opis' 3, no. 2676, p. 9v.
14. S.V. Smolensky: *Vtoroy dnevnik* (Second diary). RGIA, fond 1119, opis' 1, no. 5, p. 9v.
15. A.D. Kastal'sky: *O moyey muzïkal'noy kar'yere i moi mïsli o tserkovnoy muzïke,* in *RUSAM*, vol. 1, p. 236.
16. M. Lisitsïn: *Moskva i Sinodal'nïy khor* (Moscow and the Synodal Choir), in *Muzïka i peniye* (Instrumental Music and Song), 1906, no. 11, p. 5.
17. B.V. Asaf'yev: *Iz ustnïkh predaniy i lichnïkh moikh vstrech* (From oral legends and my personal encounters). RGALI, fond 2658, opis' 1, no. 374, p. 70v.
18. S.V. Smolensky: *Sinodal'nïy khor i uchilishche tserkovnogo peniya*, in *RUSAM*, vol. 1, pp. 88-89.

Chapter 9

Kastalsky's Discovery

His contemporaries regarded Kastalsky as having been born under a lucky star, so swift was the success of his compositions. But is it only luck that can explain the fact that from his very first steps as a composer of sacred music Kastalsky was pronounced the discoverer of a national style, whose compositions became an adornment to the repertoire of the Synodal Choir, and were applauded in Moscow, St Petersburg, Vienna, Warsaw, Rome, Dresden and Florence?

The emergence of mature compositions by a 40-year-old teacher at the Synodal School came as a great surprise to many people. Those who knew that the previous years had been filled with intensive self-improvement, however, understood that the apparent accident was in fact a natural occurrence. The clarity and conviction of the results and the way they matched the aesthetic conceptions of a national style in sacred music which had by then taken shape guaranteed that Kastalsky's compositions would become the banner of the new school and inspire many of his colleagues to creative quests along the lines he had proclaimed.

It was Boris Asafyev who described Kastalsky's discovery most precisely:

> At first by instinct and later after profoundly comprehending the essence of the arts of folksong and liturgical chant, Kastalsky strove in his arrangements of liturgical melodies to form a polyphonic texture out of the melodic (horizontal) forward movement determined by breathing. A living sonority, and not a merely mechanical distribution of the middle voices between the upper and lower ones, organizes his music. Melodic functions, not harmonic ones, produce all the part-writing. The dynamics of the voice control the sonority and the devices for forming it. In its time – and until very recently – this was all so new and out of the ordinary that there was a tendency among musicians who put their faith in the unassailable patterns of German chorale part-writing to view Kastalsky as a crank and a composer of low cultural level. Truth proved to be on his side, regardless of everything, thanks to one specific fact: his choral works always sounded better than those of his detractors. The part-writing is more intelligent vocally. When Rachmaninoff's magnificent choral

compositions (the Liturgy and especially the All-Night Vigil) emerged out of Kastalsky's art, there could no longer be any room for doubt. A melodic-polyphonic style had come into being where the immensely rich melodic inheritance of the past produced splendid new shoots.[1]

Kastalsky wrote church music over the course of his whole life as a 'serious composer', which began in 1896. (The composer himself took no account of his early experiments from the 1870s and 1880s and later destroyed them.) His first successes inspired him, and in 1902 when he was preparing to present his compositions to Emperor Nicholas II he was able to speak of 44 published works and also of 'slightly over a hundred' further unpublished stichera to special melodies in the eight church tones (*na podoben*). In the catalogue of church music compositions by Kastalsky published by P. Jurgenson in the 1910s, there are already 73 published choral items. (In reality, when different versions of the same piece are included, 88 compositions are mentioned in this list – different versions were not allocated a separate number.) This figure too, however, is far from exhausting all that the composer had written up to that time, since many of his choral items as well as new versions of already published compositions remained in manuscript and lithographed form. Since the greater part of the library of the Synodal Choir perished, with the rest scattered over the whole world, it seems impossible to establish an exhaustive list of Kastalsky's works; it remains only to name those compositions which have come to light. At present we have information about the existence of 136 sacred music compositions and arrangements written by Kastalsky in both the pre-revolutionary and post-revolutionary years.

The periodization of Kastalsky's sacred music is determined in many respects by the various stages of his career at the Synodal School, and also by his personal enthusiasms. The first period, coinciding with the final years of Smolensky's directorship (1896-1900), is marked by his most intense activity in the sacred music field. The composition of sacred music was at the forefront of his interests: in those few years everything that had been gestating over the course of many years was given birth.

This first period manifestly surpasses all the others in the quantity of music written. If one takes the information in Jurgenson's catalogue as the starting-point, then during those five years 26 compositions and arrangements for ensembles of varied size and make-up were created by Kastalsky. This period is also noteworthy for the abundance of choral works selected for performance when people wanted to show the 'image' of the new Moscow school of composers. Works which caused so much stir, such as the troparia for Matins on Holy Saturday, the ikos 'Thou alone art immortal' (*Sam Yedin*), the Old Simonov Cherubic Hymn, the 'It is meet' (*Dostoyno*) in the chant by Tsar Feodor, the Cherubic Hymn to the chant of the Cathedral of the Dormition, 'Mercy of peace' (*Milost' mira*) no. 2 and other Kastalsky masterpieces were written in these remarkable years.

One must immediately enter the proviso that the range of challenges which the artist set himself was very wide. His legacy includes works both traditional and ultra-innovative, intended for grand and ordinary services, for highly professional and amateur choirs, for mixed and single voice-type choirs, for the concert hall and the church. In Kastalsky's legacy of sacred music, however, there are no commonplaces or weak spots. The composer carried out even the humblest tasks with skill, and his fingerprints are evident on both the large and the small scales.

The liturgical texts of the eucharistic canon and the Memorial Service aroused Kastalsky's special interest. The composer was not alone in this respect. It is sufficient to recall the many hundreds of times the Cherubic Hymn, the 'Mercy of peace', the 'It is meet' and the 'Our Father' (*Otche nash*) occur in the Russian heritage of sacred music beginning in the Middle Ages. It was to these hymns that Kastalsky too turned most frequently in his early years. But the composer did not subscribe to the fashion characteristic of the new age for large-scale liturgical cycles: he composed those hymns which were needed at a given moment on the *kliros* and which attracted him emotionally. (We should remember that Smolensky and Orlov were then conducting a huge experiment in renewing the repertoire for services.) In other words, Alexander Dmitriyevich was keeping to the same principle of work as the Patriarch's Singing Clerks who had stood on the *kliros* of the Cathedral of the Dormition some centuries before. The composer was uncommonly open to the past, sensed the connection of the ages and felt the spirit of people long since departed and their creations.

Kastalsky wrote: 'I regard the *znamenny* Cherubic Hymn as the earliest of my valuable compositions, and in that respect I agree with the opinion of critics who have noted the first application in it of new devices of harmonization and new choral sonorities dependent on varied combinations of voices'.[2]

The Cherubic Hymn in *znamenny* chant – the third sacred choral item which Kastalsky composed – really did display his style in all its glory. One cannot fail to be amazed by the composer's resourcefulness in clothing the *znamenny* melody in polyphonic dress, finding ever new ways of arranging it. Thus, the first stanza 'Let us who mystically represent the Cherubim' (*Izhe Kheruvimï tayno obrazuyushche*) is treated as a juxtaposition of the two groups in the choir – the children and the men, symbolizing the worlds of heaven and earth. This device was to be used repeatedly by Kastalsky in other choral works. A *znamenny* melody, winding capriciously, is woven organically into an ornamental pattern of accompanying voices close to it in intervallic structure, forming chords of natural-mode harmony. The work's choral texture is melodic to the utmost degree. Melodic quality and the recurring use of significant intervals are characteristic of each voice, which moves in accordance with the impulse given by the principal melody, which is dissolved in abundant *divisi*. Great freedom typifies the rhythmic organization of the fabric, as a consequence of the irregularity of rhythm in the composition's primary basis even though the composer makes use of the usual time-signatures of European music.

The second line – 'And who sing the thrice-holy hymn to the life-creating Trinity' (*I zhivotvoryashchey Troitse Trisvyatuyu pesn' pripevayushche*) – is a new variant of the arrangement, treated, as far as texture is concerned, as a successive intertwining, from top to bottom, of the choral voices with the ensuing 'exclusion' of the men.

The third line – 'now lay aside all cares of this life' (*Vsyakoye nïne zhiteyskoye otlozhim popecheniye*) – is set forth in brilliant, compact chords for the children accompanied by the singing of *podgoloski* by the men. The sonority is thickened and strengthened by means of *divisi* and by the closeness in tessitura of all the parts.

The fourth line – 'That we may receive the King of All, who comes invisibly upborne by the angelic host. Alleluia' (*Yako da Tsarya vsekh podïmem, angel'skimi nevidimo dorinosima chinmi, alliluiya*) – resembles the treatment of the third line in the way it is set out. The fourth stanza, however, is preordained to have a more extended unfolding leading to an impressive climax – to a popular celebration (*alliluiya*), in fact, where a device typical of the 'Mighty Handful' is employed: the theme is set out in octaves in the upper voices, doubled also in octaves by a 'second' voice a third away in the lower voices. This kind of device, representing the heroic might of Rus, can be found in the chorus in the Prologue of Borodin's opera *Prince Igor*, and in the *Great Gate of Kiev* from Musorgsky's piano cycle *Pictures from an Exhibition*.

The finale – the concluding *alliluiya* – is rather unexpected, but is something not so very rare in Kastalsky: a perfectly Bachian preluding against a background of a long tonic pedal (Ex. 9.1).

Thus, one of the first of Kastalsky's most 'valuable' compositions did indeed prove to mark a revolution in the means of arranging monody. It is obvious that, by using the technique of varied stanzas and the *podgoloski-*

polyphonic style, the composer was starting out from the logic of the art of folksong and, moreover, relying boldly on the musical language of the 'Mighty Handful' and even elements of Bachian counterpoint. In short, all the hard work of the preceding years – the study of scores by Russian composers of the national tendency, musical folklore, compositions by great polyphonists of the past – had produced magnificent shoots on the basis of Russian medieval monody, the element native to Kastalsky. The *znamenny* chant flows through his composition freely and unconstrainedly as an organic constituent of the musical fabric, lending lively energy and sense of style to the other voices. It is perfectly obvious that the quest for a 'new antiquity' has led with this work to the birth of a long-awaited artistic style in Russian music. It is based on original compositional devices and marked by a new structure of images. This Cherubic Hymn, highly coloured, ceremonial, festive, 'regal', blossoming forth like an immense 'garden of many flowers' from stanza to stanza, was the composer's first demonstration of the 'Moscow style' he had discovered, which bore the imprint of a certain collective image of Moscow.

After the *znamenny* Cherubic Hymn Kastalsky wrote one further choral piece where he applied the technique he had worked out. The composer himself included this work among his most valuable. It is the hymn 'Open to us the doors of compassion' (*Miloserdiya dveri*) where the composer rejected the traditional path of arranging the complete (or almost complete) chant and carried out 'an experiment in developing several *znamenny* melodic cells combined in a single whole' (Ex. 9.2). This device of freely manipulating stable intervallic shapes and breeding the contrapuntal fabric of a hymn out of them would later be applied in the majority of Kastalsky's compositions. This technique was to become one of the means of treating monody most favoured by composers of the 'Moscow school'.

However, as Kastalsky himself supposed, his first compositions could not yet function as a basis on which an idea of the new direction could be formed. Therefore, when at the beginning of 1898 the publisher of the 'Russian Musical Gazette' (*Russkaya muzïkal'naya gazeta*), N.F. Findeyzen, approached him, expressing a desire for a closer acquaintance with his experiments, the composer replied:

Dear Nikolay Fyodorovich!
I ask you to forgive me for the delay in replying to your kind letter, but since there are no actions without reasons then even my silence when faced with your question 'Which of my works have been published?' can be explained very simply: of those which deserve any sort of attention (and I hope that it is only in those that musicians might be interested) just two have been published at present: the *znamenny* Cherubic Hymn and 'Open to us the doors of

compassion'. But in about two or three weeks around eight more items are due to be published, which I think are of interest, namely: two *znamenny* 'A mercy of peace' (a minor one and a major one), 'Noble Joseph' (*Blagoobrazniÿ Iosif*) with the others associated with it, the troparia and kontakia for Christ's Nativity and Baptism, the *znamenny* litanies, 'God is with us' (*S nami Bog*)... and I think that's all for the moment. That's the batch I'm waiting for from the censorship, so that I can answer you as I ought. It's difficult to see a 'direction' from only two pieces but easier with ten. And so in about two or three weeks a little collection will see the light of day. My works are on sale at Jurgenson in Moscow. I believe they are also in stock at the Petersburg Jurgenson. When the items just mentioned come out, I can send them to you if you're interested. Replying to your second question – can I send you some information about my musical activities? – is very hard for me, because going to lessons (starting with piano, choir, theory – and ending I don't know with what – maybe cycling) – are not activities anyone is interested in, and my works which are beginning to be of interest to several musicians and have been performed in public are too few in number with all too few published (the oldest of them for no more than eighteen months, I think, – for them to be able to give their composer the title 'activities', let alone 'compositional activities'. In a word, you'll have to wait a while for the 'compositional activities'. As regards sending you something to print in your journal, I don't know what would be of most interest, again, of course for musicians: 'Thou alone art immortal' appealed most to musicians in Moscow, but the fact is that I'm preparing that too for sending to the censorship and printing, and what's more the terms for placing anything in a journal are unknown territory to me. Would you be so kind as to explain to me this dark business? Excuse me for blethering. Your obedient servant, A. Kastalsky[3]

Thanks to financial assistance of 150 roubles, for which Shirinsky-Shikhmatov applied to the Synod for Kastalsky's benefit, not just the compositions mentioned in the letter to Findeyzen but also other choral pieces were published in 1898. In this way 19 published works by the composer were listed in Jurgenson's catalogue, giving a more thorough indication of the direction his creative work was taking. Among the choral pieces published was the ikos 'Thou alone art immortal', the composition which probably enjoyed the greatest popularity among contemporaries (Ex. 9.3). Even 15 years later as he recalled his début, Alexander Dmitriyevich again mentioned its resounding success and wrote that 'Thou alone art immortal', along with the Cherubic Hymn of the Cathedral of the Dormition, aroused 'great enthusiasm among the then young Sergey Rachmaninoff, Vasily Safonov and other big shots from the Conservatoire'.[4]

This composition was heard at many of the concerts of sacred music given by the Synodal Choir, though it was sung in churches as well. The performance of the ikos at the memorial service for the composer

Alexander Skryabin left an ineradicable impression. A member of the Synodal Choir who took part recalled that 'the full complement of the Synodal Choir could be accommodated on the *kliros* of the small church in Nikolo-Peskovsky Lane in the Arbat only with great difficulty. Singing there was uncomfortable and very stressful. The presence of such Moscow musicians as Taneyev and Rachmaninoff also placed an obligation upon us to sing outstandingly well. The latter had a high opinion of the Synodal Choir's singing'.[5]

The kontakion 'With the Saints give rest' (*So svyatïmi upokoy*) and the ikos 'Thou alone art immortal' made their appearance in Rachmaninoff's library of music in 1903. The copy was presented by Kastalsky and accompanied by the inscription 'To the profoundly respected Sergey Vasilyevich Rachmaninoff from A. Kastalsky to remind him that there is a realm [of music] where people are patiently but insistently waiting for Rachmaninoff to be inspired'.[6] During the 1910s Kastalsky's expectations were fulfilled. One may well suppose that the impressions Rachmaninoff obtained from his older colleague's most vivid choral canvases, including the ikos 'Thou alone art immortal', were to some extent reflected in his Liturgy and All-Night Vigil.

It is likely that the power and depth of Kastalsky's canvases were determined by the versatility of the artist's personality. As an artist in paint as well, he portrayed pictures, ideas and images of majestic liturgical rites in tone-colours; as an Orthodox believer, he expressed his religious emotions; as a person of powerful intellect and a scholar, he introduced his scholarly achievements into his artistic work; as a practical man of the *kliros*, an expert on the traditions of worship and church music, he thought in accordance with tradition and with the laws dictated by the church; and as an educated musician, he had at his disposal professional technical skills and knowledge. All these qualities allowed Kastalsky to rise to a level of mastery where an artist succeeds in creating a new canon in the musical interpretation of a series of liturgical texts.

In the opinion of contemporaries, Kastalsky's most impressive interpretation was that of the troparia for Holy Saturday. This composition's path to the *kliros* was not an easy one. The composer recalled later:

A certain misunderstanding attended 'Noble Joseph' and the other troparia for Holy Saturday; Kompaneysky went impermissibly far in his eulogies by comparing this hymn with the creations of Bach (!), but at the same time deemed it unsuitable for worship (?). There were some worshippers in Moscow who shared this way of thinking. I heard indirectly that someone was even thinking of hitting me over the head for it...[7]

And in the troparia for Holy Saturday Kastalsky had indeed given his creative imagination free range and used devices from epic symphonic writing never previously applied in choral music, which patently did not accord with the stereotypes of church music accepted at that period (Ex. 9.4). Over the course of time, however, the composer's monumental sacred choral frescoes took hold in the church, because in spite of all the freedom allowed in them they did not actually break with tradition but merely reinterpreted it.

The subject of the great mystery of death, which seems to have attracted Kastalsky at various periods in his work as a composer, called into being a number of his most expressive compositions. The general tone of the images and emotions in his sacred choral works is defined nevertheless not by dark but by bright colours; the worlds of heaven and earth predominate over the underworld in the picture of creation as the artist saw it.

And there is something else to be said about one of Kastalsky's main achievements during his first years of active work as a composer: he was the first to provide model artistic interpretations in a national spirit of the basic hymns of the central Orthodox service – the liturgy: all the liturgical cycles by composers of the New Direction, written in the 'Russian style', were to be products of the twentieth century.

Notes

1. B.V. Asaf'yev: *Khorovoye tvorchestvo A.D. Kastal'skogo* (A.D. Kastal'sky's compositions for choir), in *A.D. Kastal'sky. Stat'i. Vospominaniya. Materialï* (A.D. Kastal'sky. Articles. Reminiscences. Materials). Moscow, 1960, p. 16.
2. A.D. Kastal'sky: *O moyey muzïkal'noy kar'yere i moi mïsli o tserkovnoy muzïke* (My musical career and my thoughts about church music), in *RUSAM*, vol. 1, p. 232.
3. Letter from A.D. Kastal'sky to N.F. Findeyzen of 1898. RNB, fond 816, opis' 2, no. 1450, pp. 1-2.
4. A.D. Kastal'sky: *O moyey muzïkal'noy kar'yere i moi mïsli o tserkovnoy muzïke*, in *RUSAM*, vol. 1, p. 234.
5. A.P. Smirnov: *Pamyati direktora moskovskogo Sinodal'nogo uchilishcha i khora, kompozitora A.D. Kastal'skogo* (In memory of the director of the Moscow Synodal School and Choir, the composer A.D. Kastal'sky), in *Naslediye. Muzïkal'nïye sobraniya* (Heritage. Musical assemblies [festival]), vol. 2. Moscow, 1992, p. 70.
6. The music of Kastal'sky's compositions *So svyatïmi upokoy* ('With the Saints give rest') and *Sam Yedin yesi bezsmertnïy* ('Thou alone art immortal'), with a dedicatory inscription, is in GTsMMK, fond 18, no. 1078.
7. A.D. Kastal'sky: *O moyey muzïkal'noy kar'yere i moi mïsli o tserkovnoy muzïke*, in *RUSAM*, vol. 1, pp. 232-233.

Chapter 10

At the Crossroads

The second period of Kastalsky's biography as a composer (1901-09) began when Smolensky bade farewell to the Synodal School, leaving behind in Moscow not just the fruits of his labours but also many orphaned pupils and colleagues. But Stepan Vasilyevich managed to have some pupils and teachers transferred from the School to the Kapella along with himself. Among these lucky ones were Antonin Preobrazhensky, Nikolay Rumyantsev, Alexander Chesnokov, Pavel Tolstyakov, Alexander Smirnov, and Mikhail Klimov. Those who remained in Moscow wrote complaining letters to Stepan Vasilyevich and told him about the chaos and neglect reigning at the Synodal School after his departure.

It is difficult now to judge to what extent the tales of the School's deterioration corresponded with reality; it cannot be excluded that they contain an element of exaggeration, since they were addressed to a man who had not left Moscow of his own free will. However, the opinion that the Synodal School and Choir had surrendered their positions at the beginning of the century could be heard not only from Smolensky's followers.

It is known that Smolensky's defeat and departure resulted from intrigues by the *Prokuror* of the Moscow Synod Office Shirinsky-Shikhmatov, who drew Orlov into them as well. These two very different people concurred in their opposition to the idea of a broad musical and academic education for the School's pupils, and campaigned for a deeper specialization in church music. In reality this idea found expression in a series of experiments in collective teaching of musical disciplines: lessons in reading choral scores, piano and violin became group lessons. The number of hours of academic work too was changed in favour of specialist subjects. It seems that the problem was not so much the change in the number of hours or the form in which lessons were given, however, so much as in the absence of an active and competent School head. Orlov, the choirmaster appointed to that post, lacked any gift for organization or administration in his colleagues' opinion and, finding himself in the wrong job, suffered in morale as well as physically. The common cause also suffered accordingly. When Smolensky went to Moscow in 1902 he found the Synodal Choir not on its best form. Smolensky recalled:

> The Synodal Choir's concert did not make the same captivating impression which I used to obtain before. Of course the choir sang very well and harmoniously, but somehow with a sense of overstrain, nervously, on edge – manufactured to an unpleasant degree; the earlier good, healthy, attractive, smooth sound and animated singing had disappeared from the choir's performance and something completely weighed-down, dull, tame and unprayerful had appeared. [...] The choir's technique is as magnificent as before, and Vasily Orlov exploits it to sculpt everything that comes into his head. But Orlov himself is now far from being the elevated and inspired singer-choirmaster he used to be, and has become an unhealthily and disagreeably mannered one.[1]

Smolensky made efforts to influence the situation at the Synodal School from St Petersburg, the more so as he had connections at court and enjoyed the favour of the imperial couple. First and foremost, Stepan Vasilyevich intended to prise Orlov away from his oppressive duties as director to let him concentrate on the area where he was a great artist, that is on conducting. For the post of director, Smolensky had in mind Preobrazhensky or Kastalsky, both of whom possessed a rational, scholarly cast of mind, organizational abilities and a correct attitude, in his opinion, toward the future development of the Synodal School. In the upshot, however, neither was appointed to the directorship.

As we know, Preobrazhensky was transferred by Smolensky to St Petersburg to the post of librarian of the Court Kapella and over the following years he developed into a fine scholar of the Middle Ages, becoming Smolensky's closest successor. Kastalsky, having observed the ordeals of Stepan Vasilyevich himself, declined to enter into negotiation about taking on the directorship. 'Things have worked out now in such a way that I nonetheless enjoy freedom of conscience and some time for my own activities...', he wrote to Smolensky.[2] The composer dreamed of 'retreating into himself from the disturbed world' and busying himself with his favourite activity, but the prospect of remaining without a pension in old age forced him to think about a career in employment as well. His cherished dream was to move to the Kapella in his colleagues' wake; he also briefly considered working at the Tiflis or Sebastopol branches of the Russian Musical Society.

Kastalsky was always optimistic and keen on his work. The letters he wrote to Smolensky in the 1900s, however, are full of descriptions of the oppressive atmosphere in the School, complaints about colleagues, and anxiety about his declining health. 'As far as I am concerned, I have aged noticeably recently (even I think since last summer) and I feel psychologically not quite right', Kastalsky wrote in 1903 to Smolensky, who did as much as he possibly could to help him.[3] As early as the autumn of 1901 one of Kastalsky's first innovative compositions 'Open to us the doors of compassion' (*Miloserdiya dveri*) was performed, doing the composer no little service. In the first place 'The doors of compassion' (as it was usually known) was sung in the presence of the famous priest Father Ioann of Kronstadt, who visited the Kapella in that year, on whom it made the most powerful impression. Smolensky wrote to Kastalsky on 6 November 1901:

> Father Ioann's spontaneous, sensitive nature grasped the prayerful quality of your work and, praying fervently, he was inimitable and most affecting while he was listening to your music. His prayer must have been transmitted to the singers, and 'The doors of compassion' rang out with exceptional power and sublimity from the words 'as we have put our hope in Thee' (*nadeyushchiisya*). This increase in the performance's animation went on rising right up to the very end where, in spite of a *diminuendo* in the sound, the impression grew to an overwhelming extent.[4]

On 27 January 1902, again on the initiative of Smolensky, who had now transferred his advocacy of new ideas to St Petersburg, a public concert by the Kapella was organized. The programme was devised in such a way as to show the public the outdatedness and unacceptability to the church of music by the composers whose compositions had held undivided sway there during the previous century – Bortnyansky, Lvov and Bakhmetev. Works by these composers, to which Smolensky considered it appropriate to add Potulov's experiments, made up the first half of the programme. In the second half the Kapella performed new sacred music: works by Tchaikovsky, Rimsky-Korsakov, Ippolitov-Ivanov and Kastalsky were heard.

The public showed very great interest in the concert (mainly because a new person – Smolensky – had become the focus of the capital's attention), and the review of the concert written by the St Petersburg composer and critic Kompaneysky was extremely flattering for Kastalsky who was unknown in St Petersburg. 'Kastalsky is the first real artist among composers writing for church choirs since Bortnyansky. His compositions solve the problem of applying the strict style to our church melodies', wrote Kompaneysky.[5] And the following comparison of the reviewer's had an especially gratifying ring for Kastalsky:

Tchaikovsky's 'Blessed are they whom Thou has chosen' (*Blazheni yazhe izbral*) is a wonderfully beautiful musical treatment. But after Kastalsky's 'The doors of compassion' its instrumental character and the purely superficial link between music and words stand out. With Kastalsky, the voices form a symphony as they sing their Russian melodies; with Tchaikovsky, the chords are planned in advance for insertion at particular points, and the voices for the most part do not really sing but enter only in order to form the chords the composer needs.[6]

The work 'The doors of compassion' made a profound impression not just on Ioann of Kronshtadt and the critic Kompaneysky. On 31 March 1902 Smolensky informed Alexander Dmitriyevich: 'I wanted to write to you this very day because today we repeated "The doors of compassion" at the liturgy, and after the service the Sovereign remembered the composer's name and spoke approvingly about both the work and the performance'.[7]

Kastalsky felt grateful to Smolensky, and replied on 26 June 1902:

First and foremost of course, thank you very much for popularizing my name with the Sovereign and other highly-placed persons. At my advanced age, when you have to start thinking about the chance of being left without any money [*ne pri chom*] (or 'dealing in bricks' [*torgovat' kirpichom*], as Petrushka says, although at the present time trading in bricks is profitable, so they say – unlike composing sacred music) – when you're inclined to think that way, then getting news of the approval of the Sovereign himself is, of course, extremely pleasant.[8]

In August Smolensky suggested to Kastalsky that he present his compositions to the emperor. In February 1903 the music was sent to St Petersburg and at the beginning of May they were presented to the tsar. On 19 May the appointment of Kastalsky as choirmaster of the Synodal Choir ensued. 'I read in the newspaper today that assistant choirmaster of the Synodal Choir Kastalsky is appointed "acting choirmaster" – that means that at the age of 46 I've finally achieved something after all', the composer wrote to Smolensky on 13 May 1903.[9]

In spite of this rather grand appointment, however, Alexander Dmitriyevich had not completely given up the idea of moving to St Petersburg. Hope of leaving the Synodal School dried up completely only when Smolensky left the Kapella at the end of 1903. Alexander Dmitriyevich had to reconcile himself to his fate and carry out a role for which his nature obviously did not intend him – namely, conducting the Synodal Choir – until 1910.

During Orlov's time Kastalsky's choirmastership extended only as far as rehearsals and the *kliros*; Alexander Dmitriyevich never conducted at concerts, leaving that responsible job to Orlov, with whom he enjoyed a great friendship until the end of his days. The composer's daughter Natalia recalled:

> When we were children our family and the family of Vasily Orlov, the School's director and conductor, were very close. Orlov was a most Russian-looking man, severe in appearance, with a moustache, a beard and big grey eyes. You sensed that he did not have long to live – judging by the gloominess which sometimes overcame him. He was gentle, light-hearted and kind with children. On the concert platform he was a god and a despot! Every occasion when he appeared with the choir was an event. After concerts he and my father would embrace one another silently and tightly. Orlov was a striking figure. He was known as the 'Russian Nikisch'.[10]

Even Orlov's quarrel with Smolensky could not cast a shadow over the friendship between Kastalsky and Orlov. Immersed in his work, the composer was able to take a neutral position and was on good terms with both, the more so since after Shirinsky-Shikhmatov's departure from Moscow in 1903 the relationship between the former opponents was re-established.

Kastalsky's life did not change outwardly. As before, his working day began early in the morning and ended late in the evening; as before it was full of 'hustle and bustle from morning to evening'. The greater part of the time was swallowed up by lessons, rehearsals and church services. New tasks and commissions arose from time to time to vary the routine of normal school activities. Thus, in 1905, as a member of the Supervisory Council attached to the School, Kastalsky was instructed to 'correct all the ordinary chants, all the tone melodies, and set music to all the texts; look through all the literature published for use in churches; and devise a draft standard statute for the improvement of choirs in Moscow'; in the same year the composer embarked on preparing a complete edition of the compositions of Pyotr Turchaninov;[11] in 1907 he took part with his colleagues in compiling new school syllabuses; in 1908 he completed a self-instruction manual in church music for the ordinary people and started to write a textbook on singing from stave notation for elementary schools.[12]

Kastalsky, who occupied the second place in the School hierarchy, began gradually to leave the complex of the 'rank-and-file teacher' and the 'little man' behind and to play an ever weightier role in the life of the School. This became especially noticeable in preparing the new academic syllabuses.

The point was that the experiments of the first half of the 1900s had produced an unwelcome result: a decline in the standard of musical education, and as a consequence the transfer of the most able pupils to the Conservatoire. A new reform was introduced at the School in the spring of 1906 with the aim of raising the level of musical education at the School to that of an institution of higher learning. Forgotten slogans going back to the first years of the changes were heard again at meetings of the teaching staff: 'The Synodal School should send out church choirmasters well trained in theory (they leave other schools, church choirs and so on without training of that kind), experienced harmonizers and capable composers of sacred music, which secular musicians usually pay little attention to'.[13] It was decided in the first place to extend the course in theoretical subjects: 'It was intended, by means of a broad formulation of theoretical subjects, to round out the knowledge of Synodal School pupils so that there would be no need for them to seek to extend and deepen their theoretical knowledge of music in conservatoires and so that they would be content as far as possible with the School's course and should apply their gifts to arranging existing church melodies or to free composition in the spirit of the church without getting carried away by the prospects of purely secular music'.[14]

In his reminiscences Kastalsky links the change in the School's direction to the arrival of a new head – the *Prokuror* of the Moscow Synod Office, Filipp Stepanov, who unleashed a whirlwind of activity. Alexander Dmitriyevich also took a most active part in devising the new syllabuses. In particular, he compiled the syllabuses for the courses in Musical Forms and Folk Music. He sent the draft to Smolensky to let him see it; Smolensky was organizing a Church Choirmasters' School in St Petersburg in 1907. That scholar was attempting for the third time to realize his concept of an Academy of Church Music and was naturally interested in the changes which had taken place on Bolshaya Nikitskaya Street.

In the spring of 1907 the syllabuses and the statute were sent to the Synod, who sent them back for revision a year later. The inhabitants of the School, however, were in no state to be bothered about reforms at that time: on 10 November the conductor Orlov died, and his death represented not only a great loss for Russian art but also unsettled the Synodal School's usual régime for several years.

Smolensky made this entry in his diary over those days:

From Pasha Chesnokov I received news of the death of Vasily Orlov, my successor as director of the Synodal School in Moscow and former choirmaster of the Synodal Choir. As director the deceased is simply not open to criticism, as he was forced into becoming director and essentially was incapable of doing that job, having neither the mind for the directorship, nor the abilities, nor the education, nor even the definite career position, outside the *Prokuror*'s petty tyranny, for the directorship. I cannot even hold the dead man responsible for the fact that the Synodal School as a good school ceased to exist long ago under him. This sin is the result of Shirinsky-Shikhmatov's blows – and Orlov was not in a position to fight against them and advance the cause. But in all justice Orlov must be mentioned as a major artist-choirmaster of the front rank who raised the Synodal Choir to first place in Russia and put the artistry of that choir unquestionably higher even than the once famous singing of the Court Kapella. The period when the Synodal Choir particularly flourished was from 1895 to 1899, that is, the time from the first Historical Concerts until the trip for the consecration of the embassy church in Vienna.[15]

Smolensky viewed the future of the Synodal School with alarm: 'The loss of Orlov as choirmaster made itself felt long ago in the Synodal Choir, and I think that the talented Kolya Danilin will scarcely be able to restore the previous perfection of this choir under the late Orlov'.[16]

Soon there was more news from Moscow: under the influence of the *Prokuror* Filipp Stepanov, the successor to the late Orlov was Semyon Kruglikov, a well-known Moscow journalist and teacher.

At first sight the appointment of Kruglikov as director of the Synodal School does not seem strange, for he was a man extremely experienced in church music. Testimony to that are his many reviews of concerts of sacred music, his participation in devising the School's first syllabuses, his membership of the Supervisory Council attached to the School, and finally several years of work teaching harmony at the School. His praiseworthy position in the confrontation between Smolensky and Shirinsky-Shikhmatov should also be mentioned: Kruglikov came out on the side of the already defeated Smolensky and administered a rebuff to the *Prokuror*. In Kruglikov's opinion, turning a unique educational institution such as the Synodal School into an ordinary school for church choirmasters would be a great mistake. It was exactly that idea that was one of the fundamental ones in the conception of a transformed School after the arrival of Stepanov as *Prokuror* in 1906. The possibility cannot be excluded that Stepanov's nomination of Kruglikov for the directorship can be explained by the fact that the views of the well-known Moscow teacher and publicist coincided with his own ideas.

In the eyes of the Synodal School people, however, Kruglikov, neither a composer nor a conductor, neither a scholar nor in general terms 'a man of the *kliros*' – was actually not the right man to run such a specialized institution as the Synodal School. It was clear, besides, that, even then very sick and bereft of work as a result of the closure of many newspapers, he accepted the job offered to him not for love of the task so much as out of great material need. His appointment was even more illogical, as a general meeting of the teachers and members of the Supervisory Council had proposed Kastalsky for the job, and he had worked at the School for twenty years.

A campaign to oust Kruglikov from the School was started, which in Kastalsky's words turned into a boiling cauldron. And although work began on changing the School syllabuses and organizing the teaching on that basis, Kruglikov's directorship can be viewed only as a period when the reforms ripened, while they opened out seriously after 1910.

As far as Kastalsky was concerned, his first reaction to Kruglikov's appointment was a desire to leave the Synodal School. 'At this moment I am at a crossroads', he wrote to Smolensky in December 1907. 'Of course, if I could find other work in my field, I would not hesitate, though I couldn't say it was easy to leave "with a light heart"; after all, I've stuck it out here for twenty years, working on all sorts of commissions'.[17] The composer could not find suitable work in another institution, however, and over the following three years he had to occupy himself in earnest with the Synodal Choir. Now, on Orlov's death, both the concerts and the most crucial church services landed on Kastalsky. It fell to Alexander Dmitriyevich to direct the choir during the recording of gramophone discs in 1907 as well.

Unfortunately the few phonograms of the Synodal Choir cannot give any idea of either their singing or the skill of their choirmaster because their quality is unsatisfactory.[18] One can fairly evaluate Kastalsky as a conductor only on the basis of the statements of contemporaries who subconsciously compared him with Orlov. These statements were contradictory. Thus, after his visit to Moscow in 1904, the critic N.I. Kompaneysky wrote in the 'Russian Musical Gazette':

> The well-balanced singing of the Synodal Choir alternated on the *kliros* under the direction of two of the leading lights of church music, on the right-hand side Orlov, and on the left-hand side Kastalsky. There were two opposing characters here. Orlov commanded the singers, conducting imperiously. When a distinctive rhythm is encountered in the *znamenny* chant and the singers hesitate, he makes an impetuous movement and gives an energetic wave to compel them to carry out what he intends. Kastalsky gives the impression of a weak conductor, and his movements are lethargic. When an unexpected rhythm occurs, it looks as if he is leaving the singers to their fate, but the singers read his thoughts in an easy movement of his hand and an intent look. The singing on the left *kliros* is much calmer and more serene. As a conductor, Kastalsky is full of inner energy. [...] I noticed that the less interest the music offers, the weaker his influence over the singers, but his influence rises as the interest grows. [...] He is a great artist, but a mediocre craftsman.[19]

The assessment of another St Petersburg critic M.A. Lisitsïn, who also followed the development of church music matters in Moscow, was rather more restrained:

> I have a high regard for Kastalsky as a composer, as an artist. [...] But I cannot acknowledge Kastalsky as a conductor. Nature did not give him the necessary resources for that. His psychology is too gentle, artistic, too much that of a composer, too feminine, for him to become a conductor. [...] On some occasion or other Stepan Smolensky said to me while he was director of the School that Orlov is the bedrock of their choir, and I think he knew what he was saying. I repeat: Kastalsky is a composer – that is where his glory lies. But there is no doubt that Mr Kastalsky nevertheless conducts very well, for he is a good musician and has the temperament of an artist.[20]

Moscow musicians were of one mind in their assessment of Kastalsky as a conductor: they considered him a poor conductor. The scholar Smolensky, the conductor Bulïchev, the critic Lipayev and even the pupils of the Synodal School were all in agreement about this. If Orlov imprinted himself on the memory of everyone connected with the School as a 'tsar and a god', then Alexander Dmitriyevich, whom they christened *Yarïzhka*[21] because of his love for antiquity, struck them as a man of small stature lacking in self-confidence who on the concert platform nervously pulled up his trousers and conducted on the *kliros* in a ridiculous fashion using his glasses for a baton. After Orlov's death, when Kastalsky at last appeared on the platform as a conductor, the negative opinions of him which had previously been uttered backstage burst out on the pages of the press. Thus, the correspondent of 'The Toiler in Music' (*Muzïkalnïy truzhenik*) wrote of a Synodal Choir concert of works by Tchaikovsky given on 7 October 1908:

> The Synodal Choir sings Tchaikovsky with astounding artistic skill and refinement, taking to an exemplary extent the precision with which they reproduce his works. But that was how they sang under Orlov, not how they sang on this occasion under Kastalsky. It was the trebles' part which stood out more often than the others, and that helped weaken the fullness of the ensemble; the whole choir deserved a rebuke for their indifferent attitude to their task. The choir sang like good Moscow private choirs can sing, but not like the Synodal Choir, which has taught its admirers to listen out for something out of the ordinary when it performs.[22]

Their performance on 2 November 1908 received a similar appraisal:

The Synodal Choir gave their first concert of the current season – a programme of works by Rimsky-Korsakov and Tchaikovsky. The public go less and less to these noteworthy concerts, and perhaps they should not be blamed. The quality of the Choir's performance has become lower: they do not always sing in tune, the pronunciation of the words leaves something to be desired in clarity, there is an absence of confidence in the singing, and an air of carrying out an official duty. In short, the choir does not have sufficient vitality. Neither Rimsky-Korsakov nor Tchaikovsky stirred the choir, nor did its conductor Alexander Kastalsky. The only improvement lay in the great warmth and freedom of the singing by comparison with past concerts. These features are probably all the result of Kastalsky's choirmastership; he is evidently not at home in his new position as choirmaster at concerts.[23]

The critics replaced wrath with mercy only when Kastalsky was appointed director of the school after the death of Kruglikov in 1910 and handed over his responsibilities as choirmaster to the young Nikolay Danilin.

What the Synodal School's warmest well-wishers were waiting for has now come about. Kastalsky is the director, and Danilin the choirmaster. What can we expect from them? Both have been through the arduous school of Smolensky and Orlov, both know how to revive the School's shattered organization, how to bring the Synodal School and the Synodal Choir to life again as they were before, how to make themselves talked about, and begin to take an interest in everything outstanding that comes their way.

Those were the terms in which I.V. Lipayev welcomed the changes at Bolshaya Nikitskaya Street.[24] The well-wishers of the School and the Choir were not deceived in their prognoses: with Kastalsky's appointment to the post of director a brilliant new page, but alas the final one, opened in the history of the Synodal School and Choir.

Notes

1. S.V. Smolensky: *Sinodal'nïy khor i uchilishche tserkovnogo peniya* (The Synodal Choir and School of Church Music), in RUSAM, vol. 1, p. 124.
2. Letter from A.D. Kastal'sky to S.V. Smolensky of 19 January 1903. RGIA, fond 1119, opis' 1, no. 146, p. 30.
3. Letter from A.D. Kastal'sky to S.V. Smolensky of 26 October 1903. RGIA, fond 1119, opis' 1, no. 146, pp. 40-40v.
4. Letter from S.V. Smolensky to A.D. Kastal'sky of 6 November 1901, in Muzïka (Music), 1916, no. 248, p. 153.
5. N.I. Kompaneysky: *Kontsert Pridvornoy pevcheskoy kapellï* (A concert by the Court singing kapella), in RMG, 1902, no. 5, col. 143.

6. *Ibid.*
7. Letter from S.V. Smolensky to A.D. Kastal'sky of 31 March 1902, in *Muzïka* (Music), 1916, no. 248, p. 154.
8. Letter from A.D. Kastal'sky to S.V. Smolensky of 26 June 1902. RGIA, fond 1119, opis' 1, no. 146, p. 18.
9. Letter from A.D. Kastal'sky to S.V. Smolensky of 13 May 1903. RGIA, fond 1119, opis' 1, no. 146, p. 34v.
10. N.A. Kastal'skaya: *Nemnogoye ob ottse* (A little about my father), in *A.D. Kastal'sky. Stat'i. Vospominaniya. Materialï* (A.D. Kastal'sky. Articles. Reminiscences. Materials). Moscow, 1960, p. 107.
11. *Polnoye sobraniye dukhovno-muzïkal'nïkh sochineniy P. Turchaninova* (The complete sacred compositions of P. Turchaninov), edited by Kastal'sky, was published in five volumes in 1905.
12. As far as is known, the latter work was not brought to a conclusion.
13. *Zhurnalï pravleniya Sinodal'nogo uchilishcha za 1905/06 god* (Minute-books of the board of the Synodal School for the year 1905-06). RGALI, fond 662, opis' 1, no. 12, pp. 20v.-21.
14. *Ibid.*, p. 18v.
15. S.V. Smolensky: *Sed'moy dnevnik* (Seventh diary). RGIA, fond 1119, opis' 1, no. 12, p. 120.
16. *Ibid.*, p. 125.
17. *Ibid.*, p. 132v, verso.
18. In 1907 the Gramophone Company issued a series of records of the Synodal Choir conducted by Kastal'sky with the following repertoire: Tchaikovsky: *Svete tikhiy* ('Gladsome Light'); Kastal'sky: *S nami Bog* ('God is with us'), *Mnogoletiye* ('Many years'), *Blagoslovi, dushe moya, Gospoda* ('Bless the Lord, O my soul') to a Greek chant, *Khvalite Imya Gospodne* ('Praise the Name of the Lord') to a Kievan chant, *Dostoyno yest'* ('It is meet') to a Serbian chant; Grechaninov: *Voskliknite, Gospodevi* ('Sing unto the Lord'); Panchenko: *Vo tsarstvii Tvoyem* ('In Thy kingdom'); L'vovsky: *Tebe poyem* ('We hymn Thee'); and *Dostoyno yest'* ('It is meet') to a Kievan chant.
19. N.I. Kompaneysky: *A.D. Kastal'sky. (Po povodu 4-go vïpuska yego dukhovno-muzïkal'nïkh sochineniy)* (A.D. Kastalsky. (On the occasion of his fourth publication of sacred compositions)), in *RMG*, nos. 13-14, cols. 359-360.
20. M. Lisitsïn: *Moskva i Sinodal'nïy khor* (Moscow and the Synodal Choir), in *Muzïka i peniye* (Instrumental Music and Song), 1906, no. 12, p. 2.
21. A medieval Russian term probably chosen for its archaic sound rather than for its meaning of either a lowly servant or a good-for-nothing.
22. *Muzïkal'noye obozreniye* (A musical survey), in *Muzïkal'nïy truzhenik* (The Toiler in Music), 1907, no. 25, p. 12.
23. *Muzïkal'noye obozreniye* (A musical survey), in *Muzïkal'nïy truzhenik* (The Toiler in Music), 1908, no. 22, p. 11.
24. Samarov (I.V. Lipayev), in *Muzïkal'nïy truzhenik* (The Toiler in Music), 1910, no. 8, p. 9.

Chapter 11

The Moscow School of Ethnographers

Kastalsky's work at the Synodal School and conducting the Synodal Choir is just the tip of a vast iceberg whose underwater part is made up of composition, reflection and research. As he began to strike out along an independent path and recognized what his responsibility to society was, Kastalsky began displaying the precepts of his life and creative work not only by composing music but also through journalism, scholarship and teaching. It was at this time that his credo was finally formulated.

At the beginning of the 1900s Alexander Dmitriyevich stood at a crossroads. He had already found something new to say in the realm of sacred music, and in many respects he had given birth to what had been gestating within him over the years; now the world of secular music and orchestral music-making opened up before him, a field where every educated composer of sacred music dreamed of showing off his skill. Sensing his strength, Kastalsky wanted to subjugate that fortress too, one which had not surrendered to him in his youthful years. No less attractive to Alexander Dmitriyevich was research in musical ethnography, a field which was enjoying a period of brilliant flowering at that time. Moreover, like it or not, Kastalsky was more or less compelled to take upon himself part of Smolensky's obligations and become a bold investigator of the 'hooks'. The composer dedicated himself to all these activities with passion and forgetfulness of self.

We know that Kastalsky was a hard worker and considered work the best remedy for physical and spiritual ailments. (He even supposed that colds and influenza passed by more quickly if instead of yielding to them and lying in bed you immersed yourself in work.) It was not only his business-like approach, industry and thirst for self-affirmation that made the artist in him capture ever new heights, however. One of the main impulses in Kastalsky's life and work was a fiery patriotism and a striving to prove that Russia was heir to great treasures languishing beneath a heavy weight of 'Europeanism' from which they ought to be extricated, studied and returned to the nation. In word and deed, the artist substantiated this article of faith from his system of belief until the end of his days.

Kastalsky's earliest statement on this subject is to be found in a letter of 1898 to the composer Vladimir Rebikov. Carried away by an unusual experiment – composing choral works in sonata form, the composer suddenly remembered and repented there and then to his friend about this break with one of the new school's precepts:

> Maybe you are right that aping foreigners is a feature typical of Russians. But we too have our charming and expressive melodies (songs, the *obikhod*) which are entirely distinctive, we shall also find our own harmony (it has not all been discovered yet, but something has been found, and more will be, I am sure), and we have our own perfectly self-sufficient and original forms (both in songs – small forms, and particularly in the church *obikhodï* – our own large-scale forms), we have our own poetry (once more from the people and very attractive in its original naivety, displayed both in the epic tales (*bïlini*) as well as in the Slavonic language used in liturgical texts).[1]

As we can see, Kastalsky is not original and in many respects is merely repeating what Smolensky instilled in his pupils. In his idea of 'originality' [*samobïtnost'*], however, some fresh nuances emerged. The composer is developing his older colleague's ideas: apart from the traditional claims about national melody and poetry, he is already speaking about original harmony and forms. In subsequent years the concept continues to expand, and the subject of Russian [*narodnaya*] instrumentation arises. We find Kastalsky writing to Khristofor Grozdov in 1902: 'I am convinced that in Russia an era will soon dawn when nationalism in both harmony and instrumentation (the melodic part, thank goodness, is even now under way) will shine brightly in our music. Maybe we won't live to see it, but things are bound to move in that direction'.[2] In the same year Alexander Dmitriyevich strove to set out his ideas in an unpublished article the existence of which is known from one of his letters to Smolensky:

> For the last few days I've been preoccupied with how to take two Germans apart more scathingly – Beidler (Wagner's son-in-law) and Kes – the main reason is of course national pride, but there's more besides. The musical fraternity are strongly in sympathy with this cause, but there's an unexpected hitch: I sent the article off just today, and out of the blue I read in today's 'Moscow Bulletin' (*Moskovskiye vedomosti*) great praise from Kashkin for the same Beidler I've been cursing! So my work as a commentator on current affairs will probably be lost right at the peak of its glory![3]

Judging from all the evidence, with this article Alexander Dmitriyevich was starting out on a journalistic crusade against the German domination of

Russian music, a cause which he pursued with new vigour in what he wrote during the First World War.

Kastalsky's thoughts outlined above were a logical development of the 'Russian idea' among musicians overwhelmed by a powerful 'folklore wave' at the beginning of the twentieth century. In 1901 a Music Ethnography Commission (MEC) was established in the Ethnography Section of the Society of Lovers of the Natural Sciences, Anthropology and Ethnography attached to the University of Moscow. Many philologists and musicians became members: the ethnographers Alexander Markov, Nikolay Yanchuk, Yevgeniya Linyova, Alexander Maslov, Vyacheslav Paskhalov, Mitrofan Pyatnitsky and Dimitry Arakishvili, the composers Mikhail Ippolitov-Ivanov, Nikolay Klenovsky, Arseny Koreshchenko, Sergey Taneyev, Alexander Grechaninov and Victor Kalinnikov, the musicologists and critics Nikolay Kashkin, Georgy Konyus, Ivan Lipayev, Yuly Engel, Boleslav Yavorsky and many others. It is of interest to note that meetings of this Commission took place initially at the Synodal School of Church Music, where Smolensky, who took part in the discussions, offered his colleagues accommodation. Several members of the Commission worked as teachers at the Synodal School, while others were connected with the institution through their work; others again were pupils of Smolensky and yet others reviewed concerts by the Synodal Choir and so on. In short, the participants in the MEC formed a group involved in one way or another with the Synodal School and Choir. The problem of how to treat church chants which were regarded as folk music was, incidentally, a subject discussed at the Commission's sittings.

The MEC's activities were very wide-ranging and not confined to meetings and reports. The Commission's members transcribed folklore, organized folk choirs (the most famous was Mitrofan Pyatnitsky's choir of Voronezh and Ryazan peasants), and arranged ethnographical concerts where they acquainted the public with examples of genuine folksongs. The MEC took an interest, moreover, not just in Russian folklore but also in the musical creativity of Russia's other nations – the Georgians, the Armenians, the Kazakhs, etc. and also the legacy of ancient civilizations. The Commission was responsible for founding the People's Conservatoire (*Narodnaya Konservatoriya*) (1906-20), where Linyova, Taneyev, Yavorsky, Kastalsky, Engel and others taught.

Because many of the Commission's members were professional composers, improving the quality of arrangements of folksongs was regarded as a pressing problem. The efforts of the established composers were considered old-fashioned and out of line with one of the movement's mottos: an arrangement must reflect the rules of folk music-making and preserve the colour and character of the material as much as possible. In fits of self-assertion the ethnographers quite often accused their predecessors of adopting an insufficiently scholarly approach to folklore. Succeeding generations could not level this reproach against the members of the Commission themselves, as many of them bequeathed not only collections of sound recordings and books in music notation of the songs they had collected but also scholarly research into the theory of folklore.[4]

After the 1917 revolution the folklore movement for a time found support from the state. In 1921 an Ethnography Section was opened under the auspices of the State Institute for Musical Science (GIMN), and many participants in the MEC joined it. They included among others leading composers from the New Direction – Kastalsky, Grechaninov and Nikolsky. It was during the 1920s, after the Russian church had fallen victim to persecution, when folklore remained the only weapon in the struggle to transform musical culture on the basis of national elements, that a number of research publications on this subject appeared, where their authors' long experience was summed up. Fieldwork in folklore studies too continued. The lifetime of the Ethnography Section at GIMN was to be a short one, however. With the start of the collectivization of agriculture at the beginning of the 1930s, marking the destruction of a centuries-old peasant way of life, the outlook on peasant folklore proclaimed by the state organs of ideology changed as well, and it was pronounced a survival of the past due for eradication. It was decided to create in its place a culture of the new Soviet countryside. Just as ten years before the persecution of church art had begun, so in the late 1920s and early 1930s a campaign was launched to liquidate the Russian school of ethnography. In 1931 the Ethnography Section of GIMN was closed and its members dismissed. In the second half of the 1930s, once the former flowering of the school of ethnography had become a thing of the past, albeit not the distant past, a less rigorous attitude was adopted.

In 1942 the composer and scholar Alexander Nikolsky, who had not been evacuated from wartime Moscow, began to give two courses of lectures to the small number of Conservatoire students remaining in the capital – on sacred music and folklore respectively. One of the topics included in the plans for the courses was the history of arrangements of church chants and folksongs. Here is an excerpt from the plan for the lectures on folksong, which contains a summary of the scholar's observations on the stages of assimilation of song material by composers, starting in the 1860s:

> 1. Devices (chords and part-writing) of the common European four-part and three-part harmony in the so-called 'strict style', based on the medieval 'Greek'

or 'church' modes or on the diatonic major or minor, as a consequence of which a type of arrangement came about – a harmonization, in the narrow meaning of the word.

2. Devices of imitative counterpoint on the same modal foundations, creating a second type of arrangement – a polyphonic one – in the generally accepted European style.

3. Devices of mixed homophonic-polyphonic writing, forming a type of arrangement in which the two types are, so to speak, combined in a synthesis for the first time.

4. Folksong harmony and polyphony, realized by the *podgoloski* method – one, two and sometimes more voices, bringing about a type of arrangement usually known (most inaccurately) as 'ethnographic' – a device profoundly distinct from those mentioned above both in style of writing and in the sonorous character of such arrangements.

5. A combination of harmonic and contrapuntal elements from the common European musical language with elements from the language of folksong, leading to the formation of a distinctive type of writing and arrangement – to be precise, the 'mixed dual-style one' (compare with the 'homophonic-polyphonic' style in no. 3 above).

6. Finally, standing apart, though widely enough practised, there is the application of all the artistic and technical methods and resources of musical composition in a free and extremely varied mixing, interweaving and alternating of devices (which are generally accepted) with others (specific to folksong), and in particular in part-writing which proceeds from a modest unison to the broadest writing in seven or eight parts, with the reverse decrease of the choral parts to the original unison. By this means a special type of so-called free arrangement is guaranteed – 'free', that is, from the limitations of melodic contours specific to song, modal origins, harmony, rhythm and other features of song as the 'primary' creative material and idea.[5]

If the first three of these approaches to arranging folksong were typical of Russian music from the 1860s to the 1880s, the last three were entirely the offspring of the turn of the nineteenth and twentieth centuries. Composers involved in the MEC and the Music Ethnography Section of GIMN took part to no small extent in developing them, and thanks to their efforts a further vast stratum of creativity (besides church music) appeared in Russian music, one based on the nation's heritage.

The discovery by composers in the MEC group of a technique for harmonizing folksong material known as 'timbrification' of a choral score is not mentioned in the document quoted from; Nikolsky was the first to set out this theory in his article 'New paths in choral composition'. The essence of the theory boils down to the idea that human voices, even when they belong to the same group – sopranos, for instance – have different timbres. Accordingly, the composer, like a painter mixing his colours, has the opportunity of uniting varied timbres in one part and obtaining a choral palette of the richest colours. Nikolsky wrote:

> It follows from this that a choral score too may be compiled not of four parts only but of that number of parts which there are in actual fact, that is: either 11-12 for a mixed choir made up of male and female voices, or 15-16 when it is made up of male, female and children's voices. Such a score can show all the desired and possible nuances of timbre for every phrase and every movement of a choral composition with perfect clarity and concreteness. In writing such a score the composer must obviously act in the way he would when scoring his compositions for orchestra, as here too he has to use in effect no fewer parts than in the orchestra, parts which are diverse in quality and just as full of character.[6]

Although this definition of the essence of 'timbrification', like the term itself, appeared only at the beginning of the 1920s, the idea and development of the method go back to the start of the century, when the striving for maximum scope in the possibilities of the choir, perceived as a symphony orchestra of sorts, arose in Russian choral composition and performance. This 'orchestral tendency' is registered in the sacred work of many composers of the New Direction – Grechaninov, Rachmaninoff, Chesnokov, Panchenko, Nikolsky, Kastalsky and others. Kastalsky's archive even preserves a manuscript headed 'Various combinations of choral voices (Choral colours)' where he indicated the expressive effects of mixing timbres.[7] A brilliant example of this approach to a choir's performing possibilities was the private 'Symphonic Choir' formed by the Moscow conductor Vyacheslav Bulïchev in 1905.

It is easy to see that the evolution in approaches to folksong outlined by Nikolsky is similar in general outline to the stages in the assimilation of the church music legacy (see Chapter 3). The development of folksong also took place in the context of a reinforcing of centripetal tendencies and was conditioned by an intensifying mood of patriotism; in the same way, a qualitatively new level of arrangements was achieved as a result of intensified scholarly study of the theory of folksong; in the same way, research into folklore significantly enriched the vocabulary and range of styles in Russian music. It is also noteworthy that it was frequently the same people who took part in the assimilation of these two strata of the legacy. Thus, the artistic cultivation of monodic chants went hand in hand with the development in folklore; methods of assimilating material discovered in one of the fields inevitably enriched the other.

The aims of the activities of musicians working in the two spheres were also united; they saw the object of their lives as transforming Russia's spiritual life, strengthening features of originality in her culture and reviving primordial traditions which were becoming extinct as a result of industrialization and the pressure of western influences. The ethnographic musicians of the turn of the century understood what they were doing as serving ordinary people and trying to return to them 'property torn away artificially from them'. As a result, their creative work – whether choral items for the church or arrangements of songs – was aimed at the people who, after hearing them in church or at folk concerts, were supposed to be convinced of their own creative powers. It was not only the degree of scholarly erudition, and accordingly the degree of authenticity in the arrangements, which distinguished the creative work of the turn-of-the-century composers from their immediate predecessors in the 'Mighty Handful', who were no less disposed to patriotism and preached no less global ideals aimed at a reconstruction of musical culture. The audience towards which their work was directed was different. The compositions of the 'Handful', written not so much for the people as about the people, often did not leave the confines of the concert hall, the opera house or the fashionable salon, whereas the legacy of the turn-of-the-century ethnographical composers was heard in churches, sung by workers' choirs and performed at country shows open to all.

It was not only the ideas but also the social make-up of those taking part in this second 'movement to the people' in Russian musical history that was democratized. In the service record tables of these ethnographers the status of hereditary nobleman (*dvoryanin*) was a great rarity. One finds mainly 'from the clergy' or 'from urban tradespeople and small traders (*iz meshchan*)', and even 'from the peasantry'. If we look at the genealogies of musicians in the Synodal School circle, we see that the Chesnokov brothers were sons of a church choirmaster from near Moscow, the Shvedov brothers were sons of a coach-builder, the Tolstyakov brothers were of artisan origin (it is known that their mother was a laundress), Nikolay Danilin was the son of a porter, Vasily Orlov the son of a precentor, Victor Kalinnikov the son of a provincial policeman and Nikolay Golovanov the son of a tailor.

The group of artists who worked in the 'New Russian Style' were also, incidentally, extremely democratic in social composition. Thus, the Vasnetsov brothers were sons of a village priest from the Vyatka province. Victor Vasnetsov later recalled in a letter to Stasov how he 'lived in the village among the peasants and their womenfolk and loved them not in any idealized fashion but perfectly simply, as friends and acquaintances, listening to their songs and folk-tales, spellbound as I sat on the stove by the light and the crackling of a torch'.[8] Alexander Nikolsky, the son of a priest from the village of Vladïkino in the Penza diocese, left similar reminiscences of his childhood.

From all that has been said it follows logically that the Russian schools of sacred music and ethnography at the turn of the century represented a single direction in their ideas and creativity, united by the task of absorbing Russia's heritage and russifying her musical culture. The results of their work in this direction were exceptionally valuable, often uniting discoveries in both their ethnographical and sacred music branches. For the most part this took place in the musical language of composers who assimilated both strata of the legacy at once. Kastalsky's compositions in the secular sphere are a striking example.

Notes

1. Letter from A.D. Kastal'sky to V.I. Rebikov of November 1898. GTsMMK, fond 68, no. 274, p. 2.
2. Letter from A.D. Kastal'sky to Kh.N. Grozdov of 14 February 1902. GTsMMK, fond 370, no. 497, p. 2v.
3. Letter from A.D. Kastal'sky to S.V. Smolensky of 17 March 1902. RGIA, fond 1119, opis' 1, no. 146, p. 11.
4. Here are just a few of the publications linked to the activities of members of the MEC: *Trudï Muzïkal'no-etnograficheskoy komissii* (Proceedings of the Music Ethnography Commission), vols. 1-2. Moscow, 1906-1911; Ye. Linyova: *Velikorusskiye pesni v narodnoy garmonizatsii* (Great Russian songs in the people's harmonization), parts 1-2. St Petersburg, 1904-1909; Ye. Linyova: *Vseobshchaya perepis' narodnïkh pesen v Rossii* (General inventory of folksongs in Russia). Moscow, 1914; A. Maslov: *Opït rukovodstva k izucheniyu russkoy narodnoy muzïki* (An attempt at a guide to the study of Russian folk music). Moscow, 1911; N.A. Yanchuk: *Narodnaya pesnya i yeyo izucheniye* (Folksong and the study of it). St Petersburg, 1914; N.A. Yanchuk: *O muzïke bïlin v svyazi s istoriyey ikh sozdaniya* (The music of Russian epic tales and the history of their creation), in *Russkaya ustavnaya slovesnost'* (Russian uncial literature), vol. 2: *Bïlinï. Istoricheskiye pesni* (Russian epic tales. Historical songs), edited by M. Speransky. Moscow, 1919.
5. A.V. Nikol'sky: *Narodnaya pesnya SSSR* (The folksong of the USSR). GTsMMK, fond 294, no. 231.
6. A.V. Nikol'sky: *K voprosu o novïkh putyakh v oblasti khorovoy kompozitsii* (The question of new paths in the field of choral composition), in *Muzïkal'naya nov'* (Musical Virgin Soil), 1924, no. 6, pp. 12-13.
7. A.D. Kastal'sky: *Razlichnïye sochetaniya i kombinatsii khorovïkh golosov. (Khorovïye kraski)* (Various combinations of choral voices. (Choral colours)). GTsMMK, fond 12, no. 383.
8. Letter from V.M. Vasnetsov to V.V. Stasov of 1898, in *Viktor Mikhaylovich Vasnetsov. Pis'ma, dnevniki, vospominaniya, dokumentï, suzhdeniya sovremennikov* (Viktor Mikhaylovich Vasnetsov. Letters, diaries, reminiscences, documents, opinions of contemporaries). Moscow, 1987, p. 154.

Chapter 12

Historical Reconstructions

Kastalsky had been keen on folklore since his student years, and he put his faith in it as a source for the subsequent development of the art of music. As the composer wrote in the early 1900s:

> Ethnographic music is going to take a huge step forward in the immediate future and that will probably be strongly reflected in the direction taken by Russian music in general – and perhaps even by common European music which after Wagner is now battering its head against a brick wall, in my opinion, and does not know where to go.[1]

That statement may serve as an epigraph for Kastalsky's activities in the final 25 years of his life, when one of his main concerns was assimilating folklore in scholarly and artistic ways. It fell to Kastalsky specifically to make a massive contribution to the development of Russian ethnography and 'ethnographic music'.

The composer took his very first steps in the scholarly assimilation of the heritage of folklore and church music right at the start of the century. By the end of 1901 his first work on the harmony of folksong had been written. 'There is a valuable work of yours – Russian harmonization, which I saw when I visited you. Have you had it published?' – the composer Rebikov asked Kastalsky in a letter of 20 December 1901.[2] The work was not published, and has not survived. Likewise unknown is the fate of a brief historical investigation into the *Obikhod* which Kastalsky wrote at the beginning of the century.[3]

It is obvious, given his predilections, that Alexander Dmitriyevich could not ignore the activities of the Music Ethnography Commission. The composer wrote later in his 'Short Biography':

> From 1902 I was a member of the Moscow Ethnographical Commission (and later deputy chairman). My acquaintance with and passion for Yuly Melgunov's collection of folksongs, with their distinctive *podgoloski* and typical harmonization, dates from the same time.[4]

According to the testimony of the ethnographer Vyacheslav Paskhalov, Kastalsky was one of the people who sorted out the archive of the late Melgunov, which was placed in the hands of the Commission. Paskhalov recalled of Kastalsky's first years of attendance at the MEC:

My acquaintanceship and growing friendship with Alexander Dmitriyevich began in the spring of 1902, when on 5 February I was elected a member of the Commission. At that time Kastalsky was 46, and his solid appearance was fully in accordance with his position as director of the sacred music choir of the Moscow Synodal School. There was not the slightest hint of fuss about his movements. His gait was slow and noiseless – the gait of a conductor making his way on to a concert platform. Alexander Dmitriyevich was handsome of face, despite a low forehead. This handsome mien was partly the result of his crewcut and little wedge-shaped beard. His eyes were very expressive, and a somewhat mischievous but at the same time benevolent smile would flit across them, one that was by no means arrogant, and characteristic of people who know their own worth. [...]

Our Commission's programme of activities was apparently close to Kastalsky's heart. The problems raised by its participants appealed to him; so too did the new discoveries in the study of musical folklore, and solving the riddles of the modal structure of the folksongs of various peoples and tribes from the whole world. It is curious that while Kastalsky took an active part in the Commission's activities, he never once read a paper in public on any folklore subject. Kastalsky usually shared his impressions and achievements with us at closed sessions of the Commission and sometimes after they had officially ended.[5]

It is indeed the case that in the 1900s the composer preferred to assimilate folklore and demonstrate his ideas not in scholarly publications but in musical composition, which at times took the most unexpected forms unknown in his time. A passion for experiment was no less typical of Kastalsky than a passion for exploring music's deeps. It is precisely for that reason that when speaking about his favourite musicians, Alexander Dmitriyevich would name innovators first and foremost. 'My sympathies are always on the side of the Borodins, Musorgskys, Melgunovs, Wagners, Liszts, Berliozes, Balakirevs, Korsakovs and *tutti quanti*... With all the others, everything is so obvious!', he wrote to Rebikov.[6] The youngsters Stravinsky and Prokofiev were later added to this list. After getting to know Prokofiev's *The Gambler* in January 1917, Kastalsky wrote to Grozdov:

I've got hold of a (lithographed) vocal score of Prokofiev's *The Gambler*. He's very naughty with his harmony, but in some instances (I've only looked through 1½ acts) he's definitely a very fine naughty fellow. He has a very striking talent (for inventing chord combinations), it's a pity that he doesn't know where to stop: he bashes away at the piano, just so long as it sounds brilliant!'[7]

The 'modernist' Rebikov also enjoyed the composer's goodwill, and greatly entertained him with his talk and his music. Kastalsky's daughter Natalia recalled:

In the 1900s, when we were children, the composer Vladimir Rebikov often visited us; he was a large fat man with plump, beautiful hands and wearing a pince-nez on a broad ribbon; he played his fables (*basni*), and his opera *The Christmas Tree* (*Yolka*), which was about Hans Christian Andersen's girl with the matches; the opera greatly appealed to us children. Father liked him, but used to laugh at his 'modernism'.[8]

The following lines of a letter from Kastalsky to Smolensky confirm the last point: 'At some time or another he [Rebikov] played me his oratorio *Elijah the Prophet* (*Ilya Prorok*) – and if I didn't split my sides laughing, then it was by a miracle'.[9] Although Alexander Dmitriyevich adopted a humorous attitude to his friend's experiments, he nonetheless tried to win him over by all possible means to 'say something new' in sacred music: 'Rachmaninoff has written an entire Liturgy – we are learning it – it is a significant event in the world of music. And it's an attractive piece, though the style is a bit varied... Do you know, it would be very good if our innovators such as Rebikov, Skryabin and the others were to do something stunning with a church text – if you're going to start something, you've got to do it properly. No, seriously – do have a go'.[10] The result was Rebikov's All-Night Vigil (op. 44), composed in 1911, and it was indeed 'stunning'.

Almost the entire composition is written in parallel intervals and/or chords with one type specific to each movement – octaves, sixths and even fourths and fifths. The solo episodes in 'oriental' modes are also very original. For example, the prayer of St Simeon (the Nunc dimittis) is intended for an 'old man's timbre', the Archangel Gabriel's Annunciation to the Mother of God 'Rejoice, O Virgin' (*Bogoroditse Devo, raduysya*) is intended for a 'young person's timbre' and so on. Kastalsky probably reacted to the new opus in much the same way he had done to his friend's oratorio *Elijah the Prophet*, but for public consumption he did not break his rule of being always on the side of all that was bold and innovative in art, and in an article written in 1913 for the 'Musical Contemporary' (*Muzïkal'nïy sovremennik*) 'My career in music and thoughts on church music' he called the All-Night Vigil a 'composition of outstanding boldness'.

Rebikov was not typical of the people who gathered around Kastalsky, who were mainly colleagues from the Synodal School and Choir or members of the MEC. With Rebikov, however, Alexander Dmitriyevich was able to discuss topics on his mind at the time which would hardly have struck a chord in his own milieu, namely the newest 'leftist' directions in art. The idea that he was 'a new impressionist in art' (as Rebikov called him on account of his innovations in the field of sacred music) manifestly appealed to the composer. In a letter of 14 December 1901 to Rebikov Kastalsky writes:

If something in a piece of music surprises me – whatever it might be – I'm most likely to be on the side of the composer (Musorgsky, Grieg, Rebikov), and usually when I show somebody something new which has taken my interest I'm cursed for it. Although you and I work in rather different fields (I'm greatly interested, for instance, in musical ethnography or musical archaeology – China, Egypt, India) – because both of us seem to have turned off the beaten track and are making our way across 'virgin soil' through snow-drifts or jungle and are so bold as to 'have formed our own judgement' and to breathe air directly without wrapping ourselves up in sundry 'accepted' collars and hoods – we have become, whether we like it or not, spiritual brothers and naturally 'decadents' (as a colleague with whom I work recently christened me in an article).[11]

Thus, inspired by his faith in the treasures of the past as a panacea for contemporary art and well-disposed towards 'innovative' approaches, Kastalsky embarked at the beginning of the century on digesting the depths of history artistically. His first ethnographical compositions were the choruses *Bïlinka* and *Slava* (1900) based on folksong material. They were written in an archaic manner which was then unusual and their 'new beauty' sent Kastalsky's friend the ethnographer Khristofor Grozdov into raptures. The composer himself was not satisfied with these experiments and thought that a great deal in them had been done in a hurry.

In 1901 Kastalsky had the idea of writing a cycle of piano pieces on Georgian themes and dedicating it to the centenary of the annexation of Georgia to Russia. For this the composer asked Grozdov to send him the transcriptions of Georgian folklore which Grozdov had made during his time as director of public schools in Tiflis. (The themes were eventually taken from an article by Mikhail Ippolitov-Ivanov,[12] who had previously been director of the Tiflis branch of the Russian Musical Society.) Written in the traditional three-part *da capo* form, the pieces were intended 'for ordinary Georgian music-lovers': the composer had not set himself any greatly ambitious task.

Kastalsky had long had a soft spot for the Caucasus (as his unfinished opera *Mtsïri* based on Lermontov reminds us), and when he finally visited the area in 1902 he was stunned by what he saw. The composer turned to Georgian folklore, however, not just to 'do the Georgians a good turn' as he put it. The interest in the musical culture of the Caucasian peoples which was characteristic of Russian art acquired particular relevance at the turn of the century because of the ethnographical discoveries made in the region. This newly collected material inspired two composers in particular who worked for several years in Tiflis – Ippolitov-Ivanov, who composed *Caucasian Sketches* (1894) and *Iveriya* (1895), and Nikolay Klenovsky, who wrote a Georgian Liturgy based on Kakhetian church hymns at the end of the 1890s.

When Klenovsky's Liturgy was published in 1902, it provoked a stormy debate. Its starting-point was that the work was criticized by Kompaneysky and Arakchiyev in the 'Russian Musical Gazette' on the grounds that, in their opinion, the composer's harmonization strayed far from the fundamental character of the original hymns on which the composition was based. Kastalsky immediately spoke out in defence of the Liturgy, on 18 January 1903 sending Nikolay Findeyzen, the editor of the 'Gazette', a request that he publish his comment. Alexander Dmitriyevich thought that when interpreting folk material a composer was free in his choice of means, and that 'it is one thing to be a jealous protector of national identity, and something else altogether to bury yourself in one direction and not allow the extension of folk art beyond the bounds of its primordial type'.[13] This statement by the composer contains the key to understanding his approach to the artistic treatment of primary sources.

Let us look at Kastalsky's first experiment in reconstructing ancient Russian church hymns of the fifteenth to the seventeenth centuries. This work was carried out in 1901 for one of the Historical Concerts of the Synodal Choir, which Smolensky had decided to revive, not supposing that he would soon be leaving or that the project he had begun would have to be completed by his colleagues. Kastalsky later recalled:

> The venture was to begin with specimens from the fifteenth century. We had to supply examples with brief annotations, and there Antonin Preobrazhensky, the then superviser of our library of manuscripts, gave me some help; we had to provide striking and representative but brief examples so as not to weary the public with an undue profusion of such demonstrations and at the same time preserve their musical interest while keeping a deliberate primitiveness in the choral arrangement.[14]

In December 1901, armed with Smolensky's new work on the notation of church music,[15] Kastalsky embarked on deciphering ancient hymns. 'Thank you very much for your book', he wrote to Smolensky. 'It's exactly what I need at the moment as I pore over the "hooks"; I've compiled for myself a table of *znamenny* hooks, and started on a *demestvenny* table – and I want to transcribe the two- and three-part *strochny* chant myself for the future concert. I don't know what will come of it, but in any case I'm going to keep pestering you – is that all right?'[16]

By the end of January 1902 the materials for the Historical Concert devoted to antiquity were ready, and Kastalsky despatched them proudly to Smolensky. The result of the composer's work on church-music manuscripts from the 'little stone room' was 'Examples of church music in Rus from the fifteenth to the seventeenth centuries'; they are artistic reconstructions of the ancient chants in a kind of deliberately primitive style close to the heterophony of folksong and reminiscent of certain pages in Kastalsky's sacred choral pieces (Ex. 12.1).

Several of Kastalsky's reconstructions were performed at concerts by the Synodal Choir on 19 December 1901 and 13 January 1902, the programme of which showed 'the historical course of *partesnoye* singing in Rus'. These concerts aroused great interest among lovers of antiquity, and Smolensky 'went into a state of high emotion'.[17] Running ahead, the reader should know that the Synodal Choir introduced Kastalsky's restorations not only to Russian listeners but to listeners abroad as well during their concert in Rome on 16/3 May 1911.

In spite of the success, Kastalsky pledged himself not to repeat such archaeological ventures connected with 'painstaking digging-about in a mass of materials'. As early as October 1902, however, he was informing Smolensky of a new enterprise: 'I'm toiling over the antediluvian music of all sorts of heathens starting off with Indochina; I've got as far as the Greeks – and I think I shall find there (that is, not just with the Greeks) a good deal that's of use to me [for my campaign in favour of] antiwestern musical rules'.[18]

A month later Alexander Dmitriyevich asked Smolensky to let him have the address of Jean-Baptiste Thibaut, the researcher into Byzantine music, from whom he intended to get hold of some ancient melodies. In response to this request Smolensky sent the French scholar's published work,[19] from which the composer selected some melodies showing 'the replacement of one tonality by another as proof that this artistic operation was thought out not by learned musicians but ages ago – and by the people'.[20] From the same research publication Kastalsky also selected specimens of Byzantine reading in a manner akin to chanting for the Gospel.

By December Alexander Dmitriyevich could report to Smolensky that the new work was nearing completion:

> I have written (almost – Russia and a little bit more remain to be done) something along the lines of a history of folk music (since Adam) in brief musical pictures (for piano) with the necessary annotations and explanations. I shall finish it and let Kashkin know (I think he's interested), but the critics will probably tear it to pieces because, at variance with the historians, I regard polyphony too as a creation of the people rather than something thought up by composers'.[21]

Kastalsky was seeking in the music of the past ever new evidence of the richness of its forms and colours. With that aim in mind, he turned to the works of western historians and Russian ethnographers, in particular to a well-known book by Pyotr Sokalsky,[22] about which he wrote:

> I read Sokalsky in connection with the archaeology of Russian song and I got something out of it. There's an awful lot in it that's to the point, only his categorical assertion that choral songs are sung in unison, were so sung and can only be sung so is the most undoubted falsehood, though it cannot so much be proven as only sensed by one's inner feeling. My archaeology was not seeking an answer to precisely that question, of course, but wanted to show clearly (though not prove, for that is impossible), on the basis of albeit fragmentary and perhaps not entirely clear information, the possibility that music existed (even in ancient times) that does not at all have to be regarded as in unison. My work is similar to restorations (perhaps half-and-half with my own imagination) in other spheres of art: for instance, a picture of some ancient scene is restored on the basis of [several] separate features (a description in passing, a mention among other things, an incidental hint) or, for example, on the basis of several slivers from a whole group which have escaped destruction, the entire picture is reconstituted. That is something similar to what I wanted to achieve in music.[23]

In January 1903 work on the historical pictures in music was drawing near to completion – it remained only to put in two or three Russian folksongs and sum up Russian folk music. The composer wrote to Smolensky:

> In the note prefacing the little picture of old Russian church music, being sneaky (using your opinion on the time when church music penetrated to Rus) I shall declare that it existed in Rus perhaps from the second or third century (!?) as a result of the preaching of St Andrew the Apostle amongst 'such a pliant, simple, unwarlike and song-loving nation!' If you're going to write nonsense, you might as well do it on the grand scale![24]

To all appearances, Kastalsky understood that the fertile artistic imagination characteristic of both himself and Smolensky, the latter with his theory of the self-sufficiency (*samostiynost*) of Russian church music and its conception in Rus long before the adoption of Christianity, could do them a disservice and lead to distortion of the truth. The composer considered dry historical analysis, however, even less fruitful; in his opinion it was not capable of getting the better of the immense distances in time that divide antiquity from the present and can be overcome by artistic imagination and intuition. There remained the path of compromise: relying on fragmentary archaeological facts, to assimilate the past with the help of rational analysis, a researcher's instinct and artistic imagination.

The first three Parts of the new cycle (I. China. India. Egypt; II. Judea. Greece. The Homeland of Islam; III. The Christians) were published by Jurgenson between 1904 and 1906. As the basis for the reconstructions, specimens of the ancient music of peoples of the world were taken from the scholarly publications of J.-B. Thibaut, Louis Bourgault-Ducoudray, Hugo Riemann, François-Auguste Gevaert and others, together with historical data about the performing traditions of those times. What pictures was the composer trying to reconstitute? Here is the composer's outline of the contents of the first Part as he set it out in one of his letters to Smolensky:

1. Egypt – a scene on the Nile: pagan priests singing a hymn to the setting sun, interrupted by a funeral procession bearing the deceased to the other side of the Nile, and after the hymn is finished a song of people returning from work rings out from afar, the cries of water-drawers on the Nile are heard, and little by little all becomes quiet.

2. A scene in China; a festival of remembrance of the dead in Tai Miao, with a little preliminary scene and the following ones (as usually happens even in our day, with a crowd present).

3. India; a crowd near a pagoda. The music of the sacred dances of *bayadères* is heard – the temple maidens streaming from the depths of the temple. The singing of a Hindu rhapsodist who draws a crowd around him is interrupted by a noisy procession celebrating a festival in honour of Krishna.[25]

These contents are reminiscent of an opera libretto for scenes from the everyday life of the people. The composition was not, however, intended for the theatre: these were piano pieces meant for a music-lover wishing to become familiar with the music of antiquity in artistic form.

If we look at the music of the third Part – 'The Christians', we see that in his setting for piano the composer is reconstructing specimens of early Christian singing at the tombs of martyrs in the crypts of catacombs and during the *agape* (meal) rite. The scenes reconstructed are static and have no element of dramatic action. (The same is also true of the other Parts in the cycle.) Only liturgical singing in all its diversity of choral forms as witnessed by historians has been reconstructed. The archaic polyphony introduced occasionally is achieved by means of using sustained sounds – isons (Ex. 12.2).

Kastalsky's work belonged to a genre without precedent. It was a history of folk music illustrated by the composer himself with artistic examples accompanied by his own commentary. Thus, by the beginning of the century Kastalsky was continuing Smolensky's crusade against 'Eurocentrism' in Russian music, and starting to affirm the values of folk creativity in his own way. Unlike his senior colleague, he saw the mine of folk music not only in the Russian heritage but in that of all the world's civilizations, which accorded with the ideas discussed among the members of the MEC.

In 1904, before the cycle 'From Past Centuries' had been published, Kastalsky began to take an interest in the ancient church ritual the 'Play of the Furnace' (*Peshchnoye deystvo*), which represented a form of medieval liturgical drama and had come to Rus from Byzantium. Its literary source was the story in the biblical Book of the prophet Daniel of the three youths Ananias, Azarias and Misail who refused to worship the golden idol erected by King Nebuchadnezzar. By order of the king, the disobedient youths were cast into a burning hot furnace, but were saved from it by an angel who came down from heaven. As researchers believe, the rite came to Rus in the fifteenth century and was performed in the major cathedrals on the Sunday of the Holy Forefathers (the penultimate Sunday before Christ's Nativity).

In medieval Moscow the 'Play of the Furnace' was enacted in only one church – the Cathedral of the Dormition in the Kremlin, where it was performed by the Patriarch's Singing Clerks and the junior clerics of the Cathedral. Preparations for the performance began long before the festival itself. A 'master of the youths' specially appointed from among the senior singers taught the younger clerks the roles of the youths over several months; the props for the performance were refurbished – the 'burning fiery furnace', the canvas angel, the 'Chaldean' costumes; and the kind of grass (*plavun*) which during the performance blazed in the 'furnace' without giving off any heat was prepared. The 'Chaldeans' also rehearsed their roles, which were usually played by the Cathedral watchmen. Those present during the performance of the 'Play of the Furnace' waited with bated breath for the appearance of the saving angel lowered on ropes from beneath the cupola.

Kastalsky approached the task he had set himself both as a scholarly archaeologist and as an artist. He collected and studied the scholarly literature, sought out manuscripts containing descriptions of the Action, and even tried to decipher the 'hook' notation without cinnabar markings (*bespometnïy*). It must be admitted, however, that the work which the composer put forward was nonetheless the fruit of his artistic imagination (Ex. 12.3).

The 'Play of the Furnace' commissioned from Kastalsky by the well-known archaeological scholar Alexander Uspensky was performed for the first time on 18 March 1907 in the Diocesan House by the Synodal Choir conducted by the composer at an open meeting of the Commission for the Study of Monuments of Ecclesiastical Antiquity in Moscow and the Moscow Diocese. The performance was accompanied by a lecture given by archpriest Metallov. A dramatized performance of the 'Play of the Furnace' was given on 10 April 1909 in the hall of the Synodal School: the members of the Synodal Choir wore new ceremonial uniforms sewn using designs by Viktor Vasnetsov, and with Bishop Trifon, an auxiliary bishop of the Moscow Diocese, in the role of reader.

Thus a further page of forgotten history was made into sound in the composer's work. The 'Play of the Furnace' was no mere illustration for the scholarly papers of archaeologists, however, but was in itself a small theatrical production developed in accordance with the simple story-line and containing all the attributes of stage action in the primitive form typical of the medieval folk theatre. The composer as usual attached no great importance to his composition, although in actual fact this modest restoration became another of the steps towards the genre of the musical dramatization which was new to Russian music and would come to occupy a central position in the composer's work during the following decade.

To all appearances, Kastalsky's work on the 'Play of the Furnace' roused in him an interest in the comparative analysis of folksong and church chants – a subject being discussed by medievalists and ethnographers in those years. In a letter of October 1906, Kastalsky told Smolensky that he was seriously engaged in research into folk music and was at the stage of formulating the problems, and he was therefore asking the scholar to let him know the ways by which he arrived at the idea of a kinship between folksongs and melodies from the *obikhod*. During this period Kastalsky was also interested in deciphering medieval notation. Thus on 16 April 1908 he asked Smolensky for 'pages with the *znamenny* and *demestvenny* alphabets', and in a letter of 28 October 1908 he wrote to him again: 'Pyotr Petrov, by the way, told me about something. He says that you have found the key to reading scores in hook notation; this is very curious, because it may open the way for church *podgoloski*. This would be of special interest to me, unless it is still the "author's secret" of its inventor'.[26]

In the second half of the 1900s Kastalsky's researches in the field of ethnography were only just beginning to develop. Alexander Dmitriyevich himself recalled of this time:

> The years 1907-10 saw the deaths of Vasily Orlov, Rimsky-Korsakov, Stepan Smolensky and Semyon Kruglikov, who served as director of the Synodal School for little more than two years. During that time I was busy, among other things, researching into Russian folksong, trying to elucidate its features for myself, but, as a result of constant distractions in other directions, that work was delayed indefinitely.[27]

During those years Kastalsky was choirmaster of the Synodal Choir and a teacher at the Synodal School, and was undoubtedly very busy on his employer's behalf. Besides that work, however, and composing an as yet small number of works for the church, he was distracted by another activity entirely unconnected with his employment: Kastalsky began writing an opera.

Kastalsky was induced to compose a major 'serious' work not only by free-thinking conversations with Rebikov but also by the practice of music he observed around him. On 11 February 1903 the composer informed Grozdov that he had made the acquaintance of Rimsky-Korsakov's *Kashchey*, the Sixth Symphony of Glazunov, works by Richard Strauss, and Rebikov's 'Songs of the Heart' (*Pesni serdtsa*). Soon Kastalsky sat down once more with Gevaert's textbook on orchestration. 'I can remember my past enthusiasms for this matter; at that time it was something completely new to me, and now it is as if I am experiencing my old enthusiasms and now along comes a wicked urge – to try to find out whether I can relish something other than cabbage-soup and porridge. And now I've got Korsakov's *Kashchey* on my desk! – All it does is tempt me to do the same'.[28]

Testing himself in the genre of opera, however, was something the composer risked only in late 1906 or early 1907, or so it would appear. The first mention of work on the opera *Klara Milich* based on Turgenev's story of the same name occurs in a letter to Grozdov of 19 April 1907, where Kastalsky informs him that excerpts from the new composition were performed at one of Mariya Deysha-Sionitskaya's musical evenings. By the summer of 1907 work on the opera was going at full speed, something the holiday period made significantly easier. The composer was so enthused by his work that he wrote music even in a railway carriage, as he wrote humorously to his wife: 'In the carriage I set about the introduction out of boredom – since I was alone. The conductor was surprised: "Can you manage without a piano, then?..." I worked at the introduction until 9.30 in the evening. Then they put two fishmongers from Tver in beside me. One started to take an interest. "What sort of plan is that you're drawing?"'[29]

The first version of *Klara Milich* was completed and scored by the beginning of 1908. Orchestrating the piano score caused the composer no little difficulty, as he did not fail to inform Smolensky:

> At the moment I'm slaving away over the score all the time, and although it's coming near the end, it's going very slowly, for there's no way I could have got an orchestral technique, of course, and with the present-day style you can't afford to orchestrate just anyhow, because in that line everyone's very good – in other words, you daren't be worse than all the others. But, thank goodness, the young people are helping me out – Vasilenko, Kuper and Sakhnovsky. [...] But despite my poor technique, the orchestration has nonetheless turned out properly and by no means hopeless, contrary to expectation. The fourth act, which I'm just coming to, worries me somewhat as it needs to be orchestrated 'a little more strongly' (à la Wagner or Korsakov). But I've got something to hand for checking to see how it's done by the leading luminaries.[30]

Alexander Dmitriyevich was in a hurry to get the score ready because there was a proposal to stage the opera in the Zimin Theatre in the autumn of 1908. The première was postponed for an indefinite period, however, causing the composer much distress. New prospects of staging *Klara Milich* came along only eight years later and, dissatisfied with the first version which had been written in haste, Kastalsky took advantage of the opportunity to carry out a reorchestration and make new versions of several numbers. Nonetheless, as before the composition failed to satisfy him: 'And it's only a composer's self-esteem ... that starts to suffer at the thought that the opera is written badly, is difficult to perform, that a lot has been done thoughtlessly (in other words, the difficulties of the introductions and the intonations have been increased to no purpose); not thought out. And now it's too late! I'm simplifying here and there where I can'.[31] The long-awaited première finally took place on 11 November 1916, bringing the composer more grief than joy: in spite of a brilliant set of performers, the work's success was extremely modest.

After *Klara Milich* had been performed for the seventh time, Kastalsky told Grozdov that he had made friends with the singers, often gossiping in the dressing-rooms with them, and had even written them a lampoon to prevent them being bored during the intervals between acts; the poem ended with the composer's reflections on the composition's uncertain fate once it had been roundly condemned by the critics.

In a humorous poem, for which the composer even devised a melody, he thanked the director Fyodor Komissarzhevsky, the conductor Yevgeny Plotnikov and the performers of the principal roles Nina Koshits, Pavel Kholodkov and the other singers – in short, everyone who had worked wonderfully well on the performance of his brainchild. However, after it had given rise to a hail of newspaper criticism, *Klara Milich* has never been performed anywhere since its production at the Zimin Theatre during the 1916-17 season.

History saw to it that it was the composer's gloomy prediction, not his optimistic one, that was borne out: Kastalsky's single opera did indeed 'vanish into oblivion'.

What is this composition, to which the composer devoted so much effort and time, like? The background to the story by Turgenev is the tale of the life and death by suicide of the famous Russian singer Yevlaliya Kadmina. Kastalsky, who had worked for many years in 'impersonal' genres, chose for his new work a narrowly personal subject about the unhappy love of the singer Klara Milich and the young man Yakov Aratov.

The idea of passionate love which overcomes death is the predominant one in the opera. The composer invested all his spiritual ardour and mastery of melodic writing in developing specifically the work's lyrical-psychological and mystic-symbolist planes. Because of this, many of the opera's pages directly devoted to the main heroes are written expressively and powerfully. Such are the introduction, based on the theme of 'unhappy Klara', Aratov's ballad from the first scene, Klara's two songs from the second scene, and the duet of Klara and Aratov in the final scene. The melodic writing in the work is original and beautiful; the harmony, though traditional, is also refined. In general terms, one can sense the distant influence of Tchaikovsky's musical language (Ex. 12.4).

On the other hand, the hyperbole – in the spirit of the times – in the treatment of the subject's melodramatic and mystical features does not accord with the spirit of Turgenev's story. The inter-relationship between the two planes also seems unnatural – those of lyric drama, on the one hand, and the everyday world, devoted to depicting scenes from Moscow life and written wittily and realistically, on the other. Here, in his accustomed field as a stylizer, the composer shines brightly. Brought into being as a background against which the action unfolds, the scenes of everyday life have ripened into another one of Kastalsky's 'restorations' accorded equal status with the idea of the main heroes.

And, lastly, there is the third layer of the composition – the stylization of folk-church musical speech – linked with the portrayal of Aratov's aunt, Stepanida Ivanovna. The 'new Russian style' also makes itself felt in the melodeclamation 'The Sphinx' (based on Turgenev's 'Poem in Prose') which represents an interesting experiment in using the new language in a composition for chorus, orchestra and narrator (Ex. 12.5).

Within the framework of an opera where separable numbers are plentiful, the composer was able to say what he had to say in the realm of piano composition (in the number where a solo pianist performs a composition by Kastalsky) and in the smaller-scale vocal genres (with the many songs to words by Turgenev and other poets). The composition abounds in good music, though as a whole, however, it appears stylistically varied and dramatically illogical. Without ever becoming a serious contribution to the development of Russian opera, it marked an important stage in the biography of the composer himself and influenced his works of the 1910s.

Notes

1. Letter from A.D. Kastal'sky to Kh.N. Grozdov of 20 November 1901. GTsMMK, fond 370, no. 496, pp. 2-2v.
2. Letter from V.I. Rebikov to A.D. Kastal'sky of 20 December 1901. GTsMMK, fond 68, no. 321, p. 2v.
3. Cf. letter from A.D. Kastal'sky to Kh.N. Grozdov of 14 February 1902. GTsMMK, fond 370, no. 397, p. 2.
4. A.D. Kastal'sky: *Kratkaya avtobiografiya* (Short autobiography), in *A.D. Kastalsky. Stat'i. Vospominaniya. Materialï* (A.D. Kastal'sky. Articles. Reminiscences. Materials). Moscow, 1960, p. 134.
5. Vyach. Paskhalov: *Vstrechi i vospominaniya* (Encounters and reminiscences). *Ibid.*, pp. 19-20.
6. Letter from A.D. Kastal'sky to V.I. Rebikov of 20 November 1901. GTsMMK, fond 68, no. 273, p. 2.
7. Letter from A.D. Kastal'sky to Kh.N. Grozdov of 18 January 1917. GTsMMK, fond 370, no. 553, pp. 2-2v.
8. N. Kastal'skaya: *Nemnogoye ob ottse* (A little about my father). In *A.D. Kastalsky. Stat'i. Vospominaniya. Materialï* (A.D. Kastal'sky. Articles. Reminiscences. Materials). Moscow, 1960, pp. 106-107.
9. Letter from A.D. Kastal'sky to S.V. Smolensky of 17 March 1902. RGIA, fond 1119, opis' 1, no. 146, p. 12v.
10. Letter from A.D. Kastal'sky to V.I. Rebikov of 8 October 1910. GTsMMK, fond 68, no. 276, p. 2.
11. Letter from A.D. Kastal'sky to V.I. Rebikov of 14 December 1901. GTsMMK, fond 68, no. 275, pp. 2-2v.

12. The work in question is M.M. Ippolitov-Ivanov: *Gruzinskaya narodnaya pesnya i yeyo sovremennoye sostoyaniye* (Georgian folksong and its present-day state), in *Artist*, 1895, no. 45.

13. Letter from A.D. Kastal'sky to N.F. Findeyzen of 18 January 1903. RNB, fond 816, opis' 2, no. 1450, p. 5.

14. A.D. Kastal'sky: *O moyey muzïkal'noy kar'yere i moi mïsli o tserkovnoy muzïke* (My career in music and my thoughts about church music), in *RUSAM*, vol. 1, p. 237.

15. Apparently the work in mind is S.V. Smolensky: *O drevnerusskikh pevcheskikh notatsiyakh. Istoriko-paleograficheskiy ocherk* (Ancient Russian church music systems of notation. A historical-palaeographical outline), in *ChOIDR*, St Petersburg, 1901.

16. Letter from A.D. Kastal'sky to S.V. Smolensky of 24 December 1901. RGIA, fond 1119, opis' 1, no. 146, p. 7.

17. The second Historical Concert, which took place on 15 March 1902, was devoted to arrangements of monophonic chants made by composers of the late nineteenth and early twentieth centuries, with some by Kastal'sky.

18. Letter from A.D. Kastal'sky to S.V. Smolensky of 7 October 1902. RGIA, fond 1119, opis' 1, no. 146, p. 25.

19. Evidently the following work, the result of travels in Turkey, Jerusalem and Bulgaria, by the French Byzantine scholar is meant: Jean-Baptiste Thibaut: *Étude de musique byzantine. La notation de Koukouzéles.* In *Izvestiya russkogo arkheologicheskogo instituta v Konstantinopole* (Transactions of the Russian Institute of Archaeology in Constantinople), vol. 6, parts 2-3, 1901.

20. Letter from A.D. Kastal'sky to S.V. Smolensky of 19 January 1903. RGIA, fond 1119, opis' 1, no. 146, p. 29.

21. Letter from A.D. Kastal'sky to S.V. Smolensky of 20 December 1902. RGIA, fond 1119, opis' 1, no. 145, p. 28v.

22. P.P. Sokal'sky (Sokol'sky): *Russkaya narodnaya muzïka, velikorusskaya i malorusskaya v yeyo stroyenii melodicheskom i ritmicheskom i otlichiya yeyo ot osnov sovremennoy garmonicheskoy muzïki* (Russian folk music, Great-Russian and Little-Russian, in its melodic and rhythmic structure and its differences from the fundamentals of present-day harmonic music). Kharkov, 1888.

23. Letter from A.D. Kastal'sky to S.V. Smolensky of 28 July 1903. RGIA, fond 1119, opis' 1, no. 146, pp. 38a-38b.

24. Letter from A.D. Kastal'sky to S.V. Smolensky of 19 January 1903. RGIA, fond 1119, opis' 1, no. 146, pp. 29-29v.

25. Letter from A.D. Kastal'sky to S.V. Smolensky of 28 July 1903. RGIA, fond 1119, opis' 1, no. 146, p. 38b.

26. Letter from A.D. Kastal'sky to S.V. Smolensky of 28 October 1908. RGIA, fond 1119, opis' 1, no. 146, pp. 55v.

27. A.D. Kastal'sky: *O moyey muzïkal'noy kar'yere i moi mïsli o tserkovnoy muzïke,* in *RUSAM*, vol. 1, p. 238.

28. Letter from A.D. Kastal'sky to S.V. Smolensky of 24 February 1903. RGIA, fond 1119, opis' 1, no. 146, pp. 32-32v.

29. Letter from A.D. Kastal'sky to N.L. Kastal'skaya of 7 July 1907. GTsMMK, fond 12, no. 549, p. 1v.

30. Letter from A.D. Kastal'sky to S.V. Smolensky of 7 January 1908. RGIA, fond 1119, opis' 1, no. 146, pp. 53-53v.

31. Letter from A.D. Kastal'sky to Kh.N. Grozdov of 18 September 1916. GTsMMK, fond 370, no. 549, p. 26v.

Chapter 13

All-Night Vigil

What place did sacred music have in the second period of Kastalsky's biography as a composer? Turning to the catalogue issued by the firm of P. Jurgenson, we can see that of the 88 compositions mentioned in it, 55 individual choral pieces and choral cycles were published in precisely this first decade of the twentieth century. It is quite another matter that by no means every year was equally productive: the decline in composition of sacred music in the second half of the first decade of the twentieth century, when Kastalsky published only four pieces, is obvious. One may say that in spite of the composer's 'inclinations to the left', sacred music – by its very nature not disposed towards revolution – nonetheless continued to hold one of the leading places in his legacy from the 1900s.

By comparison with his first period of composition, his choice of hymns had changed. If in the 1890s Kastalsky had chiefly been attracted to texts from the Divine Liturgy, in his second period he gave recognition to the hymns of the All-Night Vigil and feast-days. The composer accordingly entered upon the field of hymns in 'tones', which are extremely important from the point of view of worship but offer little scope for free artistic utterance or experiment.

Kastalsky continued to organize the Synodal Choir's repertoire in a systematic manner by overhauling what was already there and filling in gaps. It is noticeable, however, that he now understood this task in a significantly broader way. Undertaking a reform of the 'tones', writing pieces to commission, arranging his own compositions for the most diverse choral forces – all these activities bear witness to the fact that the composer now saw his mission as serving not just his own school but the whole cause of church music in Russia.

Something else too is noticeable: Kastalsky was at first indifferent to the idea of cyclic form – integrating the individual movements for a church service into a large-scale entity; during the 1900s, however, he began to reveal a leaning towards unified dramatic development within the choral cycle. If between 1896 and 1900 he composed a scattering of individual miniatures, then in his works of the 1900s we observe a series of choral items which, though they may not all be heard at a single service, are united by a single idea (three sets of 'Lord, I have cried' (*Gospodi vozzvakh*), five sets of stichera, three canons, dogmatika and troparia for the Dormition) as well as cycles of hymns performed at one act of worship – the Marriage, and the Liturgy of St John Chrysostom for female choir. One can also interpret the hymns of the All-Night Vigil written between 1900 and 1905 as a choral cycle composed in the order in which they appear in the service. The composer himself never published the choral pieces of the All-Night Vigil as a single composition, although he assented to the idea of performing them in a single concert.

Kastalsky's turning to the texts of this service can be explained not just by its important position among the other Orthodox services: in the repertoire of his time he could see no examples which accorded with his ideas about the new church style. On 14 December 1901 Kastalsky replied to Rebikov's query as to which All-Night Vigil he would recommend: 'There is no decent complete All-Night Vigil, but the best one (complete) is the "Music for the All-Night Vigil in ancient chants", the Kapella's most recent publication'.[1]

Six movements from Kastalsky's All-Night Vigil were printed at V. Grosse's works at the end of 1901. Four of them were written to the text of the introductory psalm 'Bless the Lord, O my soul' (*Blagoslovi, dushe moya, Gospoda*) and two choral items to the text 'Blessed is the man' (*Blazhen muzh*) (set respectively to little *znamenny* chant and the melody of the Cathedral of the Dormition in Moscow). By 1905 a further 29 hymns from the All-Night Vigil were published, and the choir patron and conductor Leonid Vasilyev resolved to arrange a concert of them.

Thus Kastalsky began his work on the All-Night Vigil with the introductory psalm 'Bless the Lord, O my soul', which he wrote in four versions. To judge by the contents of the Synodal Choir's music books, however, the one most often performed in the Cathedral of the Dormition and at concerts was that for large choir using a Greek chant – a colourful 'symphonic' work, the pathways from which led to many settings of this text by Kastalsky's colleagues.

The psalm 'Bless the Lord, O my soul' is called 'introductory' because it opens the first part of the All-Night Vigil – Vespers, inaugurating the 24-hour cycle of acts of worship. The evening service reflects the history of the church in Old Testament times, and the beginning of it relives the first and most profound chapter of sacred history – the creation of the world. How has Kastalsky interpreted this text?

The composer has followed the structure of the text of the psalm in his treatment; it comprises verses (incipits sung by the cantor or a section of the choir) and repeated doxologies (refrains). The composition develops by means of a texture which gradually grows more complicated, with dynamic levels rising and the range of choral registers widening. From a restrained, muffled chorale in a low register to the ecstatic brilliance of all the choral colours in the concluding 'Glory' (*Slava*), woven together from a multitude of melodic lines – that is how this piece develops.

The music of the first verse concentrates reverently on the idea of the significance of the Creator of the universe (Ex. 13.1a).

This makes a distinctive introduction to the description of the picture of the creation of the world which unfolds in subsequent stanzas. The second verse 'O Lord my God' (*Gospodi Bozhe moy*) expresses the joyous amazement of men and angels at the grandeur of the Creator, conveyed by the first explosion of dynamics and texture in all the choral colours. (The 'chorus of angels' – the children, and the 'chorus of the earth' – the men, are combined in a broad, powerful and sonorous chord of C major.) Thematically akin to the first, but sounding broader and more pervaded by emotion, the second refrain leads to the third verse 'Thou makest Thine angels' (*Tvoryay angeli svoya*) – an enraptured contemplation by mankind of the mysterious and omnipotent supreme powers of heaven. The fragment of chant sung by the basses has an austere sound, and at the words 'flaming fire' (*plamen' ognennïy*) it ascends into the high soprano registers: it is as if tongues of fire had broken out from their hiding-place under the bowels of the earth. A new gentle cantilena theme for the refrain 'Marvellous are Thy works, O Lord' (*Divna dela Tvoya, Gospodi*) is sung by the trebles accompanied by the whole choir. The following fourth verse 'The waters stand upon the mountains, the waters flow between the hills' (*Na gorakh stanut vodï, posrede gor proydut vodï*) is entirely given over to word-painting: the image 'the foundations of the earth' (*tverdi zemnoy*) is symbolized by the compact, massive, dense sonority with a reliance on low registers; the flowing streams of water – by melodic *podgoloski* interweaving and coming up against one another.

The altos' cry of 'Marvellous!' (*Divna!*) rings out with dazzling brilliance, high and powerfully over the whole earth, and is taken up by the choir who exclaim in thanksgiving: 'Marvellous are Thy works, O Lord!' (*Divna dela Tvoya, Gospodi!*). A joyous comprehension of all creation's majestic grandeur is embodied in the work's climax – the universal concluding 'Glory' (*Slava*). All nations call to one another 'Glory, glory, glory' (*Slava, slava, slava*); the glorification of the Creator can be heard resounding from all the ends of the earth (see Ex. 13.1b).

The outline of the images and emotions in Kastalsky's introductory psalm given here is an abridged version of the work of a great expert in the church style and authority on the Synodal Choir traditions, Sergey Shumsky, later chorusmaster at the Bolshoy Theatre. A graduate of the Synodal School, he sang in the Synodal Choir from 1902 to 1906 when Orlov was choirmaster and left wonderful reminiscences of how the Synodal singers performed this work.

> A broad wave of sounds flows – imperious, exultant and powerful, rousing in the soul something mighty in its lofty, impassioned current. It is like watching water swelling, thundering by in an unclouded stream, with rivers and seas spilling out mightily. Joy seizes your soul. What beauty! The Lord is a great master of adorning the earth: the waters sparkle with silver in the sun's rays, the sun smiles, bright green grasses break through from under the earth towards the sun.

Thus did Shumsky express the feelings and images which this work provoked in the performers.[2]

Nikolay Golovanov, conductor at the Bolshoy Theatre, who had been a soloist in the Synodal Choir as a boy, left his recollections of how this work was performed and they have come down to us via Shumsky:

> The conductor for the All-Night Vigil was Vasily Orlov, a choirmaster of great artistic temperament but whose conducting was exceedingly restrained on the surface – 'a warm heart but cold control of the head'. Orlov behaved strictly, even severely, towards the singers. We were singing Kastalsky's 'Bless the Lord' to a Greek chant. It was one of Orlov's inspired interpretations of a work by Kastalsky. Orlov showed us, got us to understand, all the hymn's conquering power: he displayed its 'soul'. Orlov's eyes darkened, moistened and somehow smiled happily. At those points he was amazingly impressive: you could see the moisture from tears of inspiration in the conductor's eyes. We were all excited, inflamed by his fire; we were happy, experiencing an animation out of the ordinary, a feeling of unusual lightness throughout our being; we sensed that our voices, both the boys' and the adults', were making a particularly beautiful sound, powerful and moving; the sound was free, the voice seemed to have no limits and ran along sparklingly just like a brook. In this excitement, which cannot be explained in words, the faces of the singers became flushed, and one could sense the power of conviction in the words being sung.[3]

The second chapter of the Old Testament story concerns the expulsion from paradise of Adam and Eve for violating God's law. Just like the gates of paradise, the Royal Doors are closed. And like Adam and Eve repenting and praying for forgiveness, all those present in the church beg for help in the various needs of earthly life. The great litany (*Velikaya Yekten'ya*)[4] is read and sung, which in the service gives way to the singing of the kathisma 'Blessed is the man'. It tells of the life of the righteous in the Old Testament who in the midst of dishonour and unbelief never lost their hope in the Lord; this image is contrasted with the way of the 'unrighteous' which leads to perdition.

Kastalsky's musical interpretation of this text is not confined to the published versions, the best-known of which is the one for large choir using the melody of the Cathedral of the Dormition in Moscow. This artistic canvas has absorbed not just the patterns of that melody but also the special spirit of that remarkable church monument which combines features of the old and the new. Just as the cathedral's interior manages to accommodate icons painted both long ago and in the present, just as the liturgical rites integrate the ancient statute with features from the modern practice of worship, and just as the musical form of the services integrates monophonic chants with homophony – so, in just the same way, the contrast and co-existence of ancient and modern layers are a characteristic mark of the style of 'Blessed is the man' using the melody of the Cathedral of the Dormition: archaic unison verse-incipits, with a *znamenny* chant present, contrast with 'new-style' refrains – polyphonic *alliluiyas*. Resounding against a background of sustained choral pedal-points, resilient toccata-like incipits rotating within a narrow range around the reciting note are performed by the men of the choir. They are evidently an echo of the bass ensemble formed by the cathedral clergy who by long tradition performed the stichera and antiphons at All-Night Vigils.

After the singing of the kathisma and the small litany following it at the evening service, Psalm 140 is sung – 'Lord, I have cried unto Thee, hear me' (*Gospodi, vozzvakh k Tebe, uslïshi mya*), in which the psalmist asks God to accept his prayer as an evening sacrifice. Containing as it does the idea of replacing the Old Testament physical sacrifice by a purely spiritual sacrifice – the New Testament principle, this psalm signifies the transition in the service to Christian subject matter. Psalms alternate with stichera taken from the Oktoechos and the Menaion, and permanent melodies with tone melodies which can change (much like the Proper and Ordinary in the Catholic Mass).

At the turn of the nineteenth and twentieth centuries, when the aesthetic contents of Orthodox worship became a topic of widespread debate, attention was drawn to the inconsistent artistic quality between the settings of the permanent melodies and the changing ones, those set to tones. If the permanent melodies set to tones had long been material for composers' free creativity and had thus assumed the most diverse musical incarnations, the changing chants set to tones had remained inviolable, a canonical area closed off to the intrusion of composers. Moreover, the tone melodies' harmonizations introduced by Lvov and later edited in Bakhmetev's time were patently not in accordance with the style and artistic standard of the settings of the permanent chants produced by the skilled composers of the New Direction. It is therefore not surprising that Kastalsky joined in the polemics surrounding the integrity of the musical profile of worship. As the composer wrote in his booklet 'A Practical Guide to the expressive singing of stichera using varied harmonizations' published in 1909:

> One of the weakest aspects of our church music practice is the singing of the stichera. Without saying anything about bad musical grammar or the triteness of the harmonic accompaniment to the tone melodies, the distribution of grammatical, logical and declamatory accents and stopping points in the text associated with the melody is often full of anomalies in both the stichera and the verses. As regards the connection between the music (in the given instance the harmonic accompaniment of the *Obikhod* melodies) and at least the general mood (for example, joyful or grieving) of the particular sticheron text, then thanks to the single, stereotyped harmonic accompaniment of a particular tone for all occasions, this connection is often not just absent altogether but sometimes the character of the harmonization directly contradicts the general mood of the text, so that the music too, in spite of its natural power of expressiveness, kills the text's power of expression in these cases – for instance, the radiant and joyful Christmas sticheron in the 6th tone for Psalm 50 'Glory to God in the highest and on earth peace [...] today angels venerate the Newborn Child in hymns worthy of God' (*Slava v vïshnikh Bogu i na zemli mir... dnes' angeli Mladentsa rozhdennago bogolepno slavoslovyat...*) is in the ordinary minor-key, gloomy harmonic layout; or the depressed, doleful mood of the *sedalen* hymn for the Matins of Good Friday (before the third Gospel) (*Kiy tya obraz Iudo, predatelya Spasu sodela?* ('What caused you to betray the Saviour, O Judas?')) is in the cheerful major of the 7th tone – a great many examples of that kind can easily be found.[5]

In the composer's opinion, every sticheron tone should be available in at least two harmonizations: a major one for festive and joyful texts and a minor one for mournful and distressing hymns. A closer accord between the music and the text could also be obtained, Kastalsky thought, by using various artistic devices in setting the chants – for example, by introducing unison in places which 'demand greater power, austerity or unusualness of expression or energy', laying out several phrases in two parts, transferring the chant from the upper part to middle ones, or setting it against a background of sustained notes.

The composer realized the principles which he proclaimed here in four different versions of the whole complex of hymns for 'Lord, I have cried' (also know as the *vozzvakhi*) containing four psalms and the stichera following them. In the booklet mentioned above, the composer cites specimens of a minor harmonization according to the tradition of the Kievan chant tones set out in the major, intending them for the service of Good Friday (the 1st to the 5th and the 7th tones). The 6th tone, traditionally set in the minor, Kastalsky gives in a major harmonization, expecting it to be used with festive texts. In the 8th tone, the composer does not change the mode as a whole, but merely changes the minor ending to a major one, again anticipating its use on feast-days.

The settings of the Kievan chant tones are accomplished with the utmost skill, and were brought out as a booklet by the composer; in spite of all the innovations they contain, they are all within the tradition of the usual tone settings. The texture, the distribution of the voices among the parts and the placing of the melody in the upper voices are all as usual. The main new feature is the change in the traditional modal tendencies. It is interesting that this cycle was preceded by as many as three (complete) cycles of *vozzvakhi* ('I have crieds') which are far bolder in their musical language.

Reminiscing about his works from the early 1900s, the composer wrote:

> The greatest amount of time was spent, naturally, on the dogmatika and particularly the 'I have crieds'; I subsequently reworked the latter, feeling dissatisfied with the first version. In spite of the fact that in the final version I aimed for – besides typicality and artlessness in the harmonies – purely practical ends (the possibility of performing these settings with a choir made up in any way, down to and including two people), this brainchild of mine did not achieve wide dissemination. Maybe the reason was that in order to study these settings you have to do a lot of preliminary work to get a choir to unlearn the usual banal harmonization. Because of that work several choirmasters reproached me for wasting time on an 'unworthy cause' – something I disagree with, for I consider our tone melodies (corrected, of course, as far as possible) the most characteristic in our church music; and the fact that in practice they got tied up in the most hopeless clichés is, though extremely regrettable, an incontestable fact.[6]

The first three cycles of 'I have crieds' published by Kastalsky were a brave attempt to destroy the clichés. The settings of the *znamenny* chants were executed in a particularly brave and innovative manner; they were not harmonizations made in a simplified *obikhod* style to suit any text, but eight miniatures, complex in concept and performance, based on the text of Psalm 140, interpreted in the light of the individual complexion of each of them as eight states of a soul crying out to God.

The settings of the 'I have crieds' to the Kievan chant (second cycle), are treated in an austere 'ancient Orthodox' manner. The layout of the chant for basses in unison with one of the upper voices, with the others doubling in thirds, the archaic choral reciting over open fifths, the uncommon modal tendencies in the harmony – all this was bold and out of the ordinary in Kastalsky's time.

However, as the composer himself admitted in a letter of 14 February 1902 to Grozdov, the innovative 'I have crieds' were written nonetheless with an eye to public opinion and to accepted models.[7]

The dogmatika also mentioned there by Kastalsky – stichera in praise of the Mother of God, in which various aspects of the doctrine of the incarnation of the Lord Jesus Christ by the Virgin Mary are brought to light – were compiled by St John of Damascus. Kastalsky made settings of eight original tonal melodic chants (*samoglasnïye*) of the dogmatika in eight different tones. These experiments are considered the boldest in Kastalsky's sacred music. Sensitively following impulses derived from the ancient chants and their texts, the composer at times cuts loose completely not just from the canonical church style but also from academically correct music. The sound of the *znamenny* chant, preserved inviolate, is illuminated now by reflections of austere epic Russian antiquity, now by the dramatic quality of the passions of Old Testament history, events which are drawn in as a prototype to reveal the doctrine of the Incarnation, now by the calm emotion of affirming dogmas inaccessible to the mind, or again by the unearthly calm of the image of the Most Pure Mother of God praised by the hymn-writer. An elevated, pious, reverential mood prevails in these dogmatika, which represent the richest mine of national *podgoloski* polyphonic writing, based on the logic of intervallic expansion in the *znamenny* chant and using devices for colouring the musical fabric characteristic of Russian folk polyphony (Ex. 13.2).

The dogmatika and the 'I have crieds' were published in the spring of 1902 and the composer immediately sent them to his closest friends who were not slow to send in their comments. Smolensky wrote to the composer on 31 March 1902:

Dear Alexander Dmitriyevich!
I have just received your dogmatika and 'I have crieds', and a quick glance at them (and by the way I don't have a piano, because the new one from Diderikhs is late) convinced me of the need to investigate thoroughly the essence of your new ideas about how to accompany the melody harmonically, which as you write it is full of innovations and audacities of all sorts, some of which however struck me to the quick straightaway. Hail to you! [...] I am very happy for you with all my heart, even though I sense that you are beginning to lose interest in a work such as 'Thou alone art immortal' (*Sam Yedin*) or the marriage concertos [see hymns for the marriage service in List of Works] which so encouraged my best hopes for you. Why have you stopped? Or perhaps the newest pieces you have written have not reached me yet?[8]

As we can see, when Smolensky first looked at Kastalsky's dogmatika and 'I have crieds', he was somewhat concerned about their 'audacities' and 'innovations', suspecting – quite correctly – that the new compositions contained hitherto unknown ways of arranging *znamenny* chants and seeing in that the principal point of the compositions sent to him. Besides, the dogmatika and 'I have crieds', lacking the concert-platform sweep which distinguished certain of the composer's previous works, were aimed at solving a narrowly ecclesiastical problem – improving the chant set to tones – and, it seems, rather disappointed him.

Grozdov's response was more enthusiastic: 'And now, let's move on to your 'I have crieds' and dogmatika. They're extremely good, even incomparably good. The 'I have crieds' (both the old ones and the new ones) are superb, and the dogmatika are even better!'[9]

As regards the church administration, they were plunged into 'confusion', as the composer put it, when they heard one of the dogmatika sung during worship in the Cathedral of the Dormition. In spite of that, however, the dogmatika entered the repertoire of the Synodal Choir securely, as is testified by concert programmes, the very worn state of the dogmatika copies in the School library, and the reminiscences of people connected with the Choir. Thus, Alexander Smirnov, who studied at the Synodal School from 1909 to 1917, recalled that the dogmatika were considered the most difficult works in the Synodal Choir's repertoire, and singers entering the Choir were often asked at the entrance exam to sing their part in one of them.

Shortly after his enthusiastic comments about the dogmatika and 'I have crieds', Grozdov wrote the composer a letter in which he asked: 'And how is your All-Night Vigil coming along? The troparia and heirmoi await their turn, and they are no less of a challenge than the Marian items. How about 'Praise the Name of the Lord' (*Khvalite*), or the Great Doxology (*Velikoye slavosloviye*)?'[10] To all appearances, Grozdov was not quite up to date with his friend's activities, since as early as July 1902 Kastalsky had sold the publishing firm of P. Jurgenson full rights in the heirmoi for Christ's Nativity and the Exaltation of the Cross, and also the troparia for Trinity Sunday, the Dormition, and the Holy Hierarch Nicholas.

The composer prepared his next group of hymns for the All-Night Vigil for submission to the censorship in the spring of 1904. Kastalsky wrote on 21 May 1904 to Grozdov:

My dear, sincere friend Khristofor Nikolayevich!
There has been no reason for me not writing to you for so long other than the one which of course you understand well, which is that I have been hard at

work the whole time since Holy Week on what is closest to my heart – the pieces for the All-Night Vigil. A few days ago that duty to my conscience was fulfilled (though not completely, and I had counted on it being finished earlier) and now here I am boasting about it to you; I've finished and sent off to St Petersburg: three 'Gladsome Lights' (*Svete tikhiy*) (the ones you know), moreover with nos. 1 and 2 represented in 'simplified versions' as well; three 'Lord, now lettest Thou' (*Nïne otpushchayeshi*) (with nos. 1 and 3 also in two versions); three 'Praise the Name of the Lord' (*Khvalite Imya Gospodne*) (all with easier options), two Six Psalms (*Stikhi pered Shestopsalmiyem*) and one Great Doxology (I still have to do one festive Doxology and one melancholic one). In total twelve numbers, not counting simplified arrangements. I'll do the two missing Great Doxologies (or possibly just one) in a leisurely manner during the summer. I don't know about you, but I'm pleased, because all that time both exams and all the usual hurly-burly were going on as well.[11]

The works were approved by the sacred music censorship committee on 21 December 1904, and published in February 1905; one month later, in March, a concert of Kastalsky's All-Night Vigil pieces was given by Leonid Vasilyev's choir.

The 'dozen' new compositions the composer told his friend about with satisfaction began with three choral pieces on the text 'Gladsome Light' (*Svete tikhiy*), which in the service comes immediately after the dogmatikon. 'Our fathers did not want to accept the blessing of evening light in silence, and at the hour when it came they offered up praise', wrote the Holy Hierarch Basil the Great of this poetic hymn telling of Christ's advent on earth at the end of Old Testament time and of the beginning of the new day whose light the Saviour brought.[12]

The idea of light – spiritual and physical – lies at the root of Kastalsky's interpretation of the text of this evening song, and he conveys in masterly fashion all the shades of meaning in this hymn, which may be brief but is saturated with symbols and metaphors. While following the structure of the text, the composer also gives his compositions ternary form.

1. Gladsome Light of the holy glory of the Immortal One –
   The Heavenly Father, holy and blessed – O Jesus Christ!

*1. Svete tikhiy, Svyatïya slavï bezsmertnago Ottsa nebesnago,
   Svyatago, blazhennago, Iisuse Khriste.*

Just as the mystical and enigmatic play of symbols in the song's first lines concludes with the utterance of the hero's name which had merely been hinted at earlier, so the composer constructs the form of the first section of the hymn on a transition from mystery to revelation.

In 'Gladsome Light' no. 1, the first phrases performed in two parts by the men of the choir against the background of a dominant pedal maintained by the trebles, are interpreted as a concentrated, austere and measured procession which concludes with everyone pronouncing the name of Jesus Christ. In 'Gladsome Light' no. 2 (in the versions for both small and large choirs), on the other hand, it is only the children who sing of God's name, while the preceding lines, an element of whose melodic character is formed by the chant from the *fita* of the first tone, are initially performed by the whole choir and then by the children and the tenors. And the composer once more uses a pedal point as a background – first a tonic one, later one of an open fifth. A pure, sadly elegiac chorale from the children's voices opens 'Gladsome Light' no. 3. The lyrical chant sung by the children sounds like a sombre lullaby against the background of which the men recite the chant in diminution. And, finally, the tonic major bursts into flame like a ray of brilliant sunshine and the name of God proclaimed by the whole choir ascends into a high register.

2. Now that we have come to the setting of the sun,
   and behold the light of evening,
   we praise the Father, Son and the Holy Spirit – God,
   Thou art worthy at every moment to be praised in hymns by reverent voices.

2. *Prishedshe na zapad solntsa,*
   Videvshe svet vecherniy,
   Poyem Ottsa, Sïna i Svyatago Dukha, Boga,
   Dostoin yesi vo vsya vremena pet bïti glasï prepodobnïmi.

These lines from the evening song lie at the heart of the central section, which is treated as a rapturous glorification of the Creator. To convey this state of mind, the composer makes use in 'Gladsome Light' no. 1 of major-key melodic shapes characteristic of the hymns of praise (*Slavas*) in Russian operas (in the first and second lines), elements of canonic imitation as a symbol of the doxologies arising from various quarters and being woven together (third line), a severe, imperious presentation of the theme by the men affirming the dignity of the Creator, and lastly runs in thirds as the culminating doxology (fourth line). In 'Gladsome Light' no. 2 (for small and large choirs) a feature of the central section is the use of the chant of the *fita* in the first tone (in the first and third lines) and there is striking canonic imitation (fourth line). Powerful pedal points in the bass, high treble *podgoloski* and *divisi* distinguish the central section of the version for large choir from that for small choir.

But perhaps the composer's most festive and emotionally powerful treatment of the doxology is in 'Gladsome Light' no. 3, in whose central section the opening chorale-lullaby is reinterpreted as a brilliant trumpet fanfare, taken up subsequently by the whole choir.

> 3. O Son of God, Thou art the Giver of Life;
>   therefore all the world glorifies Thee.

> *3. Sïne Bozhiy, zhivot dayay,*
>   *Tem zhe mir Tya slavit.*

The final line of the hymn is treated as a varied reprise in all the variants of 'Gladsome Light'. The return to the thematic material of the first section is determined by the return in the narrative to mentioning the Son of God as the source of life. However the characteristic pacifying gentle melodic contours of the image of the Giver of Light are soon replaced by the triumphal celebration of Him associated with the concluding words of the evening song about the universal glorification of the Redeemer.

To judge by the Synodal Choir's copies, 'Gladsome Light' no. 2 for large choir and 'Gladsome Light' no. 3 were the ones most often heard at services. The first of those mentioned also formed part of the Choir's concert repertoire and was performed during their celebrated foreign tour in 1911. Another work by Kastalsky, the no less famous 'Lord, now lettest Thou' no. 1, was performed on the same trip; it was published in 1904 along with two other musical interpretations of the same prayer of St Simeon.

In his compositions on this prayer text Kastalsky was one of the first to apply the form previously unknown in Russian sacred music of a work for chorus with a large-scale part for a soloist along the lines of an aria. A form of this kind evidently arose under the influence of secular musical practice. It is also possible that the singing of the choir with the cantor was the prototype for it. That is exactly how Grechaninov's well-known 'Creed' (*Veruyu*) for choir and alto soloist from his Liturgy no. 2, first performed in March 1903, is composed.

In 'Lord, now lettest Thou' no. 1, which is based on *demestvenny* chant, a solo baritone sings the old man's monologue. The composition is perceived as an expressive operatic scene containing a broad spectrum of states of mind. In 'Lord, now lettest Thou' no. 2 a solo voice – a tenor – is also used. The composer has taken a different route, however, entrusting the soloist not with the monologue but with the epic retelling of the Gospel narrative. At the same time the soloist-narrator is linked with the hero of the event, while the choir supporting and supplementing him are associated with the people listening to the old man's words. And, lastly, in the third composition using this text, the idea of making a melody out of the bass line and giving dynamic priority to it above all the others comes into force.

The second part of the All-Night Vigil – Matins – is devoted to New Testament times and therefore opens with the doxology with which the angels hymned the infant Christ.

The composer wrote two versions of the Lesser Doxology, and each is a kind of choral scherzo typical of Kastalsky, used by him in one of his earliest sacred choral pieces – the 'It is meet' (*Dostoyno yest'*) using a Serbian chant. The light, transparent and brilliant 'orchestration' of the score, achieved thanks to the predominance of the children's choral parts where the main melodic material is concentrated, the figural and at the same time chant-derived thematic material, and the absence of contrast in dynamics and imagery are characteristic of both the first and second of Kastalsky's Lesser Doxologies. At the same time, however, the means used to embody the images of the angels' rejoicing are different in each case. Thus, in the first composition the glorification is linked with the image of fanfares from angels with trumpets; in the second the composer draws a picturesque canvas of soaring throngs of heavenly powers. In the first composition the movement of the children's voices in closely-spaced chords, with very cautious and economical use of bass colouring, was chosen as the means of realizing the images. In the second Doxology, on the contrary, the role of the bass part is very significant insofar as the basses along with the tenors form a drone of a fifth, above which refined embellishments rotate in the high voices.

Judging by the Synodal Choir's copies, no version of the 'Lord, now lettest Thou' or the Lesser Doxology was performed during worship. (According to the regulations of the Cathedral of the Dormition, these texts were read.) On the other hand, the following works by the composer on a text from the All-Night-Vigil, the three pieces 'Praise the name of the Lord', were sung very often at services in the Cathedral. Before describing these hymns, however, we should recall their meaning and position in the service, where, after the Verses before the Six Psalms, a shift in mood occurs from festivity to repentance: the light is extinguished and the Six Psalms are read out in a darkened church. From darkness to light is the direction taken by the subsequent development of Matins, where after the Six Psalms, the great Litany, the exclamation 'The Lord is God' (*Bog Gospod'*) and the kathismas the most triumphant part begins – the polyeleion, accompanied by the lighting of all the lamps, the censing of the church and the entrance of the clergy.

The idea of the uncreated light of Christ, a thread which weaves through the whole of the All-Night Vigil, is here affirmed with new force, since the radiance of the chandeliers expelling the darkness represents the threshold of the radiance of spiritual light which fills the church at the reading of the Gospel. Preceding the reading from the Gospel, stichera verses of praise from Psalms 134 and 135, known as a whole from their first line as 'Praise the name of the Lord' are heard accompanied by the refrain-doxology 'Alliluiya'.

A form of this kind is characteristic of the most festive hymns, and the composer had already had experience of realizing it in the first antiphon of the first kathisma 'Blessed is the man'. In his new works, however, he found original ways of treating it musically. In the 'Praise the Name of the Lord' no. 1, based on a Kievan chant, the principle of antiphonal performance is widely used, when the beginning (incipit) is entrusted to one *kliros* and the refrain to the other. In this case the different groups in the choir fulfil the function of the *kliroses*, with the children performing the theme in the incipits and the men in the refrains. Thus, in the course of the whole work the theme occurs four times with only insignificant modifications, with every statement linked with new variants in the arrangement of the harmony and *podgoloski* polyphony.

A *znamenny* chant is the basis for the 'Praise the Name of the Lord' no. 2, where melodic differentiation between the incipits and the refrains is not typical. Perhaps that is why the composer renounced the usual forms of contrast in this work, finding the no less ingenious solution of dividing all the performers into a 'chorus' containing the first trebles and first tenors and all the altos and basses, and a 'choral ensemble' consisting of the second trebles and second tenors. Chorus and choral ensemble perform independent versions of the musical interpretation of the psalm verses, with the whole thing merging into a substantial sound canvas of many colours.

And finally, in the 'Praise the Name of the Lord' no. 3 on a Serbian chant, written on the occasion of a visit to Moscow by the King of Serbia, the composer used the strophic form with varied refrain, employing an entirely traditional choral layout. The work's Serbian national colouring is highly conventional, and the ways of obtaining it are confined to certain devices, for instance, the flattened seventh in the major scale.

The last work included among the 'dozen' hymns for the All-Night Vigil of 1904 was the Great Doxology for small choir. In July 1905 the Moscow Committee for Sacred Censorship approved two more hymns for the All-Night Vigil – the Great Doxology no. 2 for large choir and the

Gradual antiphon in the fourth tone 'From my youth up' (*Ot yunosti moyeya*). In the service the latter hymn is sung before the reading of the Gospel. Perhaps in no single component of the All-Night Vigil did the composer invest so much expression or employ such a vivid contrast of imagery as in this miniature. The turmoil of the soul languishing under the burden of sin, the terrible predictions of the dreadful fate of those who do not believe in God – these themes in Fyodor Studit's work entailed the use of harsh dissonances, and sonority of the utmost loudness exploiting the lowest bass register (right down to low B flat) (Ex. 13.3).

In ancient times the All-Night Vigil ended with the first rays of dawn, associated with the image of God. 'Glory to Thee who hast shown us the Light' (*Slava Tebe, pokazavshemu nam Svet*), exclaims the priest, and the choir begins the angels' hymn sung at the birth of the Saviour. Thus begins the Great Doxology which is sung in the service before the dismissal – the benediction by the priest of worshippers about to leave the church. It is with this hymn that the sequence of choral movements Kastalsky wrote for the All-Night Vigil ends.

In the Great Doxology no. 1 for small choir the idea of harmonizing with a separate chord each note of the *znamenny* chant on which the work was based was taken further, and in this respect the composition retained the character typical in *znamenny* layout of uniformity through bewitching repetition. Notable neither for effects of choral sonority nor variety of means, this modest minor-key doxology is extremely characterful in mood thanks to its closeness to the structure of the original.

Very many of the choral devices found in Kastalsky's previous compositions were put into practice in his second festive major-key Great Doxology: interchanges between choral groups and brilliant 'orchestral' tuttis for the whole choir, superimposition of various melodic lines each associated with an independent text, 'pedals' in extreme voices, rapid choral reciting and sonorous fanfares in same-voice choral parts. The *znamenny* chant on which the work is based is capricious and abounds in syncopations and metrical disruptions, and demanded a broad spectrum of the most diverse resources in its arrangement. This work can with perfect justification be regarded as a model of how the composer interpreted a *znamenny* chant melody of very great length.

What, then, is the significance of Kastalsky's contribution to the legacy of Russian sacred music in the 1900s? Many of the compositions written at that time became adornments of the Synodal Choir repertoire, and their artistic merit is incontestable. Every one of these compositions marked a revolution in interpreting the traditional texts. The composer's contribution was particularly appreciable and impressive in arranging the hymns of the

All-Night Vigil, which he was in fact the first to reinterpret in the 'New Russian Style'. All the choral All-Night Vigils written by composers of the New Direction (Chesnokov, Grechaninov, Nikolsky, Rachmaninoff, Ippolitov-Ivanov and others) were written after 1905 and relied to some degree on Kastalsky's experience. A no less important undertaking in those years, however, was his reform of the tones, in which he touched the 'holy of holies' – the melodic models which give voice to a huge body of texts used in worship. Unfortunately, there proved to be no demand for Kastalsky's innovations, because it was a question of millions of singers relearning the majority of the characteristic melodies they had known since childhood – the tones. Kastalsky did not succeed in overcoming the stereotypes which in this field had become part of people's flesh and blood.

Notes

1. Letter from A.D. Kastal'sky to V.I. Rebikov, 14 December 1901. GTsMMK, fond 68, no. 275, p. 2v.
2. S.A. Shumsky: *Materialï dlya razrabotki temï 'Moskovskoye Sinodal'noye uchilishche i vozrozhdeniye natsional'noy dukhovnoy muzïki'* (Materials for developing the subject of the 'Moscow Synodal School and the revival of national sacred music'), in *RUSAM*, vol. 1, p. 618.
3. *Ibid.*, p. 628.
4. Kastalsky composed two versions of the Litany (cf. nos. 35 and 36 in List of published compositions and arrangements by Alexander Kastalsky elsewhere in this volume).
5. A.D. Kastal'sky: *Prakticheskoye rukovodstvo k vïrazitel'nomu peniyu stikhir pri pomoshchi razlichnïkh garmonizatsiy* (A practical guide to the expressive singing of stichera using varied harmonizations). Moscow, 1909, p. 3.
6. A.D. Kastal'sky: *O moyey muzïkal'noy kar'yere i moi mïsli o tserkovnoy muzïke.* (My career in music and my thoughts about church music), in *RUSAM*, vol. 1, p. 235.
7. Letter from A.D. Kastal'sky to Kh.N. Grozdov, 14 February 1902. GTsMMK, fond 370, no. 497, pp. 2-2v.
8. Letter from S.V. Smolensky to A.D. Kastal'sky, 31 March 1902, in *Muzïka* (Music), 1916, no. 248, p. 154.
9. Letter from Kh.N. Grozdov to A.D. Kastal'sky, March 1902. GTsMMK, fond 12, no. 794, p. 2.
10. Letter from Kh.N. Grozdov to A.D. Kastal'sky, 21 September 1902. GTsMMK, fond 12, no. 789, p. 4.
11. Letter from A.D. Kastal'sky to Kh.N. Grozdov, 21 May 1904. GTsMMK, fond 370, no. 500, pp. 1-1v.
12. Vasily Velikiy: *K Amfilokhiyu o Dukhe Svyatom* (St Basil the Great: To Amphilochius about the Holy Spirit), in Svyatitel' Vasily Velikiy: *Tvoreniya* (St Basil the Great: Works), vol. 1. St Petersburg, 1911, pp. 638-639.

Chapter 14

A Conservatoire for Sacred Music

'Our Kruglikov died yesterday. This morning our *Prokuror* Stepanov offered the directorship to me. I did not refuse, and indeed even thanked him', Kastalsky told Grozdov on 10 February 1910.[1] In Holy Week the order appointing Kastalsky director was signed in the Synod, and in April Alexander Dmitriyevich was already at work on the School syllabuses, which had been considered in a preliminary way by the Academic Committee in 1908 and sent back for revision. Kastalsky was very pleased about the latter, because it gave him the chance to edit them at his discretion. 'Although the work is agreeable in its rationality and usefulness, it is tedious, and I am afraid of again over-working until I get into a state of neurasthenia', he wrote to Grozdov on 28 April.[2]

The Synod's approval of the new syllabuses did not give rise to any problems: they were finally ratified and published in October 1910. More protracted and far less successful was the battle over the statutes and the rights of teachers and students, which took a great deal of Kastalsky's energy and time. Having the Synodal School confirmed as an institution of higher education was one of the composer's chief aims in the 1910s. In addition, he continued polishing and developing the syllabuses which had already been accepted, and deepening the conception of a folk-like artistic style. On 12 February 1913 Alexander Dmitriyevich wrote to Lipayev:

Since our music syllabuses have been augmented to conservatoire level in the theory of music (putting choral music, not orchestral music, at the centre of attention and also including the theory of church music), the idea has naturally arisen of seeking for graduates of the Synodal School the status of 'free artist' in their own specialism – that is in the field of church music, which is missing from the conservatoires. The syllabuses have been approved, and what is now under discussion is the statutes, as well as the rights and professional title [of graduates] and these questions must proceed through the legislative system, starting with the Synod. How the matter will be decided is not yet known, of course.[3]

The Synod's reaction to the petition from the Moscow Synod Office came only at the end of 1913, when Archbishop Sergy of Finland, the chairman of the Academic Committee at the Synod, and committee member Porfiry Mironositsky were sent to inspect the School. In May 1914 the church press carried the information that the Academic Committee had approved the new statutes and the Synod had despatched the matter to the Council of Ministers for approval and for the Emperor's ratification.[4]

The matter seemed to have been decided, and the musical community hailed the first 'institution of special higher education for church music' in Russia in the pages of newspapers and journals. According to the draft of the new statutes, the School was to comprise nine basic classes and one preparatory one. The basic classes were divided into church-music courses (years 1-5) where a musical and general education was provided for the young singers of the Synodal Choir, and senior classes in church music (years 6-9) where teachers of music for religious education institutions, church choirmasters and composers of church music were trained. The first class accepted children of Orthodox faith aged between eight and ten years, who could read Church Slavonic, write in Russian, count to one hundred and knew the basic prayers. Besides pupils at the School, young people who had completed not less than four years at a religious seminary or the entire course at a secular educational institution could now enter the senior classes.

On closer inspection it became clear that the syllabuses in theory of music at the 'Academy of Church Music' or the 'Sacred Music Conservatoire', as the School began to be known in the press, went beyond even those of the conservatoires to a certain extent. The critic V.V. Derzhanovsky wrote in the journal 'Music':

> Thus, a course in the history of folk music was introduced here several years ago, whereas at the conservatoires it is still just a proposal and will be implemented only once the new statutes have been ratified. The theory of composition (counterpoint, fugue, form, instrumentation) is studied to the same extent as at the conservatoires. But there is no class in practical and free composition. Subsidiary piano is compulsory for 9 years, not 5, plus violin and cello.[5]

The same issue of the journal carried a comparative table of the musical and general educational subjects studied at the conservatoire and at the Synodal School, which demonstrated the quantitative advantages of the School's syllabuses.[6] On the one hand, this was determined by the fact that the course lasted not seven years, as at the conservatoire, but nine (or ten with the preparatory year). On the other hand, the greater number of subjects studied could be explained also by the church emphasis of the School, which dictated some features of its syllabuses. Scripture, Russian, mathematics, geometry, general history and Russian history, the history of the arts, and aesthetics were studied at both institutions. But at the Synodal School, with its academic programme directed towards the seminary, theology, Church Slavonic, the history of Russian literature, algebra and natural history were studied besides. (Unlike the seminary, certain theological subjects and ancient languages were absent.) Among the musical subjects taught both at the conservatoire and at the School were elementary theory of music, harmony, *solfeggio*, strict and free counterpoint, musical forms, piano, choral singing, the orchestra class, instrumentation, the history of music, the history of church music and palaeography. At the Synodal School, however, some of the subjects mentioned were studied for more years and for a larger number of hours in the week. Thus, at the conservatoire *solfeggio* was studied for two years, whereas at the School it was studied for six years.

The Synodal School also offered some subjects not open to theory students at the conservatoire. They were: the forms of church music, violin, cello, church music, singing methods, voice production, conducting, the practice of music in Orthodox worship (*ustavnoye peniye*) and folk music.

The conservatoire had only one subject not taught at the School – free composition. It was precisely the desire to study composition and obtain the title of free artist which occasionally prompted former students of the Synodal School to go on to the conservatoire. After their training at the School, however, the conservatoire's demands in music-theory subjects and especially in *solfeggio* seemed to them very simplified. Sergey Vasilenko, a professor at the Moscow Conservatoire, later recalled:

> The Moscow Synodal School was one of the most important institutions of musical culture in Russia. They hunted everywhere for boys with a good ear and musical ability, and gave them an excellent general and specialized education at the School. The best Conservatoire teachers taught at the School. I immediately recognized former Synodal School pupils among new students who came to me because they were so well trained in elementary theory, *solfeggio* and harmony.[7]

One of the central courses at the Synodal School in the 1910s was the course in the Theory of Music, which was taught systematically from the second to the ninth class. It began with Elementary Theory (years 2-3) and then moved on to Harmony (years 4-6). In the seventh year Polyphony in

Strict Style began, and the first attempts were made to set chants from the *Obikhod* polyphonically in strict style. The eighth year involved Polyphony in Free Style and contrapuntal arrangements of church chants and folksongs. Fugues by Bach, Handel, Schumann, Mozart etc. were recommended as supreme models.

The course in Musical Forms, devised entirely by Kastalsky, was an independent subject. It began in the seventh year and lasted for three years. A peculiarity of it was that the forms of west European music traditionally studied were projected on to the forms of Russian church hymns. For instance, when students studied the subjects of 'phrase' and 'sentence', they had to analyse litanies, 'Holy God' (*Svyatïy Bozhe*) and other hymns of the simplest kind structurally. Simple binary form was studied by analysing Cherubic Hymns, communion verses, 'We hymn Thee' (*Tebe poyem*) and so on. In the ninth year the forms of Russian church hymns without analogies in classical music were examined, for example, great *znamenny* chant, and also the All-Night Vigil and the Liturgy as cycles of music for worship. The course in musical forms also included lessons in instrumentation.

Solfeggio was also regarded at the School as one of the fundamental subjects. Judging from the 1910 syllabuses, it began in the preparatory class and was studied continuously until the pupil transferred to the choirmasters' department, that is until the seventh class, or until his voice broke. The level at which this subject was taught can be illustrated by the fact that in the fourth year children performed at sight solo numbers and choral parts from masses and oratorios. In the sixth year, when reading music was no longer a problem, the tuition concentrated on writing dictation in harmony (using Bach chorales, etc. as examples).

Alongside Theory of Music and *Solfeggio*, one of the central courses was that in Church Music and its History. The subject of Church Music began in the preparatory class and ended in the seventh class. The students were made familiar with the ancient and later church chants (most of which had to be learned by heart), the theory of the chants was explained – features of their melodic character, rhythm and formal structure. The seventh class was devoted entirely to assimilating the language of the ancient Russian hook signs in its simple forms. The course in History of Church Music was intended to last two years. In the eighth year ancient and medieval monodic cultures were studied, and then the history of ancient Russian music and complex forms of Russian notation (*demestvenny* polyphony), and also Russian service books (palaeography of church music). And, lastly, the syllabus for the ninth year was devoted to the 'harmonic' period in the history of Orthodox church music right up to the most recent period. In the same course the historiography of Russian church music (works by Razumovsky, Smolensky, Metallov, Voznesensky, Preobrazhensky, etc.) was studied. The assimilation of the palaeography and semiography of church music also continued; in the ninth year Russian systems of notation were studied in comparison with the Byzantine ones. In its general features, the syllabus for church music and church music history adopted in 1910 was identical with that of 1897. As a result of the growth of knowledge in medieval studies, however, several new topics – for example, that of the comparative investigation of Russian and Byzantine notational systems – emerged.

As a supplement to the course in the History of Church Music, a new course in the Practice of Music in Orthodox Worship (*ustavnoye peniye*) devoted to the study of contemporary service books and the musical aspect of church services was introduced in the ninth year. The new course provided students with practical, theoretical and historical knowledge, but its objective was not limited to that. As was stated in the syllabus:

> Such comprehensive study of Russian church music not only educates new generations of singers, conductors, teachers and composers in the spirit of truly national (*narodnaya*) church music, its artistic, national and religious-ecclesiastical beauty and virtue, but will also elevate this sphere in the eyes of Russian society to its proper level and exert a broad and immensely fruitful influence on Russian Orthodox society as regards its aesthetic development, its religious and national education in the spirit of the church and the nation.[8]

A course in Folk Music also appeared in the syllabus for the ninth year of study. Generally speaking, attention was given to folksong – 'the sister of *znamenny* chant' – in the School when dealing with the most varied subjects: *Solfeggio*, Theory, Harmony, Counterpoint and so on. In the ninth year all the information about folksong obtained earlier was brought into a single system with its core in the work done by the Russian school of ethnography over the previous thirty years. Materials by Yuly Melgunov, Alexander Maslov, Vasily Prokunin, Yevgeniya Linyova, Alexander Famintsïn, Nikolay Privalov, Pyotr Sokalsky, Vyacheslav Petr etc. were used in teaching the course.

Special attention was paid to the common elements shared by folksong and church chants, which were examined on two levels – the text and the music. Attention was paid to the following common aspects of textual organization: the construction of the text in half-verses (that is, its strophic nature); the addition of 'decorative' words – 'melodic decoration' (*anenayki*) in chants and 'okh', etc. in songs; and the replacing of semi-vowels by vowels (*razdel'norechiye* or *khomoniya*) (in chants) and pleophony (full vocalism) (in songs). As regards the music, certain devices of formal construction were regarded as shared features. For example, incipits and refrains were revealed in both song and chant; the natures of *fitï* and *litsa* in the *Obikhod* and the long musical phrases to one syllable in the protracted (*protyazhnaya*) song showed similarities; in both song and chant melodic turns of phrases (*popevki*) were recorded as developing when repeated (that is, the device of melodic variation), etc. Besides, common elements were discovered in modal and metro-rhythmical organization, similar contours in melodic turns of phrase, in some cases an analogous manner of embellishment in performance (*podkhvatï, podgoloski, vavilonï*) and so on. The presence of common features in both the 'physical' properties and the conceptual attributes of folksong and chant was one of the main arguments for introducing this subject into the curriculum at the Synodal School.

Other courses mainly devoted to the study of the church music repertoire were also linked in the closest possible way with the course on Church Music and its History. For example, the course in Conducting and Simultaneous Playing (years 5-9), which originated in the old course in Simultaneous Playing in String Quartets and Directing Them. In the revised course, apart from sacred choral music, compositions from the chamber repertoire were studied, and the skills of directing choral and chamber compositions were acquired.

The course in Reading a Choral Score was concerned with mastering the repertoire of church music at the piano; it comprised two parts: the Study of a Choral Score (years 4-5) and Church Music Literature (years 6-9). Students had to absorb a significantly wider repertoire of church music, including the most recent compositions. The examples selected for study were designed to educate the student in the spirit of the new national direction.

Let us return to the course in Church Music Literature. If the names of the composers mentioned in it are distributed in accordance with the number of choral works studied, the following list is obtained: Kastalsky (44 choral items), Ippolitov-Ivanov (six choral items, Liturgy, All-Night Vigil), Grechaninov (four choral items, Liturgy no. 2, All-Night Vigil), Tchaikovsky (Liturgy, All-Night Vigil), Arkhangelsky (four choral items, Liturgy for the Dead), Rachmaninoff (Liturgy), Klenovsky ('Georgian Liturgy'), Panchenko (Liturgy), Pavel Chesnokov (16 choral items), Smolensky (Easter stichera), Bortnyansky (seven choral items), Victor Kalinnikov (five choral items), Rimsky-Korsakov (four choral items), Kopïlov (four choral items), Lvov (three choral items), Azeyev (three choral items), Lvovsky (three choral items), Balakirev (two choral items),

Glinka, Turchaninov, Poluektov, Komarov, Muzïchesku, Sakhnovsky and Arensky (one choral item each). It is easy to see that the syllabus for this course relied heavily on the repertoire performed by the Synodal Choir.

The difference between this list and the list of works recommended for study in the 1897 syllabuses is striking: the 'newest' composers there were Lomakin, Lvovsky and Arkhangelsky, with only Glinka from among the classics; preference was given to Bortnyansky, Lvov etc. In the 1910 syllabuses their works were considered rather as historical examples. The few classics of the national school – Glinka, Rimsky-Korsakov and Balakirev, who were associated with the Court Kapella, as well as other representatives of that institution – Turchaninov, Kopïlov, Azeyev and Arensky, appear to have been included for the sake of offering a rounded picture. The same may also be said of the immediate predecessors of the New Direction – Lvovsky, Poluektov and Komarov. But composers of the 'Newest Direction', connected in some way with the Synodal School, were well and truly in the lead; Panchenko from St Petersburg who had no connection with the School came into this group. From all the evidence, the works of Arkhangelsky, another figure from St Petersburg, were also prized; though he had no leanings towards the 'Russian' school, he was famed for his skill as a conductor. And it was natural that the two large cycles and some separate choral pieces by Tchaikovsky should be on the list of compositions studied. In Kastalsky's time, when the New Direction had assumed its definitive shape, Tchaikovsky was proclaimed its founder. Thus, in 1911, on the threshold of the Synodal Choir's foreign tour, Kastalsky gave the organizers of the Warsaw concerts the following information for inclusion in the programme booklet:

There are no brochures about the activities of the Synodal Choir over the last 15 years (the most interesting period), but one may say in general terms that the choir, headed by Orlov who made it famous, having begun by popularizing Tchaikovsky as a composer of church music, stood the whole time in the forefront of the Newest Direction (the national-ecclesiastical one) which was just beginning in the art of church music, for from its womb emerged Kastalsky, and Chesnokov, and Shvedov, and Tolstyakov. (Kastalsky came to the Synodal School at a tangent, though, having been engaged to teach there.) Right up to his death Tchaikovsky followed the activities of the Synodal School and Choir with the greatest interest and was a member of the [Supervisory] Council attached to the School. Grechaninov, Ippolitov-Ivanov and Kalinnikov all placed their finest inspirations at the disposal of the Synodal Choir. Developing Historical Concerts in this field was another achievement of the Synodal Choir and its directors (starting with Smolensky). Danilin, the present choirmaster, is also a former pupil of the Synodal School and a free artist of the Philharmonic School. Of the four choirmasters at the Court Kapella, two are former students of the Synodal School. The most recent outstanding new work in our literature, Rachmaninoff's Liturgy op. 31 (which is not yet in print), has already been performed this season – no less than five times – by the Synodal Choir. The composer sent the manuscript directly to the Synodal Choir to be performed, and he has also made them a gift of the autograph. In short, all that is outstanding and shows talent (but is not ugly) finds an echo first and foremost in the Synodal Choir.[9]

Thus, during those years everything that was new, 'outstanding and showed talent', mainly from Moscow, was indeed studied at the School and performed by the Choir. It remains to add the following to what has already been said about the choice of works for the course in sacred music literature. Sacred works by Russian composers were only one half of the syllabus; the other half was made up of sacred choral works by west European composers. For example, in the seventh year compositions by Josquin des Pres, Orlando Lassus and Palestrina were studied; in the eighth year choral fugues and motets by Bach; and in the ninth year vocal-orchestral scores by Haydn and Mozart. It is essential to note that the course syllabus was closely co-ordinated with the syllabuses in Harmony and Polyphony. And one final addition: the course was devised by Kastalsky.

The institution's complex curriculum required a good command of instruments, the piano in particular, and increased attention was given to studying it in the School. Students had piano lessons throughout all their years of study, and especially gifted ones (such as Golovanov and the two Shvedov brothers) were excellent pianists on completion of the course. At the final examination preludes and fugues by Bach, sonatas by Beethoven and Schubert, pieces by Chopin, Rachmaninoff and so on were played. (The syllabuses for 1897 envisaged Inventions by Bach and 'accessible' movements from sonatas by Haydn, Mozart and Beethoven being performed at the final examination.) The requirements for playing the violin were also significantly increased by comparison with the old syllabuses.

Perhaps the most interesting of the innovations made in the 1910 syllabuses was the course in the History of the Arts, a subject already introduced at the Conservatoire by that time. At the Synodal School the subject was wholly subordinated to revealing the significance of Russian art, of which Orthodox church music formed a part. Taken in the eighth and ninth years, the course opened with lectures on ancient civilizations and ended with the work of Monet, Böcklin and Rodin. But, naturally, the main accent was placed on church art and Russian church art first and foremost. The syllabus even envisaged the students drawing architectural forms and ornaments typical of Russia and going on excursions round Moscow with visits to picture galleries. Because there was no textbook on the history of the arts with an emphasis on Russian church art, the course compilers devised a very detailed synopsis which was included in the text of the syllabuses.

In concluding this review of the 1910 syllabuses of the Synodal School, one would like to give some attention to one further subject – that of Methods of Singing in Choir and School (in the Context of the Tasks of Musical Education as a Whole) which though it was not new had been completely rethought. In 1897 this course had been a section of the discipline of Pedagogy and had included wholly traditional topics linked with methods of teaching the fundamental aspects of music. According to the 1910 syllabuses, the students were offered the chance of hearing lectures on the following subjects: 'Music Criticism and the Essence of the Aesthetics of Music', 'Art for Art's Sake', 'Hanslick and his Passions', 'The Tasks and Essence of Art in General and Music in Particular (Tolstoy, Spencer etc.)', 'The Connection with Science', 'Good and Bad Music', 'Folk Music', 'The Musical Gifts of the Russian People', 'The National Direction of the Art of Music in Russia', 'Musical Ethnography' and 'Local Colour'.

As one reads the text of the 1910 syllabus, it quickly becomes evident that the approaches to individual subjects, as well as the ideas set out in the introductions to them, converge round the single theme of 'Russian style', which so enthused Kastalsky in those years. In 1913 he decided to formulate his individual observations into a special course. In several articles accompanying the campaign which unfolded in late 1913 and early 1914 for the ratification of the statutes of the Synodal School,[10] two new courses not indicated earlier in the syllabuses are named: Forms in Church Music, and Church Style; both had been devised by Kastalsky and were intended for the ninth year. 'The musical forms used in our church practice are so original in general by comparison with the widely-known forms studied in conservatoire theory classes that I thought it better to place these forms separately in a section of their own', Kastalsky wrote in his article 'From my reminiscences of recent years' about the course in Forms in Church Music, citing the syllabus for the course.[11] The composer elucidated the aims of the other new subject later on:

In my opinion, the special subject of Church Style should fill an important gap in the education of a church music artist. In our keenness to give young people an education equivalent to the conservatoire one, we have completely lost sight of the fact that an artist whom we have trained in technique and form does not hold firm views on the very essence of church music. While he knows what must be sung in accordance with the regulations and what can be sung without disgracing oneself, and while he knows the new repertoire, he is in the last resort merely a conductor on the *kliros*, who can easily perform everything he considers beautiful and striking. We have all got used to a musical jumble in concert programmes. On the *kliros* this *vinaigrette* is supplemented by adding our native music in tones on top of everything else. But meanwhile the actual definition of church style and its peculiarities in our church, establishing the boundary line between it and concert-hall style, clarifying its renunciation of amusement, with which in Russia the revelation of other genres of art is usually linked – all that will give the young artist a firm foundation for his career. In that case the symbolism and images of the rituals of worship, the burning of the lamps, the smoke of incense, the pealing of bells, the actual structure of the churches and so on – all that will pass before him in a special light. Questions about the different moods of church music and whether the ordinary repertoire of church choir music is appropriate for a house of worship; questions will be raised about nationality in our church art and purging it of currents from outside; and lastly about the boundaries of artistic freedom in choosing hymns for use in church regardless of the tastes of worshippers... The need to find answers to such questions is in my opinion urgent.[12]

As we examine the syllabuses of the Synodal School in the 1910s, there is one question which arises as a matter of course: to what extent did the level of demands made of students differ from that in the church choirmasters' classes at the Court Kapella, the oldest Russian educational institution in music, which had been headed by famous composers and conductors?

Information about the subjects studied at the Kapella may be found in the revised syllabuses ratified by the Emperor on 4 October 1908.[13] According to that document, students received eight years of training in the Kapella's choirmasters' classes. (The course at the Synodal School consisted of one preparatory class and nine basic classes.)

Students at the Kapella remained in the preparatory class for the first four years, studying Elementary Theory of Music, *Solfeggio*, Church Music, Piano and Violin. Unfortunately, the syllabuses do not show for how many years students studied these subjects or how many lessons per week were allocated to each subject.

The senior years at the Kapella comprised three special classes. The first class took two years; students who passed the examination obtained a Diploma of the Third Level and the title 'Assistant Church Choirmaster'. They studied: Harmony (first year), Reading of Choral Scores (at the Piano) (second year), *Solfeggio* (first and second years), Orthodox Church Music (first and second years), Piano (first and second years), Violin (first and second years). The second class took one year; those who passed the examination obtained a Diploma of the Second Level and the title 'Church Choirmaster'. There they studied: Counterpoint, Church Music, Reading Choral Scores, History of Church Music, Piano and Violin. The third class took one year; those completing it obtained a Diploma of the First Level and the title 'Teacher of Church Music and Music Theory'. The class involved the following subjects: Fugue, Musical General Knowledge (*entsiklopediya*), History of Music, Methods of Teaching Singing in Schools, Voice Production, Piano and Violin.

As we can see, a number of fundamental subjects existed in common at the Kapella and at the Synodal School; it is obvious that the demands made in a number of them were also similar (this relates mainly to music theory disciplines). The list of subjects at the Synodal School is, however, longer; unlike the School, the Kapella lacked Folk Music, the Practice of Music in Orthodox Worship, Cello, History of the Arts, Voice Production for new recruits and graduating students, Palaeography and Hook Notation. A large number of courses – Harmony, History of Church Music, Reading Choral Scores, Conducting, History of Music, Musical Forms – were more wide-ranging at the School. The study of certain subjects began earlier at the School than at the Kapella – Harmony, Conducting, Score-Reading. In the final examinations the demands in Violin, Piano, Reading Choral Scores, History of Church Music, History of Music, Musical Forms, etc. were appreciably lower at the Kapella than at the Synodal School. Had a graduate of the Kapella had to sit the examination in these subjects at the Synodal School, it would probably have caused him great difficulties.

The differences between the syllabuses were also determined by the differences between the practice of worship in the churches where the Synodal Choir and the Court Kapella sang, that is the Cathedral of the Dormition in the Kremlin and the court churches respectively. In a number of courses at the Kapella (Church Music, Reading Choral Scores, and even Piano), court chant was studied intensively. That also determined the choice of composers of hymns studied. Here, by way of example, is a list of the composers of hymns studied on the course in Reading Choral Scores in the special classes at the Kapella: Bortnyansky (Great Kanon, 13 choral items, six concertos), Lvov (nine choral items, two concertos), Kastalsky (11 choral items), Turchaninov (nine choral items), Tchaikovsky (six choral items), Rimsky-Korsakov and Grechaninov (four choral items each), Bakhmetev, Alexander and Pavel Chesnokov (three choral items each), Glinka, Balakirev, Ippolitov-Ivanov, Arkhangelsky, Sheremetev, Solovyov (two choral items each), Lvovsky, Arensky, Azeyev, Bogdanov, Noskov (one choral item each) and Smolensky (Easter stichera). As we can see, this list includes, alongside recognized authorities at the Kapella whose works formed the basis of its repertoire, the names of a whole series of Moscow 'stars' representing the New Direction.[14]

A secular tendency is evident in the training of the graduating third class at the Kapella who obtained the diploma of Teacher of Singing: the syllabus contained not a single purely church subject, whereas at the Synodal School it was upon the graduating class that the main burden of preparing 'the free artist in the field of church music' fell. The syllabuses of the Synodal School are distinguished generally by far greater purposefulness, because a goal had been set – to train a specialist who had at his disposal not just a superb general education and a special musical training but also a special vision of national style in all spheres of artistic endeavour. A graduate of the Synodal School had been trained to work with the heritage of church music as both composer and scholar, with the latter area developed in conjunction with the presence at the Synodal School of a unique archive.

The terseness of the Kapella's syllabuses unfortunately precludes extended comparison of its courses with those of the Synodal School, and the comments made here are thus only of the most general character.

What was the outcome of the campaign, embarked on with such vigour in 1913, to have the statutes of the Synodal School approved as an institution of higher education?

As the study of Holy Synod documents shows, the new statutes were scrutinized for about 18 months by government agencies starting in 1914, and gained the positive support of the Minister of War, the Ministers of Finance, Education, Justice, and Internal Affairs and of the State Controller and Secretary. The administrative head of His Imperial Majesty's Private Chancery also appended his observations. Finally approved by the Holy Synod, the draft statutes and staffing level were due to be sent to the legislative bodies; on 5 August 1916, however, a letter arrived from Filipp Stepanov, the *Prokuror* of the Moscow Synod Office, in which he criticized the documents prepared for ratification and proposed a draft of the statutes, staffing levels and a regulation about the Synodal School which he had devised personally. Scrutiny of the *Prokuror*'s memorandum occupied some further time, and it was only at the end of November 1916 that the Academic Committee of the Synod came to a decision to send the draft to the Council of Ministers for onward despatch to the legislative bodies and ratification by the Emperor. The statutes and staffing levels were not destined to proceed through all the remaining stages because of the revolution which broke out in February 1917.

It thus came about that several generations of Synodal School graduates ended up without legislative approval for their title of free artist. Officially the School did not change into an institution of higher education.[15] In its final years it remained nevertheless one of the best music schools in Russia. Those seven years were unique: from 1910 to 1917 the Synodal School was the first and last institution of higher education in music in Russian history to serve so purposefully the aim of turning the national Orthodox 'Russian idea' into reality.

Notes

1. Letter from A.D. Kastal'sky to Kh.N. Grozdov of 19 February 1910. GTsMMK, fond 370, no. 506, p. 1.
2. Letter from A.D. Kastal'sky to Kh.N. Grozdov of 28 April 1910. GTsMMK, fond 370, no. 507, pp. 1v-2.
3. Letter from A.D. Kastal'sky to I.V. Lipayev of 12 February 1913. RGALI, fond 795, opis' 1, no. 16, pp. 2-2v.
4. *Pribavleniye k 'Tserkovnïm vedomostyam'* (Supplement to 'Church Bulletin'), 1914, no. 22, columns 1007-1009.
5. V. Ivanov (V.V. Derzhanovsky): *Preobrazovaniye Sinodal'nogo uchilishcha* (The transformation of the Synodal School), in *Muzïka* (Music), 1914, no. 182, pp. 373-374.
6. *Sravnitel'naya tablitsa obshcheobrazovatel'nïkh i muzikal'nïkh predmetov po spetsial'nosti teorii muziki konservatoriy i Moskovskogo Sinodal'nogo uchilishcha* (A comparative table of the general educational and musical subjects in the specialty of music theory studied at the conservatoires and at the Synodal School), in *Muzïka* (Music), 1914, no. 182, pp. 384-385.
7. S.N. Vasilenko: *Stranitsï vospominaniy* (Pages of reminiscence). Moscow, Leningrad, 1948, p. 105.
8. *Programmï muzïkal'nïkh predmetov i istorii iskusstv Moskovskogo Sinodal'nogo uchilishcha tserkovnogo peniya. (V ob'yome kursa vïsshego muzïkal'no-uchebnogo zavedeniya)* (Syllabuses for musical subjects and the history of the arts at the Moscow Synodal School of Church Music. (Corresponding to a course at a higher education institution in music).) Moscow, 1910, p. 8. This document is republished in the section 'Syllabuses and statutes' in vol. 2, book 2 of *RUSAM*.
9. Letter from A.D. Kastal'sky to A.V. Zatayevich of 6 March 1911. GTsMMK, fond 5, no. 300, pp. 1-2.
10. A collection of articles, comments and reviews relating to the Synodal School and Choir covering the years from 1840 to 1918 may be found in the section 'The Periodical Press' in vol. 2, book 2 of *RUSAM*.
11. *RUSAM*, vol. 1, p. 252.
12. *Ibid.*, p. 253.
13. *Polozheniye o regentskikh klassakh Pridvornoy pevcheskoy kapellï i ikh muzïkal'naya programma* (Resolution concerning church choirmasters' classes at the Court Kapella and their music syllabus). St Petersburg, 1911. Cf. the comments made upon publication of these syllabuses in the periodical press: N.K.: *Regentskoye obrazovaniye* (Educating church choirmasters), in *Khorovoye i regentskoye delo* (Choral and Church Choirmaster Matters), 1911, nos. 3-5; *Novoye polozheniye o regentskikh klassakh Pridvornoy pevcheskoy kapellï i otklik 'pochemu?'* (The new resolution concerning church choirmasters' classes at the Court Kapella and the comment 'why?'), in

Khorovoye i regentskoye delo, 1911, no. 8.

14. From 1901 the Kapella also underwent a 'Muscovite' influence, the beginning of which was represented by the transfer there as manager (*upravlyayushchiy*) of Stepan Smolensky. In Smolensky's wake a whole galaxy of former pupils and teachers from the Synodal School appeared at the Kapella. Thus, Nikolay Klenovsky, who had worked at the Synodal School in the 1893-94 academic year, was inspector at the Kapella in 1902 and 1903, and from 1903 to 1906 was its assistant director. Pavel Tolstyakov, Alexander Chesnokov, Mikhail Klimov and Antonin Preobrazhensky were employed at the Kapella in those years in various capacities.

15. It is interesting that during the Soviet period certificates issued on graduation from the Synodal School were treated equally with diplomas from an institution of higher education.

1. Archpriest D.I. Kastalsky, the composer's father. Moscow, second half of the 1870s

2. O.S. Kastalskaya, the composer's mother. Moscow, 1860s

3. Sasha Kastalsky (Alexander) with his sister Katya, Moscow. first half of the 1860s

4. A.D. Kastalsky with his wife Natalia. Late 1880s or early 1890s

5. Teachers at the Synodal School, Seated: D.I. Kokorin (1), A.V. Preobrazhensky (2), S.V. Smolensky (3), A.K. Smirnov (4), V.S. Orlov (6), Standing: D.G. Grigoryev (2), A.D. Kastalsky (4), Yu.A. Lazarev (6). Moscow, late 1890s

6. A.D. Kastalsky. Moscow, early 1900s

7. A performance of Kastalsky's *Play of the Furnace* by the Synodal Choir in the hall of the Synodal School. Moscow, 10 April 1909

8. A.D. Kastalsky, F.P. Stepanov, N.M. Danilin in the Augusteo concert hall. Rome, 1911

9 A.D. Kastalsky and the teacher N.N. Belkin (to the left of Kastalsky) with third-year students of the Moscow People's Choir Academy. Moscow, 1923

Chapter 15

At the Height of his Fame

The third period of Kastalsky's career as a composer (1910-17) was symbolized by his directorship of the Synodal School. It goes without saying that his activities as director were not confined to editing syllabuses and gaining approval for statutes. Besides a multitude of administrative and pedagogical duties directly connected with the School, it fell to the director to chair the Supervisory Council, and during the 1910s many schemes connected with the censorship of sacred music, with education in church music, with putting church choirs in order and also with cultivating the legacy of Russian church music were evolved there. One of the projects was called 'Restoring the church music of the past' (*K vosstanovleniyu tserkovnoy starini*). Its author, the scholar of the Middle Ages Dimitry Allemanov, called on the Supervisory Council to organize further research on the legacy of manuscripts from the period before the seventeenth century, to galvanize the collecting of church music manuscripts in the Synodal School, draw together there copies of the most ancient Russian and Byzantine monuments held in other archives, and list the locations of manuscript books which for some reason could not be given to the Synodal School. Not wishing to delay the implementation of these proposals, the Supervisory Council commissioned Metallov to compile a report to the Synod with a request that it give an order to churches and monasteries to send church music manuscripts to the Synodal School. The request was edited by Kastalsky and sent to the Synod, which on 15 March 1913 published an order enjoining co-operation with the Moscow Synodal School. Russian churches and monasteries again started sending ancient manuscripts to the Synodal School, and as a result of this campaign the School archive was increased by approximately 65 church music manuscripts. Less successful, unfortunately, was Kastalsky's attempt undertaken in 1912 to get hold of copies preserved at the St Petersburg Society for Literature and Ancient Literary Texts (OLDP) of Greek music manuscripts made by Smolensky's expedition of 1906. No resources could be found to pay for the recopying, and after the revolution the collection disappeared without trace.

Publishing the 'Proceedings of the Supervisory Council of the Synodal School of Church Music' was also among the Council's projects. According to the plan approved by the Synod in July 1915, the 'Proceedings' were to consist of two sections – official and non-official. It was intended that regulations and instructions from the Synod and the government concerning church music should be published in the first section, as well as extracts from the minutes of meetings of the Supervisory Council; the material in the second section was to be set out under the following headings: history, theory, palaeography, and the forms of music for worship. Treatises and articles about the character, aesthetics, styles of music for worship and the fundamentals of liturgical studies were to be included there.[1] This scheme too, however, was never realized because of wartime financial difficulties.

Kastalsky was most active in discussing and realizing plans related to the School archive, although he left the scholarly development of questions in medieval studies to colleagues, concentrating his own attention during the 1910s on studying folksong. As far as one can judge from his correspondence, in 1910 the composer was fascinated by the idea of folk instrumentation. Thus, on 15 September 1910 Kastalsky wrote to the folklorist Nikolay Privalov in St Petersburg:

> In the midst of the usual pre-term and start-of-term hurly-burly, I've only managed to get to know your fine work in the field of folk instrumentation in fits and starts. To me your works, particularly in their full extent, are of great interest, because I have long cherished the notion of establishing (if only for myself) precise foundations for the Russian folk melodic lines with their harmony as well as the manner of instrumenting them. And in that department your name unquestionably carries immense authority, as in your researches the usual musician's fumbling progress with the question of national identity in the realm of music falls away.[2]

News that the composer had begun writing a textbook on the melody and harmony of folk music dates from March 1914. As Kastalsky recalled three years later:

> In 1914 before the war started I was successfully engaged among other things in systematizing the huge volume of material which had passed through my hands in the realm of Russian folk music. The material on harmony proved to be the most interesting of all. It had been collected over about twenty years. The beginning and the groundwork of it were the variants in the collections by Melgunov and Palchikov, then the phonograph recordings of Linyova, Listopadov and others which, unfortunately, were published in small quantities by comparison with the material actually collected and transcribed. On the

basis of this material, I think, one will be able to establish without error firm foundations for harmony in the Russian folk style, citing these foundations directly in parallel with the paragraphs which are generally accepted in harmony textbooks: starting with the combination of triads, their inversions, sevenths and ninths of all kinds, and ending with modulations and unusual progressions. But I shall have to renounce continuous academic four-part writing. An extended section on cadences, original use of passing and auxiliary notes and anticipations but a little developed section on suspensions, combined apparently with syncopations. To complete this work, however, I shall need quite a lot of time free from 'immediate work commitments', for which there is little hope at present... As it is, people express surprise to me that I contrive to work simultaneously on several fronts – both in free composition and in the bustle of a job. Need teaches many things.[3]

Intensive work on the textbook continued in 1915 too. On 23 June the composer wrote to Grozdov: 'Once again I'm sitting with my song notebooks, of course... it's one thing to pick out strikingly vivid devices, but quite another to extract rules from them'.[4] Work on folk modulation went on until the end of the year. In 1916 Kastalsky's researches in the field of folklore came to a halt because of the difficulties being experienced at that time by the School.

Another important area in which Alexander Dmitriyevich was active during the 1910s was editing the *Obikhod* of the Synodal Choir, which was meant not just to sum up the new repertoire of the era of reform but to become the Moscow alternative to the St Petersburg court *Obikhod*. In 1912 the first part of the *Obikhod* of the Synodal Choir – the All-Night Vigil – edited by Kastalsky was published in Moscow; in 1914 the second part came out – the Liturgy, the Episcopal Liturgy, the prayer services (*molebni*), memorial service, funeral service, the festive prokeimena and antiphons. Both collections, published at the expense of the Supervisory Council, were in great demand on the *kliroses*, but because of historical circumstances did not achieve the dissemination and appreciation that was their due.

One should note that the prestige of the Synodal Choir and School of Church Music in the 1910s, when they had become universally recognized as the bearers of new ideas in church music, was high not only in Russia but also abroad – greatly assisted by the concerts given by the Synodal Choir which was in magnificent form at that time. It seems that the blossoming of the choir's art is connected with the arrival as its conductor of Danilin, one of the most talented graduates of the Synodal School, as well as with the general raising of the level of teaching at the School during those years.

The first famous concerts of the Synodal Choir conducted by Danilin were associated with Rachmaninoff's Liturgy of St John Chrysostom, which was completed in the summer of 1910. As we know, while writing this work the composer turned to Kastalsky for advice, as his letters to Moscow from Ivanovka testify.[5] In one of them Rachmaninoff wrote to his older colleague: 'I have decided to disturb you in particular, because I have wholehearted faith in you and I am going to try to take the same path as you, a path which is yours alone'.[6]

The première of the Liturgy was given by the Synodal Choir in the hall of the Synodal School on 25 November 1910; the performance was repeated in the Great Hall of the Conservatoire on 16 and 21 December. The choir made a guest appearance in St Petersburg on 10 March 1911 when six numbers from Rachmaninoff's Liturgy were performed in the first half of a concert in the Hall of the Assembly of the Nobility, with selected choral pieces by Kastalsky in the second half. (Concerts with the same programme were given in Kursk on 15 March and Moscow on 27 March.) The Muscovites wanted to display the best of what had come into being in their city over recent years. The effect was unforeseen: listeners involuntarily compared the works of the two leading lights and, to judge by what appeared in the press, preferred Kastalsky. The music of Rachmaninoff's fine but somewhat eclectic composition seemed cold and brainspun in the opinion of many reviewers in comparison with the uniform style of Kastalsky's choral works.[7] The contrast between the sacred music of Kastalsky and Rachmaninoff was a subject which interested not only listeners but the 'Synodal' people themselves too. They were proud of Rachmaninoff at the Synodal School and regarded him as one of their own, since he had been a pupil of Smolensky, to whom he was to dedicate his brilliant All-Night Vigil. But they rated Kastalsky higher as a composer of sacred music, considering him to be the greater master of writing for choir and a finer stylist in using ancient Russian colouring. In the archive of the chorusmaster of the Bolshoy Theatre Sergey Shumsky, a former Synodal student, we find not only an analysis of Kastalsky's 'Bless the Lord, O my soul' (*Blagoslovi, dushe moya, Gospoda*) but also a comparison with the equivalent number in Rachmaninoff's All-Night Vigil where the author finds a series of technical errors.[8] That view was consistent with the opinion of many musicians in the Synodal School circle.

Leaving the elucidation of that question to one side, we should note that the most outstanding concerts of the Synodal Choir in the final years of its existence were connected with the works of precisely these two composers. Five brilliant performances in succession by the Synodal Choir (10, 12, 27 March and 3 and 9 April 1915) of Rachmaninoff's All-Night Vigil stayed particularly in listeners' memories, as did similar performances of selected numbers from Kastalsky's Memorial Service which were given at a concert of his works on 6 April 1916, and also at one of the final appearances in the history of the Synodal Choir on 27 May 1917. So too did a unique concert, apparently the last one of compositions by Kastalsky and Rachmaninoff which took place at the end of 1922 when the Synodal Choir had already ceased to exist. This was a performance by the Choir of the Bolshoy Theatre (made up of eighty singers), in which some former Synodal Choir members sang, under the direction of Danilin in the Church of Christ the Saviour.[9]

It seems probable that Rachmaninoff himself recognized that Kastalsky occupied the first place in the field of sacred music; he looked on Kastalsky as a senior colleague and teacher, always admiring his compositions. Kastalsky reminisced:

My friendly relations with Rachmaninoff were established at the time he was composing his Liturgy, which he sent me, a movement at a time, to have a look through and about which, I remember, we conducted a lively epistolary polemic. His sensitivity to the church style in music delighted me greatly, and the collection of *Obikhod* melodies which I sent him when he announced his intention of writing an All-Night Vigil proved highly apposite since it placed in his hands as an artist the material with which, through working on it, he started out on the true path and achieved excellent results in many cases.[10]

To all appearances, Rachmaninoff consulted Kastalsky before the first performance of the All-Night Vigil; according to the composer's son Alexander Kastalsky, Rachmaninoff brought his father a completed score to have a look at. We know something else: a few days before the première Kastalsky, remembering the Liturgy's unfavourable reception and concerned that the new composition should be successful, placed a short announcement in the newspapers:

Sergey Rachmaninoff's new work All-Night Vigil undoubtedly represents a significant contribution to our literature of church music, and the projected performance of it on 10 March is a musical event in its own right in the midst of the motley programmes of this season's Lenten concerts. By comparison with his Liturgy, the composer has taken an important step forward in the new work, rejecting the homophonic-harmonic way of composing with church melodies. He takes them straight from the *Obikhod*. But you have to hear what simple, unsophisticated melodies become in the hands of a major artist. And that's the whole secret. After all, the very same colours are equally in the palette of the dauber of icons and of the artist by the grace of God... Whether Rachmaninoff has come near the style is a matter for discussion. But the plastic simplicity of utterance in 'Bless the Lord, O my soul' (*Blagoslovi, dushe moya*) or 'Rejoice, O Virgin' (*Bogoroditse Devo*), the original poetic expressiveness in the accompaniment of the song of St Simeon, the 'peals' in the Six Psalms, the exultant 'Praise the Name of the Lord' (*Khvalite Imya Gospodne*), the powerful mood of the Great Doxology, and finally the victorious 'To Thee, the victorious Leader' (*Vzbrannoy voyevode*) – these hymns unquestionably say a good deal about Rachmaninoff. The artist's loving and careful attitude towards our old melodies is particularly precious. And therein lies the guarantee of a good future for our church music.[11]

A careful attitude towards the old chants and tactful treatment of them in sacred compositions was one of the main principles of the New Direction. This demand was made of the works of composers both great and small – for instance, of those whose sacred works came to the Supervisory Council attached to the Synodal School of Church Music for scrutiny. Distorting the melodies could be the grounds for not approving a work just as much as the musical illiteracy of their arrangers.

During his time as director Kastalsky repeatedly appeared in periodicals as the author of articles (see the Epilogue for further consideration of this subject); on several occasions the composer answered questions from the correspondents of various newspapers. In one of those interviews he spoke out on the question of purity of style in sacred music, linking it with the use of old chants in compositions, and he emphasized that treatment of them in the national style was one of the most difficult tasks for contemporary composers. To the question of whether his pupils studying composition were successful in conveying the old colouring, Kastalsky replied that, for all the young people's efforts, the desired result is often not obtained, for which they could not be reproached as the environment of sounds round about them had left its mark. Only a few could overcome the influence of contemporary music; among the latter was Pavel Chesnokov. To a question as to what the composer thought about Russian secular music, Kastalsky replied:

Our young composers have followed Skryabin and been fascinated by him – but they are only imitating him and will not themselves be as talented and artistic modernists as Skryabin was. I consider the most worthy and faithful continuer of the so-called 'old music' – the music of Borodin and Rimsky-Korsakov – to be Igor Stravinsky, but even in his latest work one notices a tendency towards modernism. We shall all, I suspect, return to the 'old music'. It is only death that carries off its continuers... One of the last of the Mohicans of ideal Russian music went to the grave in the person of Eduard Napravnik.[12]

Kastalsky was also asked questions about the Synodal Choir – for instance whether some kind of connection had been retained between the present Synodal Choir and its predecessor the patriarchal choir. The composer replied:

As regards inner things, our Choir has adopted singing in unison, which you will not find anywhere else in Russia. It sounds rather austere, though it is close to our antiquity. Then we have retained singing great *znamenny* chants and certain ancient hymns to pattern melodies (*na podoben*). That is sung only by us and in a few remote monasteries scattered about. Outwardly, we wear the uniforms of clerks. Not so long ago we adopted special kaftans with standing collars of the type worn by the clerks in the patriarchal choir.[13]

To a question as to how much interest was shown abroad in the life of the School and the successes of the Choir, Kastalsky replied: 'You are aware of our trip abroad. Apart from that, foreigners come here to visit us. As recently as yesterday some journalists from Paris arrived and we organized a little impromptu concert specially for them'.[14]

The question about interest in the Synodal Choir on the part of foreign musicians and lovers of music was not accidental, as during the 1910s the Synodal Choir made two concert tours, winning wide recognition. The first was undertaken in 1911 in connection with an invitation to the International Exhibition in Rome. The exhibition was devoted to the celebration of a national holiday in Italy – the 50th anniversary of the proclamation of Rome as capital of an independent, united kingdom – and consisted of four sections: archaeological, retrospective, ethnographic and artistic. The plans for the celebrations also included three conferences and a display of the arts of theatre and music. For the same period the Synodal Choir had received invitations from some of Europe's major cities – Prague, Warsaw, Vienna, Dresden and Florence, where it was also proposed that concerts be given.

For their appearance in Rome three programmes were prepared, which Kastalsky described thus in a letter to his friend Zatayevich – who was adviser for special projects in the office of the governor-general of Warsaw: 'A historical programme (from unison to Kastalsky), a national church programme (modern composers of national hue; first half – Kastalsky, and second half – the others), and the newest compositions (Chesnokov, Grechaninov, Rachmaninoff, Kastalsky and the rest). Roughly twelve numbers in each concert'.[15] Kastalsky suggested that Zatayevich select one of these programmes for the Choir's only concert in Warsaw. In the end a 'mixed' programme was proposed for Warsaw and Dresden.[16]

On 22 April 1911 the Synodal Choir, with 66 members, took their new ceremonial kaftans with them and set off. The Choir was on the move for a month, during which it gave twelve concerts. The correspondent of the 'Russian Word' (*Russkoye slovo*), M. Pervukhin, wrote:

> Rome is experiencing a real 'Russian week'. Wherever you might think of going, you will hear Russian spoken and see typically Russian faces. You will see typically Russian people a little perplexed by being unaccustomed to finding themselves unexpectedly in a broadly international crowd, and therefore prone to bashfulness and timidity. Even if you can't see any Russians, then at any rate you will hear about Russians. People here are saying a great deal about us, and they are saying various things: they curse us and praise us, criticize us and laud us to the skies. They speak about the nation and the people, our internal organization and our foreign policy. But most of all they speak about our art. And there are actually good grounds for that, and many sound reasons. The Russian Art Pavilion opened at the exhibition – and people started to talk about our architecture, our painting and our sculpture. People praise Repin, Serov and our young artists. They abuse the pavilion, comparing it with a rich burial-vault. They find nothing characteristically Russian about it. Our ballet performed. At first the reaction was cold. The local press had prepared the public unfavourably, intending to ruin the Russian ballet, which was in competition with Italian opera. But the impression made by the phoney hostile campaign was sufficient for only the first performance. The later ones were brilliant successes. The royal couple visited the ballet. Soon it became difficult to get tickets at the theatre, and it grew overcrowded. People started to speak of our ballet as the only artistic ballet in all Europe. Now people's attention is occupied with a fresh Russian novelty, namely our Synodal Choir, which was invited by the exhibition committee to give three concerts of sacred music in Rome. [...]
>
> As one should have expected, the first concert by the Russian choir in the colossal Augusteo Concert Hall did not attract many members of the public. Generally speaking, Italians know little about Russian music and our sacred music is almost completely unknown to them. Only with the opening of the Augusteo [in 1908] did the Roman public begin to make the acquaintance of our composers more widely at symphony concerts, and composers such as Tchaikovsky, Borodin and Rimsky-Korsakov have already become favourites of the Italians, though they do not know our performers, and particularly not choral ones. The Synodal Choir was not advertized. The newspapers said nothing. The public knew little and showed little interest. There were fewer than three thousand listeners at the first concert as a result, when the Augusteo can accommodate up to five thousand. But you had to see the amazement of the public after just a few numbers sung by our choir – amazement which rapidly turned into rapture at the purity of the performance and the wealth of vocal resources in the Synodal Choir. The applause was restrained at first, but as the performance by the choir of their programme proceeded it became more and more insistent and tumultuous, and the public just would not stop until the

morose figure of Danilin, who was unresponsive to approval, returned to the platform for encores.[17]

The Synodal Choir's success grew from one concert to the next; their appearances became triumphs of Russian choral art. Kastalsky followed events very attentively and in his letters home described what took place. He was not of course indifferent to the success of his own compositions which were very strongly represented in the concert programmes. Thus, out of 41 items selected for the tour, 11 were either original works by Kastalsky or his reconstructions of older music. Among them were 'Lord, now lettest Thou' (*Nine otpushchayeshi*) (no. 1), 'It is meet' (*Dostoyno yest'*) (Serbian chant), The Creed (*Veruyu*) (no. 1), 'Gladsome Light' (*Svete tikhiy*) (no. 3), 'Today the Virgin' (*Deva dnes'*) (*znamenny* chant), 'God is with us' (*S nami Bog*) (*znamenny* chant), 'From my youth' (*Ot yunosti moyeya*) and also four reconstructions of hymns from the fifteenth to the seventeenth centuries. To the composer's great chagrin, the Italian critics reacted to his compositions with restrained approval, considering them too serious. In Germany, Austria and Poland, on the other hand, the reception was as warm as it could possibly be. On 27/14 May Kastalsky wrote to his mother from Vienna:

Dear Granny! (*Milaya babushka!*)
We've arrived in Vienna from Rome where we gave three concerts; each time with greater and greater ovations, and at the last one people waved their hats and headscarves at Danilin and shouted at the top of their voices. Among other things they had to sing my 'Lord, now lettest Thou' (with the bass solo) again, and some scribbler wrote all about me as if he understood something. Tchaikovsky's brother kept calling me 'our pride and joy' to everyone. In Florence my Serbian 'It is meet' was encored. A famous artist wants to do a picture for me for the dust-cover of my works. And yesterday we had a concert, also with huge success, in Vienna. Generally, we're doing a bit to bring lustre to our fatherland. In Vienna Danilin was presented with a garland. The ambassador in Rome presented Danilin and me with a gold cigarette-case each, and I asked him for as many cigarettes as possible. I kiss your hand, your son, A. Kastalsky.[18]

The Synodal Choir's next foreign tour, to Leipzig and Berlin, took place from 30 September to 11 October 1913. It was undertaken on the occasion of the dedication of the Russian church of St Aleksey in Leipzig, built as a memorial to Russian glory, and of that of the monument in memory of those who fell in the Battle of the Nations in 1813. To be sure, Kastalsky did not go on that tour, though his compositions were performed both during the solemn act of worship and at the concerts. We know that they made a deep impression on the German Kaiser Wilhelm, who first heard the Synodal Choir's singing in 1911 and became a great admirer of their art.

In the 1910s the Synodal Choir and School were spoken of in the New World, where under the patronage of Charles R. Crane a choir and school for boys was established on its model at the Russian Cathedral of St Nicholas in New York.[19]

Charles Crane was the son of a factory-owner who received a brilliant education and had a command of many European and eastern languages; he was one of the most cultured Americans of his time. He was the president of the company he had inherited from his father, a director of the National Bank of the Republic and at the same time an authoritative specialist about the East and Russia. Over the course of many trips to Russia at the beginning of the century as a businessman and diplomat, he had acquired many friends among Russia's artistic world and came to know and genuinely love her art. Russian church music was a particular passion of Crane's, and the American patron decided to popularize it in his own country. He approached Kastalsky for help in organizing a Russian church choir in the New World. As a result, in 1911 Crane invited the Moscow choirmaster Ivan Gorokhov whom Kastalsky had recommended and six adult singers to work in America, and they formed the basis of the future choir which sang at services in the Cathedral of St Nicholas in New York. Boy singers were recruited from among the Russian-speaking population in America and, like the young singers in the Synodal Choir, received a general and musical education while with the choir. During the summer the children were taken for a holiday to the state of Massachusetts, where on the seashore there was a biology laboratory maintained by Crane.

In 1913 the Russian cathedral choir, made up of six men and twelve boys, dressed in kaftans reminiscent of the Synodal Choir's ceremonial dress, began giving concerts, which were attended by resounding success. On 24/11 July 1913 Gorokhov wrote to Kastalsky in Moscow:

> The Americans are very interested in Russian music generally and church music in particular. Your compositions make the very best impression on them. The Americans express their delight and their regret that until now they have not had the chance of hearing Russian church music. Choirmasters (organists) besiege me with requests to give them copies of the compositions which I perform with my choir. Critics write lots of articles about my choir and hold it up as an example to American choirs. All the newspaper and journal reviews so far have been very complimentary both about the choir and about the church music. So far everything is fine, but nostalgia for Russia often bothers us.[20]

Concerts by Ivan Gorokhov's choir took place in Harvard University and Carnegie Hall; they toured towns on the eastern seaboard. On 2 February 1914 the choir performed in Washington before President Wilson and other high state officials.

Thanks to the concerts given by the choir of the Cathedral of St Nicholas, Americans found out not just about Russian church music but also about the very finest Russian church choir – the Synodal Choir. The following letter from Yevdokim, Archbishop of North America, to Kastalsky testifies to this:

> Your Excellency,
> Dr Mott, the bearer of this letter, is a personal friend of President Wilson. After the President, he is the most influential person in the whole of America. He wishes to attest to you his deepest gratitude for the wonderful singing which he has heard in America at the Russian cathedral, where a pupil of yours is the choirmaster. Please receive him. I rejoice that the glory of your name and your choir has spread so far round the world. May God preserve you for many years. Your admirer who prays for you, Archbishop Yevdokim.[21]

Unfortunately Ivan Gorokhov's choir continued in existence for only three years after this letter was written: after the revolution the Synod stopped funding parishes abroad, and the Cathedral of St Nicholas was sold at auction. The choir broke up. Several of its members continued with their musical education, some became clergymen, while others took up careers in business or other secular professions. Gorokhov himself continued his career in choral work from 1918 to 1945 at Smith College in Massachusetts. He never returned to his homeland and died in America in 1949.

Notes

1. Information about these unrealized initiatives taken by the Supervisory Council was discovered in the following document: RGADA, fond 1183, opis' 9, part 2, no. 22.
2. Letter from A.D. Kastal'sky to N.I. Privalov of 15 September 1910. RNB, fond 615, no. 506, p. 1.
3. A.D. Kastal'sky: *Iz vospominaniy o poslednikh godakh* (From my reminiscences of recent years), in *RUSAM*, vol. 1, p. 251.
4. Letter from A.D. Kastal'sky to Kh.N. Grozdov of 23 June 1915. GTsMMK, fond 370, no. 532, p. 4.
5. S. Rakhmaninov: *Literaturnoye naslediye* (Literary legacy), vol. 2, *Pis'ma* (Letters). Moscow, 1980, pp. 14-16, 18, 22-23.

6. Letter from S.V. Rakhmaninov to A.D. Kastal'sky of 19 June 1910. S. Rakhmaninov: *Literaturnoye naslediye*, vol. 1, p. 14.
7. *Kontsertï Sinodal'nogo khora* (The Synodal Choir's concerts), in *Khorovoye i regentskoye delo* (Choral and Church Choirmaster Matters), 1911, no. 3, pp. 12-14.
8. S.A. Shumsky: *Materialï dlya razrabotki temï 'Moskovskoye Sinodal'noye uchilishche i vozrozhdeniye natsional'noy dukhovnoy muzïki'* (Materials for developing the subject of the 'Moscow Synodal School and the revival of national sacred music'), in *RUSAM*, vol. 1, pp. 619-620.
9. Letter from A.D. Kastal'sky to S.V. Rakhmaninov of 2 January 1923. Library of Congress, Washington, D.C.
10. A.D. Kastal'sky: *Iz vospominaniy o poslednikh godakh*, in *RUSAM*, vol. 1, p. 251.
11. A.D. Kastal'sky: *Vsenoshchnoye bdeniye Rakhmaninova* (Rakhmaninov's All-Night Vigil), in *Russkoye slovo* (Russian Word), 1915, 7 March.
12. *Nashi besedï. U A.D. Kastal'skogo* (Our conversations. We call on A.D. Kastal'sky), in *Teatr* (Theatre), 1916, no. 1935, p. 6.
13. *Nasaditeli drevnego peniya. Iz besedï s direktorom A.D. Kastal'skim* (The Propagators of ancient singing. From a conversation with Director A.D. Kastal'sky), in *Ranneye utro* (Early Morning), 1911, no. 253.
14. *Ibid.*
15. Letter from A.D. Kastal'sky to A.V. Zatayevich of 18 February 1911. GTsMMK, fond 6, no. 299, p. 1v.
16. The programmes of the concerts given on the Synodal Choir's tour abroad in 1911 may be found in: ed. A.A. Naumov: *Pamyati N.M. Danilina. Pis'ma. Vospominaniya. Dokumentï* (In memory of N.M. Danilin. Letters. Reminiscences. Documents). Moscow, 1987 pp. 24-48; *RUSAM*, vol. 1, pp. 287-292.
17. M. Pervukhin: *Sinodal'nïy khor v Rime* (The Synodal Choir in Rome), in *Russkoye slovo* (Russian Word), 1911, May, no. 15.
18. A.D. Kastal'sky: *Zagranichnïye pis'ma* (Letters from abroad), in *RUSAM*, vol. 1, p. 283.
19. The name of the American diplomat Charles R. Crane occurs often in documents associated with the history of Russian church music. He is mentioned, for instance, in A.T. Grechaninov: *Moya zhizn'* (My life), New York, 1951, as an admirer of the composer's work who gave him encouragement and material support after the October coup.
20. Letter from I.T. Gorokhov to A.D. Kastal'sky of 24/11 July 1913. RGALI, fond 662, opis' 1, no. 40, pp. 22-22v.
21. Letter from Yevdokim, Archbishop of North America, to A.D. Kastal'sky of 4 May 1916. GTsMMK, fond 12, no. 319, p. 1.

Chapter 16

Musical 'Plays'

The start of Kastalsky's directorship of the Synodal School coincided with a number of anniversaries and festivities in Moscow, amongst which were the acquisition of the relics of Patriarch Hermogen, the opening of the monument to Alexander III and of the museum bearing his name, the tercentenary of the house of Romanov, and the hundredth anniversary of the war of 1812. These events, and also the beginning of the 1914 war, were accompanied by journeys of Tsar Nicholas II to Moscow. Having won great renown as a composer writing in the fashionable 'Russian style', Kastalsky received commissions for several anniversary works. The composer told Grozdov in detail about his experiences with the cantata genre.

> You and I have recently become suppliers of cantatas... I've been particularly lucky: hard on the heels of the commission that came via you (for 1912) came one (though without any money) for a cantata in memory of Hermogen, which it is proposed to celebrate here on 17 February, and then I have to concoct something similar to celebrate the 'house of Romanov' (that's for 1913). I have to admit that it's a good thing, though if there were fewer commissions it would be better. The main thing that's always needed with these concoctions is speed (there's a deadline), and that's something I'm badly equipped for in musical work. In actual fact I agreed to your proposal because I had already been told that I had to write it for 1912. When I received the proposal from you, I thought that I'd have to cook up something in any case – it's more advantageous to take whatever money is going than to write in the abstract, on the off-chance... At least now, if they begin to pester me, I can say 'I've already done it!'... I've come up with something for the beginning, but I'm thinking of digging around in [folk]songs for melodic material – to see whether it might be more coherent. The text I've been sent, although it's smooth, is very profound (as regards imagery, as our San'ka [young son Alexander] said), you can't take even a thimble's worth out of it, though cantata texts in general are always as stupid as possible ... it's a tradition all of its own. If you have a spare moment, couldn't you find somewhere to rustle up a text to commemorate Hermogen? Our Stepanov suggested that I set for choir the epistles which Muscovites sent to other cities, written under the influence of

Hermogen's epistle (!!). In actual fact, that could be done only by imagining a scene (à la Musorgsky) of the people reading out this epistle (with various phrase repetitions, even exclamations and what not). In short, the chorus would turn out theatrical – reading the epistle out rather than sending it... And, probably, there are songs of that time about those events – they would be the most suitable...[1]

In this letter Kastalsky refers to three of his compositions from the early 1910s – the cantata 'In Memory of the Year 1812' (*V pamyat' 1812 goda*) (1911), 'Three Hundred Years' ('The Great Year') (*Trista let. (God velikiy))* (1912) and 'The Reading by a Clerk to the People of Moscow of the Epistle from Patriarch Hermogen to the Tushino Traitors in 1609' (*Chteniye d'yakom lyudu Moskovskomu poslaniya patriarkha Yermogena k tushinskim izmennikam v 1609 godu*) (from Metropolitan Makary's History) (1913). The composer laid out the latter composition, written in the operatic traditions of Musorgsky, in the form of a scene for bass soloist and chorus (Ex. 16.1). The 'Reading' differed from the first two anniversary cantatas in its unusual form, and also by the absence of 'Russian' colouring: notwithstanding his initial intentions, the composer did not actually have recourse to seventeenth-century folksongs. The work was first performed by the Synodal Choir conducted by Danilin on 19 February 1912 at a ceremonial gathering in memory of Patriarch Hermogen held in the Diocesan House in Moscow.[2] Kastalsky's other choral work dedicated to this favourite saint of Muscovites was extremely traditional in form and was written on the occasion of the translation of the Patriarch's relics to a new sarcophagus. This feast took place on 11 and 12 May 1914 in the Cathedral of the Dormition where the troparion of Kastalsky's composition for Patriarch Hermogen was performed for the first time in the course of the All-Night Vigil. Victor Vasnetsov painted the icon for the celebration, the Grand Duchess Yelizaveta Fyodorovna embroidered the pall, and the cost of the new silver shrine was met by the imperial couple.

Among compositions distinguished by novelty of thinking one has to mention yet another cantata by Kastalsky composed in the early 1910s: the 'Verse about Russian Church Music' (*Stikh o tserkovnom russkom penii*) which the composer dedicated to the 25th anniversary of the reformed Synodal School.

This anniversary fell on 5-7 November 1911 and was celebrated in style. The first day was marked by the greatest solemnity, when a service (*moleben*) took place in the School Hall, an outline of the history of the Synodal Choir and School was read, salutations were received from various delegations, and Kastalsky's cantata was performed in conclusion. On the following day, 6 November, a concert of works by graduates took place:

choral pieces by Pavel and Alexander Chesnokov, Nikolay Kovin, Nikolay Tolstyakov, Konstantin Shvedov, Alexander Vorontsov, Ivan Sokolov, Vladimir Stepanov, Nikolay Golovanov and Alexander Chugunov were heard. On 7 November a student concert was organized. The celebrations on the second and third days were also crowned by repeat performances of Kastalsky's anniversary composition, which enjoyed great success with listeners. The cantata was reviewed in the press and performed a year later in St Petersburg under the direction of a former student of the School, Anastas Nikolov. The composer himself, as often happened with him, attached no great importance to this work and intended it purely for 'domestic use'. At the same time the cantata is significant if only because it is the sole composition to narrate the history of church music in the language of the Russian folk epic tale (*bïlina*). In accordance with the canon of the new school, Kastalsky based the work on consistent melodic formulas (*popevki*) and *fitï* from the *Obikhod* and fragments of familiar church melodies. In the music we can find the melodic formulas *priglaska*, *dolinka* and *kulizma srednyaya*, the *fita* of the fifth tone, an 'Old Simonov' melody, 'Eternal memory' (*Vechnaya pamyat'*), etc. (Ex. 16.2). The device of quotation beloved by the composer was applied: for instance, in the fragment telling of 'musical youth desirous of learning' (from the title-page of the 'Well-Tempered Clavier'), Bach's E-flat minor Fugue from that collection is heard. Despite the introduction of ancient and later Russian melodic turns of phrase, the work's musical language is on the whole entirely traditional and employs a moderate St Petersburg 'Russian style'. Thus, the 'New Russian Style' with a Moscow bias in which practically all Kastalsky's works for chorus a cappella were written did not work for Kastalsky in works with instrumental accompaniment. If in his ethnographic reconstructions he was able to get out of the situation by making the piano accompaniment follow the style of folk instrumental music, in the cantata the matter was complicated by the absence of instrumental analogies for the church style. Kastalsky never did succeed in transferring to the orchestra the new ideas which arose out of the heart of choral culture.

Thus, during the 1910s, after the composer had written the opera *Klara Milich*, he tried to master the genre of cantata and oratorio. Another consequence of the experience he had gained in writing the opera was his desire to introduce an element of stage action into choral music. In preparing the first three parts of the cycle 'From Past Ages' (*Iz minuvshikh vekov*) for a second edition, Kastalsky moved a very long way from the original modest piano composition and took a serious step towards staging reconstructed fragments of early Christian acts of worship. On 23

November 1911 the composer wrote to the music scholar Grigory Timofeyev in St Petersburg:

> Between two and four vocal soloists, a small choir (of five to eight people), women dancers and extras are involved in each scene. Each scene lasts from eight to ten minutes, apart from 'Judea' (five minutes), where a large unison choir is needed. These explanations will be inserted in the parts for information. The third part, 'The Christians', is provided with explanations for concert performance (chorus, soloists and accompanying harp). This number lasts from eight to ten minutes.[3]

The origin of this stage version of 'From Past Ages' lies in the fact that Kastalsky's former pupil at the School Nikolov, who organized a circle of lovers of church music at the St Petersburg Diocesan Brotherhood in 1908, had conceived the idea of giving three concerts of music by Kastalsky using the group's forces. It was proposed to give a dramatized production of 'The Christians' at one of them. As emerges from a letter from Kastalsky to Grozdov, the première of 'The Christians' in St Petersburg was a success, though it made the composer worry whether the listeners had not experienced a surfeit of unisons and isons or found the work monotonous.

The subject which Kastalsky chose for his next reconstruction took the idea of a dramatized choral play significantly further. In a letter of 23 March 1912 Kastalsky told Zatayevich of his recent activities:

> What did I get done in that time? Mostly, I wore myself out with School business, though I also did some work for the benefit of music. Incidentally, I'm still working only on material for future work. I've made a summary of various typical aspects of Russian song, and now I'm poring over ancient church manuscripts which no one has yet ventured to read or transcribe. And in the meantime, to find an answer to the questions, or rather problems, which I have set myself as a duty, these manuscripts just have to be analysed, one way or another, even if only roughly. And I consider it my duty to issue a fourth part of 'From Past Ages' entitled 'Ancient Rus' which as far as possible embraces the subject from every conceivable side – everyday life, religion, ritual and music. There is enough song material that's been worked up more or less from snippets; but there isn't any church music, as the seventeenth century (whose manuscripts can be read confidently) – well, what sort of antiquity is that? Some people express the opinion that in comparison with the previous one it is a century – they go so far as to call it a century of decline in the devout art of church music... Besides, I've been asked to make a number of church music restorations (from the eleventh and twelfth centuries!) for a music history society in St Petersburg; although at first I sniffed at a proposal of that kind, nonetheless this history interests me personally (in the depth of my heart).

Generally speaking, I have in my mind the idea of studying original folk music, since the material for it is at hand. Apart from the cantata I'm sending you, I've brewed up something to celebrate the anniversary of Patriarch Hermogen, and I've cooked up something similarly 'commemorative' for Yaroslavl (also a commission). In a word, this winter I've been busy making up orders, just like a tailor...[4]

The fourth part of the cycle 'From Past Ages', in the final version entitled 'Rus' ('A Bazaar in Ancient Times in Rus') (*Torzhishche v starinu na Rusi*), was published by the firm of P. Jurgenson in 1914. At the time Kastalsky wrote this work, he was armed with a comprehensive knowledge of folk music and strove to create a picture, of the utmost ethnographical fidelity, of life in an ancient Russian town, using transcriptions of folksongs, *bïlinï*, spiritual verses, melodized folk cries, instrumental tunes, and also transcriptions of the music of other peoples of the world. The way the music is written, in both the voice and piano parts, is of the utmost closeness to folk speech, and abounds in genuine quotations; the piano part often imitates the sound of various folk instruments – the *gudok*, the *gusli*, the *sopel'*, the *svirel'*, the bagpipes, the *balalayka* and so on (Ex. 16.3). The work was written for soloists, chorus and piano (according to the composer's directions, 20 solo singers and between 30 and 35 people in 'speaking' and 'non-speaking' parts participate in the action), and represented something like an episode in the life of remote ancestors brought to life – an episode at once highly coloured and naive. The uncomplicated story-line is set out in verbal commentaries accompanying the score. We learn from them that the action takes place in the market-square of Novgorod the Great in the centre of which stands a church. The church service comes to an end, and the square comes to life: a Moravian trader 'shouts out from his stall', a bass *skomorokh* standing in front of a booth with slave-girls ridicules a Viking trader, the 'singing of an eastern slave-girl to lute and tambourine accompaniment' is heard, 'a Venetian woman dealing in various precious stones from a tray', 'a Jew enters looking all around him', 'a keeper enters with a bear and a goat; the goat beats a drum and the bear bows', and so on. The composition is not unified by a plot of any kind, and represents a kaleidoscope of picturesque genre miniatures clad in ethnographical colours. Kastalsky's historical picture brings to mind market scenes from Russian operas, e.g. in Rimsky-Korsakov's *Sadko*, but possibly had a further model as well – the ethnographical spectacles which the composer saw at concerts given by Mitrofan Pyatnitsky's choir, who organized dramatized presentations with scenery and lighting effects in Moscow in 1910.

While he was finishing off the work, the composer gave Grozdov the following explanation:

> These last few days I've been busying myself most of all with the 'market day' in ancient Rus, where I just couldn't desist from the usual manner of including everything in a cinematographic form; and it was precisely there that I wanted to make as much of a kaleidoscope as possible, with everything constantly changing without creating the usual endings (i.e. in open form); just the same, I'm not happy with it all yet... This scene will strike a musician, of course, as the most utter chaos (just as in 'Shrovetide' (*Maslenitsa*)), and perhaps indicate a complete inability to set out musical ideas (like the prattling of some desperately self-confident amateur). And as for me, I wanted to create far more of this chaos still (that is, to make a real bazaar of sounds).[5]

To all appearances Kastalsky had a specifically cinematographic vision, and as a result he constructed the form like a chain of individual pictorial episodes. That kind of vision left its mark not only on his secular compositions but also on his sacred ones. We read in Kastalsky's letter of 9 May 1918 to Asafyev, where he tells him about his work on the hymns for Easter: 'Unexpectedly even for me (an old *kliros* rat), I find that the text 'Having come before dawn' (*Predvarivshiya utro*), which normally rushes past cinematographically in the usual Easter gallop – is supposed to be uttered in a quite special way – as a kind of fantastic narrative episode in the midst of the general rejoicing...'[6]

The composer never managed, however, to prove himself specifically in music for the cinema, though he received offers of that kind on a number of occasions. The first was in 1915. 'About two or three weeks ago Goncharov,[7] the director of the Khanzhonkov film company, came to see me, showered compliments on "Rus", which he said was just made for a film opera, and gave me a libretto for "Poor Liza" (*Bednaya Liza*) with a proposal that I write the music, but two days later he died', – Kastalsky recalled of the first such unrealized proposal.[8] The composer received a second proposal in the Soviet period, but he declined it, greatly to his regret, on the grounds of his poor general health.

There are reasons to suppose that in about 1916 Kastalsky received an even more original proposal: to write the music for a ballet 'Augmented Litany' (*Sugubaya Yekten'ya*). The evidence that an idea so seditious for its time existed consists of several sketches of a dance for a ballet by Kastalsky found in the archive of the artist Yury Annenkov.[9] It is difficult to say what Kastalsky's attitude towards this idea was; at any rate, no traces of a ballet of that name have been found in either his literary or his musical archive.[10]

At the same time, the composer's music manuscripts and letters indicate very intensive work over many years on a composition which Kastalsky himself usually called 'Celebrations' (*Prazdniki*). This was the largest-scale work of restoration undertaken by the composer in which he intended to reconstruct the annual calendar cycle of ancient peasant festivities, many of which had already been forgotten. 'Celebrations' was a work on which the composer placed special hopes.

The composer mentions 'Celebrations' for the first time in a letter of 19 August 1911 to Grozdov.

On 28 December 1912 he wrote to his wife from Kislovodsk: 'I've finished seven "Celebrations"; I'm working on "Autumn" – I'm beginning to get fed up with them...'[11]

On 11 April 1913 we read in a letter to Zatayevich: 'I've had my head down for a whole year now working on "Russian folk celebrations and rituals" – I'm going off my head with the work'.[12]

18 January 1913, from a letter to Grozdov:

The new work has dragged on for almost a whole year. [...] But when I finished working on it the idea often came into my mind: 'but what is your work needed for, and who is it for? The amount of work is huge, but the reader doesn't notice it, and what's the point of it?' Of course nobody but me would have taken it on, but that's poor consolation. Explaining the origin of lots of songs and their place in the ritual of life – that's of no interest to musicians or music-lovers, but only to ethnographical researchers and to them alone... In short, these are my gloomy thoughts on finishing the work.[13]

We read in a letter of 20 April 1913 to Grozdov:

I found in the university library Anichkov's work 'Spring Ritual Song in the West among the Slavs' (*Vesennyaya obryadovaya pesnya na zapade u slavyan*) and have found a fair amount of new material which I'm distributing here and there. [I've no idea] what it's going to be like later on, but 'Spring' (from the beginning to *Rusalii*) has turned out not bad at all, both for completeness and pictorialism... It's a shame that I can't manage to include 'solo' songs (apart from two verses, which is very little). I'm amazed by my great patience: people approach me from all quarters, asking me to continue with the *Obikhod*, or take a look at the *Prokuror*'s sacred compositions,[14] or else Sabler[15] bothers me with the troparion and kontakion for St Hermogen. It's a pity that Easter Week is coming to an end – exams will be starting and all sorts of nonsense – when am I going to get 'Celebrations' finished?[16]

30 December 1913, from a letter to his wife: 'I've finished "Celebrations", though occasionally I clean up a little bit here and there – it's a temptation. I've already done the preface'.[17]

15 February 1914, from a letter to the music historian Timofeyev: 'I have decided to call my latest work "Scenes from Russian Peasant Merrymaking in Rituals and Songs" (*Kartinï russkikh narodnïkh prazdnovaniy v obryadakh i pesnyakh*)".[18]

In one of his letters from 1914 the composer sent Timofeyev a detailed programme note about his work, on the basis of which the latter compiled the following description, which he intended to incorporate in a new article about church music:

> In this work the composer has set himself the task of giving living samples of the folk imagination in the sphere of ritual, combining music with stage production. Both the place and sequence of the action are designated in detail for each celebration separately. The (folk) instruments accompanying the songs are also designated throughout, and the preface contains a comparative table of these instruments with the orchestral ones in current use, to allow for performance by present-day orchestral resources. The libretto of these rituals has been compiled from song texts and the scenario itself is based on the researches of Sakharov and Afanasyev, Buganov, Tereshchenko, Famintsïn and others. The melodies are taken from ancient songs. The accompaniment for them was written as far as possible in the folk manner, though, in the composer's words, in places it proved impossible to get by without using the universally accepted devices of 'art music'. Since ancient ritual songs now half-forgotten by the people served as melodic material for the whole work, the composer cherishes the dream of staging these scenes in village conditions, even in the remotest places. He nourishes the hope that, by the possible return to the hearts of the people of forgotten images from their musical and poetic imagination, a stimulus may be given to reviving folk creativity.[19]

One should add that the work was laid out in the form of a two-stave piano score giving the underlay and the composer's commentaries.

At the end of 1914 'Celebrations' was passed to the board of the publisher Edition Russe de Musique for scrutiny. A fragment is quoted from a letter of the greatest interest which not only shows Kastalsky's vision of his own work but also the opinion of Rachmaninoff, a member of the board. Foreseeing a negative appraisal of the work, Rachmaninoff tried to explain the errors and show his senior colleague a way of revising it. It was obvious that Rachmaninoff did not accept the basic principle of form-construction that Kastalsky had used in the work. In other words, it was a question of a 'kaleidoscopic quality' – assembling a structure out of individual 'little pieces' not joined in a single line of development.

Moreover, the two composers did not agree in their understanding of the work's aims. Enthused by the idea of educating the people, Kastalsky tried to write a narrative accessible to all about Russian festivities through musical pictures; Rachmaninoff could not grasp that idea at all and saw in front of him merely the very richest of material which the composer had failed to transform into a work of art. Kastalsky set forth his dialogue with Rachmaninoff in detail in a letter to Grozdov:

Rachmaninoff: Yesterday (i.e. the day he received it) I received for evaluation your 'Celebrations' (he's a member of the reading panel for Edition Russe de Musique) and have come to clarify some points with you: why do you present your work as raw material, without any real arrangement, not in the form of a score and not even as a real piano score? I've come to persuade you to take the job in hand and work up the material fully... It's so new and interesting; what astounding details there are in the rituals (even in the text). I'd like to undertake it myself... Anyone will give you whatever you ask for this work (that is, for the material), as much as you want, if you surrender it. Look at Stravinsky – it'd be a real treasure for him! He'd give you a hundred thousand for it! But in the form in which you present it, although I shall defend your work, – I'm afraid that it will prove unacceptable. (The matter is decided by a majority of votes – using closed envelopes each containing the opinion of a member of the jury – it's terrific fun!) Get on with it – work up even part of it, develop it, redo it as a piece for orchestra (this piece throughout is asking for orchestra and development!). Surely you can't leave work like that in such an unfinished form?! After all, you often break your own rule, now and then you begin to develop, you add something of your own, now here, now there, and so on and so forth...

Me: I'm quite prepared for the possibility of the jury rejecting my work on the grounds that it does not meet the demands of 'symphonic development' and so on because the thought occurred to me right from the start... But what can I do? That's the way things are! I prepared my work:

1) for the music-lover who can sit at the piano and over an evening or two run through the whole annual cycle of folk rituals with both ritual and music concentrated into one whole thing;

2) I prepared this work for country shows in the audacious hope that the people, on observing their forgotten offspring, might perhaps see that their peasant art is not after all so primitive and uncouth and that there is actually nothing about it to be ashamed of...

Rachmaninoff: But what happens then? What's this about music-lovers at their pianos and country shows? You consider the music-lover too primitive – don't you want to give him a real piano score with the vocal parts fully written out, with a proper artistic accompaniment... After all, you yourself are always wanting to break away from these constant fragments and more fragments!

Me: Fragments – that's actually the character of folk art, the fragments take on a different appearance because each fragment (that is couplet, or verse) is repeated many times, and they (the people) vary it when it is repeated. And if I sometimes break my own rule, it means I couldn't restrain myself.

Rachmaninoff: It ought to have been you who did the varying.

Me: And then my work would have been four times longer – and it would be impossible to perform it in one evening... And if it had been commissioned from me, another three years would have been spent on it.

Rachmaninoff: But what a wonderful work it would be! I'm overcome with envy that I don't have such material.

Me: Well, what about it? My material gives you the chance of composing whatever you want... And if you want to see that this style of writing is nothing new to me, then take a look at my 'From Past Ages' – it's in the same manner. Historians use the piece in their lectures, and try to reproduce it in concert form – and no one's ever told me it lacks development!

Rachmaninoff: That's very interesting.

From the whole dialogue you can see there's a real possibility of my 'Celebrations' not being accepted by Koussevitzky's firm. For if Rachmaninoff can't accept it in such a 'raw' form, there's no hope for any of the others. There's still a couple of weeks before the decision is made (it's a difficult work, and the people concerned are all very busy...). 'I can't fathom giving a work of this kind to Jurgenson', said Rachmaninoff; I answered 'Goodness, I've given my fourth part "Bazaar in Ancient Rus" to Jurgenson – in other words if you don't want it, then the devil take you'. But in general it was an interesting conversation, giving me some ideas.[20]

We know that when the manuscript was discussed at Edition Russe de Musique Rachmaninoff did indeed defend Kastalsky's work, giving his opinion that, although the material was raw, the material in itself was greatly needed and very interesting. But the critic A.V. Ossovsky was opposed to publication and asserted that Kastalsky's work was 'of no ethnographical interest, no scientific significance and no artistic value'.[21] As a result, the manuscript was rejected, and the composer had to seek funds to publish it himself. On 8 April 1914 Kastalsky informed Grozdov that he would prefer to revise the 'Celebrations' and then inquire about having them published by Shmidt. During 1915 Kastalsky really did revise the work substantially, the more so as Sergey Zimin, the proprietor of the Private Opera, began to take an interest in a stage production. In the spring of 1917 Kastalsky was already discussing with Asafyev the idea of orchestrating the 'Celebrations' and informed him that he had had the idea of a stage version, inspired by Melnikov-Pechersky's novel 'The Forests' (*Lesa*).

That is where the pre-revolutionary history of 'Celebrations' comes to an end. Without having been completed, the work lay in the composer's archive waiting for the time when he would again return to revise it.

As far as the remaining works of restoration were concerned, while they provoked perplexity on the part of several 'serious' composers and critics, they struck a chord with the young Asafyev, who saw in these musical scenes made up of a multitude of illustrations in small pictures a new genre in Russian music, which he described as a musical play. As Asafyev wrote,

> The essence of a play as it is taking shape in its modern conception amounts to rejecting the usual elements of drama, with an opening, a build-up of conflict and then its resolution – in short, any development of the action determined by the plot devised. What used to be the background or framework (everyday life) in a drama or a comedy now becomes a self-sufficient value, on condition that the religious basis, the primordial essence, of everyday life and ritual concealed in their outer forms is revealed. Personal feelings are removed or are possible not in contrast to the single *dramatis persona* – the people, but as individual expressions of the ordinary joys and sorrows known to everyone and felt by everyone.[22]

Kastalsky's experiments in restoring folk theatrical spectacles went unperformed; they were known basically only among musicians. But in itself the idea of plays on the stage proved viable, and was embodied in Stravinsky's brilliant works of the second half of the 1910s: *Renard* (*Bayka*) (A Burlesque Story about the Fox, the Cock, the Cat and the Ram) (a jolly presentation with song and instrumental music), *L'Histoire du Soldat* (Tale of a Fugitive Soldier and the Devil, to be read, played and danced), and *Les Noces* (*Svadebka*) (Russian Choreographic Scenes with Song and Instrumental Music, on folk texts). In the creative output of Kastalsky himself, the genre of the play found an outlet in one further work – the 'Requiem for Fallen Brothers'.

Notes

1. Letter from A.D. Kastal'sky to Kh.N. Grozdov of 12 October 1911. GTsMMK, fond 370, no. 512, pp. 12-13.
2. In the same concert pieces specially composed by Mikhail Ippolitov-Ivanov were performed: 'Troparion from the service to Our Holy Father Dionisy, compiled by his pupil Simon Azar'in' and 'Spiritual verse about patriarch Germogen' (*Dukhovnïy stikh o patriarkhe Germogene*).
3. Letter from A.D. Kastal'sky to G.N. Timofeyev of 23 November 1911. RNB, fond 423, no. 1510, pp. 1-1v.
4. Letter from A.D. Kastal'sky to A.V. Zatayevich of 23 March 1912. GTsMMK, fond 6, no. 314, pp. 1-2.
5. Letter from A.D. Kastal'sky to Kh.N. Grozdov of 18 January 1913. GTsMMK, fond 370, no. 520, pp. 1-1v.

6. Letter from A.D. Kastal'sky to B.V. Asaf'yev of 9 May 1918. RGALI, fond 2658, opis' 1, no. 581, p. 19v.

7. Ivan Goncharov was the director of the first Russian feature-length film *Osada Sevastopolya* (The Siege of Sebastopol), made in 1911. The film opera based on Nikolay Karamzin's story 'Poor Liza' was his last, unfortunately unrealized, project.

8. Letter from A.D. Kastal'sky to Kh.N. Grozdov of 9 October 1915. GTsMMK, fond 370, no. 533, p. 6.

9. Yu.P. Annenkov: *Nabroski tantsa k baletu A.D. Kastal'skogo 'Yekten'ya sugubaya'* (Sketches for a dance for A.D. Kastal'sky's ballet 'Augmented Litany'). RGALI, fond 2618, opis' 2, no. 4.

10. For evidence of a ballet entitled *Liturgie* under consideration at much the same time with which the names of Diaghilev, Massine and Stravinsky are associated, see, *inter alia*, Richard Taruskin: *Stravinsky and the Russian Traditions*. Oxford, 1996, vol. 2, p. 1379, footnote 64.

11. Letter from A.D. Kastal'sky to N.L. Kastal'skaya of 28 December 1912. GTsMMK, fond 12, no. 565, p. 1v.

12. Letter from A.D. Kastal'sky to A.V. Zatayevich of 11 April 1913. GTsMMK, fond 6, no. 315, p. 2.

13. Letter from A.D. Kastal'sky to Kh.N. Grozdov of 18 January 1913. GTsMMK, fond 370, no. 520, pp. 1v-2.

14. The person directly responsible for the Synodal Choir and School of Church Music – the *Prokuror* Filipp Stepanov – composed distinctly mediocre church choral pieces.

15. The person mentioned in the letter is the *Ober-Prokuror* of the Holy Synod, Vladimir Sabler.

16. Letter from A.D. Kastal'sky to Kh.N. Grozdov of 20 April 1913. GTsMMK, fond 370, no. 521, p. 3.

17. Letter from A.D. Kastal'sky to N.L. Kastal'skaya of 30 December 1913. GTsMMK, fond 12, no. 572, p. 1v.

18. Letter from A.D. Kastal'sky to G.N. Timofeyev of 15 February 1914. GTsMMK, fond 12, no. 440, p. 1.

19. G.N. Timofeyev: *[O tserkovnom penii]* (About church music). RNB, fond 773, no. 196, pp. 5-6.

20. A.D. Kastal'sky: *Iz vospominaniy o poslednikh godakh* (From reminiscences of recent years), in *RUSAM*, vol. 1, pp. 258-259.

21. A.V. Ossovsky: *S.V. Rakhmaninov*. In *Vospominaniya o Rakhmaninove* (Recollections of Rachmaninoff), vol. 1. Moscow, 1974, p. 382.

22. Igor' Glebov (B.V. Asaf'yev): *Ot 'opïtov' k novïm dostizheniyam. Po povodu muzïkal'nïkh 'restavratsiy' Kastal'skogo* (From 'experiments' to new achievements. Kastalsky's musical 'restorations'), in *Muzïka* (Music), 1915, no. 28, p. 413.

Chapter 17

'Requiem for Fallen Brothers'

But now an unprecedented war has burst out upon us... Who has not been carried away by it? Although in days of old I did my military service as an artilleryman, it was at the time when I was studying at the Conservatoire; the days when I was of any use as a soldier are long gone... I've had to respond to events only 'professionally', since there was nothing I could actually do. I started work simultaneously on both a musical 'battle' for orchestra taking national anthems as the themes, and 'Requiem for heroic brothers who have fallen in the Great War' using funeral melodies from the allied nations taking part. I've also orchestrated the greater part of a third work – a kind of processional also using national anthems as thematic material,

recalled Kastalsky of the beginning of the First World War.[1]

The 'Battle' and the 'Processional' he mentioned were never finished. Concentrating his attention on the 'Requiem for Fallen Brothers', and then on preparing for the première of his opera *Klara Milich*, the composer was in no hurry to finish them. 'In fact, there's no point in rushing', he wrote to a friend. 'Now those sons-of-bitches the Turks have joined in; maybe they too will have to be brought into the free-for-all? Therefore my composition is being written subject to political horizons'.[2] In 1917 those horizons changed to such an extent that Kastalsky was obliged to stop work altogether, because after the February revolution there was no demand for Aleksey Lvov's national anthem which he had used widely in these works. Judging by the materials in Kastalsky's literary archive, the 'Battle' (also known as the 'Battle of the Nations'), which had been conceived at first as the introduction to the 'Processional', gradually grew into an independent musical picture based on the development and collision of musical themes of the nations in the Entente and German songs such as 'Deutschland über alles', 'Wacht am Rhein', etc.

The composition of the monumental score of the 'Requiem for Fallen Brothers' developed using the same logic as in the works just mentioned – namely, it was determined by the contents of the military reports about the entry into the war of one or other of the allied countries. Consequently, there are several versions of the 'Requiem for Fallen Brothers', whose musical themes fully correspond with historical information about the membership of the anti-German coalition in the years 1916 and 1917.

Probably no other single composition gave the composer so much difficulty or was accompanied by such bouts of depression as the 'Requiem for Fallen Brothers'. In the spring of 1916, tired of the many alterations and additions, Kastalsky wrote to Grozdov:

> I'm completely demented! Accursed be the job of composing! What on earth's the point! Newspaper fame! You're dependent on messrs. conductor and impresario – whether they like you or not, whether they want to make you happy or not, that's what the whole thing hinges on, both fame and popularity – that's where the deception lies.[3]

Inclined even earlier to curse his profession from time to time, Kastalsky had never before been so much on edge as he was in these years. 'Requiem for Fallen Brothers' was of course the first experiment in his life at creating a monumental cyclical canvas. But the difficulties were not purely of a technical character: for the first time in history a composer was faced with the task of creating a form of funeral composition which would be acceptable in honouring the memory not just of people of different Christian denominations but also of other creeds.

The need for such a composition was self-evident. As Kastalsky wrote in the preface to the published edition of the 'Requiem', 'the unbroken brotherhood and unity of the nations of the Entente and their mutual fraternal help during the present war naturally gives rise to the idea of a fraternal service of remembrance for soldiers who have fallen for the common cause'. But what form should such a work take, when the idea of it so lacks any foundation from a canonical point of view? Kastalsky racked his brains over this for four years, starting out with the model which he had devised of a 'Russian Requiem'. Taking as his model the form of the Catholic Requiem Mass for the Dead, the composer decided to russify it in accordance with his views on 'the national distinctiveness of Russian music'.

As befitted a true representative of the new school, Kastalsky started his work by collecting genuine material. He set himself the task of obtaining the melodies heard during the funeral ceremonies of the various churches. One of his first steps was to tackle the organist of the Catholic cathedral in Moscow.

As Kastalsky wrote to a friend in Petrograd[4] in October 1914:

> I've begun the memorial service. I've made some plans, and been successful in my approach to the organist for musical themes from the service. We could

scarcely understand one another: 'the themes are different in Mozart and Schumann, after all', but he nevertheless gave me a little book (during the service he played the organ as well as speaking to me; he even showed me where I could tear off a piece of manuscript paper). I copied out what I needed for myself: the 'Dies irae' (which is well known) and the 'Lux perpetua', and it seemed there wasn't anything else. I found some funeral melodies – the Serbian ones – they'll also be useful, by the way.[5]

The form of the Catholic Mass for the Dead was well known to Kastalsky from his experience of teaching the Requiems of Mozart and Schumann to the Synodal Choir in the 1890s. And therefore his selection of numbers for inclusion in his own Requiem, where such movements as the 'Dies irae' and the 'Tuba mirum' are absent, certainly cannot be explained by lack of knowledge. The choice was obviously determined by considerations of artistic planning; movements corresponding in imagery and meaning to movements of the Russian memorial service (*panikhida*) were perhaps favoured in the selection, since the textual underlay in the choral parts was originally inserted in Latin and Church Slavonic.

The preliminary draft version of the 'Requiem' was ready by January 1915 and comprised the following movements: 'Requiem aeternam', 'Kyrie eleison', 'Rex tremendae', 'Confutatis', 'Lacrimosa', 'Domine Jesu', 'Hostias', 'Agnus Dei', 'Kyrie eleison' and 'Requiem aeternam'. The absence of certain Requiem numbers is conspicuous, and so is the untypical repetition of the 'Kyrie eleison' movement before the work's finale.

The first six months of 1915 were spent on composition, and in the middle of the year Kastalsky was able to show the piece to Grozdov, who at that time was working as inspector of the Court Kapella. While on holiday in the summer, however, Kastalsky suddenly realized that in his work he had forgotten about Anglicans who had died, and that 'it was awkward to write a work of remembrance without the participation of, so to speak, the crafty English'. For that reason a new round of research was begun, and a letter was despatched from Kimri to Moscow to the organist of the Anglican church with a request that he send on some popular church melodies. During that time Kastalsky inserted an English underlay into the score with the help of his wife Natalia and introduced an organ accompaniment. In October, after the composer's return to Moscow and his meeting with the English organist Don, two further movements of the 'Requiem', 'Ingemisco' and 'Sanctus', came into being.

Towards the end of 1915 the score of the first version of the work laid out for choir and organ was completed;[6] the Requiem movements were arranged in the following order: 1. 'Requiem aeternam', 2. 'Kyrie eleison',

3. 'Rex tremendae', 4. 'Ingemisco', 5. 'Confutatis', 6. 'Lacrimosa', 7. 'Domine Jesu', 8. 'Hostias', 9. 'Sanctus', 10. 'Agnus Dei', 11. 'Kyrie eleison', 12. 'Requiem aeternam'.   The idea of making a simplified arrangement of the composition for performance in Catholic churches occurred to Kastalsky at that time, but when the idea did not find support from Grozdov it was dropped.

In October 1915 Kastalsky began to consider the difficulties which might lie in store for the work as a result of the use in it of canonical Church Slavonic texts and the necessity arising from that of obtaining permission to print and perform it.   Moreover, the concluding major-key finale-apotheosis was based on the melody of the kontakion 'With the Saints give rest' (*So svyatïmi upokoy*), which might even induce outrage in Synodal circles where shortly before this an instruction had been drawn up which made the rules on giving concerts of sacred music much more rigorous.

In the meantime, the composer's fertile imagination was taking the idea of the composition ever further and further beyond the boundaries of any canonical framework: while discussing the severities of the censorship with friends, he shared his idea that the non-Christian nations taking part in the war against the Germans had been undeservedly forgotten in his Requiem, and asked Grozdov to trouble the famous scholar of the Middle Ages Preobrazhensky with a request to search in the Public Library in Petrograd for funeral melodies of the Hindus, the Singhalese and others. (We need to remember that in the course of the war the Entente, which was originally made up only of Russia, France and Great Britain, was joined by Belgium, Bolivia, Brazil, China, Cuba, Ecuador, Greece, Guatemala, Haiti, Hejaz, Honduras, Italy, Japan, Liberia, Nicaragua, Panama, Peru, Portugal, Rumania, Serbia, Siam, Uruguay and the USA.) Kastalsky himself took a zealous part in searching for themes from the oriental allies, having decided to refer to them in instrumental interludes (inserted after the 8th and 11th numbers).   By this point it was perfectly clear that there could be no question of obtaining permission of any kind from the church censorship.

Trying to avoid a collision with the Synod, the composer decided in December 1915 on an extreme measure – removing the Church Slavonic text and leaving only the Latin and English.   This decision was rapidly overturned by him, however, because it led to the open abandonment of the idea born in the depths of his soul of a 'Russian Requiem' in favour of a Requiem which was 'non-Russian'. Imagining the reaction of the public, which would probably reason that Kastalsky had obviously got bored with composing Orthodox chants, and had therefore written a Requiem, the composer, continuing his torrents of irony and measuring his Requiem against its French translation – 'Commémoration fraternelle', wrote to Grozdov: 'Something extremely odd it would be – especially for Kastalsky – it's funny even to me; like walking along the Nevsky with bare thighs and wearing a red toga, or, even better, in a red cardinal's robe with red skull-cap'.[7] Literally a few minutes after he had written these lines, a new idea came to Kastalsky, an idea which gave the work a chance of avoiding all the tribulations of censorship: he decided to replace the church text with a free translation into Russian, falling back on the paraphrases of A.K. Tolstoy, Bazhanov and the priest Slobodskoy, with some home-made text. The new Russian underlay was skilfully inserted into the manuscript vocal score, and it is in that form that the 'Requiem' has come down to us via its 1916 publication.

Having effected such an abrupt modulation towards a secular genre, Kastalsky had not, though, given up the idea of hearing the work in a church version, and decided that in due course he would create another version for a cappella choir in Church Slavonic which would be intended specifically for performance during worship in Orthodox churches. Thus was born the idea of the third version of the 'Russian Requiem'.

While this church version, later to be entitled 'Eternal Memory to the Heroes' (*Vechnaya pamyat' geroyam*), was awaiting its time, the second version with the free Russian translation entered a stage which was difficult for the composer – that of orchestration – in the winter of 1916. In the interim, circumstances forced Kastalsky to rush to complete the work, since the prospect of Count Alexander Sheremetyev's choir performing it had arisen unexpectedly; Grozdov had sought this, and helped Kastalsky to put the proofs in order and hastened along the orchestration. Under his friend's pressure, at the end of December 1915 the composer embarked on setting out the score, complaining to Grozdov: 'That's all you ever say to me – "orchestrate! get on with the orchestration!" Who do you think I am – Rimsky-Korsakov, or somebody? A couple of hours and it's in the bag? That's not the way it is at all: I sit from morning to night, entering things in the draft and thinking things out'.[8] While complaining to Grozdov that the work was 'not going very swiftly', Kastalsky was busy writing the organ part – not without satisfaction – which, in his own words, he had introduced in some places to support the choir and in others to bind the instrumental colours together. (One should add that the 1910s are noteworthy for Kastalsky's unusually close attention to the organ. In one of his letters from those years he even confessed that he had had to sell his harmonium at home because he had been too much attracted to its 'ethereal sonorities' at the expense of composing.)

In the winter of 1916, however, the composer had had to abandon both experiments with the organ and the work on orchestration for a certain period. The reason was that the choirmaster of the Synodal Choir, Danilin, who had come to know the 'Requiem', suggested performing some numbers from it at a concert devoted to Kastalsky. After giving his consent, however, the composer ran into an unanticipated problem: since during the war years a field hospital had been accommodated in the Moscow Conservatoire, the organ in the Great Hall had been boarded up, and the organ in the Small Hall had been worn out by students studying on it intensively. Moreover, the student orchestra of the Synodal School was too feeble to perform a complex score. Kastalsky was left with no alternative but to make an arrangement of three movements of the 'Requiem' for choir a cappella, which were performed for the first time on 6 March 1916 in the hall of the Synodal School. The première of three 'choral extracts' from the 'Requiem' – 'With the Saints give rest' (*So svyatïmi upokoy*), 'Give rest with the just, O our Saviour' (*Pokoy Spase*) and 'Eternal memory' (*Vechnaya pamyat'*) – was interpreted as an important public event and left an ineradicable impact on listeners: many crossed themselves or wept, and for the last movement those present in the hall stood.[9]

Meanwhile, the Petrograd première of the 'Requiem for Fallen Brothers' by Count Sheremetyev's forces was cancelled, and the composer had to look for another performance opportunity. Recalling that the conductor Alexander Siloti gave concerts in the Mariinsky Theatre regularly, Kastalsky resolved to entrust negotiations with him to Serge Rachmaninoff, Siloti's cousin. Learning at the beginning of April that Rachmaninoff's mission had been successful and Siloti had agreed to perform his new opus, Kastalsky got down to completing the work eagerly, the more so as Moscow musicians had also begun to take an interest in the 'Requiem' and an offer to perform it had reached the composer from Emil Kuper, conductor of the Bolshoy Theatre, and Mikhail Ippolitov-Ivanov, the director of the Moscow Conservatoire.

By the end of April the adaptations of the work were complete, and so were the two new interpolated numbers dedicated to the memory of Buddhist soldiers. Kastalsky, completely exhausted, wrote to his friend:

> Joking apart, if the idea of a fraternal union in the struggle with the Germans had not been firmly in my mind, I'd have discarded it, without batting an eyelid – the whole of the 'Requiem' with all of its entrails! I'm so fed up with it! You can hardly find two or three numbers which have remained intact – everything has had alterations made to it over and over again (thank goodness that at least the choir part has stayed the same – of course, in general though not

in the details, which also crack at the seams in alterations). The second movement is redone from scratch, the seventh as well, the ninth is lowered a semitone and has had a new accompaniment added (new introduction). And in addition I've cooked up the Japanese national anthem (as an Interludium), as I couldn't find any funeral melodies and seized on the fact that the Japanese have hardly suffered any human losses. I have concocted another Interludium out of a Hindu hymn to Indra, since again I couldn't find anything for funerals, and seized on the idea that Indra receives fallen soldiers on her couch. My wife, of course, is cursing me, saying that all this is neither fish nor fowl, and why just Hindus, and so on. For me it's important to show that even the Asians are not forgotten. I was on the point of dragging in a New Zealand funeral song – it was also aboriginal – and I gave up. I want to visit the Japanese consulate to see if they can't find something.[10]

The most important thing for Kastalsky in his composition was historical truth, and also the necessity to give their due to the memory of all the soldiers who fell in the struggle with the enemy without regard to their nationality or creed. Concerns about the artistic form took second place, and that form took shape in association with the entry of allies to the coalition and in line with how the composer himself perceived events.

While composing the 'Requiem', Kastalsky liked to seek advice from friends and colleagues, but there were very few among them who shared his 'civic' approach to the creation of a work of art. Many musicians examined the score at different stages of preparation; they included Kashkin, Vasilenko, Zatayevich, Grozdov, Asafyev, Derzhanovsky, Kuper, Safonov, Ippolitov-Ivanov, Sakhnovsky and others. In one of his letters Kastalsky wrote in detail about the encounter with the three last-named 'generals' which took place in February 1916 and amounted to a kind of exam for Kastalsky. The presentation of the work took place in the Director's office at the Conservatoire late one evening, when the work was played on two pianos by the composer and his friend Zatayevich. As Kastalsky summed up his impressions, Safonov had arrived tired after a rehearsal, and was not very attentive: he livened up only when he heard some familiar Old Believer melodies, and suggested publishing the composition with a London publisher whom he knew. Ippolitov-Ivanov praised the accompaniment as a 'cute little item', and Sakhnovsky approved of the score and heard in the 'Requiem' a special kind of style combining influences from Borodin, Rimsky-Korsakov, Musorgsky, Bach and Handel. On the whole, it seemed to Kastalsky that the 'pure sons of art' had failed to understand the most important thing: 'The actual idea itself (the most precious thing) remained in the background as far as they were concerned; none of them picked up any scent of brotherhood – music was the only thing that mattered to them'.[11] This meeting was not in vain for the composer, however, because during the presentation of the work a happy thought came to him – to begin the 'Requiem' with a bass monologue, which he composed immediately (Ex. 17.1). 'Every cloud has a silver lining: the generals who sensed nothing about music brought me a happy idea', as Kastalsky consoled himself.[12]

Thus, by the beginning of May the 'Requiem for Fallen Brothers' was finally in the form in which Kastalsky decided to submit it to the publisher Jurgenson. The vocal score and parts were published on 10 November 1916, and by the end of the year the orchestral score had also been lithographed.

A long-awaited important event took place on 7 January 1917 – the première of the 'Requiem for Fallen Brothers' in the Mariinsky Theatre in Petrograd.[13] It made a big impression on the public, but left the composer dissatisfied. When reviewing this concert, Asafyev was obliged to say that:

> in Petrograd they don't understand Kastalsky and don't know how to sing his music. The performance was like reading out a document written in a language the performers didn't understand, without any hint of phrasing, or dividing the music up into phrases, or distributing accents, even if one supposes that there was at least a desire to understand an unknown composer. And there was no one to blame, since each was as perplexed as the other (the conductor, the soloists, the choir, the orchestra) and shuffled along as if they were blind. There was only one course left – to blame the composer. That was what they did, without even having made any effort to represent his ideas as they should have done.[14]

Despite reading many reproaches in the press, Kastalsky did not give up. Inspired by the entry of the Americans to the anti-German alliance in the summer of 1917, and also by the proposal of the Jurgenson firm to publish a second edition of the vocal score, as the first had sold out, he wrote another three new numbers for the 'Requiem for Fallen Brothers'. One of them arose as a consequence of his meeting with the members of an American Extraordinary Mission which arrived in Petrograd in the summer of that year.

His acquaintance with John Mott and Cyrus McCormick took place through the mediation of Kastalsky's old admirer Charles Crane. The composer put many detailed questions to the Americans about how funeral ceremonies were carried out in America, asked them for funeral melodies and there and then, in Petrograd, composed the American number 'Rock of ages', which was performed in the Winter Palace before the envoys. He described the latter event to his wife:

Taking advantage of free evenings up to Sunday, I wrote the American number of the 'Requiem' [...] in which motives from Chopin's funeral march go in alternation and even together with two American (genuine American!) funeral melodies. McCormick (to whom I played it in the Winter Palace on an upright piano with mother-of-pearl keys) was amazed and went into raptures. Even while deeply moved, he brought his little sheets of manuscript paper on which he sketched their melodies in an inspired way ('even on the train I was writing melodies!'). He suggested that he might 'help' me publish my American number with Jurgenson. [...] I'm pleased, however, that I've done it (I'll have to orchestrate more simply). I was on the point of introducing Prokofiev to the Americans, – but it didn't come off!...[15]

Having paid his respects to the Americans, Kastalsky decided to refer to the presence in the anti-German coalition of the French, the Rumanians, the Greeks and the Portuguese, by using elements from the musical material of those nations in two new numbers 'Beati mortui' (*Blazheni usopshiye*) and 'Dies irae' (*Kakaya sladost' v zhizni sey*), to a text by A.K. Tolstoy from 'St John of Damascus' (*Ioann Damaskin*). Besides political considerations, the composer was also guided by the demands of artistic strategy, candidly admitting in a letter to Asafyev:

These two numbers should introduce a degree of animation into the majority of the other movements which are rather slow in tempo. Work on these pieces proceeded with difficulty, because I had to put up with some very strong sounds in competition: every evening from the house opposite the despairing cries of a lady singing interspersed with a no less despairing tenor (with gipsy repertoire) came freely through my open windows (and even now they're coming in a little). And from the gates across from them came the sounds of balalaykas and concertinas, with each piece never lasting less than half an hour. But I struggled on valiantly, did not desert my post, and ... got to the end.[16]

In June 1917 Kastalsky submitted three new numbers to the publisher Jurgenson which over the course of the second half of the year were published lithographically.[17] (The choral items in the 17-movement version of the Requiem were in the following sequence: 1. 'Requiem aeternam', 2. 'Kyrie eleison', 3. 'Rex tremendae', 4. 'Ingemisco', 5. 'Confutatis', 6. 'Lacrimosa', 7. 'Domine Jesu', 8. 'Beati mortui', 9. 'Hostias', 10. Interludium, 11. 'Sanctus', 12. 'Agnus Dei', 13. 'Dies irae', 14. 'Rock of ages', 15. 'Kyrie eleison', 16. Interludium, 17. 'Requiem aeternam'.)

The prospect of a second edition of the vocal score, and also the interest taken in the composition by the conductor Yevgeny Plotnikov, formerly of the Zimin Opera Theatre, who had expressed a desire to perform the work at Easter 1918, inspired Kastalsky to make a new version of the orchestration, and also to write a programme for the performance. The latter was no doubt linked with his recollection of the unsuccessful Petrograd première and with the intention of explaining his conception in more detail to performers and public this time.

It has to be said that the view of the work in performance took shape over a number of months and went hand in hand with the changes which the score itself and the composer's opinions underwent. The question of the form in which the new work ought to be performed was one which Kastalsky had asked himself as early as 1915, when he could see the prospect of the work being completed. The idea of how the previously unknown remembrance ceremony should be conducted had been put to Kastalsky by Bishop Anastasy, who was popular in Moscow, often officiated in the Cathedral of the Dormition and knew well and approved of Kastalsky's compositions. When he met the bishop at one of the concerts where Rachmaninoff's All-Night Vigil was performed, the composer told him about his new work, which prompted the hierarch, as Kastalsky wrote, to exercise his imagination freely: 'If it were to be performed at the mass graves of fallen brothers in the presence of allied troops, banners and with military music – that would be absolutely terrific'.[18] This 'fantasy' was obviously close to Kastalsky because a description of a picture of a performance similar to it is found in the manuscript vocal score of 1916. The only divergence lay in the fact that the ceremony ought to be conducted not by the graves of fallen brothers but in a church, around which military units had taken up position. But against the background of discussions about the Synod's tightening-up of the regulations for the conduct of religious concerts and the possible prohibition on publishing the work, a church as performance venue looked unrealistic. For that reason, when all was said and done the composer preferred not to be specific about where the action should take place.

In the vocal score published in 1916 the description of the 'solemn religious ceremony' reads as follows:

> around the place where the act of worship is conducted units of allied troops are assembled; funeral melodies are heard – now Russian, now Catholic, now Serbian, now English; one language succeeds another; from time to time trumpet-calls of the different armies, drum-beats, and cannonades can be heard; bereaved wives and mothers sob their lamentations in the distance; to the sides where the Asian soldiers are to be found the sounds of Japanese and Hindu national anthems ring out. At the proclamation 'Eternal memory' military bands join in, artillery salutes ring out and the music takes on the bright colours of the apotheosis of the fallen heroes.

One can see that the description of the surroundings which accompany the actual act of worship is very reminiscent of the remarks in the section *Rus* from Kastalsky's cycle 'From past ages'. But nevertheless, in spite of the lamentations, trumpet-calls and cannonades etc. envisaged at the performance of the 'Requiem for Fallen Brothers', the composer regarded his composition in 1916 as ritual music, deciding not, however, to discuss what the worship setting of this international Requiem ought to be. This topic was thus never developed by the composer, since the theatrical stage not only did not lend itself to such a treatment of the subject, but also dictated its own laws. It was those that Kastalsky followed in his description for the programme of the performance of the 'Requiem for Fallen Brothers' prepared for the Moscow première in 1917, which was fated not to take place. In the form in which it was cast in that programme, the composition had very little in common with a religious ceremony and appeared to be 'a kind of oratorio' with elements of stage action whose heroes were a cardinal, youths in white attire, English, Rumanian and Italian nurses, a Greek clergyman, groups of Russian peasant women, Montenegrins and Serbs, some Americans, Hindu soldiers and priests, a Japanese religious procession, and also a choir.[19] A church was present on the stage as an element of décor: the cardinal emerged from it with the processions, and chants could be heard. But this stage-prop church was only a symbol of the real church which Kastalsky spoke about in 1916 when imagining his composition as a religious ceremony. One year later the 'Requiem for Fallen Brothers' had turned into a stage spectacle with elements of church ritual and become a continuation of the composer's series of dramatic actions.

The final 17-movement version of the 'Requiem for Fallen Brothers' was not in fact performed in Zimin's Theatre.[20] Plotnikov, the conductor, anticipating complications with the new authorities, who, in his words, 'have nothing in common with art', renounced his intention, and emigrated from Russia altogether in 1918. The political situation too worked against the composition: in March 1918 rumours about the imminent arrival of the Germans circulated around Moscow, and soon even former allies turned into enemies. Thus ended Alexander Kastalsky's tribulations over the creation of an immense musical chronicle of the First World War.

Notes

1. A.D. Kastal'sky: *Iz vospominaniy o poslednikh godakh* (From my reminiscences of recent years) in *RUSAM*, vol. 1 p. 251.

2. Letter from A.D. Kastal'sky to Kh.N. Grozdov of 21 October 1914. GTsMMK, fond 370, no. 530, p. 14v.

3. Letter from A.D. Kastal'sky to Kh.N. Grozdov of 1 April 1916. GTsMMK, fond 370, no. 546, p. 19.

4. The name St Petersburg, with its German sound, was changed to Petrograd soon after the start of hostilities in 1914. After the death in 1924 of the leader of the October revolution, the city which had been the cradle of that revolution was renamed Leningrad in his honour.

5. Letter from A.D. Kastal'sky to Kh.N. Grozdov of 21 October 1914. GTsMMK, fond 370, no. 530, p. 14v.

6. The dispersed incomplete manuscript of this original version is now preserved in RGALI, fond 952, opis' 1, no. 269. It lacks the 'Sanctus'.

7. Letter from A.D. Kastal'sky to Kh.N. Grozdov of 19-20 January 1916. GTsMMK, fond 370, no. 542, p. 9v.

8. Letter from A.D. Kastal'sky to Kh.N. Grozdov of 26 December 1915. GTsMMK, fond 370, no. 536, p. 11v.

9. For this concert, see *'Otkrïtiye' Kastal'skogo* (Kastal'sky's 'Discovery'), in *Muzïka* (Music), 1916, no. 249, pp. 172-173.

10. Letter from A.D. Kastal'sky to Kh.N. Grozdov of 25 April 1917. GTsMMK, fond 370, no. 547, pp. 22-22v.

11. Letter from A.D. Kastal'sky to Kh.N. Grozdov of 3 February 1916. GTsMMK, fond 370, no. 545, p. 17.

12. *Ibid.*, p. 18.

13. On 22 November 1917 the 14-movement version of the 'Requiem for Fallen Brothers' was performed in Birmingham by the Festival Choral Society conducted by Sir Henry Wood. In the composer's native land this version has been heard only once – with a new secular patriotic text; it was performed by the USSR State Symphony Orchestra and the Large Chorus of the All-Union Radio conducted by Yevgeny Svetlanov on 12 March 1977, when it was recorded live.

14. Igor' Glebov (B.V. Asaf'yev): *'Bratskoye pominoveniye' A. Kastal'skogo* (A. Kastal'sky's 'Requiem for Fallen Brothers'), in Chronicle of the journal *Muzïkal'nïy sovremennik* (Musical contemporary), 1917, no. 15, p. 5.

15. Letter from A.D. Kastal'sky to N.L. Kastal'skaya of 20 June 1917. GTsMMK, fond 370, no. 583, p. 1v.

16. Letter from A.D. Kastal'sky to B.V. Asaf'yev of June 1917. RGALI, fond 2658, opis' 1, no. 581, p. 13.

17. Authorized manuscripts of the numbers 'Beati mortui' and 'Rock of ages' are preserved in RGALI (fond 952, opis' 1, no. 266, pp. 4-5v and 8-9v.). Page proofs of the lithographed version of all three numbers are in GTsMMK (fond 12, nos. 447, 448 and 451).

18. Letter from A.D. Kastal'sky to Kh.N. Grozdov of 23 February 1915. GTsMMK, fond 370, no. 535, p. 10.

19. This programme is also in GTsMMK (fond 12, no. 506). In 1990 it was published by A.T. Tevosyan in the symposium *Naslediye. Muzïkal'nïye sobraniya* (Heritage. Musical assemblies). Moscow, 1990, pp. 13-20.

20. The first and so far only performance of the 17-movement version of 'Requiem for Fallen Brothers' was given in 1992 by the New Moscow Symphony Orchestra and the Large Choir of the Radio conducted by Konstantin Krimets.

Chapter 18

The Late Sacred Choral Music

What place did sacred music occupy in Kastalsky's work in the years immediately before the revolution? In the catalogue of the composer's work published by P. Jurgenson, and also in the periodical publications where sacred music compositions were announced, only ten sacred music compositions are listed. Included among them are arrangements entirely within the *kliros* tradition but carried out with immense skill: the festal Hymn to the Theotokos (*zadostoynik*) for Trinity Sunday, and the troparion for the holy martyr Hermogen, attempts at ethnographic stylization (the 'We hymn Thee' (*Tebe poyem*) to a Georgian chant), the inspired extended scenes for soloist and choir 'Thy bridal chamber' (*Chertog Tvoy*) and 'Gladsome Light' (*Svete tikhiy*) no. 4, intended for the great tenor Leonid Sobinov, and other works.

Reviewing the composer's final choral works, Asafyev wrote:

> All these works by Kastalsky bear witness to imaginativeness, originality, and profundity – to that blossoming of creativity which occurs after a composer has found and mastered the means of expression necessary to reveal his creative persona, and is now able to reveal with assurance and in full the powers concealed within him. Radiant, expressive and beautiful – the description fits any of the compositions listed above.[1]

Later in his review, the critic analyses the troparion for the holy martyr Hermogen, 'O Heavenly King' (*Tsaryu nebesnïy*), the festal Hymn to the Theotokos for Trinity Sunday, the Georgian 'We hymn Thee' and 'Christ is risen' (*Khristos voskrese*) dedicated to the boy choristers of the Court Kapella, and points to the simplicity, naturalness and at the same time lack of formality in the harmonic devices, the ingenious stratification and expansion of the voices, and to the distinctive but always well founded false relations and chromaticisms.

The hymn 'The good thief' (*Razboynika blagorazumnago*) particularly delighted Asafyev and he considered it one of the pearls among Kastalsky's compositions (Ex. 18.1). The critic wrote:

It is impossible to imagine a simpler or more modest conception. Over a sustained pedal point (a low fifth in the tenors and basses), the trebles and altos (soloists, or else two or three performers per part) sing a doleful melody bathed in tender heartfelt sorrow harmonized in a fascinating manner. The religious contemplation of the Russian, the purely Russian soul which has plumbed the depths of folk creativity, can be heard in this melody. There are only twelve bars, but to create them it was necessary for an unknown force to insert in the artist's soul some remote bygone mourning endured perhaps over the course of centuries by several generations, and it is also necessary that the person through whom this was revealed just did not know what he was creating. Possibly some personal grief was making itself felt here. Who can tell?... But in any case, the completeness, conciseness and expressiveness of 'The good thief' are qualities so significant, the mastery with which the composition is carried out so perfect, and the sincerity and heartfeltness of the music – move one so much that one cannot fail to number it among the most significant achievements in the realm of church music.[2]

Thus, sacred choral pieces are rare phenomena among Kastalsky's compositions of the years between 1910 and 1916. Burdened by work obligations, attracted by research into folklore and constructing a theory of folk style, seized by the idea of composing choral music with accompaniment, the composer seemed to have abandoned the field where he had won recognition as one of the best. At the end of 1916, however, on the threshold of the great catastrophe, he returned once more to a cappella sacred music and composed a work which worthily crowned his career as a church composer. The work in question is the cycle for a cappella choir 'Eternal Memory to the Heroes' (Selected Hymns from the Memorial Service) (*Vechnaya pamyat' geroyam. (Izbrannïye pesnopeniya Panikhidï)*), which represents the third version of the 'Requiem for Fallen Brothers'.

This work is based on the first, unpublished version of 'Requiem for Fallen Brothers' for choir and organ of 1915. Why did the composer take the first version with organ as the basis for the third version, rather than the fuller, second version with orchestra? It is possible that he felt that in the orchestral version, which he had reworked and extended many times, many of the improvements had been made in vain. Thus, he preferred to go back to the original version, which had been composed 'in a single breath' and which probably struck him as being closer to the concept of the canonical memorial service. The church genres imposed discipline on Kastalsky, leaving relatively little scope for 'arbitrariness'. And for that reason in the new version of the Requiem he tried to avoid elements of historical and ethnographical stylization.

Altering the organ version of 'Requiem for Fallen Brothers' to create 'Eternal Memory to the Heroes' did not take long. Judging from the material preserved in the Russian State Archive for Literature and Art, the adaptation was carried out very quickly using the manuscript of the first version of 'Requiem for Fallen Brothers'. The changes amounted mainly to crossing out what was superfluous and writing new endings for movements. This can be explained by the fact that the organ part, which links the movements in the cycle, had been eliminated, and the need arose to assign its functions to the choir. The composer had only to write one number from scratch – 'I will pour out my petition' (*Molitvu proliyu*), while the three movements performed at the Synodal Choir's concert in March 1916 required no amendments at all.

The changes in the choral parts of the first version amounted to the following: the 'Ingemisco' and 'Sanctus' movements were eliminated altogether; the two movements 'Requiem aeternam' and 'Lacrimosa' were significantly shortened; both 'Kyrie eleison' (both times), 'Rex tremendae', 'Confutatis', 'Domine Jesu', 'Hostias' and 'Agnus Dei' underwent small editorial corrections.

Thus, in 'Eternal Memory to the Heroes', also known as his Memorial Service (*Panikhida*), the composer returned to the work's original conception. What differed very sharply in musical language was subject to shortening – namely, the two numbers 'Sanctus' and 'Ingemisco', which were marked by the weighty magnificence and depth of feeling typical of oratorio. The elimination of the organ, the main instrument of stylization, also helped smooth out the ethnic colouring. The work became more of an entity, more compact, as a result; the mosaic quality was softened, and a sense of a 'painted fresco' on the grand scale arose. The Memorial Service appears still more integral in dramatic plan and stylistically unified in comparison with the final orchestral version in 17 movements of the 'Requiem for Fallen Brothers' in 1917, which includes 'Asian' interludes and 'American', 'Portuguese', 'Greek' and 'Rumanian' thematic material.

A certain kaleidoscopic element is nonetheless inherent in 'Eternal Memory to the Heroes', however. This manifests itself first and foremost in the Litany and the Triple Litany, which originate in nos. 2 and 11 respectively of the 'Requiem for Fallen Brothers'. These movements are remote from any traditional genre – as they were initially, and represent extended programmatic canvases. In this regard the composer inserted indications in the score of the Memorial Service that in the event of it being performed during worship it would be necessary to retain only certain choral responses. A mosaic quality is inherent too in another movement – 'Give rest, O Lord' (*Pokoy, Gospodi*), whose origin lies in the 'Lacrimosa' movement. The 'Catholic' fragment and the 'Russian lament', the latter without words in the 'Requiem for Fallen Brothers', remained in the Memorial Service as the central section of the movement; in the new version it was provided with a stanza from the canon for the deceased. In the a cappella version of this movement another innovation attracts attention – the prolonged pedal point in the basses which stems from the orchestral part of the second version. The pedal point in the movement 'Thou art the God' (*Ti yesi Bog*) also goes back to the orchestral part of the 'Requiem for Fallen Brothers', which adorned by its presence the troparion narrating the descent into hell (the low basses in the choir have to go down to a low G at this point). In this way the orchestral stage in the life of this composition did not pass by without leaving a trace in the Memorial Service.

In the concluding number of the Memorial Service the composer could not relinquish the idea of a finale-apotheosis which had taken his fancy. To be sure, the major-key funeral march based on the theme of the kontakion 'With the Saints give rest' (*So svyatïmi upokoy*) from the 'Requiem for Fallen Brothers' did not find its way into the Memorial Service; on the other hand, the 'Eternal memory', sounding so unusual in the major, remained.

And, lastly, the principal innovation in the second version must be mentioned – the new movement 'I will pour out my petition unto the Lord', written at the end of December 1916, replacing the lyrico-dramatic movement 'Ingemisco' (an 'Anglican' number for solo soprano). The penitential monologue for solo tenor with choral accompaniment became the only manifestation of a personal element in the Memorial Service. Unlike the 'Ingemisco', based on independent material, the monologue of the tenor is tightly bound up with the fabric of the Memorial Service and is a treatment of the chant 'With the Saints give rest'. The soloist's part, which initially developed as the pathetic speech of a man sensing the horrors of approaching hell, flows at the end of the movement into the common current of the chant element of the kontakion (Ex. 18.2).[3]

As a result of the re-ordering of the movements to correspond with the sequence of the Memorial service, the items from the former Requiem emerged in the following order: 1. Litany (*Yekten'ya*), formerly the 'Kyrie eleison' (no. 2); 2. Alliluiya and 'O Thou who with wisdom profound' (*Glubinoyu mudrosti*), formerly the 'Domine Jesu'; 3. 'Give rest with the Just, O our Saviour' (*Pokoy, Spase*), formerly the 'Hostias'; 4. 'Give rest, O Lord' (*Pokoy, Gospodi*), formerly 'Lacrimosa'; 5. 'I will pour out my petition' (*Molitvu proliyu*), formerly 'Ingemisco'; 6. 'With the Saints give rest' (*So svyatïmi upokoy*), formerly 'Requiem aeternam' (no. 1); 7. 'Thou alone art immortal' (*Sam Yedin yesi bezsmertnïy*), formerly the 'Rex tremendae'; 8. 'Thou art the God' (*Ti yesi Bog*), formerly 'Confutatis'; 9.

'Give rest, O Lord' (*Upokoy, Bozhe*), formerly 'Agnus Dei'; 10. Triple Litany (*Troynaya yekten'ya*), formerly 'Kyrie eleison' (no. 11); 11. 'Eternal memory' (*Vechnaya pamyat'*), formerly 'Requiem aeternam' (no. 12).

The dramatic plan of the music in the Memorial Service took shape spontaneously, but it looks well proportioned and well regulated nonetheless. As a result of the re-ordering of the movements, the dramatic and tragic pieces (nos. 5-8) are placed at the centre of the composition, while the movements characterized by calm, radiant hues are concentrated at the beginning and end of the cycle.

With the writing of 'Eternal Memory', it also became clear that the choral score of the 'Requiem for Fallen Brothers' was self-sufficient and capable of surviving as an independent composition.

'Eternal Memory to the Heroes', published in early 1917, brought to a worthy conclusion a whole era in Russian sacred music, which for many years thereafter was to be an art 'without the law'. The fate of one of the finest creations in the heritage of Russian church music proved dismal: it was first heard complete only fifty years after the composer's death.[4] As regards the bibliography for this work, it amounts to just a few phrases of Asafyev, who during the Second World War recalled this 'Russian Requiem' in the following words:

> The same 'ticking of the clock of history' in the heat of the flames of the First World War roused in the heart of the composer Kastalsky a sorrowful threnody, a great lament for the fallen heroes, in accordance with the customs of the Russian people – for the heroic warriors who had fought for the Russian nation and her allies. This Requiem, 'Requiem for Fallen Brothers' (for choir and orchestra), entirely Russian in its sources and its choral style, made a very deep impression: the music of the tears of many nations – that is how the whole 'Requiem' was interpreted. When in its compressed version – in an edition for a cappella choir – the separate choral movements were brought together with one another, the 'Requiem' became yet more profound – it became the epic bearer of universal grief, attaining Homeric majestic simplicity and sustained lyricism.[5]

Notes

1. B'as (B.V. Asaf'yev): *A. Kastal'sky. Dukhovno-muzïkal'nïye sochineniya. Notografiya* (A. Kastal'sky. Sacred music compositions. Music publications), in *Muzïka* (Music), 1916, no. 248, p. 158.
2. *Ibid.*, p. 159.
3. The autograph of this movement, dated 27 December 1916, is preserved in RGALI, fond 952, opis' 1, no. 266, pp. 6-6v.

4. The première of the complete 'The Eternal Memory of the Heroes' was given on 18 February 1996 by the male-voice choir of the Academy of Choral Art conducted by Viktor Popov, who made a new version of the work for same-voice choir. In the composer's original version for mixed choir, this work was performed in 1997 for the first time by an American amateur choir, the Russian Chamber Chorus, conducted by A.V. Rudenko, in a church in the Boston suburb of Cambridge.

5. B.V. Asaf'yev: *Ne zaklyucheniye, a prolog* (Not a conclusion – rather, a prologue). Academician B.V. Asaf'yev: *Izbrannïye trudï* (Selected works), vol. 5. Moscow, 1957, p. 96.

Chapter 19

The End
of the Synodal School's History

In 1916, on the threshold of revolutionary events, the Synodal Choir and School of Church Music were going through hard times. Because of the high cost of living during the war years, the Synod's financial managers suggested to the School that, like other educational institutions under the church's control, they 'shorten teaching' by two or three months. The discussion of this proposal at the School's board on 12 December 1916 ended with the passing of a resolution that teaching could not be discontinued: 'Closing the school would not only deprive the choir of the chance of improvement but would also destroy choral work put into shape over centuries. After about a year, the choir would have to be created again right from the beginning'.[1]

The School board was supported by the senior priest of the Cathedral of the Dormition Nikolay Lyubimov, who sent in a report to the Synod Office saying that even the temporary closure of the School would lead to the cessation of singing at services in the Cathedral of the Dormition: the adult singers could not shoulder the responsibilities of the whole choir, the more so since 11 out of 30 of them had already been called up for military service. As a result it was decided to end the academic year a few weeks earlier – on 18 March. The School faced the serious problem of how to survive, as the money allocated for the academic year 1916–17 had already been spent by the beginning of the year and it was necessary to seek additional resources. It was decided to increase the charges for the rent of flats in houses which had long been the property of the Synodal Choir. Other sources of income included renting out the School's large hall, selling copies of the Synodal Choir *Obikhod*, charging for examinations for the title of church choirmaster, and being paid for outside services where the Choir was asked to sing. The reintroduction of the last charge, which had been dispensed with in Smolensky's time, became inevitable during the First World War.

Because of the call-up, the adult membership of the choir had fallen to two thirds of the usual, and the director of the School was obliged in January 1917 to petition the *prokuror* of the Synod office that the choir sing at services in the cathedral only when the senior priest was taking part and not at ordinary ones. There could be no question of extended concert activity; according to the information available, the Synodal Choir sang in concerts on only four occasions in the 1916–17 season.

A difficult situation also arose in relation to the call-up of persons working in the School. On 15 July 1916 the directorate of the Synodal School was even obliged to send a request to the commander of the Moscow Military District N.N. Obolensky to send 18 prisoners-of-war who were Slavs whom it was intended to use in the dining room, kitchen and dormitories as attendants and as classroom assistants and boilermen.

The academic year came to an end a great deal earlier than had been anticipated.

> One fine day the 'final bell' rang and we were all assembled for prayer in the large hall. They began to sing the processional 'It is meet' (*Dostoyno*), which by tradition marked the end of the academic year. This time, however, the 'final bell' marked not just the end of the academic year – it marked – as, of course, we could not conjecture at that time – the closure of the Synodal School. Soon, literally within a few days, the graduation ceremony took place. Prayers were held on that occasion in the small hall (the large hall was rented out). The results of the academic year were announced: contrary to the usual practice, no one was excluded. Filipp Stepanov addressed some parting words to us. I recall him saying that the February revolution was just the beginning, that many historic events lay ahead and that we should be prepared for trials and hard work.

That is what Alexander Smirnov, who was completing the fifth class at that time, remembered.[2]

In the meantime Moscow was rejoicing, celebrating the February revolution which had occurred several weeks before. On 14 March 1917 Kastalsky described to Grozdov his impressions of the revolutionary events:

> I still feel as if I'm living in a fairy-tale! The way Moscow behaved was particularly fairy-tale-like in its improbability; on the eve of the coup squads armed with machine-guns were prepared everywhere in 'reliable' places ready to shoot rebels. And all of a sudden a miracle happened – the armed soldiers hoisted red flags and fraternized with the rebels, and now they're all walking along together singing *Vstavay, podïmaysya* ('Get up, arise'). And it's the same everywhere. [...] On 4 March they organized a vast act of worship and

parade for the troops on Red Square. A great many clergy were there; during the prayers an aeroplane flew low over Red Square and dropped red flags and bouquets of red flowers. Minin was also holding a red flag in his hand.[3] And the soldiers and officers were festooned with red bows and flowers. Bright sunlight flooded everywhere... On the 12th there was another holiday – this time a purely popular one. It would seem that where you are too they celebrated the revolution (one would like to replace it with 'coup'). Life settled down into a peaceful existence here a long time ago now; there are meetings of people to form associations by profession. We 'Synodal folk' have already joined up with the Union of Religious Educational Institutions and yesterday we signed up for the Union of the Clergy, where a frenzied purge of the old stable is going on.[4]

The city seethed with all kinds of meetings, assemblies and congresses. The intelligentsia were discussing plans for restructuring artistic life – it was proposed to create an independent Ministry of the Arts, to reform a number of major institutions, the conservatoires and music schools in particular, which before had come under the now abolished Imperial Russian Musical Society. The fates of the Imperial Theatres, the Court Kapella and the Court Orchestra were discussed.

The euphoria of freedom, combined with hopes for a better life, gripped not just the liberal intelligentsia but also the clergy. A significant part of the Moscow clergy approved of the new régime, as is testified to if only by the following resolution of the Moscow City Council of 7 March 1917 which stated that the clergy welcomed with all joy the announcement by the *Ober-Prokuror* of the Synod Vladimir Lvov of a new direction in church activities and supported the Provisional Government regardless of its political foundations. The opposition to the new course, however, consisting of representatives of clergy with monarchical inclinations, was no less strong. One of the key figures was the Metropolitan of Moscow Makary, who was declared by the new church authorities to be a protégé of Rasputin. Lvov made many visits to Moscow, and won the Moscow clergy and laity round to the idea of appealing to the Metropolitan to take voluntary retirement. Not without a struggle, the bishop withdrew to the Nikolo-Ugreshsky Monastery. On 19 June 1917 the Moscow Diocesan Congress of Clergy and Laity elected Tikhon archbishop of Moscow and Kolomna; he had previously been archbishop of Lithuania and Vilna. The Petrograd Metropolitan Pitirim was also sent into retirement, accused of connections with Rasputin, and the future new martyr Metropolitan Veniamin took his place. The whole membership of the Rasputin Synod was renewed, with only Sergy, Archbishop of Finland, remaining of the old membership. The purge apparently affected the lowest ranks in the church with monarchical inclinations as well.

The name of Lvov, the new *Ober-Prokuror* of the Synod, was associated not only with the renewal of the ranks of the clergy but also with modernizing the church's organization. In particular he fought for a new form of appointment of bishops and above, who from now on were not appointed by the Synod but chosen by the votes of representatives of the diocese. Lvov was also a champion of restoring the patriarchate in Russia. Moderate liberal projects stood side by side, however, with radical proposals. For instance, an All-Russian Union of Democratic Orthodox Clergy and Laity was created in Petrograd in March 1917, headed by the future leader of the modernist 'Renewal' church Alexander Vvedensky, who called for a review of the basic statutes of canon law. Lvov himself later became an active participant in the 'Renewal' movement, which regarded itself as a new revolutionary church.

After the February revolution Lvov frequently travelled to Moscow with the aim of implementing ideas of democracy in church life. He visited the Synodal School too, where he met Kastalsky who tried to exploit any opportunity to establish a higher folk-church choir school. As he told Grozdov,

> *Ober-Prokuror* Lvov called on us yesterday. I read through for him a certain 'explanation' of the essence of the national church art where I well and truly tore strips off the court chant and mentioned that even Wagnerites had made their appearance in church music and mentioned the fight with them. He seemed to be very sympathetic to this idea, and sometimes made notes in pencil on my report (it included, by the way, the phrase: 'but, because of its independent path both in choice of repertoire and the way it was performed, the Synodal Choir received an unexpected and unwarranted rebuff from the former head of state, which people in the Synod did not fail to note with malice'.[5] Lvov promised to do everything in his power to further the improvement of the Synodal School and Choir. But I'm fed up with all this chopping and changing – it's time to get down to some real work! There's an infinite number of things needing to be done – it's not a time for just wagging your tongue.[6]

There was reason for Kastalsky to be worried, because he knew better than anyone the true state of affairs with the Synodal School, which was on the edge of bankruptcy. On 27 March 1917 he passed on his fears to Grozdov:

> Our Synodal livelihood is also hanging in the air. Over the past year we've overspent by 40,000 (we're not paying off our debts, in spite of the Synod's categorical demand that we settle them). In three months we run through our

annual grant, and one fine day we'll go broke in the most spectacular manner. After all, the *Ober[-Prokuror]*'s promises are essentially a repetition of the same promises made by previous *Obers* – they tie nobody down to anything, and are equivalent to saying – you're living in a fashion that no one's given you permission for, and that can be dealt with very simply: you don't know how to live properly – so don't live, die, and the devil take you![7]   And that's why, seeing that I've probably got five months (until September) in reserve – to try to change my speciality and look for a job where people are needed now, in a field where I might be able to be useful. In music, as I see it, there's no point in looking, because nobody's got time to worry about music.[8]

In spite of bouts of pessimism, however, Kastalsky saw real possibilities of making his dream come true in the new political conditions. Like many people, he accepted the February revolution with enthusiasm; it seemed to him that it would be followed by a time of great reforms and the construction of a national musical culture, the Synodal School's finest hour would come – after all, children from the poorest strata of society had received a higher education in music there, and then returned to the people. Kastalsky preached his ideas in every possible forum – first and foremost in the periodical press and at the congresses of all kinds so frequent at that time.

The question of what the musical culture of the new free republic should be like was one of concern not only to Kastalsky. Many musicians joined in the widespread polemic about the lines along which it should be constructed.   In the opinion of Alexander Dmitriyevich, however, most people were thinking mainly about the then generally accepted forms of educating a nation who, as the proponents of such forms got indignant about, 'could not even sing the *Internationale* in four parts'. The composer therefore took a 'revolutionary' step and wrote a 'proclamation', that is, a poem, where he called for 'non-Russian' textbooks on music to be 'overthrown' and for new textbooks based on ordinary people's musical creativity to be written specially for them.

Kastalsky's colleagues who read or heard this 'summons' were bewildered. 'The majority of those to whom I read my summons winced in silence, and that was all...', the composer recalled.[9]   But Alexander Dmitriyevich did not give up, having probably decided to accomplish his reforms even if it was only in his own Synodal School. According to Kastalsky's idea, in the new conditions the School ought to become 'the sole and completely original national artistic academy of music for church and choral singing in general'. He wrote in one of his articles:

At the School national art has already been laid as the corner stone – in the form of church melodies; national secular music is studied, national architecture, painting, ornament and so on are all dealt with (in the History of Art course). Having set itself the goal of studying widely the nation's creativity both in those fields and in poetry, literature, ritual, everyday life and national life in general – an academy of this kind could be an institution standing guard over the artistic and musical interest of its people, defending the purity and originality of the native art, training young people permeated with democratic ideas in their own specialty...[10]

Kastalsky developed similar ideas in a further article of that time entitled 'Church Music and the Moscow Synodal School' which he prepared for a trip to Petrograd for the Congress of Religious Schools in mid-May 1917. While he was in the capital, the composer tried through Alexander Siloti to have it published in 'Russian Freedom' (*Russkaya volya*) and also in the 'Church and Community Herald' (*Tserkovno-obshchestvennïy vestnik*), whose editor, however, rejected the material on the grounds that it 'concerned a matter that was too specialized'.[11] The article was eventually read out by its author as a report to the All-Russian Congress of Clergy and Laity, which took place in Moscow from 1 to 13 June 1917, and was devoted to working out new forms of administration for the Orthodox Church. Kastalsky's address was given on 2 June at the evening session, which was held in the Synodal School and devoted to the question of the significance of church music in a democratic society. The composer's address preceded a concert by the Synodal Choir which was, it seems, the final public appearance in its history.

Kastalsky's aim was to convince society of the need to show the utmost care for church music which along with folk music went back to a common source. (To prove this thesis the composer cited concrete results from a comparative analysis of song and chant.) From this premise was deduced the idea of the need for the state to support the Synodal School whose mission was:

to serve the special interests of precisely that art which nourishes not less than 60 per cent of the population of Russia (or 69 per cent including Old Believers of all types), i.e. about a hundred million inhabitants. The overwhelming majority of them are, of course, peasants. And those who prize and sincerely love this art are in the main the working people of the countryside, and not that public which fills the theatres and concert halls. This art is a folk one, and moreover it is free of charge to listeners, just like its sister – the folksong. I consider that neither of them is cheapened in consequence, and nor is their value or the need for them reduced. We do not know what will spring from the attitude of the Constituent Assembly to the church and the clergy, but the attitude of worshipping people cannot be unfavourable towards an art created by the people themselves which has been preserved over the course of centuries.[12]

To his immense sadness, however, the composer did not have occasion to take part in compiling new 'democratic' statutes and syllabuses for the Synodal School. '...My role in the final reform of the School was confined primarily to dreaming, wishing and making official speeches along the same lines', Kastalsky wrote in an autobiographical article.[13] A new statute and list of school subjects, compiled evidently by his colleagues, he later described as 'completely useless' and in December 1917, in a different historical situation, he tried to replace their documents with new ones. The reason underlying what took place is as follows.

One of the features typical of life in Russia after the February revolution was the formation of multifarious professional associations; this occurred within the Synod's jurisdiction too. Thus, a Union of Deacons and Psalmodists was formed in Moscow, and they saw their Union's principal aim as a struggle against episcopal authority; on 14 March a Society of Moscow Sacred Music Singers (of both sexes) was established who discussed measures to abolish the power of patrons who supported choirs of their own. The organization of local societies of choir directors and drawing them together in an All-Russian Union was the theme of the All-Russian (sixth) Congress of People Active in Choral Music, which opened in Moscow in the building of the Synodal School on 23 May 1917. Kastalsky was elected honorary chairman of this latter Russian choral forum, with Alexander Nikolsky as chairman. A large share of the forum sessions was taken up with discussion of the lack of rights involved in the social position of church choirmasters, who suffered oppression from the clergy and churchwardens. The Congress instructed its representative Dmitry Zarin, a music teacher and substantial figure in the choral world, to give a report on this subject at the forthcoming All-Russian Congress of Clergy and Laity in June 1917. A number of resolutions were passed by the delegates, in particular about recognizing the right of church choirmasters and teachers of church music to a pension, and the obligatory introduction of tuition in singing into the syllabuses of all educational institutions. Concerts were given, incidentally, within the framework of the Congress – by the Synodal Choir (27 May) and by the choir conducted by Mitrofan Pyatnitsky.

Nor did the Synodal School escape 'democratic reforms': work started on devising a system of self-administration and, in all probability, a struggle with the autocracy of the director. An executive committee was elected by ballot, and Kastalsky was not a member of it. He was so greatly offended by his colleagues' behaviour that he even mentioned their 'gift' in the preliminary version of his article 'From reminiscences of recent years'.[14]   His letters of 1917-18 contain many complaints about the executive committee which was made up of non-musicians who did not understand the features peculiar to an exclusively musical educational institution. The feud between Kastalsky and the inspector of the Synodal School Konstantin Uspensky continued even after the October revolution. Uspensky's views – he was a doctor and theologian by profession – differed from those of Kastalsky, who took a sharply negative attitude towards Uspensky's aspiration to equate the general education at the School with the course at a *gimnaziya*, which in the composer's opinion would lead to a lowering of standards in the disciplines of music.

In the meantime a special instruction arrived from the Synod about the cessation of teaching at the School until further notice: the School building began to be made ready for the Local Council of the Russian Orthodox Church, which opened on 15 August 1917. Some of the delegates who arrived from other cities were accommodated in the Synodal School. No further special instruction followed on 1 September, when the new academic year should have begun, and teaching was not resumed.

As far as the Synodal Choir was concerned, it continued to sing for services in the Cathedral of the Dormition, and earned money mainly by hiring itself out to sing. Certain means were found by renting out property, including the School hall. Thus, in the autumn of 1917, the hall was let to the Soviet of the All-Russian Co-operative Union, the Soviet of Soldiers' Deputies, the 'Polish House' Society, the Ukrainian Military Regiment, Ivan Yukhov's choir, etc.[15] These resources, however, were insufficient, and in September 1917 the Synodal singers and some School employees organized a strike. The directorate had to try to justify itself. On 15 September 1917 Kastalsky reported to Lyubimov, the senior priest of the Cathedral of the Dormition: 'A general assembly of the School teaching staff, convened specially by the School administration for the purpose on 14 September, considers it essential to announce that teaching staff, with their moral and cultural level, cannot allow themselves even to think of the possibility of reinforcing their requests by such means as a strike'.[16] But the report had not a word to say about singers in the Choir: they really did go on strike.

The day of the October coup – 25 October/7 November – was marked by Muscovites by prayer in the Cathedral of the Dormition by the shrine of the Holy Father Hermogen, which the day before had been desecrated by two soldiers. Worship was conducted by the Metropolitan of Moscow Tikhon, thirty bishops and many married and monastic clergy, with the Synodal Choir singing. Before the service the Metropolitan said a few words to the worshippers, calling on them to offer penitence before God and pray to the saint for forgiveness and protection for their native land.

A few days later many of Moscow's inhabitants were no longer taking the risk of leaving their own homes: the armed coup had started in Moscow. For residents of the Synodal School gunfire in the street was nothing new, because in 1905 Bolshaya Nikitskaya Street had also been a battle zone. Ivan Smïslov, who was studying at the School at that time, recalled that during the night the staff would carry sleeping children into the furthest corner of the dormitory for safety. During the Moscow battles in 1917 the School did not risk leaving in their dormitory those children who had not been dispersed to their family homes, and they were moved to the stage of the School hall to sleep. Kastalsky described the events of the 'carnage' in Moscow in detail in letters to his friends in Petrograd:

> The end of the battle was marked for us by all the panes of glass flying out from the half-house along Kislovka Street, because ten paces away from us a shell struck the flat of Ippolitov-Ivanov (just the pier, thank goodness) who was sitting quietly at home at the time; but, as a result of the blast of air, almost all the glass blew out both in the Conservatoire and in our building opposite (only two in my flat). The shell was fired, so I'm told, from the Sparrow Hills. On Bolshaya Nikitskaya Street (where there was a cannonade and firing round the clock every day without a break) eight or ten windows in the Synodal School were shattered by bullets in the children's dormitory (during the afternoon, thank goodness). We moved them on to the concert hall stage to sleep. They put in new glass quickly, by the way (at a cost of about 3½ thousand). In several of our flats on Kislovka Street the bullets broke the glass to the diameter of the thickness of a finger – that doesn't count (it's a mere trifle!). On Kislovka bullets and shells must have been flying more over the buildings. To avoid any 'misunderstandings' I too moved my bed into a corridor because for some reason I didn't want to get a bullet while I was asleep.[17]

The fate of their son Alexander also caused the Kastalskys no little anxiety; on the day of the coup he returned to Moscow from Peterhof and was detained without explanation by Red soldiers who beat him up with their rifle-butts. After spending several days under arrest in the Dresden Hotel the young man was released and waited at a friend's until the fighting was over, since he could not get home because of the powerful exchange of fire on the streets adjoining the School.

Kastalsky in his letters was not exaggerating the scale of the 'carnage'. The 'Russian Musical Gazette' (*Russkaya muzïkalnaya gazeta*) wrote about the destruction on Bolshaya Nikitskaya Street:

As we know, the civil strife took on more threatening dimensions in Moscow, since many buildings (even the Kremlin!) were subjected to bombardment, as if the first capital were experiencing the horrors of a foreign enemy! The latter, though, would hardly create so much devastation. We are told that, of the buildings on Bolshaya Nikitskaya Street, the Moscow Conservatoire suffered particularly severe damage.'[18]

A few days later the fighting stopped, but the sense of alarm was no less. The composer's daughter recalled an event which took place soon after the October coup:

I remember an event which occurred in the first few days after the revolution: two armed soldiers appeared in our flat with a menacing shout of 'Where are the priests here, then?' (apparently someone had pointed out our address – or was tempted by our flat, perhaps?). Mum jumped out at them 'wearing only her pince-nez' and put a degree of fear into them, threatening to phone Lenin 'on the hotline' and so on, and the lads hummed and hawed for a while and then took themselves off. Dad was standing sideways in the doorway and looked over his spectacles at the soldiers with a faint smile. It must have been his unpretentious appearance in his felt boots and smock sewn by Mum that made an 'impression' on them and they realized that there had been a mistake...[19]

In the interests of safety, the inhabitants of Middle Kislovka (the lane running parallel to Bolshaya Nikitskaya, where the School's living accommodation for the teaching and service staff was located) decided to organize a system of guard duty in their street at night-time. In that connection the director of the Synodal School and the chairmen of the house committees made a request to the Committee for Public Safety at the Aleksandrovsky Military School for eight rifles and four revolvers to be issued to protect the building.[20] Several people did guard duty for two or three hours at a stretch; Kastalsky took his turn on the watch along with the others.

Incidentally, some graduates of the Synodal School entered the Aleksandrovsky Military School during the First World War. On completing short training courses, they were awarded junior officer ranks. Several people from the Synodal School subsequently turned up in the White army – for example, the future conductor of the famous émigré Don Cossack choir Serge Jaroff, who was enrolled at the Aleksandrovsky school from 1 April 1917.

In the meantime, a new misfortune was approaching the country – famine. In his efforts to feed his family, Alexander Dmitriyevich had begun to sell off personal possessions – books, piano scores and his painting equipment. The idea of leaving the School and turning his back on Moscow haunted him more and more persistently. The composer even formed the intention of writing to various music schools in the south about teaching vacancies. Dreams of moving to the south were soon abandoned, however, when news reached Moscow about the bloodshed flaring up there. In March 1918 Kastalsky began to develop another idea which had come to him the previous summer: he intended to emigrate and decided to send a request to the Metropolitan of Petrograd Veniamin to give him the chance of a position as a psalmodist in some parish abroad. Together with Alexander Dmitrievich his friend Grozdov also intended to serve abroad as a sacristan; he too expected the imminent closure of the Court Kapella where he worked as director. It is difficult to say how seriously the two friends tried to bring about their 'sacristanship'; judging from their letters their attitude to the prospect was both humorous and serious. In any case, it was too late to petition the church authorities about the matter – the church did not have the resources to keep up its parishes in Russia, let alone abroad.

At the end of 1917 many people, Kastalsky among them, still hoped that the nightmare would soon come to an end, and life would somehow settle down one way or another. At the Church Council which took place in Moscow and lasted right up to September 1918 discussions continued about ways of organizing church life and even about the future of church music; Kastalsky participated in the Council's work both as a member of the Conference on Finances and Management attached to the Council Board and as chairman of the Supervisory Council attached to the Synodal School. On 8 December an unusual question appeared on the Council's agenda, which in the 1910s had been the subject of lively debate in the press – the possibility of using the organ in Orthodox worship. Its inclusion on the agenda for sessions of the Council can be explained in part by the fact that in conditions of revolutionary terror it was becoming more and more difficult to maintain complete choirs in the churches, and in cases of dire necessity they could be replaced by an instrument. Besides participants in the Council, members of the Supervisory Council were present at the session: Kastalsky, Allemanov, Nikolsky and Danilin, as well as the composer Grechaninov who had been specially invited and was given the chance to speak first.

Grechaninov spoke with passion in favour of introducing the organ into the service, believing that 'the musical impressions which the Orthodox service can give at present are, in his opinion, too primitive and uncultured and therefore incapable of uplifting the spirit of worshippers to the necessary extent'. The composer declared that 'any time he wants to pray he goes to the Roman Catholic church and finds there the religious and musical atmosphere which allows him to enjoy the artistic quality with which religious music is performed'.[21]   Kastalsky's position was much more moderate and pragmatic:

> Introducing an organ would be impractical for a country church because of both the cost of such an instrument and the absence of competent performers. Training good organists requires special schools and a very long time. In our conditions we can restrict ourselves to a good harmonium, which would have to be put on the *kliros*. The purpose of this harmonium would be to support the singers in performing hymns during the service. As country choirs would not be singing difficult musical compositions, an extensive harmonium technique would not be required. Any church choirmaster, country teacher or psalmodist would be able to cope with the task. The singing of the choir would gain significantly from harmonium accompaniment, and the pronunciation of the words would become more distinct for listeners.[22]

Kastalsky's opinion was supported by Allemanov, a teacher at the Synodal School. The majority of contributors to the session spoke out categorically against the proposal, however, justifying their position with reasons based on history, church politics and art.   For instance, the participant in the Council Pavel Kladinov said: 'I wholly disagree with both opinions – with what Alexander Grechaninov proposes and with Alexander Kastalsky's view. Introducing a musical instrument into our service would kill the further development of our choral art – and not only in its elementary form of communal singing, but also in the higher form of organized choral performance'.[23]   As a result, the question of introducing instrumental music into Orthodox worship was decided at the Council in the negative.

Even while he was taking part in the sittings of the Council, Kastalsky nonetheless made an attempt in December 1918 to clear the Synodal building of the members of the Council and officials of the Council secretariat.   Alexander Dmitriyevich intended to resume classes with the students who had arrived if only in the second half of the year, to enrol children in the preparatory class and allow the students completing the ninth class to graduate.   He even had the idea of transferring the boy-singers from the disintegrating Court Kapella into the Synodal School. The attempt met with no success, and all that the director managed to achieve was to get teaching restarted in the second half of the year for the ten graduating students, to administer their exams and issue their certificates. On 18 January 1918 Kastalsky wrote to Asafyev about the state of affairs:

Our School and Choir are in a critical condition. There is no teaching – because of the absence of resources to maintain it. I want to arrange at the very least a graduation this year, because the students are of course in no way at fault. Recruiting boys to renew the choir is something else we can't do because there aren't the resources to keep them. The School has been filled up with officials of the Synod, who've arrived to run the Council office. We rent out our hall for concerts and other things – we at least get something from that. The financial breakdown is complete. How are we going to last through the winter? Thank goodness – January has been warm so far – firewood has become twelve times more expensive![24]

By the end of 1917 Russia's other most important choral institution – the former Court Kapella – was also in a critical condition. The 'Russian Musical Gazette' wrote:

'New Times' (*Novoye vremya*) reports that the future of the former Court Kapella is completely unknown. The budget provides funds only until January. No teaching is being done in the Kapella's classes at the present time. Some of the pupils have been dispersed, while the others (about 60 people) are still in Petrograd and are somehow sheltered in the accommodation of the former Kapella hospital, since all the class-rooms and pupils' dormitories are occupied by the Committee of the Black Sea fleet and the military bodyguard of Minister Kerensky (numbering 200), who incidentally have ruined all the musical instruments belonging to the Kapella – grand pianos and so on. Although the fate of the Kapella has not yet been decided and new decisions are taken practically every day by Messrs Golovin and Kalugin, they propose nonetheless to evacuate them. First of all, they wanted to send them to Rostov (Yaroslav province), but the two hotels they rented in a small county town proved insufficient. They approached Novocherkassk who gave a favourable reply, which they don't know how to use to advantage without knowing whether only the pupils are to be evacuated, with their teachers, or without them, whether to send the adult singers, for whom there will of course be nothing to do in Novocherkassk – still less in Rostov, where they will not be able to find any work or earnings.[25]

As we can see, the position of the Kapella was not easy. It is, however, apparent that in regard to it, unlike the Synodal School, the state at least showed some concern. That was probably because the Kapella came under a department of the state, not the church. Later on, like the former imperial theatres, museums and conservatoires, it became the property of the state.

Meanwhile, the anti-church terror was gathering strength. The church press was full of announcements about the murder of clergymen and outrages committed against churches. Life for residents in the Synodal School became more and more dangerous. In a letter of 19 January 1918

Kastalsky informed Grozdov: 'Yesterday evening about 20 armed soldiers held council by our entrance, wondering whether ours was the building they were looking for. In any event, they went away – they had evidently decided that it was not the right one, even though they said it was next to the Conservatoire. We don't know who they were looking for'.[26]

On 19 January the famous encyclical from Patriarch Tikhon was published pronouncing an anathema on the Bolsheviks and calling on the flock to rise to the defence of the faith and the church. On 23 January Soviet power replied with a decree on freedom of conscience and church and religious societies; thereafter a decree from *Narkompros* was published about the subordination to it of institutions for religious education which were to be turned into secular schools. On 15/28 February the resolution of the Patriarch and the Synod came out which called for the organization of unions to oppose the destruction of churches, and suggested ways of offering resistance to the removal of objects of value. The document also recommended to those in charge, employees and students of institutions of religious education and their parents, to close ranks to defend religious schools from seizure and secure their activities for the future.[27] The state replied to this with new repressions and issued a decree nationalizing all church property not used for worship.

For church educational institutions this meant that they were deprived of the opportunity of obtaining their earlier income, for example, from renting out accommodation. Shortly afterwards even the buildings themselves used for education were nationalized. Simultaneously religious schools were not permitted to obtain any money from the state treasury; financing was resumed only on condition that the school was transferred to the jurisdiction of *Narkompros*. In this way in the Moscow Diocese the threat of abolition hung over the Moscow Theological Academy, the Moscow and Bethany Theological Seminaries, the Filaret and Synodal Schools and other educational institutions, which feverishly sought a way out of their predicament. A special Committee was set up to seek funds for the needs of institutions of religious education in the Moscow Diocese, which, after trying many ways of obtaining resources, addressed the following despairing appeal to believers:

Orthodox Christians!
Our motherland is on the verge of ruin. The Orthodox Church is in peril. We are on the eve not only of physical slavery but, what is far more terrible, even of religious slavery, for our enemies are preparing to take away from us – partly by criminal agitation, partly by means of simple violence – that which is more precious to us than anything: our sacred Orthodox faith. We must fight for it to our last breath. But we must not only stand up for our holy faith: the further

great and unalterable obligation has been imposed upon us of training future warriors for the preservation and flourishing of the Orthodox Church, for true freedom and the good of the Russian nation. [...] In fact even those religious schools which exist, with the most insignificant exceptions, are on the verge of being closed because of insufficiency of funds. [...] A hopeless situation is being created, and if help does not come from outside, then the beginning of the end will soon come for religious instruction. At this terrible time we, the spiritual guides to our young people, who are our hope and the future buttress of Holy Russia, we appeal to you with this fervent and tearful prayer to come to our aid in the name of Christ and His eternal commandments and spare part of your substance to save a cause which is perishing.[28]

One way of preserving religious educational institutions was seen as taking them out of church jurisdiction and organizing them as private schools. Even the possibility of transforming them into classical *gimnazii* was not excluded. The teaching staff of the Synodal School also agonizingly sought a way out of the cul-de-sac. Two routes were considered. One involved the newly elected Patriarch Tikhon; in that case it was proposed to reorganize the School as the Patriarchal School of Church Music. The second route involved an independent judicial and financial existence. It proved impossible to bring either of these ideas into reality.

In March the situation of the Synodal School became even more complicated because a resolution came out requisitioning the building for the needs of the revolution. The houses and trading stalls belonging to the Synodal School, the hiring out of which allowed the School to exist, were also nationalized.

On the morning of 6 March Kastalsky wrote to Grozdov:

Three 'organizations' have already been in the Synodal School to requisition the building – we've no idea what's going to happen. They make threats. I've complained to the Soviet of Workers' and Soldiers' and Peasants' Deputies about three or four times, and they promised to defend us, but let's see – though they've seized half our income already and there's no money to live on or sing on. The boys sometimes just arrive from their parents' homes, and go right back again. I have, incidentally, got together for a month eight students who're finishing the course so we can let these blameless souls graduate with diplomas that will get them jobs – let them earn their bread, or learn to starve.[29]

By 7 March the matter was decided and Kastalsky informed Grozdov:

Yesterday our Synodal School building was requisitioned for the needs of the Commissariat for War (I just don't know how they're going to chase me out of the flat and where). Pavel Meskhi, who lives with us, assures me that we won't be chased out of the flat. [...] But all the same the Soviet of Workers and Soldiers have informed me that they are taking away our 'singing' things – it looks as if my salary's down the drain! They advise transferring the Synodal School to the Commissariat of Education 'if they recognize the usefulness of your School' (doubtful!). As you can see, if you find yourself between two stools, you naturally look for a point of support...[30]

The 'Church Bulletin' (*Tserkovnïye vedomosti*) published the following note: 'The building of the Moscow Synodal School was requisitioned recently, and the Commissariat for Military Affairs is now accommodated there. Commissar Trotsky and his wife are housed in the former office of the Minister for Religious Denominations A.V. Kartashov'.[31] But things were changing as in a kaleidoscope and on 20 March Kastalsky gave Grozdov the following piece of news: 'Trotsky's office has been transferred away from us, and in its place it seems the office "for military communications" is moving in...'[32]

For the School's teachers, March was a time of uncertainty: it became clear that the church was unable to maintain the School, yet they were all afraid of being transferred to the Commissariat of Education. At the beginning of April the senior priest of the Cathedral of the Dormition, Nikolay Lyubimov, informed the School directorate in the name of the church authorities that there was no money in the Synodal treasury, and that it was necessary for employees to look for other work. The School was thus obliged either to close or transfer to the Commissariat's jurisdiction. The latter option was chosen, and Kastalsky set off to demonstrate the Synodal School's 'usefulness' to Anatoly Lunacharsky, the People's Commissar for Education.

The composer decided to expound to Lunacharsky his idea of the 'self-determination' of national art and his ideas about the role which the Synodal School could play in the process. Kastalsky told Grozdov:

I made Lunacharsky's acquaintance in a very simple manner. I've long nursed the idea of the necessity of the 'self-determination' of Russian national art in all its forms. (What's more, I wrote about it in an article as well as speaking at congresses – all to no avail...) [...] I wrote some report on the subject: Does the government of workers and peasants consider it important to convince the Russian proletariat that the Russian people long ago created its own independent art in all fields, that it died out and now awaits revival?! I proposed the simplest means to convince them of this: to hang up in all places where the people gather (even in tea-rooms) large-size copies of architectural, pictorial, ornamental and other specimens of folk creativity, so that the proletariat could see more often what had been created by their ancestors and how to approach it (for 'a tree cannot grow without roots'). I regard it as very important to direct the proletarian's gaze on to himself, and not to ape the bourgeois: operas, ballets (only patented works of art and not their own, folk forms).[33]

This conception, hastily edited in accordance with 'the spirit of the age' where the proletarian figured with his original art and the bourgeois westernizer with his operas and ballets replacing the Orthodox nation and cultivated musicians, roused Lunacharsky's complete sympathy. The article where Kastalsky set forth his theory of 'self-determination' also won the approval of the People's Commissar.

The composer later, having decided shortly before his death to compile an autobiographical album, reminisced in the third person about this event:

Soon after the revolution [...] Alexander Kastalsky presented Anatoly Lunacharsky with a well-argued report on the need for concern on the part of the workers' and peasants' government for the preservation and cultivation of the people's achievements (monuments of folk art – architectural, pictorial, ornamental, literary, musical, objects for domestic use, costumes, etc.) and of the desirability of creating a House of Folk Art where it could be shown in all its forms (on the stage, on the concert platform, in talks, films and so on) with the aim of reviving folk art. The report was prompted by apprehension that folk art would be infected with the brand of 'culture' that involved modernist, futurist perversions of artistic taste and the hiding-away from the people of original art with its clarity and artistic independence (which could already be demonstrated in a scholarly manner).[34]

The report was in many respects similar to Kastalsky's article of 1917 'Church Music and the Moscow Synodal School'. The two articles differed in that in the earlier one the value of church music was proved in detail, and only after that the value of her 'sister' folksong; in the 1918 article 'brother' and 'sister' had exchanged places, and moreover the 'brother' was now called 'church-ritual song'. In both the first and the second article the conclusion was the same: Russia needed an educational institution to attend to the preservation of the heritage and to train musicians brought up on that basis. Thus was born the idea of transforming the Synodal School into a People's Choir Academy. The democratic nature of the old and the new school was obvious: both the School and the Academy were full of children from the poorest strata of society and served ordinary people who had no chance of buying a musical instrument but who loved singing. It was therefore unnecessary to spend long demonstrating the continuity of the old and new schools; the only essential thing was to correct the teaching syllabuses.

The conception of the choir attached to the People's Choir Academy was somewhat different:

> The Choir attached to such an institution as the Choir Academy must first and foremost be set the task of promoting folksongs both in a cultivated style and in a non-artificial folk style by means of concerts.   Then artistic choral compositions by Russian composers for choirs variously constituted.   Then comes our sacred choral literature, primarily recent.   These concerts may be enlivened by introducing melodeclamation, soloists and instrumental accompaniment.   With educational ends in view, parallels may be drawn in the programmes of these concerts between purely folksong and artistic compositions, or Russian music contrasted with European, or our sacred music compared with Catholic sacred music, etc.   Besides its general educational objectives, a choir of that sort could serve as a permanent model for young students devoting themselves to the art of choral music as well.[35]

As Kastalsky wrote to Grozdov,

> My article apparently made an impression on Lunacharsky, because in the newspapers they wrote (they garbled it, the swine) about his report to the Executive Committee that Lunacharsky had said that in a conversation with me the composer Kastalsky had declared that according to his belief the Russian people will now 'start singing' (from hunger?).   Since I said nothing of the kind (I did say, incidentally, that at the moment no great wave of Russian song is to be heard in the towns...).   Well, the devil take them.[36]

Kastalsky's visit to Lunacharsky and the inaccurate quotation by the latter of what the composer had said to him provoked ironic comment in the church press. But the matter did not end there. At the beginning of May 1918 Kastalsky informed Asafyev: 'The Synodal authorities plan to kick me out of here (for having connections with the Bolsheviks)'.[37] Gradually a new image of Kastalsky began to take shape in church milieux – as a 'red professor' who had betrayed Orthodoxy, which in actual fact did not correspond to reality. The composer probably tried to defend himself, as is attested by a fragment of a letter from him preserved in the Synodal School archive to the senior priest of the Cathedral of the Dormition Lyubimov, where he explains that he was forced into appealing to the secular authorities.[38]

And so the Synodal School changed into a secular institution. And once again, for the umpteenth time, Kastalsky set about compiling statutes and syllabuses, cursing his wretched fate. 'I've got to reform the Synodal School again in a new way. Confound it! Since I've been director, this is about the fifth or sixth time!   You curse your bitter fate', Alexander

Dmitriyevich complained to Grozdov.[39] At the same time he understood that he had been given another chance to realize his dream of a higher Russian choir school and was extremely glad about it. Lunacharsky, who was working consistently at taming the old intelligentsia, as far as he could, softened the School's transfer from religious to secular jurisdiction if only in that, contrary to the state's anticlerical policy, he did not abolish church music as a discipline to be studied at the Choir Academy.

The loyalty of the People's Commissar to church music is attested not only by the reception he gave Kastalsky but also by the contents of a speech he made at the first concert given by the former Court Kapella since the revolution. According to the reminiscences of a relative of the Kapella's conductor Mikhail Klimov,

> the concert by the Kapella was scheduled for 21 February 1918. The People's Commissar for Education Anatoly Lunacharsky was supposed to be making a speech at the concert. The Kapella's repertoire contained only sacred music, and for that reason, Klimov refused to conduct a programme of that kind. A delegation from the choir called on him at home and appealed to him to conduct the concert, telling him that 'if you perform with us, you will support us'. And he agreed. As a musician, to be sure, it was hard for him to conduct a programme like that, but Lunacharsky made it easier for him to perform by what he said in his introductory address.[40]

It was said in the press of those years that Lunacharsky dwelt in detail on 'the beauty created in church art and music' and promised that in restructuring Russian life the Soviet government 'will not allow the artistic inheritance – the purest gold of folk art' – to be lost.[41]

Thus, the Court Kapella was preserved and became a state institution. What was the fate of the Synodal Choir?

Soon after the October coup a most important event took place in Russian church life: after two centuries of 'Synodal' existence a patriarchate was again established in Russia. At the enthronement of Tikhon as patriarch in the Cathedral of the Dormition in the Kremlin on 21 November 1917 the Synodal Choir sang, even though its ranks had been thinned out by the call-up, and from now on it was often referred to in the press as the patriarchal choir. In truth, however, the Synodal singers did not become the patriarch's choir. According to documents in the Synodal School archive, and also to the church periodical press of the time, the Choir took part in patriarchal worship rather rarely, receiving money for individual services, like a hired choir. Thus, it is known that at the end of December and in January the Synodal singers sang at only three services in which the patriarch participated: on 17 December 1917 – for the liturgy in the church of Saint Nicholas in Golutvin and received 1,000 roubles; at the Epiphany in 1918 – for the All-Night Vigil and liturgy in the Church of the Theophany in Yelokhov, for which they received 3,000 roubles, out of which it was decided to give 1,627 roubles to the children who had taken part in the service; and on 21 January 1918 the Choir took part in the liturgy in the Alekseyev Monastery, for which they were given 1,000 roubles.[42] It is possible that the Synodal Choir's singing cost the church authorities too much for them to be able to afford their services more often. Moreover, the artistic manner in which the Synodal Choir sang and its repertoire did not find adherents among the patriarch's closest associates, who discussed the idea of forming a choir of deacons and psalmodists and reviving the older strict church music at patriarchal services.[43] As a result, the choirs of the churches where the worship was taking place sang for patriarchal services. (The following fact is testimony that those close to the patriarch nourished a special passion for clergy singing: on 21 June 1917, at the consecration of Tikhon the Archbishop of Moscow as Metropolitan of Moscow in the Church of Christ the Saviour, it was not the Synodal Choir that sang, nor the choir of the church, but a gathered choir made up of 600 priests and deacons conducted by deacon Vasily Bogoslovsky.)

On 22 April/5 May 1918 the final service before its closure took place in the Cathedral of the Dormition in the Kremlin.[44] Matins and the liturgy of the radiant Resurrection of Christ were concelebrated by Patriarch Tikhon and many clergy as the patriarchal choir sang. As the 'Moscow Church Bulletin' wrote,

> On account of the circumstances we are enduring at this time the celebration of Easter in Moscow this year was not as triumphal as it used to be in previous years. In the first place, after the First of May holiday street lighting at night was discontinued, and worshippers setting out for Easter Matins in the Cathedral of the Dormition were therefore compelled to move about in darkness, which of course was attended with significant discomforts. And then Muscovites did not know whether access to the Kremlin without tickets would be permitted, and therefore not as many people gathered for Easter Matins in the Cathedral of the Dormition as used to before, although from 10pm everyone who wished was allowed to enter by the Trinity Gate – without tickets of any sort.[45]

The Synodal singers bade farewell to the cathedral on whose *kliroses* their predecessors had stood for many centuries. On 27 April/10 May they were already singing for Easter Vespers, with the patriarch participating, in the Church of St John the Baptist in Serebrenniki by the Yauza Bridge. The Choir did not return to the cathedral again. Soon all mention of the patriarch's choir in documents and the church press came to an end. Later on one could find Synodal singers in the ranks of various state and church choirs; a few of them changed to other professions.

The destruction of the Synodal Choir, which was a personal tragedy for many of its singers and choirmasters, was often discussed by lovers of church music. We know that even in emigration Rachmaninoff asked about the fate of the Synodal Choir.[46] During these discussions the question was often asked: why could the Synodal Choir not be saved? Among its members a legend was current that the Choir was abolished because the singers had refused to sing revolutionary songs. Danilin is supposed to have told this story to his pupils at the Moscow Conservatoire in Soviet times.[47] It is difficult to say to what extent this tradition corresponds to reality. Whatever the truth might be, along with the history of the 'old' Russia, the centuries-long history of the patriarchal choir also came to an end in 1918.

Notes

1. *Delo po predlozheniyu Khozyaystvennogo upravleniya pri Sv. Sinode o sokrashchenii zanyatiy v Sinodal'nom uchilishche v 1917 godu* (The proposal of the Holy Synod administrative management to shorten teaching at the Synodal School in 1917). RGADA, fond 1183, opis' 9, part 2, no. 36.
2. A.P. Smirnov: *Vospominaniya o Sinodal'nom uchilishche i khore* (Reminiscences of the Synodal School and Choir), in *RUSAM*, vol. 1, pp. 494-495.
3. The writer of the letter refers to the monument on Red Square to the leaders of the national militia Koz'ma Minin and Dmitry Pozharsky. The monument is the work of the sculptor Ivan Martos, and was erected in 1818 in honour of the 200th anniversary of the victory over Polish troops as well as the victory over Napoleon's armies in 1812.
4. A.D. Kastal'sky: *Iz pisem 1917-1918 godov* (From the letters of 1917-1918), in *RUSAM*, vol. 1, p. 293.
5. The reference is to the disfavour of Nicholas II which Kastalsky incurred during the sovereign's visit to Moscow in 1914. The author of an article published in one of the church newspapers describes the incident as follows: 'Nicholas II was extremely agitated at the service in the Cathedral of the Dormition and at the end summoned the director of the Moscow Synod Office Filipp Stepanov. A witness to this scene told me that in a state of great agitation Nicholas II shouted at Stepanov: "the Empress and I were not able to pray, and that's an outrage. It's you and your Kastal'sky who've spread these operatic motives from Warsaw to Perm." My ordinary soldiers at Tsarskoye Selo sing better than your learned singers'. *Khronika moskovskoy yeparkhial'noy zhizni* (Chronicle of Moscow diocesan life), in *Moskovskiye tserkovnïye vedomosti* (Moscow Church Bulletin), 1918, no. 11, p. 4.
6. A.D. Kastal'sky: *Iz pisem 1917-1918 godov*, in *RUSAM*, vol. 1, pp. 293-294.
7. The composer was correct in thinking that his conversations with the new *Ober-Prokuror* were unlikely to lead to anything. L'vov's time in the Provisional Government was brief: on 21 July 1917 he resigned along with A.F. Kerensky.

8. A.D. Kastal'sky: *Iz pisem 1917-1918 godov*, in *RUSAM*, vol. 1, p. 295.
9. A.D. Kastal'sky: *Iz vospominaniy o poslednikh godakh* (From reminiscences of recent years), *Ibid.*, p. 254.
10. *Ibid.*, p. 257.
11. The article was finally published in 1918 in the second issue of the annual 'Melos'.
12. A.D. Kastal'sky: *Tserkovnoye peniye i Moskovskoye Sinodal'noye uchilishche.* (Church music and the Moscow Synodal School), in *RUSAM*, vol. 1, p. 265.
13. A.D. Kastal'sky: *Iz vospominaniy o poslednikh godakh*, *RUSAM*, vol. 1, p. 257.
14. In the final version the composer crossed out the section of his manuscript text where he set out his grievances against his colleagues. Cf. A.D. Kastal'sky: *Iz vospominaniy o poslednikh godakh* (From reminiscences of recent years). GTsMMK, fond 171, no. 90.
15. *Dokladï direktora Sinodal'nogo uchilishcha i ordera prokurora Sinodal'noy kontorï po khozyaystvennoy chasti* (Reports of the director of the Synodal School and the orders of the *prokuror* of the Synod Office regarding administrative matters). RGALI, fond 662, opis' 1, no. 102, p. 187.
16. *Perepiska po Sinodal'nomu uchilishchu* (Correspondence about the Synodal School). RGADA, fond 662, opis' 1, no. 101, p. 41.
17. A.D. Kastal'sky: *Iz pisem 1917-1918 godov*, in *RUSAM*, vol. 1, pp. 296-297.
18. *Ibid.*, p. 308. The Cathedral of the Dormition suffered particularly badly during the bombardment of the Kremlin; it was there, in the singers' chamber, that the Synodal Choir's outfits and part of its music library were housed.
19. N.A. Kastal'skaya: *Vospominaniya* (Reminiscences), p. 5v.
20. *Perepiska po Sinodal'nomu uchilishchu* (Correspondence about the Synodal School). RGADA, fond 662, opis' 1, no. 101, p. 50.
21. *Protokol Soyedinyonnogo zasedaniya chlenov podotdela po tserkovnomu peniyu Pomestnogo sobora pravoslavnoy russkoy tserkvi i Nablyudatel'nogo soveta Moskovskogo Sinodal'nogo uchilishcha tserkovnogo peniya ot 8 dekabrya 1917 goda* (Minutes of the combined session of members of the subcommittee on church music of the Local Council of the Russian Orthodox Church and the Supervisory Council of the Moscow Synodal School of Church Music, held on 8 December 1917), in *Tserkovnïye vedomosti* (Church Bulletin), nos. 15-16, pp. 88-89. *Ibid.*, in *RUSAM*, vol. 3, pp. 808-816.
22. *Ibid.*, p. 89.
23. *Ibid.*, p. 90.
24. A.D. Kastal'sky: *Iz pisem 1917-1918 godov*, in *RUSAM*, vol. 1, p. 298.
25. *Ibid.*, p. 308.
26. *Ibid.*, p. 299.
27. A joint letter from the parents of children studying at the Synodal School has survived. It asks that a unique educational institution be safeguarded.
28. *Vozzvaniye komiteta po izïskaniyu sredstv dlya nuzhd dukhovno-uchebnïkh zavedeniy Moskovskoy yeparkhii* (Appeal from the committee seeking means to meet the needs of religious educational institutions in the Diocese of Moscow), in *Moskovskiye tserkovnïye vedomosti* (Moscow Church Bulletin), 1918, no. 6, pp. 4-5.
29. *RUSAM*, vol. 1, pp. 300-301.
30. *Ibid.*, p. 301.
31. *Ibid.*, p. 311.
32. *Ibid.*, p. 302.
33. *Ibid.*, pp. 302-303.
34. A.D. Kastal'sky: *Avtobiograficheskiy al'bom* (Autobiographical album). GTsMMK, fond 12, no. 503, p. 72.

35. A.D. Kastal'sky: *K proyektu uchrezhdeniya narodnoy akademii khorovogo peniya* (A plan for the establishment of a People's Academy of Choral Music). GTsMMK, fond 12, no. 308, p. 2.

36. Letter from A.D. Kastal'sky to Kh.N. Grozdov of 5 April 1918, in *RUSAM*, vol. 1, p. 303.

37. Letter from A.D. Kastal'sky to B.V. Asaf'yev of 9 May 1918. RGALI, fond 2658, opis' 1, no. 581, p. 18.

38. RGALI, fond 661, opis' 1, no. 103, p. 64.

39. A.D. Kastal'sky: *Iz pisem 1917-1918 godov*, in *RUSAM*, vol. 1, p. 304.

40. O.M. Klimova: *Zametki o M.G. Klimove* (Notes about M.G. Klimov). RNB, fond 1127, no. 91, pp. 12-12v.

41. V. Yefimov: *Letopis' zhizni i deyatel'nosti A.V. Lunacharskogo* (Chronicle of the life and career of A.V. Lunacharsky), vol. 1. Dushanbe, 1992, pp. 70-71.

42. *Dokladï direktora Sinodal'nogo uchilishcha i ordera prokurora Sinodal'noy kontorï po khozyaystvennoy chasti* (Reports of the director of the Synodal School and the orders of the *prokuror* of the Synod Office regarding administrative matters). RGALI, fond 662, opis' 1, no. 102, pp. 204 and 214.

43. *Khronika moskovskoy yeparkhial'noy zhizni* (Chronicle of Moscow diocesan life), in *Moskovskiye tserkovnïye vedomosti* (Moscow Church Bulletin), 1918, no. 11, col. 4.

44. On 11 March 1918 the Bol'shevik government, with Lenin at its head, moved from Petrograd to the Kremlin in Moscow. Thereafter, entry to the Kremlin was possible only by special passes. The Kremlin's churches and monasteries were closed down soon after.

45. *Moskovskiye tserkovnïye vedomosti* (Moscow Church Bulletin), 1918, no. 8, p. 6.

46. *Interv'yu s L. L'vovïm* (Interview with L. L'vov), in *Rossiya i slavyanstvo* (Russia and the Slavonic peoples, [Paris], 1930, 26 April.

47. L. Sakharov: *Vospominaniya* (Reminiscences*)*, in *Pamyati N.M. Danilina. Pis'ma. Vospominaniya. Dokumentï* (In memory of N.M. Danilin. Letters. Reminiscences. Documents). Moscow, 1987, pp. 166-167.

Chapter 20

'Wretched Old Age has set in'

The decree establishing the People's Choir Academies of Moscow and Petrograd on the basis of the Synodal School and the Court Kapella was signed on 22 July 1918. Kastalsky, who had made the suggestion that the two institutions might be combined, was appointed director of the new choir schools. Kastalsky also became rector of the Moscow People's Choir Academy. 'The intention is to create institutions of musical culture which are to give a firm cultural foundation for the creative musical element of the Russian people, flowing from the very essence of the people's creative image', wrote V. Derzhanovsky in 'News of the Day' (*Novosti dnya*).[1]

The Academy was an institution of tertiary education. It was proposed that the teaching of adults would be limited to five courses, and that of children would involve two preparatory years and ten basic classes. Those who completed the entire course at the Academy were to be awarded the title 'free artist' with the right to be conductors and instructors of choirs and teachers of church music.

The roots of the Choir Academy lay in the Synodal School: many teachers and pupils continued working and studying within the old walls; although in a deformed fashion, the training of young musicians in the national heritage did in fact come about. To be sure, in the new conditions Kastalsky had the chance of basing his conception principally on musical folklore. Having dedicated the preceding twenty years of his life to investigating folksong, the composer now intended to give effect to his ideas, knowledge and discoveries with the utmost fullness in the new educational institution. It proved possible to include church music in the syllabuses, because at that time the senior staff at *Narkompros* regarded it as an achievement of the people. All this is borne witness to by an 'Outline table of subjects and activities at the People's Choir Academy' compiled by Kastalsky and ratified by Lunacharsky and the head of the Music Department of *Narkompros*, the composer Arthur Lourié, in July 1918.

The People's Choir Academy opened on 19 December 1918 and by the end of the first academic year 291 pupils had enrolled. It was possible to get studies organized, however, only in the 1919–20 academic year. We know this from an article about the new Choir Academy written by Kastalsky at the request of the Music Department of *Narkompros*. It is interesting that the larger part of it is devoted to the glorious pages of the Synodal School's history, and not to the People's Choir Academy at all. Among other things, it gives the names of a number of graduates of the School who had made careers in music in recent times. They included Nikolay Kovin, Mikhail Klimov, Alexander Chesnokov, Pavel Tolstyakov, Nikolay Danilin, Nikolay Golovanov, Konstantin Shvedov, Pavel Ippolitov, Pavel Chesnokov, Vladimir Stepanov, Alexander Grebnev and others. It also indicated that many of the choral instructors in the Moscow *Proletkult* were former pupils of the School.

It follows from the article that teaching at the Choir Academy followed the syllabuses of the Synodal School, with a few corrections made. For instance, new subjects such as performance on folk instruments, acoustics, vocal hygiene, and the general history of culture in conjunction with musical culture were introduced. It was proposed that the structure of the institution would also be similar: it was intended to organize boarding accommodation for children and preparatory classes as well.

And finally, at the end of the article the true state of affairs at the Academy was described:

> where, because of the requisition by the military administration of the teaching accommodation and the ruination of the majority of the grand pianos, it proved possible to organize classes only from January 1919, forming two groups of students – one in the morning (for the young ones) and another in the evening for listeners who were predominantly adults. Lessons were held mainly in the flats of members of the administration. The Academy's concert hall was damaged by fire in October 1919 and has not as yet been renovated...[2]

There is also mention here of the fate of two of the Synodal School's notable assets – the library of church music manuscripts, which it had been intended to transfer to the Historical Museum for safekeeping, and the Synodal Choir. It says of the latter:

> The famous Synodal Choir which used to exist at the School gradually fell away as a result of the general destruction and the absence of material support. At the present time there exists at the Academy only a students' choir made up of pupils from the morning group and listeners from the evening group. The choir has performed several times at Soviet celebrations.[3]

We can note that by 1923 lessons were being conducted only on the ground floor; the first floor remained closed, because it required disinfection after one of the officials who had previously occupied it had fallen ill with a severe infectious illness.

It is perfectly obvious that Kastalsky regarded the Choir Academy as a Synodal School reformed yet again. But it is also clear that he had to set up what was in fact a new educational institution. For a sick man who was getting old and had been weakened by hunger, this was an intolerable burden. The composer's final decade, however, was unusually productive. Work truly saved Alexander Dmitriyevich during a difficult time. He was so carried away by his work that he felt life's many problems less sharply and recommended this method to Grozdov: 'All the same, immersing yourself in intensive brainwork is better in my opinion than moping about and thinking how hard times are'.[4]

Kastalsky's 'medicine' was his research into folksong, which he resumed soon after the October revolution and never stopped till the end of his days, looking on it as his final duty. On 18 April 1918 the composer informed Grozdov: 'My "Fundamentals" (*Osnovï*) are making progress. I've almost finished the first part. The number of examples is huge, which is amazing even to me...'[5] The aim of the first part of the book, which was nearing completion, was 'to establish as a fact the existence of a Russian system – independently of the one generally accepted in the world of scholarly musicians of common European music'. Asafyev intended to copy the manuscript and prepare it for publication; Suvchinsky offered to subsidize its publication. The work was sent to Petrograd, though after Suvchinsky's departure from Russia the manuscript was given to the Music Sector of the State Publishing House, by whom it was indeed published in 1923 under the title 'Peculiarities of the Russian folk musical system' (*Osobennosti narodno-russkoy muzïkal'noy sistemï*).

Kastalsky meanwhile worked on further parts of this book. The second part, entitled 'Peculiarities of part-writing and chord formation' (*Osobennosti golosovedeniya i soyedineniya sozvuchiy*) was to be devoted to investigating the laws of polyphony, the melodic lines of folk music and musical forms. 'After all, we know nothing at all about Russian melodic lines (despite the amazingness of Borodin, Musorgsky and Korsakov), still less about rhythm. [...] And in the section on musical forms (including there probably the church forms in the *Obikhod*), there is plenty that is original and unprecedented in art music', the composer wrote to Asafyev.[6] It was intended to place material about the folk orchestra and bell-ringing in the second part. 'It will be something along the lines of a textbook on Russian folk harmony', Kastalsky wrote of his plans; he meant 'to flabbergast those self-confident [classical] musicians'.[7]

The composer was destined, however, neither to flabbergast his colleagues, nor to see in print the continuation of his book. He died when the work was nearly finished. On 2 January 1927 Natalia Kastalskaya wrote to Asafyev: 'Already ill, Alexander Dmitriyevich was on no account willing to lie in bed, regardless of what the doctor had ordered, and looked through what had been copied, since it remained for me to copy and look over about ten pages with insertions, or about 15 pages of normal writing. Our son is fully aware of his father's intentions and keeps me right'.[8] Even while Kastalsky was still alive, the work was copied by his former pupil at the Synodal School, the Moscow Conservatoire teacher Nikolay Belkin, and was almost completely ready for publication. The book was published, however, only 22 years later.[9]

Similarly the author did not learn the fate of another of his works – the long-suffering 'Celebrations' (*Prazdniki*) (the composer's informal name for nos. 114-116 in the worklist), on which he had embarked as long ago as 1911. Let us recall that after Edition Russe de Musique had rejected the first version, which was later partially destroyed, the composer made a second version in 1916, which soon also met the same fate as the first: except for a few numbers, it served as fuel in the stove one cold day. A year later, however, Kastalsky embarked on a third, orchestral version, work on which had been initiated by the head of *MUZO* at *Narkompros*, Arthur Lourié. It was apparently expected that 'Celebrations' would be heard at mass popular celebrations. It is known that one movement was suggested by Kastalsky himself for performance in Petrograd on 1 May 1918; it seems, however, that the work was not in fact performed. The composer nonetheless continued to work on 'Celebrations' without having any clear idea of who might find his composition of interest. In 1924 the composer, having lost faith in the prospects for publication of the work, conceived the idea of a new, fourth version, which his death prevented him finishing.

After Alexander Dmitriyevich's funeral, his widow wrote to Asafyev that 'Celebrations' remained in a very chaotic state. 'To tell the truth, it is not difficult to restore "Spring", "St George's Day", *Rusalii*, *Semik*, *Kupalo* and Yarilo's Day which were completed a few years ago, but *Osenini*, "Winter" and "Cheese Week" (*Maslenitsa*), though they too are finished, have not been edited to give the fluidity on the stage that the others have', Natalia Kastalskaya wrote to Asafyev.[10] To his mother's letter the composer's son, who had helped him in his work, considered it essential to add explanations of his own:

> I want to add something as far as 'Celebrations' is concerned. Dad could see that this piece could not be published in the USSR, because it contains too

much of 'God' in various forms – and for that reason he undertook to wrench it
round into the present-day manner: with committees, Young Communists,
Executive Committees etc., but he did not have enough time to finish it. He
wanted to bring out some aspect of the subject, ending with a wedding, – but
that too is unfinished. Perhaps it's possible to substitute other texts for those
with God and other 'ideology'? Although I think it's better not to proceed with
that and possibly try to get a performance abroad, if it doesn't come off here.[11]

In the end Kastalsky's son prepared some numbers from 'Celebrations'
for publication himself, and published them in a collection of documents
and materials which came out in 1960 (Ex. 20.1).

Besides working at the People's Choir Academy, investigating folksong
and re-working 'Celebrations', the composer managed to get an improbably
large amount of work done during the Soviet period. On 1 September 1919
he sent Asafyev a detailed account of what he had achieved in his first year
of work after the revolution:

What have I done in the last year? Apart from rushing around to various
meetings and lectures (I even had to go along and show some grown-up
brethren piano keys and how to play music from notation on them) – out of
financial need – all the same, I contrived (much to my own surprise) 1) to
harmonize the *Internationale* twice (for four-part choir and choir with
orchestra, where my son who is experienced in orchestration helped me), and
the second version turned out not bad and even had some success, although the
accompaniment has more to do with *Dubinushka* and other specifically Russian
turns of phrase [than with the *Internationale*]... 2) I wrote music for the play
Stenka Razin by Vasily Kamensky, who tried very hard to persuade me to make
an opera out of it (the libretto is not bad – I'd probably have done it if I'd
known for certain that it would be staged). The orchestra was made up of
domras + woodwind. In places it sounded quite respectable. The play had lots
of performances – to the point where I got fed up with it. 3) I wrote music for
Shakespeare's *King Lear*, for small orchestra (with choir in places), – it won't
be staged for a bit – during the winter. 4) A few days ago I finished the first
scene (I reworked it) of 'Peasant Celebrations' at the insistence of Arthur
Lourié: a) 'Invocation and celebration of spring'; b) *Radonitsa* and c) 'St
George's Day' – I've written the piano score (my son is orchestrating it). 5) I
gave an address about 'Urgent tasks for proletarian art' at a public meeting of
the 'Palace of Art'. After me came Balmont, who started to sing the praises of
the 'unity of art' and it became the fiasco he deserved. 6) I compiled some
notes about methods of musical education in school and outside school. The
work awaits copying and receipt of monetary recompense for it, without which
it is impossible to live on account of the [high] prices of flour, groats and other
objects the bowels need. I declined work for the cinematograph (foolishly) –
Lev Tolstoy's *Polikushka*, because it would have paid well. I was not well, and
my nerves were in a mess, which was why I declined it. Maybe I'll accept the

commission for music to [Gerhart Hauptmann's play] *Hanneles Himmelfahrt* (I've not come to an agreement yet); what choice is there? You have to live, you must eat, even if you're actually half-starving; then there's the family...[12]

Another very curious project which remained unrealized dates from this period. In 1919 Asafyev gave Kastalsky to understand that Chaliapin wanted to see him. The meeting took place on 1 September, and Kastalsky told Asafyev all about it:

Dear Boris Vladimirovich!
I went to see Chaliapin myself today, although he had promised to come to see me, which I didn't place much confidence in. As far I could understand, he was talking about some religious play (*deystvo*) ('profoundly tragic', in Chaliapin's words) which would be produced in an artistic manner, rather than in the fashion of the clergy as usually happens... There's a great deal to think about and let your imagination loose on here: you could ennoble the ritual of our worship, make it more sincere, more deeply felt (using all the resources of art for the purpose). Have I understood the idea correctly? Chaliapin said that it would unavoidably draw people reduced to a beastly existence towards real warmth, warm-heartedness, 'we shall embrace one another...' I'd like to hear something about this from you...[13]

In the subsequent years the intensity of his work showed no decline. It would seem that the composer himself particularly liked his 'Summons to Russian Musicians' (*Vozzvaniye k russkim muzïkantam*), composed in 1921 when starvation broke out in Russia, for bass 'accompanied by a mumbling, wordless chorus (or harmonium). The text is [my] own (Russian, translated into English, French and other languages), endorsed by Lunacharsky and others. The contents deal with hunger and all that Russia in her time has done to help others... And now she just watches and waits'.[14] (Ex. 20.2)

The greater part of what Kastalsky wrote after the revolution consisted of choral compositions *à la russe*, and also arrangements of folksongs. Alexander Dmitriyevich regarded his (unpublished) 'Agricultural Symphony' (*Selskokhozyaystvennaya simfoniya*) as one of his greatest 'sins' of that time. In this work, in the words of the composer,

all the themes are songs which begin with a reference to various forms of work in the country, which when they first appear are sung by a solo singer and are then usually taken up in a symphonic statement. I actually prepared it for an agricultural exhibition, but nothing came of it at the time. I also wrote seven choruses entitled 'Agricultural work in folksongs' accompanied by balalaykas (for the ensembles in workers' clubs). I believe a second edition has come out.

I've only heard some of them. I'm told that *Troyka* to words by Oreshin is popular, but I've not heard it myself. I've also written eight songs (also for choir and balalayka). *Rus* (Nekrasov's words *Tï i ubogaya...*) dedicated to Stasov (for his centenary, which has got bogged down) is pretty difficult. My latest opus is 'By Lenin's Tomb' (*U groba Lenina*) (declamation + choir and piano), words by Kirillov.[15]

Kastalsky pursued his speech-making with uncommon intensity after 1917, and continued preaching his message with a will. As Nadezhda Bryusova recalled:

> One might say that Kastalsky was in love with the ancient peasant songs; what he loved about them was both their style and their contents, as they conveyed the way of life and the labour of the peasant. He made settings of folksongs, introduced their melodies into his own compositions, wrote up his research into the structure of Russian folksong, and promoted folksong everywhere he possibly could. It seemed as if there was no productive meeting he didn't take part in, speaking up 'to defend' folksong. At some point this modest quiet man would get up, ask for permission to speak and then read out an appeal prepared in advance, calling for attention to be concentrated on folk art.[16]

In the statement just quoted an 'appeal' is mentioned which is neither more nor less than the 'proclamation' written shortly after the February revolution which had made many of Kastalsky's colleagues wince. Under the new régime the composer made one more attempt to convince the musical community of the need to restructure culture on folk foundations. He had changed not just the title of the poem but also some of its lines, expanding on the idea of folk culture's ideological opponents. Thus, in the 1918 variant, the following words appeared:

> Not the Germans, nor the French will develop our art,
> They will foster their classical modernist style.[17]

The fact that the subject of 'modernism' in contemporary art worried Kastalsky in the Soviet period is evident from several of the composer's literary manuscripts.[18] Thus, in lectures for the Choir Academy Alexander Dmitriyevich developed his ideas about the losses suffered by an art torn from its roots and become elitist. He listed among the losses the endless diversity and deep religious content, the beauty of form and sincerity, instead of which there appeared mannerism, coldness and rationalism.

Kastalsky's judgements about contemporary music were not by any means the result of abstract philosophizing: they were based on a careful study of the musical language of present-day composers and the latest systems of musical theory, as is testified once again by materials in his archive[19] and the reminiscences of musicians. Thus, the composer Alexander Davidenko, who had been a pupil of Kastalsky, wrote:

> Several of the teachers and students at the Conservatoire, when they spoke about the compositions of Alexander Dmitriyevich, considered him a conservative; they asserted that he did not know the contemporary literature of music. In my lessons with him I became convinced that that was untrue. I often had occasion to speak to him about Stravinsky, Schoenberg, Hindemith and *Les Six*, and he displayed very great erudition about all of them. All musicians can confirm that no concert of any significant interest went by without Kastalsky's hardly noticeable, rather grey figure appearing at it.[20]

In short, Kastalsky was far from accusing all modern composers who had 'non-proletarian' tendencies of 'modernism and futurism'. His criterion for evaluating a particular composer was not so much stylistic direction as talent. And there is one further factor which should not be neglected when examining Kastalsky's predilections in the Soviet period. The fact is that all the composer's critical utterances about contemporary art are found in the materials for his public speeches or lectures, not memoirs or letters.

In 1925 the composer compiled an autobiographical album into which he gathered several reviews and articles and summed up the results of the Soviet period. Kastalsky did not pass up the chance of letting Asafyev know the results of his statistical calculations:

> I myself was surprised by the final outcome: sundry jobs and memberships after the Synodal School – 16 headings; papers and various syllabuses – 16 entries; research papers and articles on folk music – 8 titles. There are 57 (!) compositional works since 1918, of which only half are published. This figure includes complete sets of music, for example for *Stenka Razin*, *Lear*, *Hannele*, the symphony, Lunacharsky's 'Heroic Sonata' (choral declamation), and so on. Of course, some works (for instance, 'Celebrations', 'Folk Polyphony', work on which is making very slow progress because of my ardent desire that the materials be complete, 'Diplomatic Notes and Concerts' – using the melodies of national anthems) – are far from being complete and need to be looked through again, but..., nonetheless, one may say that over those years I did not consume Soviet bread in vain... Of course, the greatest quantity of reviews relate to my sacred compositions (which are counter-revolutionary) and 'From Past Ages' – and every one of the reviews is complimentary (even perhaps too much so!).[21]

In the same letter, besides giving a joyful report of what he had done, Kastalsky informed Asafyev that the press rarely wrote about compositions of his written after the revolution and linked that with the hostile attitude towards him of 'revolutionary' musicians as a former composer of sacred music. 'I hear indirectly: he's a writer of "Cherubic Hymns", but now he sets revolutionary words just like everybody else!', the composer complained to Asafyev.[22]

Kastalsky's position in the musical world after the revolution was indeed a complicated one. Finding himself, in his own words, 'between two stools', he did not rise up in opposition to the new authority, and, like many people of his circle, he tried to adapt to the new régime. In spite of the fact that Alexander Dmitriyevich was a member of a number of Soviet institutions and commissions and wrote compositions with Soviet subject-matter, the composer never regarded himself as a revolutionary. On 10 March 1924 Kastalsky wrote in a letter to Asafyev about some mutual acquaintance in Petrograd:

> We've got enough of our own such people who dress themselves up as 'revolutionaries' in Moscow too (starting with Sabaneyev...), and, what's more, as an old man I don't number myself among them, since from the outset (and even earlier) I've gone in the direction of not individualizing my own person but of dissolving it in contact with the mass of the people, which you don't get a whiff of with the modernists. Maybe for that reason, while I don't present myself as such, people link me with the Association of Proletarian Musicians and with the 'Red Professors' (a 67-year-old ruin!). And I really am going to pieces: my heart's not fit for anything, there's a lot of emphysema in my lungs (an extension, is it?). I gasp for breath every night.[23]

And in fact his desire 'to dissolve his person in the mass of the people' manifested itself even in the composer's outward appearance. Alexander Davidenko described his first encounter with his teacher thus:

> At the exam (I had enrolled at the Choir Academy) I was very surprised when, expecting to see the famous Kastalsky, who was renowned not only in Russia, but also abroad for his works on Russian song, I beheld not a venerable, distinguished professor but a modest, rather grey little old man who held himself so that you would not notice him, who asked the candidate the questions in a business-like and simple way. His unusual modesty and simple everyday appearance at a solemn entrance exam amazed me. [...] Alexander Dmitriyevich had a special manner of his own: he addressed students in the [less formal] second-person singular and spoke directly, using the same language which I used to hear and still hear in workers' clubs.[24]

At the same time, in church circles Kastalsky was firmly branded a traitor. The composer was deeply offended and regarded this as black ingratitude. In 1924 he wrote to Asafyev: 'There can of course be no question of "religious" music now, and that public itself (that is the priests of the cult) have become so diabolical that it is disagreeable even to remember them, to say nothing of their swinish attitude towards old Kastalsky (with a few exceptions)'.[25]

A sense of grievance towards specific individuals did not mean that Kastalsky had become an atheist, however; several letters and people he associated with bear witness to the contrary. Despite the fact that after the revolution a choice was made, the composer did not break the link with the creation of sacred music, although of course compositions for the church were very rare phenomena in the Soviet period. Thus at the beginning of the first post-revolutionary year the choral cycle 'From the Vesting of Patriarchs and Bishops' (*Iz patriarshego i arkhiyereyskogo oblacheniya*) which included the choral pieces *Ot vostok solntsa* (From the rising of the sun), a processional 'It is meet' (*Dostoyno*), 'To our master' (*Ton despotin*), 'Thou didst enter into the temple' (*Voshel yesi vo tserkov'*) and 'Many years, Master' (*Ispolla eti despota*). On 18 January 1918 the composer wrote to Asafyev: 'I have just done the "Bishops' Vesting" out of need – to the text and melody given to me to deal with by the Patriarch, but harmonized by some priest called Zinovyev, which (not enamoured by its laurels) I replaced with one of my own. I think it will sound satisfactory. I'm adding to it the *Ispolla* to a *demestvenny* chant'.[26] The 'Vesting' was performed for the first time by the remnants of the Synodal Choir on 21 January 1918 at a patriarchal service in the Alekseyev Monastery. During the 1920s they were also performed in other churches where the choirmasters were ex-Synodal Choir people or admirers of the Synodal Choir who continued to hold Kastalsky's name in high regard for many years to come. In particular, the 'Vesting' was performed in the church of the Transfiguration of the Lord where the choir was directed by Nikita Drachev, a friend of Pavel Chesnokov. (It was for this choir that Kastalsky wrote a troparion for the Transfiguration of the Lord to great *znamenny* chant in 1921.) The work was performed from manuscript copies, because 'for lack of time' Alexander Dmitriyevich had delayed handing it in to the publisher, which was nationalized soon afterwards.

In 1921 Kastalsky again began thinking about the fate of his sacred compositions, the greater part of which had been published at his own expense, and he decided to sell ownership of them to the publisher Belayev, based in Leipzig; he asked Asafyev for his advice on the matter: 'It's of course impossible to have them printed here now (or even to run off a few more copies). And meantime there are some items of which I don't have even a single copy. And here's another thing: do you still have the copy of

my Great Doxology which I corrected and reworked for Suvchinsky? If
you do, please be so kind as to send it to me for copying. I'll return it
unharmed'.[27]   Kastalsky asked his American friends Crane and
Rachmaninoff for their help in selling the rights to publish his sacred
compositions (288 pages according to Kastalsky's calculation) and at the
same time selling the printing plates for them.[28]   To all appearances
Alexander Dmitriyevich was doubtful about the benefit of this operation
and tried to find out from Rachmaninoff if he thought there would be any
demand for his compositions abroad. He was reckoning not so much on
poor Russian emigrants as on Americans who, as Kastalsky had heard,
loved Russian sacred music and could play his choral compositions at
home on the piano or in church on the organ. The composer did not even
exclude the possibility of applying a new text in Latin or other languages to
his compositions.   Alexander Dmitriyevich offered the services as
translator of his wife, who as we know, had carried out that task for
'Requiem for Fallen Brothers'.[29]

In a letter to Rachmaninoff of 21 March 1922 Kastalsky candidly
admitted that the enterprise of selling the publishing rights was explained
by his wish to have some funds abroad in case he emigrated. The idea,
uttered with a degree of irony in 1917, of becoming a psalmodist in some
foreign parish sounded wholly serious in 1922, and Kastalsky delicately
asked Rachmaninoff for his co-operation in this. It was perfectly obvious
that the composer was overwhelmed by circumstances and was behaving
like a drowning man clutching at a straw. Asafyev, who visited Kastalsky
in the summer of 1922, wrote to Suvchinsky in Berlin: 'Kastalsky's
behaving oddly – he's abandoned his real work. He's aged a great deal and
looks poorly'.[30]   In letters to friends Alexander Dmitriyevich himself
confessed that he felt terribly tired and had been worn out by his half-
famished existence, cold, deprivations and fear for the fate of those dear to
him. A line from one of his letters to Rachmaninoff – 'Wretched old age
has set in' – may serve as epigraph to the Soviet period of the composer's
life.

Sad appeals 'to foreign brethren' had their effect: several foreign friends
and acquaintances (including Rachmaninoff and Mott) began to provide the
composer's family with very significant material aid. By the end of 1923,
thanks to receiving parcels and being 'pampered with dollars', the
Kastalskys, in the words of the head of the household, 'had started to be in
clover as regards provisions'. Even cheese, white sturgeon and the pie with
rice and fish (*kulebyaka*) which had been a favourite since childhood
appeared on the table from time to time. The approaching cold period gave

rise to alarm: the situation with clothing and firewood remained critical and the only hope was that the winter would be warm.

While everyday life was improving, the state of Alexander Dmitriyevich's health was getting worse: the hard years had aggravated his heart and lung ailments dramatically. (In his final years the composer suffered from asthma, emphysema of the lungs, myocarditis, and atherosclerosis.) And although in 1923 the 67-year-old Kastalsky could still find strength to joke about his illnesses, he understood that the time had arrived to bring an end to big enterprises: the idea of a 'posthumous' edition of his compositions and writings did not elicit great enthusiasm from him. As Vyacheslav Paskhalov remembered:

The deprivations suffered during the civil war finally shattered Alexander Dmitriyevich's health, but in spite of that, he continued his teaching at the Choir Academy and the Moscow Conservatoire. [...] And meanwhile a monstrous shortness of breath (the result of his progressive illness) made it difficult for him to work. I found him at home in the posture typical for someone with a heart condition: he was kneeling on a chair, resting with his whole body and his left elbow on a table, his head inclined low. He was holding a pen in his right hand as he wrote his latest work. Asphyxia pursued him outside the house too. I recall a journey I made with him to the Conservatoire. The gates of the Choir Academy and the Conservatoire both opened out on to Herzen Street [the former Bolshaya Nikitskaya]. I walked along the pavement alongside Alexander Dmitriyevich and was astounded by the difficulty he had walking these twenty or thirty steps to the Conservatoire, where he was going for some concert that interested him.[31]

Kastalsky's life in the Soviet era conceals many mysteries which it is now too late to unravel. The composer who had previously been very open in his correspondence was restrained and cautious in his letters of the Soviet period, and allowed himself to speak from the heart only on extremely rare occasions. The quantity of letters written during this period is also sharply reduced; this related first and foremost to the deaths of two of his closest friends – Grozdov (who died in 1919) and Rebikov (who died in 1920). Fate scattered former friends and acquaintances across the whole world: Rachmaninoff was in America and Suvchinsky in Germany; Zatayevich, who lived with the Kastalskys for several years after the revolution, moved to Orenburg in 1920.

It is difficult to say what compelled the brilliant assistant to the governor of Warsaw to set off for the backwoods, where, like Kastalsky, he became engrossed in collecting and investigating local folklore, until he acquired in due course the status of Merited Art Worker of the Kazakh SSR. It was in his few letters to Zatayevich that Kastalsky stayed the same emotional, open, sharp-tongued and critical person he had been in earlier years.

The composer gave his support in every possible way to his friend who was now remote from the cultural centres, the more so since the latter was accomplishing heroic feats in collecting folksongs. Thus in 1922 Kastalsky came to an agreement with the Ethnographical Commission attached to *MUZO* of *Narkompros* for Zatayevich to send 350 of his transcriptions for publication. To be sure, he warned his friend frankly that he was unlikely to be able to obtain any fee for them: 'As regards payment, I don't think you'll find things anywhere any more satisfactory than they are in Kirgizia. I'm judging by my own experience: for six months of writing, both to commission and without, for folk orchestra, for choir, for music with choral declamation (an entire sonata), in general, about fifteen compositions, and so far – not a penny!'[32]

Naturally, the friends discussed the fate of former acquaintances in their correspondence. On 6 January 1921 Kastalsky wrote to Zatayevich: 'I've heard that Rachmaninoff has turned into the complete American – become a planter, a landowner; I'm not going to assess to what extent it's true. He's certainly giving concerts. [...] A few days ago I received a letter from Asafyev telling me that Prokofiev had written from America saying that he had got himself excellently set up there, and that they were even staging his new opera *The Love for Three Oranges* there'.[33] In the same letter the composer tells him about Koussevitzky, who was living in Paris and had written to Kastalsky that many things were better there than in Russia, and that he did not intend going back to his motherland.

As regards Zatayevich, he was dreaming of returning to Moscow, as he informed Kastalsky. The latter warmly supported this idea and reasoned that in the capital Zatayevich would be able to find work as a teacher or school inspector. 'In our Choir Academy I've introduced additional lessons in reading music for the pupils – in all classes, both morning and evening. Almost everybody reads extremely badly. Because of the enormous importance of this subject, maybe I'll be able to organize a post of inspector in that subject'.[34] According to Kastalsky, the main problem about returning to Moscow would be finding a place to live.

Accommodation was a sore point for Kastalsky himself, since he had been able only with difficulty, thanks to the protection of Lunacharsky and Yenukidze, to save his flat from being 'consolidated' – that is, reducing the amount of space allowed per person. It appears that Alexander Dmitriyevich had an attitude of great sympathy and gratitude towards Lunacharsky, keeping in his archive a copy of the following telephoned telegram from the People's Commissar to the head of the Moscow Central Housing and Land Department:

> One of the most famous Russian musicians, Kastalsky, is overloaded with all kinds of commissions from the state and is having his flat, which is in the City Area, consolidated. I wrote to the Housing and Land Department there, saying that it was quite improper to touch individuals like that. We incurred real unpleasantnesses from Vladimir Ilich [Lenin] on these grounds on account, for example, of Glazunov and Pavlov. It will be just the same in this case – there will be an enormous scandal, possibly on a European scale. In the meantime, the Housing Department for the City Area have paid no attention to the letter. I request that you give instructions that Kastalsky be left in peace. I count on your assistance, but I must warn you that this case is such that, if you do not give me your help, then I shall have to take the matter to VTsIK [the All-Union Central Executive Committee] and to the Party TsK [Central Committee]. It would be very good if you and the Areas would finally realize that it is politically criminal to irritate the most important representatives of culture, people with European reputations, with [petty] restrictions.[35]

In the spring of 1922 a threat once more hung over the Kastalskys' flat, as he wrote to Zatayevich: 'They're threatening us again both with consolidation and particularly with the endless millions for space in flats, of which millions I receive very few. But for my academic food ration, I'd peg out right away!'[36] The situation was repeated a year later, even though by then lodgers were already living in the flat: 'I've got an engineer Tambiyev (a Kabardinian) and a writer Tarabukin staying with me. A worker with five children was sent along with an order for two rooms!.. I managed to fight them off and the rooms are still registered in my name for the time being'.[37]

That same spring (of 1922) there were other serious causes of alarm. 'Our Choir Academy has been cut back to the very bone', Alexander Dmitriyevich wrote to the same correspondent, 'and besides that, it seems that in a few days it is going to lose all state funding (!), and what perhaps lies ahead is merger with the Moscow Conservatoire, and I shall change from being "Academy Rector" into the devil only know what!'[38]

Despite all his efforts, Kastalsky was not successful in averting the Academy's abolition: in 1923, having failed to comply with the reforms in musical education then being conducted in the country, it was converted into the Choir Sub-Department of the Moscow Conservatoire. (The main architect of the reform was none other than Boleslav Yavorsky, at one time a favourite pupil of Smolensky, who in 1921 had been appointed by Lunacharsky to the post of head of the department of music education institutions at *Glavprofobr* [Main administration of professional education].)   It is possible that there was also another reason for the abolition of the Academy: even without its choir and child boarders, it continued to preserve the remnants of the pre-revolutionary traditions of choirtraining and teaching.   Kastalsky had often had to justify the 'church spirit' which reigned there to the authorities.

In the spring of 1923 Alexander Dmitriyevich informed Zatayevich about the closure of the Academy as a matter which had been decided:

> Here's a new misfortune now: they're merging our Choir Academy with the Conservatoire (amalgamating smaller institutions into larger ones is in fashion), and perhaps your humble servant (Rector of the Choir Academy) is demoted to ... the devil knows what – in a word, a subordinate figure at the Conservatoire (where, incidentally, instead of Ippolitov-Ivanov the rector is to be Goldenveyzer, and where Nazar Grigoryevich Raysky is to be specially in command – he's married to the sister of Sergey Zimin, for whom Ippolitov-Ivanov is one of the conductors.   But the main thing is that the Conservatoire has a special appetite for our building with the flats on Kislovka Street so that it can provide its employees with flats there (and who knows, they may start by evicting the likes of us).   From this year I am a Conservatoire professor of folk music (there's one person who attends my lectures).   In short, my immediate prospects are – poor...[39]

Soon, while the property – furniture, library, firewood etc. – which had belonged to the Academy was transferred to the Conservatoire, the building itself was 'seized' by Moscow University.   In 1925 it was decided to transfer the choral singers into the vocal department, leaving only the choirmasters; the sub-department was deprived of a proper choir made up of good voices.   By the academic year 1926-27 all that remained of the People's Choir Academy was the department of general musical education in the faculty for training instructors, to which choral conductors were assigned.

In the life of Kastalsky, who had ceased to believe in the good intentions of the new authorities, the 1920s were filled with battles to hold on to the remnants of his school.   His last memorandum on this subject was written four months before his death.   The composer wrote there that:

> There is in the Choir Sub-Department a fundamental subject which unites singers and [choir] directors – choral singing and its repertoire.   It is the actual sound of a choir that educates them, just as the orchestra in which they once played has educated many symphonic and operatic conductors.   The finest practitioners of the art of choral conducting were educated in the good choirs in which they sang.   [...]   If the cause of choral singing was looked on before as a

secondary species of art, then that view is a strange one at the present time. Closing the Choir Academy serves that point of view exactly.[40]

On 17 December 1926 Kastalsky died. Five years after his death, in 1931, a Department of Choral Conducting was to be organized at the Moscow Conservatoire, with former 'Synodal' people on its staff: Chesnokov, Danilin and Nikolsky. However, the students in the Choral Department were to be educated not on *znamenny* chant, and not even on peasant song, which came under a cloud at the beginning of the 1930s as a 'relic of the past', but on the Soviet mass [song] repertoire. The 'Russian' period in the nation's choral music was to die along with Kastalsky; the triumph of the 'Soviet' choral school was about to begin. Fate decreed, however, that no choir similar to the Synodal one was to emerge. History had proved that a phenomenon of such artistic dimensions could emerge only as the result of a church and folk choral culture lasting many centuries.

Notes

1. V. Derzhanovsky: *K proyektu Kastal'skogo* (Kastal'sky's project), in *Novosti dnya* (News of the Day), 1918, 26 November.
2. *V Informotdel MUZO Narkomprosa dlya spravochnika 'Muzïkal'naya Moskva'* (Sent to *Informotdel MUZO Narkompros*a for the handbook 'Musical Moscow)'. GTsMMK, fond 12, no. 249, p. 1v.
3. *Ibid.*
4. A.D. Kastal'sky: *Iz pisem 1917-1918 godov* (From letters from the years 1917-1918), in *RUSAM*, vol. 1, p. 301.
5. *Ibid.*, p. 304.
6. Letter from A.D. Kastal'sky to B.V. Asaf'yev of 9 May 1918. RGALI, fond 2658, opis' 1, no. 581, p. 19.
7. *Ibid.*, p.34.
8. Letter from N.L. Kastal'skaya to B.V. Asaf'yev of 2 January 1927. RGALI, fond 2658, opis' 1, no. 592, pp. 4-4v.
9. Kastal'sky's work *Osnovï narodnogo mnogogolosiya* (Fundamentals of folk polyphony) was published in 1948 edited by V.M. Belayev.
10. Letter from N.L. Kastal'skaya to B.V. Asaf'yev of 2 January 1927. RGALI, fond 2658, opis' 1, no. 582, p. 5.
11. Letter from A.A. Kastal'sky to B.V. Asaf'yev of 12 January 1927. RGALI, fond 2658, opis' 1, no. 582, p. 5v.
12. Letter from A.D. Kastal'sky to B.V. Asaf'yev of 1 September 1919. RGALI, fond 2658, opis' 1, no. 581, pp. 34-35v.
13. Letter from A.D. Kastal'sky to B.V. Asaf'yev of 1 September 1919. RGALI, fond 2658, opis' 1, no. 581, p. 34.
14. Letter from A.D. Kastal'sky to B.V. Asaf'yev of 12 August 1921. RGALI, fond 2658, opis' 1, no. 581, p. 37v.

15. Letter from A.D. Kastal'sky to B.V. Asaf'yev of 10 March 1924. RGALI, fond 2658, opis' 1, no. 581, pp. 41-41v.
16. N.Ya. Bryusova: *Khorovaya kul'tura v perviye godï posle Oktyabrya. Kastal'sky i Davidenko* (Choral culture in the first years after October. Kastal'sky and Davidenko). RGALI, fond 2009, opis' 1, no. 110, p. 23.
17. A.D. Kastal'sky: *Vozzvaniye k russkim muzïkantam* (Summons to Russian musicians). GTsMMK, fond 12, no. 186.
18. Cf. for instance: A.D. Kastal'sky: [*Zametki o sovremennom iskusstve*] (Notes about contemporary art). GTsMMK, fond 12, no. 188.
19. A.D. Kastal'sky: *Yavorsky i drugiye garmonicheskiye izïskaniya i postroyeniya. Obobshcheniye muzïkal'nïkh form* (Yavorsky and other harmonic investigations and structures. A generalization about musical forms). GTsMMK, fond 12, no. 194.
20. A.N. Davidenko: *Uchitel'* (My teacher), in *A.D. Kastal'sky. Stat'i. Vospominaniya. Materialï* (A.D. Kastal'sky. Articles. Reminiscences. Materials). Moscow, 1960, p. 121.
21. Letter from A.D. Kastal'sky to B.V. Asaf'yev of 1 May 1925. GTsMMK, fond 171, no. 97, pp. 1v-2.
22. *Ibid.*, p. 2.
23. Letter from A.D. Kastal'sky to B.V. Asaf'yev of 10 March 1924. RGALI, fond 2658, opis' 1, no. 581, pp. 40-40v.
24. A.N. Davidenko: *Uchitel'*, in *A.D. Kastal'sky. Stat'i. Vospominaniya. Materialï*, p. 120.
25. Letter from A.D. Kastal'sky to B.V. Asaf'yev of 10 March 1924. RGALI, fond 2658, opis' 1, no. 581, p. 41v.
26. A.D. Kastal'sky: *Iz pisem 1917-1918 godov*, in *RUSAM*, vol. 1, p. 298.
27. Letter from A.D. Kastal'sky to B.V. Asaf'yev of 12 August 1921. RGALI, fond 2658, opis' 1, no. 581, p. 37v.
28. Letters from A.D. Kastal'sky to S.V. Rakhmaninov of 21 March 1922, 2 January, 23 March and 7 December 1923 are housed in the Rachmaninoff archive at the Library of Congress in Washington, D.C.
29. It is difficult to say whether Kastal'sky carried out his intention to sell the publication rights. The one thing that is clear is that the engraved plates of his compositions have disappeared without trace, which cannot be said of the archive carefully preserved in the Kastal'sky family and sections of the already published editions of sacred compositions. The composer's archive was subsequently given by his children to GTsMMK, with his music library going to the Publishing Department of the Moscow Patriarchate.
30. Letter from B.V. Asaf'yev to P.P. Suvchinsky of 23 July 1922. Bibliothèque Nationale de France, Paris, Res. Vm. Dos. 91-94. (Information provided by L.Z. Korabel'nikova.)
31. V. Paskhalov: *Vstrechi i vospominaniya* (Encounters and Reminiscences), in *A.D. Kastal'sky. Stat'i. Vospominaniya. Materialï*, p. 25.
32. Letter from A.D. Kastal'sky to A.V. Zatayevich of 14 April 1922. GTsMMK, fond 6, no. 322, p. 1v.
33. Letter from A.D. Kastal'sky to A.V. Zatayevich of 6 January 1921. GTsMMK, fond 6, no. 321, p. 1v.
34. Letter from A.D. Kastal'sky to A.V. Zatayevich of 28 October 1921. GTsMMK, fond 6, no. 320, p. 1v.
35. Telephonogram from People's Commissar A.V. Lunacharsky to the head of the Central Housing and Land Department M. Merkulov of 15 July 1921. GTsMMK, fond 12, no. 499.
36. Letter from A.D. Kastal'sky to A.V. Zatayevich of 14 April 1922. GTsMMK, fond 6, no. 322, p. 2v.
37. Letter from A.D. Kastal'sky to A.V. Zatayevich of 10 April 1923. GTsMMK, fond 6, no. 323, p. 2.

38. Letter from A.D. Kastal'sky to A.V. Zatayevich of 14 April 1922. GTsMMK, fond 6, no. 322, p. 2v.
39. Letter from A.D. Kastal'sky to A.V. Zatayevich of 10 April 1923. GTsMMK, fond 6, no. 323, pp. 2-2v.
40. Memorandum of A.D. Kastal'sky of 25 August 1926 concerning the report of N.Ya. Bryusova about reorganizing the Choir Sub-Department at the Moscow State Conservatoire. GTsMMK, fond 12, no. 268, pp. 2-2v.

Epilogue

Kastalsky and Asafyev

I had occasion to know well and to mourn the passing of three grand old men – men of past ages, but who never lost their link with the life of the young. They were Vladimir Stasov, Nikolay Kashkin and now Alexander Kastalsky. It is difficult to convey in a short note just what I gained as a result of being in their company. From no one did I learn to love human life and creativity more than those three – who were very different but each in his own way was profoundly experienced and wise and had 'seen an entire era come and go'. And when you realize with sorrow that you are never again going to hear such a person's voice, it seems disappointing that you did not have more time to profit from their company, you met them but seldom, and did not ask them many questions,

wrote Asafyev soon after Kastalsky's death in 1926.[1]

Asafyev, it appears, was the only critic and scholar who fully understood and appreciated the worth of the one and indivisible Kastalsky, whose life was divided into two mutually exclusive parts.

The revolution created a fissure in the biography of Asafyev too, who was younger than Kastalsky – in 1917 he was 33. By that time Asafyev had made a name for himself as a brilliant music critic who supported the most striking, the most talented and advanced composers. He developed an intense interest at the same time in church music and became a genuine connoisseur and expert. In Soviet times he was famous for a number of outstanding publications and was rightly recognized as the founder of the Soviet school of musical scholarship. He accommodated himself to the Soviet era's conditions of intellectual and physical survival, not without effort or sacrifice of principle, and became one of the most influential figures in the world of music; he was the only music historian to be awarded the status of a full member of the Academy of Sciences of the USSR, and twice won Stalin Prizes. The most important Russian composers were often the subject of Asafyev's work in the Soviet period. But a more modest hero – Alexander Kastalsky – was also among his favourites.

Until the end of his days Asafyev dreamed of shedding adequate light on the composer's legacy, but did not live to see the day when recognition of that kind became possible.

Asafyev's 'immersion in Kastalsky' began in 1915, when his article about the genre of 'musical restoration' which the composer had invented was published in the journal 'Music' (*Muzïka*). The cycle 'From Past Ages', in which Kastalsky reconstructed scenes from the life of past ages on the basis of music archaeological materials, thrilled the young critic 'with its sincerity and thoughtful insight into the depths of the nation's soul' and evidently heightened his interest in the composer, whose acquaintance he made during Asafyev's visit to Moscow in 1916.

The reason for their meeting was so that Asafyev could get to know Kastalsky's recently completed composition 'Requiem for Fallen Brothers', dedicated to victims of the First World War. Several lines in one of Kastalsky's letters are devoted to this meeting: 'Derzhanovsky pestered me the other day to come and introduce this little thing to Igor Glebov (a pseudonym) who had arrived to visit him. I played the "Requiem" through in piano duet with Asafyev. Derzhanovsky, who was behind me, scribbled something (probably for "Music"), and fantasized about "letting Diaghilev hear it"'.[2]

The upshot of the visit soon made itself felt, and in the March issue of 'Music', along with a note about new sacred choral works by Kastalsky, there was Asafyev's article about 'Requiem for Fallen Brothers'.[3] After the work's première in 1917, the critic published a more extended review in 'Musical Contemporary' (*Muzïkal'nïy sovremennik*) which besides analytical points contained the aesthetic and philosophical reflections typical of Asafyev. The reaction of Kastalsky, who was not overfond of either 'scribblers' or 'aestheticizing', was extremely sarcastic. It may be judged from a letter to his friend in Petrograd:

And about the article by Igor Glebov (who was here the day before yesterday with Suvchinsky – they're organizing 'Musical Contemporary' concerts in the Synodal School), I can only say: Thank you, I wasn't expecting it – but that's all. I've read his long review... Fancy him imagining for some reason that I intended to produce or create some kind of 'brotherhood of nations' or 'religious unity of nations based on religious art' with the 'Requiem'! After all, I think, I say specifically (in the Preface) how I regard the 'Requiem' – as a possible picture – but it didn't turn out that way. (Him): No, you're deceiving us, my friend. You wanted 'to create a work in which present-day religious trends find an echo' (do you like that, then?) 'and a dream about religious art is embodied'. That's just too clever by half! I thought he (Igor) was simple, that's true... He talks an awful lot of nonsense – God save us! And generally he cursed me more than he felt satisfied. [...] But Asafyev in person is an

attractive, unassuming lad. But, the devil take him, what does it matter to me –
I don't have to share my flat with him, do I?[4]

Thus, to begin with, the relationship between Asafyev and Kastalsky
developed on the 'composer and critic' model with all that it entails.

In 1917 a lively correspondence arose between them, prompted by the
fact that after Asafyev and Suvchinsky left the staff of the Petrograd
'Musical Contemporary' they organized a journal entitled 'Musical
Thought' (*Muzïkal'naya mïsl'*) and were starting to recruit authors for their
publication. It was intended to introduce an extended section on church
music into the annual, and the editors placed church music on the same
footing as the 'elite' forms of art. They proposed to publish materials on
church music, in particular Smolensky's famous *Reminiscences* in full and
writings by Kastalsky. 'Kastalsky has an absolutely inexhaustible wealth
of material!', Asafyev wrote to Suvchinsky, – 'but he's pretty hard to edit'.[5]

After negotiating at Asafyev's request with the Moscow authors Dimitry
Allemanov and Konstantin Shvedov about them taking part in the journal,
Kastalsky informed Petrograd:

> As regards publishing yours truly's work in the prospectus for the new journal,
> I'm in complete agreement, though I should tell you that with me 'literature',
> that is my tongue-wagging ability, is not at all developed. What I prepared for
> the 'Musical Contemporary' starts off with the war against German domination
> in music (I can't do anything until I've got that out of the way), which may not
> fit in with your plans (I'll move on to church music when I've had my fill of
> being rude).[6]

Kastalsky's article 'Simple art and its not-so-simple tasks', devoted to
church music in democratic Russia, was published in 1918 in the second
number of 'Melos'. (Suvchinsky and Asafyev began publishing the
almanac of that name instead of 'Musical Thought'.) A year later the
annual ceased to exist, and another article by Kastalsky written for it was
published only sixty years later.[7]

The correspondence between Asafyev and Kastalsky lasted until the
composer's death and dealt mainly with professional matters. The letters'
contents, however, testify to the two men's growing friendship at this
difficult time. In letters written in the period between the two revolutions,
when Alexander Dmitriyevich was carried away with the idea of the
renewal of art, he shared his plans with Asafyev. In a letter of 16 April
1917 he wrote: 'How one ought to be stirring up the idea of the musical
renaissance of Mother Rus at the moment, especially the cause of music
education! How much wholly original material there is – melodic and

structural as well as harmonic! When will all this begin to rise to the surface?'[8] After writing his 'proclamation' in verse, Kastalsky sent it among others to Asafyev, asking him to read it out at a folk concert-meeting on the subject of 'Art for the People' at the People's Conservatoire.

The October events of 1917 which broke out soon thereafter turned the composer's life and frame of mind in a quite different direction. Hunger, destruction, deprivations and the absence of prospects dealt both Kastalsky and Asafyev painful blows. In the composer's letter of 18 January 1918 the topic of folk creativity is replaced by a completely different subject: 'I read today that they want to give you half-a-pound of bread each a day (can that be for long?) We've been on a ration of a quarter of a pound a day for ages now. You see, I've started talking about bread straightaway!...'[9] In June 1918, when Asafyev called on Kastalsky during a trip to Moscow, he was struck by how he had changed and shared his impressions with Suvchinsky: 'Kastalsky is a wonder, he's just amazing. But, poor soul, he's got a lot older and is exhausted'.[10]

As was said in previous chapters, Russian folklore helped the composer cope with the crisis, which was so severe as to cause him to think about emigrating. As far as we can understand from Kastalsky's letters, Asafyev tried to promote the publication of his work in Petrograd, which Alexander Dmitriyevich was very pleased about, supposing that publication would 'proceed from loving hearts'. In those years Asafyev truly became someone who thought the same way as Kastalsky insofar as after the revolution he entered heart and soul into propagating and studying Russian folksong in the belief that it should be the basis of the country's musical education and the art of composition. In 1920, as head of the Music History section at the Institute for the History of the Arts in Petrograd, Asafyev put forward the idea that the area of priority for that institution ought to be folk art. To demonstrate this idea, he gave a series of lectures about Russian folksong, began writing a book about the folksong foundations of the style of Russian classical opera, and organized a folklore expedition to the north of Russia.

During the 1920s the subject 'The creative work of Kastalsky' (and following it the subjects 'Tchaikovsky' and 'Rimsky-Korsakov and Wagner') appeared on a list of scholarly projects planned by Asafyev. In 1925 Asafyev made the composer aware of his intention, and in a letter the latter supplied a full account of his activities, starting in 1918, remarking though that he could not see how it was possible to make do with only 'his secular doings, even though the "religious" part is now unacceptable'. It looks as if in his desire to give Asafyev material for his book Kastalsky also began compiling a very extensive autobiographical album, fragments of which have been cited in previous chapters.

Apparently, Asafyev himself finally came to the conclusion that the time was not altogether suitable for writing about Kastalsky, and decided not to outline the composer's significance only on the basis of the work of his late period. All that Asafyev did was to formulate for the first time the importance of Kastalsky's work for Russian music in an article of 1926. He did it in connection with Prokofiev's Third Piano Concerto:

> The texture of the Third Concerto rests on an intuitive premise that melody is the foundation of music's dynamic. [...] Has the time not come for music in western Europe to improve its health again from the sources of melody, as at the dawn of its history? In Russia there is only one composer who long ago sensed and was able to understand, through profound artistic insight, the meaning of the process taking place. From the heights of their greatness many Russian-European musicians were inclined to pass by the 'clumsy escapades' of this folksy dreamer (I mean Kastalsky). It has always struck me that people – particularly musicians – are afraid of everything that forces them to extend their horizons; they pronounce one system of musical thought perfect and deny the right of others to exist. For that reason they did not know or support the system sought by Kastalsky of Russian diatonic harmony (in essence not Russian at all, but belonging to all mankind from time immemorial), a harmony which flows from the construction and dynamics of *znamenny* chant and folksong. It is time to examine seriously what Kastalsky did. It will then turn out that the idea he assimilated will rise to the surface in the work of many musicians and researchers – in fact, of all those who seek a healthy way out of the dead-end of over-refined emotionalism and subjectivism'.[11]

After the composer's death Asafyev, who as everyone knew meant to write a book about him, received letters from his widow, his son and his friends.[12] In one such letter Zatayevich described Kastalsky's last journey:

> Sincerely respected and dear Boris Vladimirovich!
> I have just visited Natalia Kastalskaya, from whom I learned both your address (is it temporary?) and – something that's particularly important – of your intention to write a fitting monograph about the late Alexander Dmitriyevich! This news gave me so much joy that I'm picking up my pen to write you a few words! I know how highly you valued the late Kastalsky and therefore made a point of buying the 'Evening Red Gazette' (*Vechernaya Krasnaya gazeta*) hoping to find an article written by you. But, alas – maybe because I did not manage to find every issue – I could not find a single line about poor Alexander Dmitriyevich in the paper!
> And then all of a sudden came word of your intention to write a really solid piece of research about him and his work! How that delights me! I shall await

your booklet with the greatest impatience! [...] He was destroyed by an influenzal inflammation of the lungs, which could not fail to overwhelm his sickly nature worn out by a long-term heart ailment, although his temperature did not exceed 38 degrees. According to his widow Natalia, for the last four days his life was maintained artificially by camphor and oxygen. He died, thanks be to God, perfectly peacefully and without suffering. He lay in his coffin just as when he was alive, but he somehow struck me as bigger and more imposing.

His funeral service took place at the church of Boris and Gleb on Arbat Square. A huge crowd of people was there: musicians, church choirmasters, church singers and students. About eight priests conducted the funeral service, with superb protodeacons. The famous bass Tolkachov recited the Epistle, and Danilin surpassed even himself with his choir and performed a number of hymns by the deceased 'maker of hymns Alexander' with astounding power and freedom: the *znamenny* Cherubic Hymn (*Kheruvimskaya*), the 'It is meet' (*Dostoyno yest'*) to the chant by Tsar Feodor and much more. 'With the Saints give rest' (*So svyatïmi upokoy*) from the 'Requiem for Fallen Brothers' and 'Eternal memory' (*Vechnaya pamyat'*), also from the 'Requiem', which as you know ends with a powerful major chord, made a particularly strong impression.

He was buried in the new cemetery at the Novodevichy Convent. I saw Myaskovsky, Ippolitov-Ivanov, Igumnov, Vasilenko and others in the church. There, if you want them, are my immediate impressions of the funeral!

There was a good deal of talk among the mourners there about arranging large-scale concerts of Alexander Dmitriyevich's sacred compositions to help his family. Danilin declared that all the best church singers in Moscow would respond with enthusiasm to such an appeal, if permission were given for concerts of that kind! But he is convinced that permission will not be forthcoming![13]

As the musicologist Yekaterina Lebedeva wrote in her unpublished obituary article about Kastalsky, his friends and admirers decided even at the time of the funeral not just to arrange a concert of works by the composer but also to organize a Society of Friends of Alexander Kastalsky and a memorial museum. They supposed that the object of the Society would be to publish and perform Alexander Dmitriyevich's unpublished works.

The Moscow musical community remembered Kastalsky repeatedly during the first half of 1927. On 8 February 1927 the administration of the Moscow Conservatoire took a decision to rename the committee established to arrange the celebrations for the composer's 70th birthday, which he did not live to see, as a committee to perpetuate his memory. The members of the committee were Nikolay Danilin, Vladimir Stepanov, Nikolay Belkin, Nikolay Golovanov, Mikhail Ippolitov-Ivanov, Alexander Davidenko and Mikhail Shorin. On 28 March a memorial session was held at the State Institute for Musical Science where Kastalsky worked; on 10 May a concert of his compositions took place, before which several speeches were made. Secular compositions by the composer were performed at the concert; the performers were the soprano Antonina Nezhdanova, the folksong singer Olga Kovalyova and the choir of the Association for Contemporary Music conducted by Ivan Kalinin. On 21 May a session and concert in memory of Kastalsky took place at the Conservatoire too. No other initiatives of any kind were taken, however, to popularize the composer's ideas and works.

Nor was Asafyev's book about Kastalsky written, and in the 1930s the subject of Kastalsky, just like the subject of folksong inseparable from it, disappeared from the scholar's research altogether.

That in brief is the history of the relationship between these two most interesting people united by a profound sympathy and mutual understanding who discovered similar ideas and evaluations. Both artists, like their immediate predecessors and teachers the 'Mighty Handful', were distinguished by a patriotic attachment to everything Russian – nature, history, everyday life, Russian ethnic creativity; they saw their main objective as serving Russia and reviving her national traditions, irrespective of the colour of the flags fluttering in the wind above their heads. They were at the same time open to all that was new and talented in art, and in that respect there were no restrictions of idea or nationality – with the sole exception of an anti-German tendency which revealed itself most strongly during the wartime years.

Unlike Kastalsky, Asafyev was destined to survive the two wars. And if he was on the sidelines during the First World War, he was at the epicentre of events during the Second World War – in besieged Leningrad.[14] A sense of the calamity which had befallen his motherland stirred up in him an interest in the question of the distinctive value of Russian music, and in his declining years the scholar came to a fresh understanding of the significance of his country's musical heritage, admitting that when the journal 'Melos' had been created he had only begun intuitively to understand his path, 'still a long way from recognizing all the wealth of content in Russian melodic patterns (*intonatsii*) and the superlative musical culture brought to life out of them by the people'.[15] Like Kastalsky, Asafyev completed his path through life on a note of praise for the song-creativity of his native land, once again including in this concept not just musical folklore but also *znamenny* chant. In the wave of patriotic fervour of the 1940s, Russian music appeared in the sum total of all her historical forms in Asafyev's late works.

The subject of Kastalsky also returned to Asafyev's writings in those years: the scholar revived his idea of comprehending the methods of folk creativity with the aim of renewing composers' practice and russifying their musical language. What Asafyev wrote about the composer is not large in extent. To him, the most important thing was to describe Kastalsky's unusual musical language as an attempt to construct national traditions in his composition and to grasp the essence of his discoveries in the field of part-writing.

As regards Kastalsky – a composer whom it was customary in Soviet musicology to consider 'not of the front rank' – for Asafyev particular criteria operated, as a result of which Kastalsky's name occurs in the same company as those of Glinka, Musorgsky, Rimsky-Korsakov and Tchaikovsky in the scholar's writings. The composer's capacity to express a Russian spirit in music and to understand the laws of national musical speech served Asafyev as criteria of value in constructing this hierarchy. It is no coincidence that interest in Kastalsky and Kastalsky's popularity grow in periods when a mood of patriotism is intensified in Russian society – during the 1910s, the 1940s and the 1990s, when the name of Kastalsky, like those of the classic Russian composers, becomes a symbol of the 'Russian idea'.

In the first winter of the siege of Leningrad, Asafyev did not merely remember Kastalsky, but even attempted to express himself in the language of his favourite genre – sacred music. On 4 December 1941, on the Feast of the Entry into the Temple of the Most Holy Mother of God, a choral item 'Gladsome Light' (*Svete tikhiy*) composed by Asafyev appeared in his music notebook; this is one of the most poetic texts in the evening service, where the Saviour is linked to the calm light of evening.[16] The work contains many corrections by the composer and was clearly not finished, but this 'trying-out of his pen' displays a very interesting interpretation of the hymn, undoubtedly akin in style to Kastalsky. The way the musical fabric develops dramatically is genetically similar, where over the course of the whole work the initially thinned-out texture is gradually consolidated and saturated with *podgoloski* and *divisi*, and blossoms forth towards the end in a brilliant simultaneous flowering of the choral *tutti*. Also unquestionably in the line of succession to Kastalsky is the type of polyphonic statement, close to the folk drawn-out (*protyazhnaya*) song and designated in its time by Asafyev 'melodic-polyphonic', as well as the striving to saturate the fabric with turns of phrase using melodic patterns of national colouring. Unlike Kastalsky, however, Asafyev introduces some generalized contours of melodic patterns in which one can discern the turns of phrase of folksong, but not ancient church chants. The bolder manipulation of dissonant chords and tonal contrasts is undoubtedly new.

This first experiment apparently prompted the composer to express himself on a larger scale without any intention of publication or performance. Sacred music was an outpouring of his soul, a reminiscence of a departed world and a beloved composer who lived on inside him. 'To the unforgettable memory of Alexander Dmitriyevich Kastalsky. "Kants" (*Kanti*) for mixed chorus a cappella (Sketches)' – those are the words on the title-page of a music manuscript containing ten sacred choral works by Asafyev written between 5 December 1941 and 7 January 1942.[17] The completion of the manuscript on Christmas Day, and the presence among the pieces of four Christmas hymns prompts the thought that the composer was marking the great festival by choosing to complete his manuscript on that date.

In these 'Kants' the composer was not laying claim to any artistic quality, although several of the sketches are of indisputable interest. The composer's religious feeling can be sensed in these compositions, thanks to which these pieces could actually be used during worship. It is obvious, however, that we are dealing, not with a phenomenon from a living church tradition, but with a reminiscence in quite extraordinary conditions of something that used to exist, in the form in which it was preserved in Asafyev's compositional consciousness. And it should be pointed out that the ideas and forms remained securely in his memory, but not the language of the melodic patterns, and the essence of composing music for the church remained outside his range.

One should mention that the statements made here as a result of analysing the music do not reflect the meaning of the phenomenon to its fullest extent. And it is not just the fact that the 'Kants' are unique and represent one of only a few attempts at composing in this area from Stalin's time. Asafyev's choral pieces are not simply a creative act: they represent a phenomenon laying bare the subconsciousness of a man on the brink of death and in the grip of reveries and visions, and demand a different set of analytical tools.

Here are the circumstances in which the compositions were created, as related by the composer himself, who was with his family in the bomb-shelter of the Pushkin Theatre at the time:

A kind of creative existence had taken shape in the corridors of the theatre's bomb-shelter by the beginning of December. We had encounters, conversations and a lively exchange of both joys and sorrows. [...] I tried not to waste any time and worked untiringly. But December made itself felt, and it brought with it both cold and hunger and with them came a terrible darkness.

The Aleksandrinsky Theatre [the earlier name of the Pushkin Theatre] froze up. The light went out more and more often. The heating system ceased functioning. Without losing its prevailing tone of good spirits, the mood in the shelter changed depending on a whole range of complex influences from the outside. Problems made themselves felt constantly. Instances of people dying grew more frequent. Yet I wanted to work as I had never done before. I began recalling the whole course of my life. [...]

My general state and that of my family began to give way. Midday meals (if that's what they really were!) tapered off to less than a bare minimum. Oil-cakes were introduced into our food: they proved to be the most dangerous of foes. But there was still boiling water [for drinking]. Then it was decided that we should spend more time lying down, so as to conserve the warmth in our bodies and do without extra lighting. As I lay in the darkness I tried to compose music, applying my experience of making up theme-intonations into living forms of vocal music. January grew savage. But things became quieter as regards the bombardments. And calm set in generally. Toboggans and hand-carts stretched out one after another in doleful files with corpses shrouded like mummies. You just had to keep hold of your will-power – that was all.

Music is a strange thing: as I lay in semi-oblivion, I remember how I thought through my [book on] 'intonation', recalling lots of 'musics', but in order to restrain the surge of power within myself I started composing music of my own, sometimes fixing my impressions of announcements from the front I'd heard on the radio in short, aphoristic pieces, at other times listening attentively to a line of choral part-writing and enjoying the beauty of the logic in the scores' imagined sounds. Suddenly there were some short 'rebirths of light round about' – and my thought illuminated for me the ending of my book about intonations.[18] After writing it down, I could not come to my senses from my weakness. Again darkness, again cold – I don't remember for how long. My heart-beat began to fade, and suddenly music arose in my brain, and in the midst of a complete absence of distinction as to whether we were living during the day or at night, I remember, I began to compose a symphony 'the changing seasons' surrounding the everyday life of the Russian peasant. I can barely recall fragments of the sound-ideas in this symphony, and that doesn't actually matter. The important thing is that this desperate attempt at composing a work in a strict and well-proportioned form saved my moribund willpower in the midst of cruel suffering. Soon we moved from the darkness into the building of the Institute for Theatre and Music, on the square by St Isaac's Cathedral. We were taken out of the theatre on sledges and were literally saved by the now deceased director of the Institute, the unforgettable Aleksey Ivanovich Mashirov.[19]

In the winter of 1943 Asafyev was taken across Lake Ladoga to Moscow, a city dear to him as the place where the premières of several of his compositions had been given, where his pseudonym Igor Glebov had been born, and where he had met Kastalsky, following in whose footsteps he had composed, exerting his last ounce of strength, in a city under siege, a symphony 'the changing seasons in the life of the Russian peasant', consciously or otherwise repeating the concept of *Scenes of Peasant Merrymaking in Rus* left unfinished by his favourite composer. Work on this composition saved his dying willpower from extinction, as Asafyev thought. Who knows? Perhaps during that terrible winter the prayers resurrected in his memory were also heard.

Notes

1. B.V. Asaf'yev: *A.D. Kastal'sky*, in *A.D. Kastal'sky. Stat'i. Vospominaniya. Material ï* (A.D. Kastal'sky. Articles. Reminiscences. Materials). Moscow, 1960, p. 7.
2. Letter from A.D. Kastal'sky to Kh.N. Grozdov of 3 February 1916. GTsMMK, fond 370, no. 545, p. 17v.
3. Igor' Glebov (B.V. Asaf'yev): *Samoye sovremennoye sochineniye. Po povodu Requiem'a A.D. Kastal'skogo* (A most contemporary composition. The Requiem of A.D. Kastal'sky), in *Muzïka* (Music), 1916, no. 248.
4. Letter from A.D. Kastal'sky to Kh.N. Grozdov of 4 February 1917. GTsMMK, fond 370, no. 554, pp. 3v-4.
5. Letter from B.V. Asaf'yev to P.P. Suvchinsky of 9 June 1918. Bibliothèque Nationale de France, Paris. Res. Vm. Dos. 91-94. (Information provided by L.Z. Korabel'nikova.)
6. Postcard from A.D. Kastal'sky to B.V. Asaf'yev of 19 February 1917. RGALI, fond 2658, opis' 1, no. 581, p. 31.
7. A.D. Kastal'sky: *Iz vospominaniy o poslednikh godakh* (From reminiscences of recent years), in *SovM*, 1977, no. 6.
8. Postcard from A.D. Kastal'sky to B.V. Asaf'yev of 16 April 1917. RGALI, fond 2658, opis' 1, no. 581, p. 5.
9. Letter from A.D. Kastal'sky to B.V. Asaf'yev of 18 January 1918, in *RUSAM*, vol. 1, p. 298.
10. Letter from B.V. Asaf'yev to P.P. Suvchinsky of 13 June 1918. Bibliothèque Nationale de France, Paris. Res. Vm. Dos. 91-94. (Information provided by L.Z. Korabel'nikova.)
11. Igor' Glebov (B.V. Asaf'yev): *Tretiy fortep'yanniy kontsert S. Prokof'yeva* (S. Prokof'yev's Third Piano Concerto). *Sovremennaya muzïka* (Contemporary Music), 1925, no. 10.
12. It should be noted that in the 1920s Asafyev, as head of the Music History section of the Russian Institute for the History of the Arts and a professor at the Leningrad Conservatoire, was very active in proclaiming the need to study the heritage of church music, gave lectures on the subject and lent his support to research projects in the field of ancient Russian music. For that reason, Asafyev was regarded as a champion of the interests of the heritage of church music, and viewed with hope not only by Kastal'sky's relatives but also by other people, whose letters come to light in Russian archives.
13. Letter of A.V. Zatayevich to B.V. Asaf'yev of 4 January 1927, in *RUSAM*, vol. 1, pp. 315-316.
14. The blockade of Leningrad by German armies, which began in September 1941 and lasted 880 days, was the most bloody siege in the history of mankind. In the course of it at least 642,000 people perished.

15. Igor' Glebov (B.V. Asaf'yev): *Mezhdunarodnoye znacheniye russkoy muzïki* (The international significance of Russian music). RGALI, fond 2658, opis' 1, no. 374, p. 85.

16. B.V. Asaf'yev: *Notnaya zapisnaya knizhka* (Music notebook). RGALI, fond 2659, opis' 1, no. 208, pp. 32v-33.

17. B.V. Asaf'yev: *Dukhovnïye pesnopeniya dlya smeshannogo khora* (Sacred hymns for mixed choir). RGALI, fond 2658, opis' 1, no. 171.

18. The second part of Asaf'yev's well-known book *Muzïkal'naya forma kak protsess* (Musical form as a process), *Intonatsiya* (Intonation), published in Moscow in 1947, was written in Leningrad under siege.

19. B.V. Asaf'yev: *Moya tvorcheskaya rabota v pervïye godï Velikoy Otechestvennoy voynï* (My creative work during the first years of the Great Patriotic War), in *SovM*, 1946, no. 10, pp. 91-92.

List of Kastalsky's Published Compositions and Arrangements

This list provides information about the first publication of works. In the case of sacred choral works, the number assigned to a work in the catalogue of Kastalsky's compositions published by the firm of Jurgenson is given in addition to the number in the present list. 'C. d.' stands for 'Censorship date' – that is, the date on which the censor approved an item for publication; in the absence of other data about the time of composition, this date assumes a certain importance. 'Composer' indicates 'published by the composer'. Unless stated otherwise, the place of publication is Moscow.

Sacred Choral Works

Hymns of the All-Night Vigil

1. *Blagoslovi, dushe moya, Gospoda* ('Bless the Lord, O my soul'), *znamenniy* chant for small choir (melody from Potulov's Handbook, abridged). (No. 24a). C. d. 21 December 1900. Composer.
2. *Blagoslovi, dushe moya, Gospoda* ('Bless the Lord, O my soul'), *znamenniy* chant for large choir. (No. 24b). C. d. 21 December 1900. Composer.
3. *Blagoslovi, dushe moya, Gospoda* ('Bless the Lord, O my soul'), variant of a Greek chant used in the Moscow diocese, for small choir. (No. 25a). C. d. 21 December 1900. Composer.
4. *Blagoslovi, dushe moya, Gospoda* ('Bless the Lord, O my soul'), variant of a Greek chant used in the Moscow diocese, fuller arrangement for large choir. (No. 25b). C. d. 21 December 1900. Composer.
5. *Blazhen muzh* ('Blessed is the man'), little *znamenniy* chant, first version. (No. 26a). C. d. 21 December 1900. Composer.
6. *Blazhen muzh* ('Blessed is the man'), little *znamenniy* chant, second version. (No. 26a). C. d. 21 December 1900. Composer.
7. *Blazhen muzh* ('Blessed is the man'), melody from the Cathedral of the Dormition, Moscow. (No. 26b). C. d. 21 December 1900. Composer.
8. *Gospodi vozzvakh* ('Lord, I have cried') and *Da ispravitsya molitva moya* ('Let my prayer arise'), *znamenniy* chant. (No. 27). C. d. 10 December 1901. Composer.

9. *Gospodi vozzvakh* ('Lord, I have cried') and *Da ispravitsya molitva moya* ('Let my prayer arise'), usual Kievan melody. (No. 27). C. d. 10 December 1901. Composer.

10. *Gospodi vozzvakh* ('Lord, I have cried') and *Da ispravitsya molitva moya* ('Let my prayer arise'), simplified arrangement of the Kievan melody. (No. 27). C. d. 10 December 1901. Composer.

11. *Dogmatiki bogorodichnï vos'mi glasov* (Dogmatika of the Mother of God in eight tones), *znamennïy* chants. (No. 28). C. d. 10 December 1901. Composer.

12. *Svete tikhiy* ('Gladsome Light') no. 1, for small choir. (No. 45). Written late 1903 or early 1904. C. d. 21 September 1904. Published February 1905. Composer.

13. *Svete tikhiy* ('Gladsome Light') no. 2, for small choir, with indications for performance by same-voice choir. (No. 46a). Written late 1903 or early 1904. C. d. 21 September 1904. Published February 1905. Composer.

14. *Svete tikhiy* ('Gladsome Light') no. 2, for large choir. (No. 46b). Written late 1903 or early 1904. C. d. 21 September 1904. Published February 1905. Composer.

15. *Svete tikhiy* ('Gladsome Light') no. 3. (No. 47). Written late 1903 or early 1904. C. d. 21 September 1904. Published February 1905. Composer.

16. *Svete tikhiy* ('Gladsome Light') no. 4. (No. 73). Published 1908. Composer.

17. *Svete tikhiy* ('Gladsome Light') no. 4, for solo tenor and choir. (No. 73a). Published 1914. Composer.

18. *Nïne otpushchayeshi* ('Lord, now lettest Thou') no. 1, *demestvo*, for solo baritone and large choir. (No. 48a). Composed early 1904. Published February 1905. Composer.

19. *Nïne otpushchayeshi* ('Lord, now lettest Thou') no. 1, *demestvo*, for small choir. (No. 48b). Composed early 1904. C. d. 21 September 1904. Published February 1905. Composer.

20. *Nïne otpushchayeshi* ('Lord, now lettest Thou') no. 1, *demestvo*, for same-voice choir (women or men). (No. 48v). Composed early 1904. C. d. 21 September 1904. Published February 1905. Composer.

21. *Nïne otpushchayeshi* ('Lord, now lettest Thou') no. 2, melody from an old manuscript, for solo tenor and choir. (No. 49). Composed early 1904. C. d. 21 September 1904. Published February 1905. Composer.

22. *Nïne otpushchayeshi* ('Lord, now lettest Thou') no. 3, Kievan chant, for large choir. (No. 50a). Composed early 1904. C. d. 21 September 1904. Published February 1905. Composer.

23. *Nïne otpushchayeshi* ('Lord, now lettest Thou') no. 3, Kievan chant, for small choir. (No. 50b). Composed early 1904. C. d. 21 September 1904. Published February 1905. Composer.

24. *Stikhi pered Shestopsalmiyem* (Verses before the Six Psalms) no. 1, with indications for performance by same-voice choir. (No. 51). Composed early 1904. C. d. 21 September 1904. Published February 1905. Composer.

25. *Stikhi pered Shestopsalmiyem* (Verses before the Six Psalms) no. 2. (No. 52). Composed early 1904. C. d. 21 September 1904. Published February 1905. Composer.
26. *Khvalite Imya Gospodne* ('Praise the Name of the Lord') no. 1, from Kievan chant. (No. 53a). Composed early 1904. C. d. 21 September 1904. Published February 1905. Composer.
27. *Khvalite Imya Gospodne* ('Praise the Name of the Lord') no. 1, from Kievan chant, for small or same-voice choir. (No. 53b). Composed early 1904. C. d. 21 September 1904. Published February 1905. Composer.
28. *Khvalite Imya Gospodne* ('Praise the Name of the Lord') no. 2, *znamennïy* chant, for small or same-voice choir. (No. 54a). Composed early 1904. C. d. 21 September 1904. Published February 1905. Composer.
29. *Khvalite Imya Gospodne* ('Praise the Name of the Lord') no. 2, *znamennïy* chant, arrangement for small choir. (No. 54b). Composed early 1904. C. d. 21 September 1904. Published February 1905. Composer.
30. *Khvalite Imya Gospodne* ('Praise the Name of the Lord') no. 3, Serbian chant, for small choir. (No. 55a). Composed early 1904. C. d. 21 September 1904. Published February 1905. Composer.
31. *Khvalite Imya Gospodne* ('Praise the Name of the Lord') no. 3, Serbian chant, for female choir. (No. 55b). Composed early 1904. C. d. 21 September 1904. Published February 1905. Composer.
32. *Ot yunosti moyeya* ('From my youth'). (No. 58). C. d. 6 July 1905. Composer.
33. *Velikoye slavosloviye* (Great Doxology) no. 1, for small choir. (No. 56). Composed early 1904. C. d. 21 September 1904. Published February 1905. Composer.
34. *Velikoye slavosloviye* (Great Doxology) no. 2, for large choir. (No. 57). Composed early 1904. C. d. 6 July 1905. Published February 1905. Composer.

Hymns of the Liturgy

35. *Yektenii* (Litanies), *znamennïy* chant. (No. 5). Written 1898. C. d. 17 April 1898. Composer.
36. *Yektenii*. (Litanies). New edition. (No. 65). Written 1905. Composer.
37. *Yektenii. Yedinorodnïy Sïne* (Litanies. 'Only begotten Son') no. 1, Serbian. (No. 66). Composer.
38. *Yektenii. Yedinorodnïy Sïne* (Litanies. 'Only begotten Son') no. 2, Bulgarian melody. (No. 67). Composer.
39. *Slava, Yedinorodnïy Sïne* ('Glory, only begotten Son') no. 3, *demestvo*. (No. 68). Composer.
40. *Vo Tsarstvii Tvoyem* ('In Thy Kingdom'). Written 1926. *Journal of the Moscow Patriarchate* (English-language edition), 1972, no. 1.
41. *Svyatïy Bozhe. Krestu Tvoyemu. Yelitsï vo Khrista krestistesya* ('Holy God'. 'Before Thy cross'. 'As many as have been baptized in Christ'), *znamennïy* chant. (No. 18). C. d. 15 October 1898. Composer.

42. *Kheruvimskaya pesn'* ('Cherubic Hymn'), *znamennïy* chant. (No. 3). C. d. 5 July 1897. Composer.
43. *Staro-Simonovskaya Kheruvimskaya pesn'* (Old Simonov 'Cherubic Hymn'). (No. 12). C. d. 15 October 1898. Composer.
44. *Staro-Simonovskaya Kheruvimskaya pesn'* (Old Simonov 'Cherubic Hymn'), for male-voice choir with or without alto. (No. 12). C. d. 15 October 1898. Composer.
45. *Staro-Simonovskaya Kheruvimskaya pesn'* (Old Simonov 'Cherubic Hymn'), for female-voice choir (monastic or ordinary). (No. 12). C. d. 15 October 1898. Composer.
46. *Sofroniyevskaya Kheruvimskaya pesn'* ('Sofrony Cherubic Hymn'), melody from the Glinskaya hermitage. (No. 13). C. d. 15 October 1898. Composer.
47. *Sofroniyevskaya Kheruvimskaya pesn'* ('Sofrony Cherubic Hymn'), for male-voice choir. (No. 13). C. d. 15 October 1898. Composer.
48. *Sofroniyevskaya Kheruvimskaya pesn'* ('Sofrony Cherubic Hymn'), for female-voice choir. (No. 13). C. d. 15 October 1898. Composer.
49. *Kheruvimskaya pesn' 'na razoreniye Moskvï'* ('Cherubic Hymn "on the ravaging of Moscow"'), melody by an unknown composer. (No. 15). C. d. 15 October 1898. Composer.
50. *Kheruvimskaya pesn' napeva moskovskogo Uspenskogo sobora* ('Cherubic Hymn on a melody from the Cathedral of the Dormition in Moscow'). (No. 19). C. d. 15 October 1898. Composer.
51. *Kheruvimskaya pesn'* ('Cherubic Hymn'), Serbian melody. (No. 30). C. d. 18 November 1902. Composer.
52. *Kheruvimskaya pesn'. 'Vladimirskaya'* ('Vladimir Cherubic Hymn'). (No. 39). Sold to the publisher P. Jurgenson 3 July 1902. C. d. 17 April 1903. Jurgenson.
53. *Veruyu* ('I believe', the Creed), no. 1. (No. 69). Composer.
54. *Veruyu* ('I believe', the Creed), no. 2. (No. 70). Composer.
55. *Veruyu* ('I believe', the Creed), no. 3. (No. 71). Composed c. 1909. Composer.
56. *Milost' mira* ('Mercy of peace'), Serbian melody. (No. 1). C. d. 17 March 1897. Composer.
57. *Milost' mira* ('Mercy of peace'), no. 1, *znamennïy* chant. (No. 6). C. d. 17 April 1898. Composer.
58. *Milost' mira* ('Mercy of peace'), no. 2, *znamennïy* chant. (No. 10). C. d. 17 April 1898. Composer.
59. *Milost' mira* ('Mercy of peace'), Ipat'yev melody. (No. 14). C. d. 15 October 1898. Composer.
60. *Milost' mira* ('Mercy of peace'), Ipat'yev chant, for male or female choir. (No. 14). C. d. 15 October 1898. Composer.
61. *Milost' mira* ('Mercy of peace'), known in Moscow as the 'Nevskaya'. (No. 16). C. d. 15 October 1906. Composer.
62. *Milost' mira* ('Mercy of peace'), Kievan chant. (No. 40). Sold to the publisher P. Jurgenson 3 July 1902. Jurgenson.
63. *Tebe poyem* ('We hymn Thee'), Georgian. (No. 78). Jurgenson, 1915.

64. *Dostoyno yest'* ('It is meet'), Serbian melody. (No. 2). C. d. 17 March 1897. Composer.

65. *Dostoyno yest'* ('It is meet'), Kievan. (No. 17). C. d. 15 October 1898. Composer.

66. *Dostoyno yest'* ('It is meet'), Mount Athos (the melody is a variant of the *Dostoyno* for *Ob'yatiya otcha*). (No. 17a). C. d. 15 October 1898. Composer.

67. *Dostoyno yest'* ('It is meet'), chant by Tsar Feodor. (No. 23). C. d. 21 December 1900. Composer.

68. *Otche nash* ('Our Father'), melody from an old manuscript. (No. 33). C. d. 18 November 1902. Composer.

69. *V pamyat' vechnuyu* ('Memory eternal'), melody from the *Obikhod*. (No. 29). Composed 1902. Composer.

70. *Blazheni yazhe izbral* ('Blessed are they whom Thou hast chosen'), in memory of Yekaterina Dmitriyevna Kastal'skaya. (No. 22). C. d. 21 December 1900. Composer.

71. *Miloserdiya dveri otverzi nam* ('Open to us the doors of compassion'), an experiment in setting *Obikhod* melodies. (No. 4). C. d. 5 July 1897. Composer.

72. *Ne imamï inïya pomoshchi* ('We have no other help'). (No. 21). C. d. 21 December 1900. Composer.

73. *Liturgiya Sv. Ioanna Zlatousta* (Liturgy of St John Chrysostom), selected hymns from the Liturgy for women's chorus: *Yekteniya velikaya* (Great Litany), *Yedinorodnïy Sïne* ('Only begotten Son'), *Vo tsarstvii Tvoyem* ('In Thy kingdom'), *Svyatïy Bozhe* ('Holy God'), *Yekteniya sugubaya* (Augmented Litany), *Kheruvimskaya pesn'* (Cherubic Hymn), *Yekteniya prositel'naya* (Litany of Supplication), *Milost' mira* ('Mercy of peace'), *Dostoyno yest'* ('It is meet'), *Otche nash* ('Our Father'), *Miloserdiya dveri* ('Open to us the doors of compassion'). Sold to the publisher P. Jurgenson 17 May 1905. C. d. 6 July 1905. Jurgenson.

Hymns for the Marriage Service

74. *Venchaniye* (Marriage): *Vstrechnoye pesnopeniye zhenikhu* (Entrance hymn for the bridegroom), *Pesnopeniye pri vkhode nevestï* (Entrance hymn for the bride), *Amin'* (Amen) *Sugubaya yekteniya* (Augmented Litany), *Slava Tebe, Bozhe nash* ('Glory to Thee our God'), *znamennïy prokimen* (Prokimenon in znamennïy chant), *Isayye likuy* ('Rejoice, O Isaiah'), *Po okonchanii venchaniya* (At the conclusion of the service). (No. 32). C. d. 18 November 1902. Composer.

Hymns for the Panikhida (Memorial Service)

75. *So svyatïmi upokoy* ('With the Saints give rest'). (No. 20). C. d. 15 October 1898. Composer.

76. *Sam Yedin yesi bezsmertnïy* ('Thou alone art immortal'). (No. 20). C. d. 15 October 1898. Composer.

77. *Vechnaya pamyat' geroyam* ('Eternal Memory to the Heroes'), selected
    hymns from the Memorial Service (*Panikhida*): *Yekteniya* (Litany), *Alliluiya*
    and *Glubinoyu mudrosti*, ('Alliluiya' and 'O Thou who with wisdom
    profound'), *Pokoy, Spase nash* ('Give rest with the Just, O our Saviour'),
    Pokoy, Gospodi ('Give rest, O Lord'), *Molitvu proliyu* ('I will pour out my
    petition'), *So svyatïmi upokoy* ('With the Saints give rest'), *Sam Yedin yesi
    bezsmertnïy* ('Thou alone art immortal'), *Tï yesi Bog* ('Thou art the God'),
    Upokoy, Bozhe ('Give rest, O Lord'), *Troynaya yekteniya* (Triple Litany),
    Vechnaya pamyat ('Eternal memory'). Written in late 1916. Jurgenson, 1917.

Hymns for the Great Feasts

78. *Stikhirï na podoben na Vozdvizheniye Chestnago Kresta* (Stichera *podoben*
    for the Exaltation of the Holy Cross). ('*O preslavnago chudese, zhivonosnïy
    sad*' ('O most glorious wonder, the lifegiving garden'), '*O preslavnago
    chudese, yako grozd' ispolnen zhivota*' ('O most glorious wonder, like a
    cluster of grapes full of life'), '*O preslavnago chudese, shirota Kresta*' ('O
    most glorious wonder, the breadth and length of the Cross')). (No. 61). Sold
    to the publisher P. Jurgenson 12 April 1906. Jurgenson.
79. *Irmosï na Vozdvizheniye Chestnago Kresta* (Heirmoi for the Exaltation of the
    Holy Cross), with a refrain [*pripev*] to the ninth song, ordinary chant. (No.
    34). Sold to the publisher P. Jurgenson 3 July 1902. C. d. 17 April 1903.
    Jurgenson.
80. *Tropar' Rozhdestvu Khristovu* (Troparion for the Nativity of Christ),
    znamennïy chant, fourth tone (*Rozhdestvo Tvoye Khriste Bozhe nash* ('Thy
    Nativity, O Christ our God')). (No. 7a). C. d. 17 April 1898. Composer.
81. *Deva dnes'* ('Today the Virgin'), third tone, *znamennïy* chant *podoben*. (No.
    7b). C. d. 18 November 1902. Composer.
82. *Deva dnes'* ('Today the Virgin'), *znamennïy* chant, for large choir. (No. 7b).
    C. d. 18 November 1902. Composer.
83. *Deva dnes'* ('Today the Virgin'), *znamennïy* chant, for small choir
    (simplified arrangement of Jurgenson No. 7b). (No. 80). C. d. 24 November
    1916. Jurgenson.
84. *Deva dnes'* ('Today the Virgin'), *znamennïy* chant, for small mixed choir
    (revision of preceding item). Written 1921. *Journal of the Moscow
    Patriarchate* (English-language edition), 1972, no. 1.
85. *Avgustu yedinonachal'stvuyushchu na zemli* ('When Augustus reigned alone
    upon the earth'), sticheron for the Vespers of Christ's Nativity, melody from
    the *Glinskaya* hermitage. (No. 36). Sold to the publisher P. Jurgenson 3 July
    1902. C. d. 17 April 1903. Jurgenson.
86. *S nami Bog* ('God is with us'), *znamennïy*. (No. 9a). C. d. 18 April 1898.
    Composer.
87. *Mnogoletiye na navecheriyakh Rozhdestva Khristova i Bogoyavleniya* (Many
    years for Vespers of the Nativity and the Theophany), ancient
    mnogoletstvovaniye ('many years') melody. (No. 9b). C. d. 18 April 1898.
    Composer.

88. *Pervïy kanon na Rozhdestvo Khristovo* (First canon for Christ's Nativity), *znamennïy* chant, first tone. (No. 43). Sold to the publisher P. Jurgenson 3 July 1902. C. d. 17 April 1903. Jurgenson.

89. *Vtoroy kanon na Rozhdestvo Khristovo* (Second canon for Christ's Nativity), *znamennïy* chant. (No. 44). Sold to the publisher P. Jurgenson 3 July 1902. C. d. 17 April 1903. Jurgenson.

90. *Tropar' na Bogoyavleniye Gospodne* (Troparion for the Lord's Theophany), *znamennïy* chant, first tone ('*Vo Iordane kreshchayushchusya Tebe, Gospodi*' ('When Thou wast baptized in the Jordan, O Christ Lord')). (No. 8a). C. d. 17 April 1898. Composer.

91. *Kondak na Bogoyavleniye Gospodne* (Kontakion for the Lord's Theophany), *znamennïy* chant, fourth tone ('*Yavilsya yesi dnes' vselenney*' ('Thou hast appeared today to the inhabited earth')). (No. 8b). C. d. 17 April 1898. Composer.

92. *Zadostoynik v nedelyu Vaiy* (Zadostoynik for the week of Palm Sunday), *znamennïy* chant ('*Velichay, dushe moya*' ('Magnify, O my soul')). (No. 37). Sold to the publisher P. Jurgenson 2 July 1902. Composer.

93. *Khristos voskrese* ('Christ is risen'), for same-voice choir, dedicated to the boy choristers of the Court Kapella. (No. 77). Composed 1911. Jurgenson, 1915.

94. *Zadostoynik Sv. Paskhi* (Zadostoynik for the Holy Resurrection), melody of *znamennïy* chant ('*Angel vopiyashe*' ('The Angel cried')). (No. 31). C. d. 18 November 1902. Composer.

95. *Stikhirï na Vozneseniye Gospodne. Na Khvalitekh glas 1-y podoben 'Nebesnïkh chinov'*. (Stichera for Ascension. Lauds, first tone *podoben* 'Joy of the ranks of heaven') (*Angel'ski izhe v mire torzhestvuim* ('Let us that are in the world now keep the feast angelically'), *Nachal'nitsï angelov, smotryayushche* ('The leaders of the angels were bewildered'), *Galileyane, zryashche Tya voznesenna* ('The Galileans beheld Thine ascension')). (No. 63). Sold to the publisher P. Jurgenson 2 May 1907. Jurgenson.

96. *Tropar' i velichaniye v den' Sv. Troitsï* (Troparion and 'We magnify' for the day of the Holy Trinity), *znamennïy* chant, eighth tone (*Blagosloven yesi, Khriste Bozhe nash* ('Blessed art Thou, O Christ our God')). (No. 35). Sold to the publisher P. Jurgenson 3 July 1902. Jurgenson.

97. *Tsaryu nebesnïy* ('O Heavenly King'), sticheron for the day of the Holy Trinity. (No. 75). Jurgenson, 1914.

98. *Zadostoynik v den' Sv. Troitsï* (*Zadostoynik* for the day of the Holy Trinity), ('*Raduysya, Tsaritse*' ('Rejoice, O Queen')). (No. 76). Jurgenson, 1914.

99. *Stikhirï na podoben na Preobrazheniye Gospodne. 'Na khvalitekh'*, fourth tone, *podoben 'Zvannïy svïshe'* (Stichera *podoben* for the Transfiguration of Our Lord. Lauds, fourth tone, *podoben* 'Called from on high') (*Prezhde chestnago Kresta Tvoyego* ('Before Thy precious Cross'), *Izhe prezhde vek sïy Bog Slovo* ('O, Thou who from all eternity art God the Word'), *Ot devicheskago oblaka Tya rozhdenna* ('Born from a Virgin')). (No. 60). Sold to the publisher P. Jurgenson 12 April 1906. Jurgenson.

100. *Iz sluzhbï na Uspeniye Presvyatïye Bogoroditsï* (From the service for the Dormition of the Most Blessed Mother of God): (*Bog Gospod'* ('The Lord is God'), troparion *V Rozhdestve devstvo sokhranila yesi* ('In giving birth Thou hast preserved thy virginity') in versions for same-voice and mixed choirs, *velichaniye* ('We magnify'), refrains for the ninth verse of the canon). (No. 42). Sold to the publisher P. Jurgenson 3 June 1902. Jurgenson.

101. *Bogonachal'nïm manoveniyem* ('By the Divine command of God'). Sticheron for the Dormition of the Most Blessed Mother of God, *znamennïy* chant, first tone. (No. 41). Sold to the publisher P. Jurgenson 3 June 1902. C. d. 17 April 1903. Jurgenson.

Hymns for the Feasts of Great Saints

102. *Tropar' svyatitelyam moskovskim Petru, Aleksiyu, Ione, Filippu.* (Troparion for the Moscow hierarchs Pyotr, Aleksy, Iona and Filipp). Published as a supplement to the journal *Khorovoye i regentskoye delo* ('Choral and Church Choirmaster Matters'), 1909, no. 1.

103. *Tropar' i velichaniye Sv. Nikolayu (6 dekabrya)* (Troparion and 'We magnify' for St Nicholas (6 December)), fourth tone *znamennïy* chant (*Pravilo verï i obraz krotosti* ('Rule of faith and icon of meekness')). (No. 38). Sold to the publisher P. Jurgenson 3 June 1902. C. d. 17 April 1903. Jurgenson.

104. *Tropar' svyashchennomucheniku Yermogenu* (Troparion for the hieromartyr Hermogen), *znamennïy* chant. (No. 79). Written c. 1914. Jurgenson, 1915.

105. *Stikhirï svv. Kirillu i Mefodiyu. Maya 11-go 'na khvalitekh', glas 4-y podoben 'Yako doblya'* (Stichera to Sts. Cyrill and Methodius. 11 May, Lauds, fourth tone *podoben* 'As valiant as the martyrs'), (*Kirille i Mefodiye bogomudrii* ('The divinely wise Cyrill and Methodius'), *Vinograda Khristova delateliye* ('Labourers in Christ's vineyard'), *Svyatïya Troitsï pobornitsï* ('Defenders of the Holy Trinity')). (No. 62). Sold to the publisher P. Jurgenson 2 May 1907. Jurgenson.

106. *Stikhirï svv. apostolam Petru i Pavlu* (Stichera for the Apostles Peter and Paul), (*Kiimi pokhval'nïmi ventsï* ('What laudatory wreaths'), *Kiimi pesennïmi dobrotami* ('What beautiful hymns'), *Kiimi dukhovnïmi pesn'mi* ('What spiritual songs')). (No. 64). Sold to the publisher P. Jurgenson 2 May 1907. Jurgenson, c. 1909.

Hymns for Holy Week

107. *Chertog Tvoy* ('Thy bridal chamber'), for tenor solo with choir. (No. 72). Written in the early 1910s. Composer.
108. *Razboynika blagorazumnago* ('The good thief'). (No. 74). Written 12 April 1913. Jurgenson, 1914.
109. *Bog Gospod' i tropari v Velikuyu Subbotu na utreni* ('The Lord is God' and troparia for Great Saturday at Matins), Bulgarian and *znamennïy* chants. (No. 11). Written in 1897. C. d. 17 April 1898. Composer.

Musical Restorations

110. *Iz minuvshikh vekov. Opït muzykal'nïkh restavratsiy* (From past ages. An experiment in musical restorations). Book I No. 1 *Kitay* (China). No. 2 *Indiya* (India). No. 3 *Yegipet* (Egypt). For piano (or voice and piano), Jurgenson, [1904]. Book II No. 4 *Iudeya* (Judea). No. 5 *Ellada* (Greece). No. 6 *Na rodine Islama* (In the homeland of Islam). For piano (or voice and piano). Jurgenson, [1906]. Book III *Khristiane* (The Christians). For piano (or voice and piano). [1910]. Book IV Rus'. *Torzhishche v starinu na Rusi* (Rus'. A bazaar in ancient times in Rus'). For vocal performance on stage or piano. Jurgenson, [1914].
111. *Peshchnoye deystvo. (Starinnïy tserkovnïy obryad)* (The Play of the Furnace. (Ancient church ritual)), for choir and bass solo. Composed using melodies preserved in manuscripts. Jurgenson, [1909].
112. *Iz zapisey A.D. Kastal'skogo* (From A.D. Kastal'sky's transcriptions): a) *Vïkrik nishchego sleptsa* (The cry of a blind beggar); b) *Peniye sleptsov* (Blind people's song); c) *Otrïvok iz ulichnoy simfonii, tvorimoy po vremenam na uglu Bol'shoy i Sredney Kislovki, v Moskve, k vesne 1910 g.* (Excerpt from the Street Symphony, created at various times on the corner of Great and Middle Kislovka [Streets] in Moscow, in spring 1910). *Trudï Muzïkal'no-etnograficheskoy komissii* (Proceedings of the Music Ethnography Commission), vol. 2, 1911.
113. *Obraztsï tserknogo peniya na Rusi v XV-XVII vekakh. Materialï dlya istoricheskikh dukhovnïkh kontsertov* (Examples of church music in Rus' from the fifteenth to the seventeenth centuries. Materials for historical sacred concerts). Jurgenson, 1915.
114. *Iz tsikla 'Narodnïye prazdnovaniya na Rusi'* (From the cycle 'Peasant merrymaking in Rus''), [*Yur'yev den' (pastushiy naigrïsh)* (St George's day (shepherd's tune), *Stikh o Yegorii khrabrom (tekst dukhovnogo stikha)* (Verse about Yegory the bold (text of a spiritual verse))]. In *V pomoshch' zhertvam voynï. Sbornik obshchestva Muzïkal'no-teoreticheskaya biblioteka v Moskve* (In aid of war victims. A collection published by the Music Theory Library Society in Moscow). Jurgenson, 1916.
115. *Kartinï narodnïkh prazdnovaniy na Rusi* (Scenes from peasant merrymaking in Rus') (Excerpt). For mixed choir with piano. Muzsektor Gosizdata, 1927.

116. *Kartinï narodnïkh prazdnovaniy na Rusi* (Scenes from peasant merrymaking in Rus') (Excerpts edited by A.A. Kastalsky). For mixed choir and piano. In *A.D. Kastal'sky. Stat'i. Vospominaniya. Materialï* (A.D. Kastalsky. Articles. Reminiscences. Materials). Moscow, 1960, pp. 174-266.

Cantatas

117. *V pamyat' 1812 goda* (In memory of the year 1812). Cantata. Words by P. Zuyev. St Petersburg, Geynts, 1911.
118. *V pamyat' 1812 goda* (In memory of the year 1812). Cantata. For 3-part same-voice choir. Words by P. Zuyev. St Petersburg, Geynts, 1911.
119. *Stikh o tserkovnom russkom penii* (Verse about Russian church music). Cantata. For mixed choir with orchestra (or piano). Piano score. Text by A. and N. Kastal'sky. Moscow, Jurgenson, 1912.
120. *Trista let* (Three hundred years). *Kantata-gimn* (Cantata-anthem) for mixed choir. Words by S. Shambinago. St Petersburg, Geynts, 1912.
121. *Trista let* (Three hundred years). *Kantata-gimn* (Cantata-anthem). For 3-part same-voice choir. Words by S. Shambinago. St Petersburg, Geynts, 1912.
122. *Chteniye d'yakom lyudu moskovskomu poslaniya patriarkha Yermogena k tushinskim izmennikam v 1609 godu* (The reading by a clerk to the people of Moscow of the epistle from Patriarch Hermogen to the Tushino traitors in 1609). For bass solo and mixed choir. Moscow, Jurgenson, [1913].
123. *Bratskoye pominoveniye* (Requiem for Fallen Brothers). For soprano and bass soloists, choir and orchestra. Arrangement for voices and piano. 1. Requiem aeternam. 2. Kyrie eleison. 3. Rex tremendae. 4. Ingemisco. 5. Confutatis. 6. Lacrimosa. 7. Domine Jesu. 8. Hostias. Interludium. 9. Sanctus. 10. Agnus Dei. 11. Kyrie eleison. Interludium. 12. Requiem aeternam. Jurgenson, 1916.
124. *Bratskoye pominoveniye* (Requiem for Fallen Brothers). For soprano and bass soloists, choir and orchestra. Arrangement for voices and piano. 1. Requiem aeternam. 2. Kyrie eleison. 3. Rex tremendae. 4. Ingemisco. 5. Confutatis. 6. Lacrimosa. 7. Domine Jesu. 8. Beati mortui. 9. Hostias. Interludium. 10. Sanctus. 11. Agnus Dei. 12. Dies irae. 13. Rock of ages. 14. Kyrie eleison. Interludium. 15. Requiem aeternam. Jurgenson, [1918].
125. *1905 god* (The year 1905). Words by A. Bezïmensky [For mixed choir with piano accompaniment]. MONO Muztorg, 1925.

Opera

126. *Klara Milich*. Opera in four acts after the novella of the same title by Ivan Turgenev. Vocal score. [1908]. Composer.

Accompanied Choral Works and Choral Cycles

127. *Internatsional* (The *Internationale*). Arrangement for choir and orchestra. Moscow, Gos. muz. izd-vo., 1919. Full score. Also: vocal score. Muzsektor Gosizdata, [n. d.].

128. *Proletariatu na 1 Maya 1920* (To the proletariat on 1 May 1920). Words by I. Filipchenko. For mixed choir and trumpets. Published by the Music Section of Moscow Proletkul't, 1920. Cf. also the collection: *Pesni revolyutsii* (Songs of revolution), first issue. Published by Proletkul't, 1923.

129. *K zarubezhnïm brat'yam* (To foreign brethren). For basses accompanied by choir (or bass solo accompanied by harmonium). Gos. muz. izd-vo., 1921.

130. *Gimn truda* (Hymn of labour). Words by I. Filipchenko. For choir accompanied by brass and percussion instruments. Muzsektor Gosizdata, 1923.

131. *Pervomayskiy gimn* (Hymn for the 1st of May). For choir with piano accompaniment. Also for mixed choir unaccompanied. Cf. collection *Pesni revolyutsii* (Songs of revolution), first issue. Published by Proletkul't, 1923.

132. *Sten'ka Razin* [folksong]. Arrangement for choir accompanied by an orchestra of folk instruments. Muzsektor Gosizdata, [1923].

133. *Sel'skiye rabotï v narodnïkh pesnyakh. V pamyat' Vserossiyskoy sel'skokhozyaystvennoy vïstavki v Moskve v 1923 godu.* (Work in the countryside in folksongs. In honour of the all-Russian agricultural exhibition in Moscow in 1923). Arrangement [for mixed choir] accompanied by Russian folk instruments. Folk words. Book I No. 1 *Posev* (Sowing). No. 2 *Senokos* (Haymaking). Book II No. 3 *Na pashne* (Ploughing). Book III No. 4 *Zhito* (Corn). No. 5 *Lyon* (Flax). Book IV No. 6 *Zhatva* (Reaping). No. 7 *Dozhinki* Harvest festival. Moscow, Petrograd, [1924].

134. *Troyka* (Russian carriage drawn by three horses). Words by P. Oreshin. For mixed choir, three trumpets, triangle and cymbals. In the collection: *Krasnïy Oktyabr'* ('Red October'), issue no. 1, Moscow, Muzsektor Gosizdata, 1923. Also: For mixed choir accompanied by triangle, cymbals, and three trumpets. Muzsektor Gosizdata, 1927.

135. *V. I. Leninu. U groba* (To V. I. Lenin. By the tomb). Words by V. Kirillov. For declamation and choir with piano accompaniment. Muzsektor Gosizdata, 1924. Also: for declamation and choir with orchestral accompaniment. Muzsektor Gosizdata, 1926.

136. *Pesnya pro Lenina.* (Song about Lenin). For choir accompanied by clarinet and domras [or piano]. Muzsektor Gosizdata, 1924. Also: for mixed choir accompanied by clarinet and orchestra of Russian folk instruments [balalaykas and domras]. Score. Orchestration by A. Chagadayev. Muzsektor Gosizdata, 1926.

137. *Kuma* (Godmother). Folksong. Arrangement for choir accompanied by orchestra of folk instruments. Muzsektor Gosizdata, [1924].

138. *Pesnya tovarishchey Razina* (Song of Razin's comrades). Words by V. Kamensky. For choir and orchestra of folk instruments. Muzsektor Gosizdata, 1924.

139. *Krasnaya Rus'* (Red Rus'). Words by N. Tikhomirov. For [mixed] choir accompanied by orchestra of folk instruments. Muzsektor Gosizdata, 1924.
140. *Poyezd* (Train). Words by P. Oreshin. For mixed choir, trumpets, and percussion instruments. In the collection: *Krasnïy Oktyabr'* (Red October), issue no. 2, Muzsektor Gosizdata, 1924. Also: for mixed choir accompanied by large symphony orchestra. Muzsektor Gosizdata, 1927. Also: for mixed choir accompanied by piano, trumpet, cymbals, side drum, bass drum, triangle. Gos. muz. izd-vo., 1931.
141. *Rïbolov* (Fisherman). Folksong. Arrangement for choir and orchestra of folk instruments. Muzsektor Gosizdata, 1924.
142. *Starinka* (The old customs). For choir and orchestra of folk instruments. Muzsektor Gosizdata, 1924.
143. *Kumach* (Red calico). Words by N. Aseyev. For mixed choir accompanied by piano, tambourine, cymbals and bass drum. Muzsektor Gosizdata, 1925.
144. *Pesnya o klade* (Song about the treasure). Words by D. Bednïy. One-part choir accompanied by piano, side drum, bass drum and cymbals. Muzsektor Gosizdata, 1925.
145. *Dunya.* Russian folksong. Arrangement for mixed choir with piano. Muzsektor Gosizdata, 1926.
146. *Khorï iz muzïki k drame 'Sten'ka Razin' V. Kamenskogo* (Choruses from the music for V. Kamensky's drama 'Sten'ka Razin'). For male choir. 1. Historical Cossack song about Stenka Razin. Accompanied by oboe and cor anglais. 2. *Oy li nam, sokolikam* ('O, if we falcons').With piano accompaniment. 3. *Rebyata, na strugi ('Fellows, to the boats')*. With piano accompaniment. 4. *Pogodushka* (Weather). Unaccompanied. Muzsektor Gosizdata, 1927.
147. *Zhatva (Bratchina)* (Reaping (Comradeship)). Russian folksong. Arrangement for mixed choir accompanied by violin, domras and balalaykas. Moscow, Leningrad, Muzgiz, 1949.

A cappella Choruses and Choral Cycles

148. *Dve russkiye narodnïye pesni* (Two Russian folksongs), for mixed choir. No. 1 *Bïlinka.* No. 2 *Slava.* Jurgenson, [1902].
149. *Pesni k Rodine* (Songs for the Motherland). No. 1 *Polya neoglyadnïye* ('Fields too wide for the eye to take in'). No. 2 *Ekh, troyka* ('Ach, troyka'). Words by N. Gogol [from *Dead Souls*]. No. 3 *Pod bol'shim shatrom.* ('In a large tent'). Words by I. Nikitin. For mixed choir. Jurgenson [1904].
150. *Dve velikorusskiye pesni* (Two Great-Russian songs). No. 1 *Nadoyeli nochi* ('I'm tired of the nights'), No. 2 *Poduy, nepogodushka* ('Start to blow up, bad weather') [From M. Balakirev's collection]. Izd. Muzïkal'no-etnograficheskoy komissii, 1912.
151. *Detskiy gimn svobode* (Children's hymn to freedom). Words by I.A. Belousov. Jurgenson, 1917.

152. *Internatsional* (The *Internationale*). Arrangement for mixed choir. Gos. muz. izd-vo., [1918].
153. *Khor iz 'Sten'ki Razina'* (Chorus from 'Sten'ka Razin') [play by V. Kamensky]. Music Section of Proletkul't, 1920.
154. *Rus'. Pamyati smelogo glashataya russkogo iskusstva Vladimira Vasil'yevicha Stasova (1824-1924)* (Rus'. To the memory of the bold herald of Russian art, Vladimir Vasil'yevich Stasov (1824-1924)). Words by N.A. Nekrasov. For mixed choir. Moscow, Petrograd, Muzsektor Gosizdata, 1923.
155. *Krasnoarmeyskaya* (The Red Army song). MONO Muztorg, 1924.
156. *Ti, ryabinushka* ('You, little rowan-tree'). Russian folksong. Muzsektor Gosizdata, 1924.
157. *Vrangel'. Denikin. Krasnoarmeyskiye chastushki* (Vrangel'. Denikin. Red Army satirical songs). In the collection: *Krasnoarmeyskiye pesni* (Red Army songs). MONO Muztorg, 1925.
158. *U vorot, vorot batyushkinïkh* ('By the gates, the gates of my father's house'). Folksong. Muzsektor Gosizdata, 1927.
159. *Dunya-tonkopryakha* ('Dunya the fine seamstress'). Russian folksong. In the collection: *10 russkikh narodnïkh pesen* (Ten Russian folksongs). Muzizdat, 1933.

For Voice with Accompaniment

160. *Kolïbel'naya* (Lullaby). Words by A. Dorogoychenko. For voice and piano. Moscow, Muzsektor Gosizdata, 1925.
161. *Ne odna vo pole dorozhen'ka* ('There's more than one path through the field'). Folksong. For voice and piano. Muzsektor Gosizdata, 1927.

Compositions for Piano

162. *Po Gruzii* ('Across Georgia'). Eight pieces for piano on Georgian folk melodies. Jurgenson, 1901.

List of Kastalsky's Published Writings and Interviews

1. *Pis'mo v redaktsiyu* (Letter to the editor), in *RMG*, 1903, nos. 7-8, cols. 206-207 (concerns the Georgian Liturgy by N.S. Klenovsky).
2. *Zhenshchinï v tserkovnïkh khorakh (otvetï na voprosï redaktsii)* (Women in church choirs (answers to the editors' questions)), in *Muzïkal'nïy truzhenik* (The toiler in music), 1906-1907, no. 16, p. 5.
3. *Sredi regentov* (Among church choirmasters), *Muzïkal'nïy truzhenik* (The toiler in music), 1906-1907, no. 16, pp. 9-10.
4. *Obshchedostupnïy samouchitel' tserkovnogo peniya. S prilozheniyem notnoy tetradi* (An easy teach-yourself church singing. With a notebook in music notation appended). Published by A.F. and N.A. Fyodorov, Moscow, 1909.
5. *Prakticheskoye rukovodstvo k vïrazitel'nomu peniyu stikhir pri pomoshchi razlichnïkh garmonizatsiy* (A practical guide to the expressive singing of stichera using varied harmonizations). Moscow, 1909.
6. *[Interv'yu s A.D. Kastal'skim o zarubezhnïkh gastrolyakh khora 1911 goda]* (An interview with A.D. Kastal'sky about the choir's foreign tour in 1911), *Golos Moskvï* (The Voice of Moscow), 1911, 24 May.
7. *Nasaditeli drevnego peniya. (Beseda s A.D. Kastal'skim)* (The propagators of ancient singing. A conversation with A.D. Kastal'sky), in *Ranneye utro* (Early morning), 1911, 3 November.
8. *Muzïka v pravoslavnïkh khramakh. (Beseda s direktorom Sinodal'nogo uchilishcha A.D. Kastal'skim)* (Music in Orthodox churches. (A conversation with the director of the Synodal School A.D. Kastal'sky), in *Ranneye utro* (Early morning), 1911, 2 December.
9. *Zagranichnïye pis'ma* (Letters from abroad), in *RUSAM*, vol. 1, pp. 269-292 (selected letters of 1911).
10. *Narodnïye prazdnovaniya na Rusi* (Peasant merrymaking in Rus), in *Muzïka* (Music), 1914, no. 196, pp. 519-521. *Ibid.*, entitled *Predisloviye k Kartinam narodnïkh prazdnovaniy na Rusi* (Preface to Scenes of peasant merrymaking in Rus'), in ed. D.V. Zhitomirsky: *A.D. Kastal'sky. Stat'i. Vospominaniya. Materialï* (A.D. Kastal'sky. Articles. Reminiscences. Materials). Moscow, 1960, pp. 171-173.
11. *O moyey muzïkal'noy kar'yere i moi mïsli o tserkovnoy muzïke* (My career in music and my thoughts about church music), in *Muzïkal'nïy sovremennik* (Musical Contemporary), 1915, no. 2, pp. 31-45. The same, entitled My Musical Career and my Thoughts on Church Music, translated by S.W. Pring,

in *Musical Quarterly*, 1925, no. XI/2, pp. 231-247. *Ibid.*, in *RUSAM*, vol. 1, pp. 227-249.

12. *Vsenoshchnoye bdeniye Rakhmaninova* (Rakhmaninov's All-Night Vigil), in *Russkoye slovo* (Russian Word), 1915, 7 March, no. 54.

13. *[Nashi besedï]. U A.D. Kastal'skogo* (Our conversations. Calling on A.D. Kastal'sky), in *Teatr* (Theatre), 1916, no. 1935, p. 6.

14. *Tserkovnoye peniye v Moskovskom Sinodal'nom uchilishche. (Doklad, prochitannïy na Vserossiyskom s'yezde dukhovenstva i miryan v Moskve 2 iyunya 1917 goda)* (Church music at the Moscow Synodal School. (Report read at the All-Russian Congress of Clergy and Laity in Moscow, 2 June 1917)), in *Melos*, vol. 2, pp. 126-129; in *RUSAM*, vol. 1, pp. 265-268.

15. *Iz pisem 1917-1918 godov* (From letters from the years 1917-1918), in *RUSAM*, vol. 1, pp. 293-312.

16. *Prostoye iskusstvo i yego neprostïye zadachi* (Simple art and its not-so-simple tasks), in *Melos*, vol. 2, 1918, pp. 122-126.

17. *Iz vospominaniy o poslednikh godakh* (From reminiscences of recent years), *SovM*, 1977, no. 6, pp. 107-111 (abridged). *Ibid.*, in *RUSAM*, vol. 1, pp. 250-264 (abridged).

18. *O vechere narodnostey v Bol'shom teatre* (A nationalities evening in the Bol'shoy Theatre), in *Muzïkal'naya nov'* (Musical Virgin Soil), 1923, no. 2, pp. 25-26.

19. *Osobennosti narodno-russkoy muzïkal'noy sistemï* (Peculiarities of the Russian folk musical system). Moscow, Petrograd, 1923. *Ibid.*, Moscow, 1961 (ed. T.V. Popova).

20. *[Iz zapisok]* (From notes), in ed. B.M. Yarustovsky: *I.F. Stravinsky. Stat'i i materialï* (I.F. Stravinsky. Articles and materials). Moscow, 1973, pp. 207-213.

21. *Pervïye shagi* (The first steps), in *Muzïkal'naya nov'* (Musical Virgin Soil), 1924, no. 11, pp. 8-10.

22. *Posleduyushchiye shagi* (Subsequent steps), in *Muzïkal'naya nov'* (Musical Virgin Soil), 1924, no. 12, pp. 9-10.

23. *Russkaya narodnaya pesnya. (Narodnaya pesnya – kharakteristika natsii)* (Russian folksong. Folksong – a feature of a nation), in *A.D. Kastal'sky. Stat'i. Vospominaniya. Materialï* (A.D. Kastal'sky. Articles. Reminiscences. Materials), pp. 136-170.

24. *Vstupleniye k sborniku: A. Zatayevich. 1000 pesen kirgizskogo naroda (napevï i melodii* (Introduction to the collection: A. Zatayevich. 1,000 songs of the Kirgiz people (tunes and melodies)), Orenburg, 1925.

25. *Kratkaya avtobiografiya* (Short autobiography), in *A.D. Kastal'sky. Stat'i. Vospominaniya. Materialï* (A.D. Kastal'sky. Articles. Reminiscences. Materials), pp. 133-134.

26. *V.M. Metallov*, in *Muzïkal'noye obrazovaniye* (Musical Education), 1926, nos. 3/4, p. 92-93. (Obituary.)

27. *Osnovï narodnogo mnogogolosiya* (Fundamentals of folk polyphony). Moscow, Leningrad, 1948; ed. V.M. Belayev.

Bibliography

1896

Teatr i muzïka (Theatre and Music). [Synodal Choir concert on 15 December 1896]. *Moskovskiye vedomosti* (Moscow Bulletin), 1896, 18 December. (Kastal'sky's compositions '*Dostoyno yest*'' (It is meet) and '*Miloserdiya dveri*' (Open to us the doors of compassion).)

1897

Kruglikov, S.: *Posle tryokh dukhovnïkh kontsertov* (After three concerts of sacred music). *Sem'ya* (Family), 1897, 6 April, no. 14. (Concerts by the Synodal Choir, L.S. Vasil'yev's Kapella and the Chudov Choir.)

Lipayev, I.: *Moskva. Ot nashego korrespondenta* [Synodal Choir concert, 2 March 1897]. *RMG*, no. 4, cols. 678-680.

[Synodal Choir concert, 18 December 1897]. *Moskovskiy listok* (Moscow Leaflet), 1897, 20 December, no. 350. (Concerns Kastal'sky's '*Bog Gospod*'' (The Lord is God) and '*Milost' mira*' (Mercy of peace).)

[Synodal Choir concert, 20 December 1897]. *Moskovskiye vedomosti* (Moscow Bulletin), 1897, 21 December, no. 351. (Kastal'sky's style and his '*Bog Gospod*'' (God is the Lord) and '*Milost' mira*' (Mercy of peace).)

Teatr i muzïka (Theatre and Music). [Concerns the Synodal Choir concert on 2 March 1897]. *Moskovskiye vedomosti* (Moscow Bulletin), 1897, 5 March, no. 63. (Kastal'sky's '*Kheruvimskaya pesn*'' (Cherubic Hymn) using *znamennïy* chant and '*Miloserdiya dveri*' (Open to us the doors of compassion).)

1898

[The concert by the Synodal Choir, 20 December 1898]. *Moskovskiye vedomosti* (Moscow Bulletin), 1898, 23 December, no. 351. (Chesnokov, who is 'following in Kastal'sky's footsteps'.)

Findeyzen, N.F.: *Sinodal'noye uchilishche tserkovnogo peniya v Moskve* (The Synodal School of Church Music in Moscow). *RMG*, 1898, no. 4, cols. 343-349.

Lipayev, I.V.: *Muzïkal'naya zhizn' Moskvï. Sinodal'noye uchilishche, yego idealistï, khor. G-n Kastal'sky. Dukhovnïye kontsertï Vorotnikovskoy kapellï i [kapellï] Ivanova* (The musical life of Moscow. The Synodal School, its idealists, choir. Mr Kastal'sky. Sacred music concerts by Vorotnikov's choir and Ivanov's) *RMG*, 1898, no. 4, cols. 399-401. (The style of Kastal'sky, which is compared with that of the artist V. Vasnetsov, his choruses '*Sam Yedin*' (Thou alone art immortal) and '*Miloserdiya dveri*' (Open to us the doors of compassion) sung at the Synodal Choir concert on 15 March 1898.)

1899

Dmitriyev, N. [Kashkin, N.D.]: *Venskiye vpechatleniya* (Viennese impressions). *Moskovskiye vedomosti* (Moscow Bulletin), 1899, 11 April, no. 100. (Synodal Choir concert in Vienna, 17/5 April, and Kastal'sky's choral pieces '*Miloserdiya dveri*' (Open to us the doors of compassion) and '*Dostoyno yest*'' (It is meet) to a Serbian chant.)

Lipayev, I.: *Kak pishut znatoki* (How the experts write). (Reply to a feuilleton in *Novoye vremya* (New Time), 1899, 4 October, no. 8478). *RMG*, 1899, no. 42, cols. 1029-1036. (Kastal'sky, and a statement by N. Kashkin about his music.)

Lipayev, Iv.: *Iz Moskvï: kontsert Sinodal'nogo khora* (From Moscow: a concert by the Synodal Choir)[28 March 1899]. *RMG*, 1899, nos. 15/16, cols. 479-480.

K. N. [Nelidov, K.]: *Dukhovno-muzïkal'nïye sochineniya i perelozheniya A. Kastal'skogo* (Sacred music compositions and arrangements by A. Kastal'sky). *RMG*, 1899, nos. 16/17, cols. 517-519.

[The Synodal Choir concert, 28 March 1899)]. *Moskovskiye tserkovnïye vedomosti* (Moscow Church Bulletin), 1899, no. 15, pp. 206-207. (Kastal'sky's choral piece '*Ne imamï inïya pomoshchi*' (We have no other help).)

Vox [Chereshnev, G.Ya.]: [Synodal Choir concert, 19 December 1899)]. *Russkoye slovo* (Russian Word), 1899, 21 December, no. 352. (Kastal'sky's compositions '*Blazheni yazhe izbral*' (Blessed are they whom Thou has chosen) and '*Tebe poyem*' (We hymn Thee).)

1900

N. K. [Kashkin, N.D.]: *Dukhovnïy kontsert* [Synodal Choir concert, 17 December 1899]. *Moskovskiye vedomosti* (Moscow Bulletin), 1900, 20 December, no. 351. (Kastal'sky's choruses '*Milost' mira*' (Mercy of peace) and '*Blazhen muzh*' (Blessed is the man) to a melody from the Cathedral of the Dormition.)

Lipayev, I.: *Iz Moskvï* (From Moscow) [Synodal Choir concert, 30 March 1900]. *RMG*, 1900, no. 15, cols. 439-441. (Kastal'sky's style, his '*Dostoyno yest*'' (It is meet) to a melody by Tsar Fyodor and the sticheron to a pattern melody '*O preslavnoye chudese*' (O most glorious wonder) to a Kievan chant.)

1901

Kochetov, N.: *Dukhovnïy kontsert* [Synodal Choir concert, 19 December 1901]. *Moskovskiy listok* (Moscow Leaflet), 1901, 22 December, no. 355. (The concert presented the 'historic course of *partesnoye* singing in Rus''; Kastal'sky's 'Vstrechnoye pesnopeniye zhenikhu' (Entrance hymn for the bridegroom) was performed.)

Kompaneysky, N.I.: *O stile tserkovnïkh pesnopeniy* (Concerning the style of church hymns). *RMG*, 1901, no. 37, cols. 854-860, no. 38, cols. 886-896, no. 39, cols. 925-930.

Kontsert Sinodal'nogo khora (Concert by the Synodal Choir) [on 11 March 1901]. *Russkiy listok* (Russian Leaflet), 1901, 12 March. (Kastal'sky's '*Sam Yedin*' (Thou alone art immortal), '*Blagoobraznïy Iosif*' (Good Joseph) and the *zadostoynik* for the week of Palm Sunday.)

1902

Kompaneysky, N.: *Kontsert Pridvornoy pevcheskoy kapellï (the Court Kapella concert)* [29 January 1902]. *RMG*, 1902, no. 5, cols. 141-145. (Kastal'sky in connection with the performance of his chorus '*Miloserdiya dveri*' (Open to us the doors of compassion).)

Kompaneysky, N.: *Sovremennoye demestvo* (Present-day *demestvo*). *RMG*, 1902, no. 6, cols. 161-170 (Tchaikovsky, Balakirev, Rimsky-Korsakov, Kastal'sky and Grechaninov, who have opened 'a new present-day era in church and *demestvenny* hymns and of national rebirth'); no. 38, cols. 878-885, no. 49, cols. 1227-1235 (analysis of '*Bog Gospod*'' (God is the Lord) and the troparia for Great Saturday, performed at a concert of combined St Petersburg choirs conducted by A. Arkhangel'sky on 1 December 1902, and about Kastal'sky as the creator of a 'church-music symphony in Russian church style'); no. 50, cols. 1258-1264 (completion of the analysis of Kastal'sky's '*Bog Gospod*'' and the troparia.)

Lisitsïn, M.A.: *Tserkov' i muzïka. Po povodu novïkh techeniy v muzïkal'nom iskusstve* (The church and music. New trends in the art of music). St Petersburg, 1902. (Panchenko, Kastal'sky and Grechaninov.) *Ibid.*, expanded, St Petersburg, 1904.

Metallov, V.M.: *O sovremennom sostoyanii i nuzhdakh tserkovnogo peniya* (The present condition of church music and its needs). *Moskovskiye vedomosti* (Moscow Bulletin), 1902, nos. 348-352.

1903

Kompaneysky, N.I.: *Vozrazheniye svyashchenniku V.M. Metallovu* (An objection to Father V.M. Metallov). *RMG*, 1903, no. 4, cols. 107-114, no. 5, cols. 135-144, no. 6, cols. 166-174. (The New Direction and its representatives.)

Livin, A.: *Moskva* (Moscow). [A musical evening (9 February) at the Synodal School]. *RMG*, 1903, no. 9, cols. 267-268. (Performance of Kastal'sky's *Dve russkiye narodnïye pesni* (Two Russian Folksongs): *Bïlinka* and *Slava*.)

Livin, A.: *Moskva* (Moscow). [Review of Synodal Choir concert, 16 November 1903]. *RMG*, 1903, no. 48, cols. 1204-1205. (The concert in its entirety was devoted to compositions and arrangements by Kastal'sky.)

[Synodal Choir concert made up of compositions by Kastal'sky, 16 November 1903]. *Russkiy listok* (Russian Leaflet), 1903, 17 November.

St. F.Ye. [Stepanov, F.P.]: [Synodal Choir concert, 16 March 1903]. *Muzïka i peniye* (Instrumental music and song), 1902/03, no. 6. (The difficulty of performing Kastal'sky's compositions.)

1904

N.F. B[ukreyev]: *Dukhovno-muzïkal'nïye sochineniya dlya smeshannogo khora, muzïka A.D. Kastal'skogo* (Sacred music compositions for mixed chorus, music by A.D. Kastal'sky). *Izvestiya Sankt-Peterburgskogo obshchestva muzïkal'nïkh sobraniy* (Proceedings of the St Petersburg Society of Musical Assemblies), 1904, January-February.

Kompaneysky, N.I.: *Kastal'sky istochnik* (Kastal'sky as source). *RMG*, 1904, nos. 6/7, cols. 161-169.

Kompaneysky, N.I.: *A.D. Kastal'sky (po povodu 4-go vïpuska yego dukhovno-muzïkal'nïkh sochineniy)*. *RMG*, 1904, nos. 13/14, cols. 359-364; no. 15, cols. 391-398; no. 16, cols. 425-429; nos. 17/18, cols. 457-465.

K. Ch-v.: [Review of A. Kastal'sky's piano cycle *Po Gruzii* (Across Georgia)]. *RMG*, 1904, no. 42, col. 957.

1905

V. D. [Derzhanovsky, V.V.]: *Operï i kontsertï* (Operas and concerts). [Synodal Choir concert, 19 December 1904]. *RMG*, 1905, no. 1, col. 34. (Kastal'sky's 'Marriage Concertos'.)

Kashkin, N.D.: [Concert comprising compositions from Kastal'sky's All-Night Vigil given by L.S. Vasil'yev's choir, 27 March 1905]. *Russkiye vedomosti* (Russian Bulletin), 1905, 12 April.

Maslov, N.: *Tserkovnaya i svetskaya muzïka v Rossii i narodnoye tvorchestvo* (Church and secular music in Russia and folk musical creativity). *RMG*, 1905, no. 1, cols. 6-11, no. 2, cols. 48-52.

1906

Kompaneysky, N.I.: *Protest kompozitorov dukhovnoy muzïki* (A protest by composers of sacred music). *RMG*, 1906, nos. 23/24, cols. 569-574. (Grechaninov, Kastal'sky, Chesnokov etc.)

Lisitsïn, M.: *Moskva i Sinodal'nïy khor* (Moscow and the Synodal Choir). *Muzïka i peniye* (Instrumental Music and Song), 1906, no. 11, pp. 4-5, no. 12, pp. 1-3.

Lisitsïn, M.: *O novom napravlenii v russkoy tserkovnoy muzïke* (About the new direction in Russian church music). *Novoye vremya* (New Time), 1906, no. 10974.

[The singing in the Cathedral of the Dormition]. *Veche* (Popular assembly), 1906, 12 September. (Abusive article about Kastal'sky's compositions.)

1907

[How Kastal'sky composed the opera *Klara Milich*]. *Teatr* (Theatre), 1907, no. 28.

Kruglikov, S.: [Review of concert given by an amateur choir conducted by P.G. Chesnokov)]. *Golos Moskvï* (Voice of Moscow), 1907, 31 October.

Novïye proizvedeniya nashikh kompozitorov (New works by our composers). *Obozreniye teatrov* (Review of the Theatres), 1907, no. 164. (Kastal'sky's opera *Klara Milich*.)

[Performance by the Synodal Choir in the hall of the Diocesan House, 18 March 1907]. *Moskovskiye tserkovnïye vedomosti* (Moscow church bulletin), 1907, 1 April, no. 13, pp. 401-402. (Première of Kastal'sky's *Play of the Furnace*.)

Preobrazhensky, A.V.: *Kratkiy ocherk istorii tserkovnogo peniya v Rossii* (Brief outline of the history of church music in Russia). *RMG*, 1907, separate supplement. *Ibid.*, entitled: *Ocherk istorii tserkovnogo peniya v Rossii* (Outline of the history of church music in Russia). St Petersburg, 1910.

1908

[Information about a music publication]. *A. Kastal'sky. 'Iz minuvshikh vekov'. Opït muzïkal'nïkh restavratsiy. Tetradi I-II* (A. Kastal'sky. 'From past ages'. An experiment in musical restorations. Books I and II). *Muzïka i zhizn'* (Music and Life), 1908, no. 1, p. 13.

[Kastal'sky's work on the orchestration of the opera *Klara Milich*]. *Moskovskiye vedomosti* (Moscow Bulletin), 1908, 6 January.

M.: [Information about a music publication]. *A. Kastal'sky. Stikhirï svv. Kirillu i Mefodiyu, app. Petru i Pavlu i na Vozneseniye* (A. Kastal'sky. Stichera to Sts. Cyrill and Methodius, for the Apostles Peter and Paul, and for Ascension. For mixed choir. Moscow, 1908. *Muzïka i zhizn'* (Music and Life), 1908, no. 11, p. 23.

A. N-y. [Nikol'sky, A.V.]: *Korrespondentsiya iz Moskvï* (Correspondence from Moscow). *Khorovoye i regentskoye delo* (Choral and Church Choirmaster Matters), 1909, no. 11, pp. 290-291. (Concerns *'Veruyu'* (The Creed) no. 3 by Kastal'sky.)

Veritas: *Dukhovnïye kontsertï khorov: Sinodal'nogo, L.S. Vasil'yeva i P.G. Chesnokova* (Sacred concerts by choirs: the Synodal Choir, the choirs of L.S. Vasil'yev and P.G. Chesnokov). *Muzïka i zhizn'* (Music and Life), 1908, no. 11, p. 12.

1909

Allemanov, Dim.: *Russkoye khorovoye tserkovnoye peniye* (Russian choral church music). *Muzïkal'nïy truzhenik* (The Toiler in Music), 1909, no. 24, pp. 4-17. *Ibid.*, Moscow, 1910.

Kh. G[rozdov]: *Novïye knigi i muzïkal'nïye sochineniya. Veruyu No. 1, 2, 3 Kastal'skogo.* (New books and compositions. The Creed nos. 1, 2 and 3 by

Kastal'sky.) *Khorovoye i regentskoye delo* (Choral and Church Choirmaster Matters), 1909, no. 11, pp. 293-294.

Kastal'sky. [Biographical sketch]. *Muzïkal'nïy truzhenik* (The Toiler in Music), 1909, no. 2, p. 2.

D.K.: *Novïye knigi i muzïkal'nïye sochineniya. Devyat' stikhir, perelozhennïkh A.D. Kastal'skim dlya smeshannogo khora* (New books and compositions. Nine stichera arranged by A.D. Kastal'sky for mixed choir). Published by P. Jurgenson, 1909. *Khorovoye i regentskoye delo* (Choral and Church Choirmaster Matters), 1909, no. 1, p. 30.

Lisitsïn, M.A.: *O novom napravlenii v russkoy tserkovnoy muzïke. Referat, prochitannïy v Sankt-Peterburgskom obshchestve pisateley o muzïke 9 noyabrya 1908 goda* (The new direction in Russian church music. A paper read to the St Petersburg Society of Writers about Music on 9 November 1908). Moscow, 1909.

Lisitsïn, M.: *Letniye vpechatleniya* (Summer impressions). *Muzïka i peniye* (Instrumental Music and Song). 1908/09, nos. 10, 11 and 12. (*'Kastal'sky teper' krome sebya, kazhetsya, nikogo ne poyot...* (Kastal'sky conducts only his own compositions nowadays, it seems...').)

Novïye knigi i muzïkal'nïye sochineniya. A. Kastal'sky. Peshchnoye deystvo (New books and compositions. A. Kastal'sky. The Play of the Furnace). *Khorovoye i regentskoye delo* (Choral and Church Choirmaster Matters), 1909, no. 10, p. 262.

1910

Bukreyev, N.F.: *K voprosu o tserkovnosti dukhovnoy muzïki* (The question of the church-like quality of sacred music). *Khorovoye i regentskoye delo* (Choral and Church Choirmaster Matters), 1910, no. 4, pp. 83-89.

[Information about a music publication]. A.D. Kastal'sky. *Prakticheskoye rukovodstvo k vïrazitel'nomu peniyu stikhir pri pomoshchi razlichnïkh garmonizatsiy* (A practical handbook to the expressive singing of stichera with the help of varied harmonizations). Published by P. Jurgenson, 1909. *Khorovoye i regentskoye delo* (Choral and Church Choirmaster Matters), nos. 5/6, p. 151.

Kashkin, N.: *Liturgiya Rakhmaninova* (Rakhmaninov's Liturgy). *Russkoye Slovo* (Russian Word), 1910, 26 November, no. 273. (Kastal'sky's influence on Rakhmaninov.)

Samarov [Lipayev, I.V.]: *Pro Sinodal'noye uchilishche* (About the Synodal School). *Muzïkal'nïy truzhenik* (The Toiler in Music). 1910, no. 8, pp. 8-9.

Universal-Handbuch der Musikliteratur aller Zeiten und Völker. Wien, Pazdirek und Co., 1904–1910, alphabetical index in 14 vols. Vol. K-L, pp. 49-50. (List of Kastal'sky's early published works.)

1911

Arkhangel'sky, An.: *Kontsert Moskovskogo Sinodal'nogo khora v Vene* (The Synodal Choir's concert in Vienna). *Muzïka i zhizn'*, 1911, nos. 6/7, pp. 7-9.

D. A.: [Information about a music publication]. A. Kastal'sky. *'Iz minuvshikh vekov': 'Khristiane'* (From past ages: the Christians). *Muzïka i zhizn'* (Music and Life), 1911, nos. 1/2, p. 27.

[Derzhanovsky, V.]: *Sinodal'nïy khor. 6 noyabrya* (The Synodal Choir. 6 November). *Muzïka* (Music), 1911, no. 50, p. 1118. (Kastal'sky's anniversary cantata *Stikh o tserkovnom russkom penii* (Verse about Russian church music).)

Dukhovnïye kontsertï Moskovskogo Sinodal'nogo khora (Sacred concerts by the Moscow Synodal Choir). [Rome, 3 May 1911]. *Moskovskiye vedomosti* (Moscow Bulletin), 1911, 14 May.

Dukhovnïye kontsertï Moskovskogo Sinodal'nogo khora: v Varshave, v Rime (Sacred concerts by the Moscow Synodal Choir: in Warsaw and Rome). *Khorovoye i regentskoye delo* (Choral and Church Choirmaster Matters), 1911, no. 5, pp. 126-132.

Dukhovnïye kontsertï Moskovskogo Sinodal'nogo khora: v Drezdene, v Vene (Sacred concerts by the Moscow Synodal Choir: in Dresden and Vienna). *Khorovoye i regentskoye delo* (Choral and Church Choirmaster Matters), 1911, nos. 6/7, pp. 152-156.

Ivanov, V.: *K yubileyu Sinodal'nogo uchilishcha tserkovnogo peniya* (For the anniversary of the Synodal School of Church Music). *Muzïka* (Music), 1911, no. 49, pp. 1066-1069.

Ivanov, M.: *Moskovskoye Sinodal'noye uchilishche* (The Moscow Synodal School). *Novoye vremya* (New Time), 1911, 21 March, no. 12580.

Metallov, V.M.: *Iz istorii Moskovskogo Sinodal'nogo uchilishcha tserkovnogo peniya* (From the history of the Moscow Synodal School of Church Music). *Khorovoye i regentskoye delo* (Choral and Church Choirmaster Matters), 1911, no. 12, pp. 251-260.

Kontsert moskovskogo Sinodal'nogo khora v Peterburge (Concert by the Moscow Synodal Choir in St Petersburg) [10 March 1911]. *Khorovoye i regentskoye delo* (Choral and Church Choirmaster Matters), 1911, № 3, pp. 12-14.

Konyus, G.E.: *V kontsertakh* (At concerts). *Utro Rossii* (Russia's Morning), 1911, 8 November. (The 25th anniversary of the Synodal School; Kastal'sky's cantata *Stikh o tserkovnom russkom penii* (Verse about Russian church music).)

K poyezdke Sinodal'nogo khora za granitsu. (Ot nashego korrespondenta) (The Synodal Choir's journey abroad. (From our correspondent)). *Moskovskiy listok* (Moscow Leaflet), 1911, 12 May.

K poyezdke Sinodal'nogo khora za granitsu (The Synodal Choir's journey abroad). *Moskovskiy listok* (Moscow Leaflet), 1911, 25 May. (Excerpts from Viennese newspapers about the Synodal Choir's performances; reviews of compositions by Kastal'sky.)

Lisitsïn, M.: *Kontsert Sinodal'nogo khora* (Concert by the Synodal Choir) [10 March 1911]. *Kolokol* (The Bell), 1911, 12 March, № 1488.

S.M.: *Dukhovnïy kontsert Sinodal'nogo khora* (Sacred concert by the Synodal Choir) [10 March 1911]. *Novoye vremya* (New Time), 1911, № 12573. (Compares compositions by Rakhmaninov and Kastal'sky performed at this concert.)

Metallov, V.M.: *Sinodal'noye uchilishche tserkovnogo peniya v yego proshlom i nastoyashchem* (The Synodal School of Church Music in its past and present). Moscow, 1911. *Ibid.*, in *RUSAM*, vol. 2, book 1, pp. 99-196.

Petrov, A.: *25-letniy yubiley Moskovskogo Sinodal'nogo uchilishcha tserkovnogo peniya* (The 25th anniversary of the Moscow Synodal School of Church Music). *Khorovoye i regentskoye delo* (Choral and Church Choirmaster Matters), 1911, no. 12, pp. 265-268.

Sakhnovsky, Yu.: *Kantata A.D. Kastal'skogo k 25-letnemu yubileyu Moskovskogo Sinodal'nogo uchilishcha* (A.D. Kastal'sky's cantata for the 25th anniversary of the Moscow Synodal School). *Russkoye slovo* (Russian Word), 1911, 8 November.

Sinodal'nïy khor v Rime (The Synodal Choir in Rome). *Russkoye slovo* (Russian Word), 1911, 15 May.

[The Synodal Choir's concert in Rome, 13 May/30 April 1911]. *Moskovskiy listok* (Moscow Leaflet), 1911, 7 May. (Concert at the reception given by the Russian ambassador Prince Dolgoruky; among the works performed were Kastal'sky's '*Nïne otpushchayeshi*' (Lord, now lettest Thou) no. 1 and '*Veruyu*' (The Creed) no. 1.)

B. T[yuneyev]: *Nepostavlennaya opera Kastal'skogo* (Kastal'sky's unproduced opera). *RMG*, 1911, no. 1, cols. 12-16, no. 2, cols. 36-39.

Vladimirsky, F.: *O 'novoy' tserkovno-muzïkal'noy literature* (About 'new' church music literature). *Khorovoye i regentskoye delo* (Choral and Church Choirmaster Matters), 1911, no. 2, pp. 33-38.

Vladimirsky, F.: *'Staroye' i 'novoye' v tserkovnoy muzïke* ('Old' and 'new' in church music). *Muzïka i zhizn'* (Music and Life), 1911, nos. 1/2, pp. 17-19.

Yubiley Sinodal'nogo uchilishcha (The Synodal School's Anniversary). *Muzïka i zhizn'* (Music and Life), 1911, no. 10, pp. 12-13.

Zatayevich, A.: *Dukhovnïy kontsert Moskovskogo Sinodal'nogo khora* (Sacred concert by the Moscow Synodal Choir). *Varshavskiy dnevnik* (Warsaw Diary), 1911, 26 April/9 May.

Zatayevich, A.: *Vtoroy kontsert Moskovskogo Sinodal'nogo khora v Varshave* (Second concert by the Moscow Synodal Choir in Warsaw). *Varshavskiy dnevnik* (Warsaw Diary), 1911, 24 May/6 June.

Z[atayevich] A.: *Vtoroy kontsert Moskovskogo Sinodal'nogo khora v Varshave* (Second concert by the Synodal Choir in Warsaw). *Khorovoye i regentskoye delo* (Choral and Church Choirmaster Matters), 1911, no. 9.

25-letniy yubiley Moskovskogo Sinodal'nogo uchilishcha tserkovnogo peniya (The 25th anniversary of the Moscow Synodal School of Church Music). *Khorovoye i regentskoye delo* (Choral and Church Choirmaster Matters), 1911, no. 11, pp. 233-241.

1913

Dukhovnoye pesnopeniye (A sacred hymn). *Moskovskiye vedomosti* (Moscow Bulletin), 1913, 4 January, no. 3. (Review of performance by the Synodal Choir conducted by Danilin of compositions by Chesnokov, Kastal'sky, Stepanov and Shvedov, with Nezhdanova and Sobinov taking part.)

Kanevtsov, A.: *Dukhovnïy kontsert kapellï M.A. Nadezhdinskogo* (Sacred concert given by M.A. Nadezhdinsky's choir [of compositions by A.D. Kastal'sky]). *Kiyevlyanin* (The Kievan), 1913, 23 November.

Nikol'sky, A.V.: *S.V. Smolensky i yego rol' v Novom napravlenii russkoy tserkovnoy muzïke* (S.V. Smolensky and his role in the New Direction in Russian church music). *Khorovoye i regentskoye delo* (Choral and Church Choirmaster Matters), 1913, no. 10, pp. 151-156. *Ibid.*, in *RUSAM*, vol. 1, pp. 158-159. (Smolensky, Orlov and Kastal'sky as founders of the New Direction.)

Novïye knigi. Kastal'sky. Pamyati svyatitelya Germogena (New books. Kastal'sky. In memory of Patriarch Germogen). *Khorovoye i regentskoye delo* (Choral and Church Choirmaster Matters), 1913, no. 12.

G. T[imofeyev]: *Dukhovnïy kontsert iz sochineniy A.D. Kastal'skogo* (Sacred concert of A.D. Kastal'sky's compositions). *Rech'* (Speech), 1913, 19 December.

1914

V. Ivanov [Derzhanovsky, V.V.]: *Preobrazovaniye Sinodal'nogo uchilishcha* (The transformation of the Synodal School). *Muzïka*, 1914, no. 182, pp. 373-376.

Opera Zimina (Zimin's Opera). (Run-through of Kastal'sky's opera *Klara Milich* at Zimin's Opera). *Ranneye utro* (Early Morning), 1914, 16 January.

[Review of the publication of compositions by Kastal'sky, Nikol'sky and Myakinnikov]. *Khorovoye i regentskoye delo* (Choral and Church Choirmaster Matters), 1914, no. 9, pp. 175-176.

[Run-through of Kastal'sky's opera *Klara Milich* at Zimin's Opera]. *Teatr* (Theatre), 1914, no. 1433.

Yu. S[akhnovsky]: *'Klara Milich'. Opera A.D. Kastal'skogo* ('Klara Milich'. Opera by A.D. Kastal'sky). *Russkoye slovo* (Russian Word), 1914, 9 November. (Concerns the forthcoming première.)

G. T[imofeyev]: [About the performance of Kastal'sky's *Iz minuvshikh vekov: Khristiane* (From past ages: the Christians)]. *Rech'* (Speech), 1914, 14 January. (Concert by a choir of lovers of church music conducted by A.N. Nikolov in St Petersburg.)

G. T[imofeyev]: *Vecher dukhovnogo peniya A. Kastal'skogo* (An evening of sacred music by A. Kastal'sky). *Rech'* (Speech), 1914, 28 March, no. 85.

1915

B'as. [Asaf'yev, B.V.]: [Bibliographical note]. *A. Kastal'sky. Obshchedostupnïy samouchitel' tserkovnogo peniya. S prilozheniyem notnoy tetradi. Izd. A.F. and V.A. Fyodorovïkh.* (An easy teach-yourself church singing book. With a notebook in music notation appended. Published by A.F. and V.A. Fyodorov.) *Muzïka* (Music), 1915, no. 231, 17 November, pp. 479-482.

Igor' Glebov [Asaf'yev, B.V.]: *Ot 'opïtov' k novïm dostizheniyam. Po povodu muzïkal'nïkh 'restavratsiy' Kastal'skogo* (From 'experiments' to new achievements. Kastal'sky's musical 'restorations'). *Muzïka* (Music), 1915, no. 228, 17 October, pp. 412-417. *Ibid.*, B. Asaf'yev: *O khorovom iskusstve* (On choral art). Leningrad, 1980, pp. 86-101.

[Information about a music publication.] *Obraztsï tserkovnogo peniya na Rusi v XV-XVII vv. Materialï dlya istoricheskikh [dukhovnïkh] kontsertov* (Examples of church music in Rus' from the fifteenth to the seventeenth centuries. Materials for historical sacred concerts). *Khorovoye i regentskoye delo* (Choral and Church Choirmaster Matters), 1915, no. 10, p. 189.

Sakhnovsky, Yu.: *Vsenoshchnoye bdeniye S.V. Rakhmaninova* (S.V. Rakhmaninov's All-Night Vigil). *Russkoye slovo* (Russian Word), 1915, 11 March, no. 57. (Première of Rakhmaninov's All-Night Vigil, and also its continuation from the work of Kastal'sky.)

1916

B'as. [Asaf'yev, B.V.]: [Information about a music publication.] A. Kastal'sky. *Dukhovno-muzïkal'nïye sochineniya: no. 74 'Razboynika blagorazumnago', no. 75 'Tsaryu nebesnïy', no. 76 Zadostoynik v den' Sv. Troitsï, no. 77 'Khristos voskrese', no. 78 'Tebe poyem', no. 79 Tropar' svyashchennomucheniku Yermogenu* (A. Kastal'sky. Sacred compositions: no. 74 'The Good Thief', no. 75 'O Heavenly King, no. 76 *Zadostoynik* for the day of the Holy Trinity, no. 77 'Christ is risen', no. 78 'We hymn Thee', no. 79 Troparion for the hieromartyr Hermogen). *Muzïka* (Music), 1916, no. 248, 5 March, p. 158-159.

B'as. [Asaf'yev, B.V.]: [Information about a music publication.] A. Kastal'sky. *Obraztsï tserkovnogo peniya na Rusi v XV-XVII vekakh* (Examples of church music in Rus' from the fifteenth to the seventeenth centuries). *Muzïka* (Music), 1916, no. 248, 5 March, pp. 159-160.

Chereshnev, G.: *'Klara Milich' Kastal'skogo* (Kastal'sky's 'Klara Milich'). *Moskovskiye vedomosti* (Moscow Bulletin), 1916, 18 November.

Derzhanovsky, V.V.: *Kastal'sky. Utro Rossii* (Russia's Morning), 1916, no. 68.

Derzhanovsky, Vl.: *'Klara Milich'. Opera Kastal'skogo na stsene teatra Zimina* ('Klara Milich'. Kastal'sky's opera on the stage of the Zimin Theatre). *Utro Rossii* (Russia's Morning'), 1916, 12 November.

[Dress rehearsal of Kastal'sky's opera 'Klara Milich' at the Zimin Theatre]. *Ranneye utro* (Early Morning), 1916, 10 November.

Engel', Yu.: *Opera v Moskve. 'Ole iz Nordlanda' Ippolitova-Ivanova (Bol'shoy Teatr). 'Klara Milich' Kastal'skogo (teatr Zimina)* (Opera in Moscow. 'Ole from Nordland' by Ippolitov-Ivanov (Bol'shoy Theatre). 'Klara Milich' by Kastal'sky (Zimin Theatre)). Chronicle of the journal *Muzïkal'nïy sovremennik* (Musical Contemporary), 1916, nos. 9/10, pp. 20-23.

Engel', Yu.: *'Klara Milich' A.D. Kastal'skogo (teatr Zimina)* ('Klara Milich' by A.D. Kastal'sky (Zimin Theatre)). *Russkiye vedomosti* (Russian Bulletin), 1916, 13 November.

Florestan [Derzhanovsky, V.V.]: *Kontsert Sinodal'nogo khora iz proizvedeniy Kastal'skogo* (A Synodal Choir concert of compositions by Kastal'sky) [3 March]. *Utro Rossii* (Russia's Morning), 1916, 16 March. *Ibid., Muzïka* (Music), 1916, no. 249, pp. 172-173.

Igor' Glebov [Asaf'yev, B.V.]: *Samoye sovremennoye sochineniye. Po povodu Requiem'a A.D. Kastal'skogo* (A most contemporary composition. The Requiem of A.D. Kastal'sky). *Muzïka* (Music), 1916, no. 248, 5 March, pp. 149-152.

Grinevsky, A.: *Opera S. Zimina* (S. Zimin's Opera). *Rampa i zhizn'* (The Footlights and Life), 1916, no. 47.

Kurov, N.: *'Klara Milich'. Teatr* (Theatre), 1916, no. 1935, p. 6.

Kurov, N.: *'Klara Milich' (Opera Zimina)* ('Klara Milich' (Zimin Opera), *Ranneye utro* (Early Morning), 1916, 12 November.

[List of sacred compositions by Kastal'sky]. *Muzïka* (Music), 1916, 5 March, no. 248, pp. 145-146.

Ne muzïkant (Non-musician): *'Real'naya muzïka'* ('Real music). *Teatr* (Theatre), 1916, no. 1936, p. 4. (Mention of Kastal'sky's opera.)

Opera A.D. Kastal'skogo 'Klara Milich' (A.D. Kastal'sky's opera 'Klara Milich'). *Ranneye utro* (Early Morning), 1916, 12 November.

[Production of Kastal'sky's opera at the Zimin Theatre]. *Russkiye vedomosti* (Russian Bulletin), 1916, 12 November.

Prokof'yev, Gr.: *Moskovskiye kontsertï Sinodal'nogo khora* (The Moscow concerts of the Synodal Choir). *RMG*, 1916, no. 13, cols. 310-311. (Première of three choruses from Kastal'sky's *Vechnaya pamyat'* (Eternal Memory) at concert, 6 March 1916.)

Prokof'yev, Gr.: *Kontsert Sinodal'nogo khora iz proizvedeniy Kastal'skogo* (The Synodal Choir concert of compositions by Kastal'sky) [3 March]. *Russkiye vedomosti* (Russian Bulletin), 1916, 8 March. *Ibid., Muzïka* (Music), 1916, no. 249, p. 173.

Sabaneyev, L.: *Muzïka v Moskve* (Music in Moscow). Chronicle of the journal *Muzïkal'nïy sovremennik* (Musical Contemporary), 1916, no. 21, pp. 34-36. (Synodal Choir concert of compositions by Kastal'sky on 6 March 1916.)

Sakhnovsky, Yu.: *'Klara Milich'. Prem'yera operï Zimina* ('Klara Milich'. A première of the Zimin Opera). *Russkoye slovo* (Russian Word), 1916, 12 November.

Sredi pechati. 'Otkrïtiye' Kastal'skogo (Press review. Kastal'sky's 'discovery'). *Muzïka* (Music), 1916, № 249, 12 March, pp. 172-173.

Tideböhl, E. von: *Alexander Dmitrijevich Kastalsky and the Moscow Synod Choir. The Monthly Musical Record*, 1916, vol. XLVI, p. 166.

Tri otkrïtki S.V. Smolenskogo A.D. Kastal'skomu (Three postcards from S.V. Smolensky to A.D. Kastal'sky). *Muzïka* (Music), 1916, 5 March, no. 248, pp. 153-154.

B. T[yuneyev]: *Kastal'sky. 'Bratskoye pominoveniye'* (Requiem for Fallen Brothers). *RMG*, 1916. Bibliographical leaflet, no. 8, pp. 58-59.

1917

Igor' Glebov [Asaf'yev, B.V.]: *'Bratskoye pominoveniye' A. Kastal'skogo* ('Requiem for Fallen Brothers' by A. Kastal'sky). Chronicle of the journal *Muzïkal'nïy sovremennik* (Musical Contemporary), 1917, no. 15, pp. 1-5.

Igor' Glebov [Asaf'yev, B.V.]: *Vpechatleniya i mïsli* (Impressions and thoughts). *Melos*, 1917, book 1, pp. 78-100. (About Kastal'sky: pp. 88-90.)

Newmarch, Rosa: *A Requiem for the Allied Heroes. The Musical Times*, 1917, vol. 58, November, pp. 496–497.

B. T[yuneyev]. *Khronika. Kontsertï v Petrograde* (Chronicle. Concerts in Petrograd). *RMG*, 1917, no. 3, cols. 72-74. (Review of the sixth concert in A. Ziloti's subscription series, when Kastal'sky's 'Requiem for Fallen Brothers' was performed.)

1918

Music in the Provinces (by our own correspondents). The Musical Times, 1918, vol. 59, January, p. 33. (Review of performance of 'Requiem for Fallen Brothers' in Birmingham, 22 November, 1917.)

Derzhanovsky, Vl.: *Muzïkal'naya reforma. K proyektu Kastal'skogo* (Musical reform. Kastal'sky's project). *Novosti dnya* (News of the Day) (evening newspaper), 1918, no. 69, 26 June. (About the establishment of the People's Choir Academy.)

Igor' Glebov [Asaf'yev, B.V.]: *Puti v budushcheye* (Pathways to the future). *Melos*, 1918, book 2, pp. 50-96.

Protokol soyedinyonnogo zasedaniya chlenov Podotdela po tserkovnomu peniyu Pomestnogo Sobora Pravoslavnoy Russkoy Tserkvi i Nablyudatel'nogo soveta Moskovskogo Sinodal'nogo uchilishcha tserkovnogo peniya ot 8 dekabrya 1917 goda. (Ob upotreblenii organa za pravoslavnïm bogosluzheniyem.) (Minutes of the combined session of members of the sub-committee on church music of the Local Council of the Russian Orthodox Church and the Supervisory Council of the Moscow Synodal School of Church Music, held on 8 December 1917. (About the use of the organ in Orthodox worship.) *Tserkovnïye vedomosti* (Church Bulletin), 1918, no. 15/16, pp. 88-94. *Ibid., Bogoslovskiye trudï* (Theological Proceedings). Vol. 34: *Yubileynïy sbornik. K 120-letiyu so dnya rozhdeniya Svyateyshego Patriarkha Aleksiya I. K 80-letiyu vosstanovleniya Patriarshestva.* (Anniversary symposium. For the 120th anniversary of the birth of the Most Holy Patriarch Aleksy I. For the 80th anniversary of the re-establishment of the Patriarchate.) Moscow, 1998, pp. 203-209. *Ibid.*, in *RUSAM*, vol. 3, pp. 808-816. (Kastal'sky's opinion about introducing the organ into Orthodox worship.)

1923

Bugoslavsky, S.: [Information about a music publication.] *'Krasnïy Oktyabr'. Sbornik muzïkal'no-revolyutsionnogo tvorchestva. Muzsektor Gosizdata, 1923.* ('Red October'. Symposium of musical-revolutionary creativity. Published by the Music Section of the State Publishing House, 1923). *Muzïkal'naya nov'* (Musical virgin soil), 1923, no 1, pp. 45-46. (Kastal'sky's chorus *Troyka* and the style of his mass songs.)

1924

Abakumov: [*'V Moskovskoy gosudarstvennoy konservatorii khorovoy podotdel...'* ('At the Moscow State Conservatoire a choral sub-department...')]. *Muzïkal'naya nov'* (Musical virgin soil), 1924, no. 10.
Bugoslavsky, S.: [Information about a music publication.] *Muzïkal'no-revolyutsionnaya literatura (izdaniya Muzsektora, mart-avgust 1924)* (Musical-revolutionary literature (publications of Muzsektor, March-August 1924). *Muzïkal'naya nov'* (Musical virgin soil), 1924, no. 9. (Kastal'sky's choral compositions published in 1924.)
M.-D. C[alvocoressi]: *'Peculiarities of Russian Folk-Music'. By P.* [sic] *Kastalsky. The Musical Times*, 1924, vol. 65, November, p. 999. (Review.)
Preobrazhensky, A.V.: *Kul'tovaya muzïka v Rossii* (Religious music in Russia). Russian Institute for the History of the Arts. *Russkaya muzïka* (Russian Music): a non-periodical series published by the Department for the History of Music, issue 2, Leningrad, 1924. *Ibid.,* in German: Antonij V. Preobraženskij. *Die Kirchenmusik in Rußland. Von den Anfängen bis zum Anbruch des 20. Jahrhunderts.* Herausgegeben von Andreas Wehrmeyer. Aus dem Rus. übers. v. Ernst Kuhn und Andreas Wehrmeyer. Berlin, 1999.
Tsenovsky, A.: [Information about a music publication.] *Sbornik 'Krasnïy oktyabr'* (Symposium 'Red October'). *Muzïkal'naya nov'* (Musical virgin soil), 1924, no. 10, p. 30.

1925

Bugoslavsky, S.: *Kontsert v Teatre revolyutsii (13 dekabrya 1925)* (Concert in the Theatre of Revolution (13 December 1925). *Izvestiya* (News), 1925, 19 December. (Review of the performance of Kastal'sky's *Derevenskaya simfoniya* (Agricultural Symphony) on 13 December 1925.)
'Derevenskaya simfoniya' (Agricultural Symphony)**.** [About the concert in the Theatre of Revolution]. *Izvestiya* (News), 1925, 12 December.
Igor' Glebov [Asaf'yev, B.V.]: *Tretiy fortep'yannïy kontsert S. Prokof'yeva* (S. Prokof'yev's Third Piano Concerto). *Sovremennaya muzïka* (Contemporary

music), 1925, no. 10, pp. 57-63. (Kastal'sky's diatonic harmony.) *Ibid.*, in Academician B.V. Asaf'yev: *Izbrannïye trudï* (Selected works), vol. 5, Moscow, 1957, pp. 109-112.

1926

Braudo, Ye.A.: *Kastal'sky* [Obituary]. *Pravda* (Truth), 1926, 21 December.

Bugoslavsky, S.A.: *A.D. Kastal'sky. Muzïka i Oktyabr'* (Music and October), no. 3, 1926, pp. 4-6.

Bugoslavsky, S.A.: *Kastal'sky* [Obituary]. *Izvestiya* (News), 1926, 21 December.

Drozdov, A.: *Simfonicheskiy kontsert v teatre Revolyutsii 13 dekabrya* (Symphony concert in the Theatre of Revolution on 13 December). *Muzïka i revolyutsiya* (Music and Revolution), 1926, no. 1, p. 45. (Performance of the *Derevenskaya simfoniya* (Agricultural Symphony).)

1927

A-o.: *A.D. Kastal'sky* [Obituary]. *Zarya Vostoka* (Dawn of the East), 1927, 16 January.

Davidenko, A.A.: *Vospominaniya ob A.D. Kastal'skom* (Reminiscences of A.D. Kastal'sky). *Muzïkal'noye obozreniye* (Music Review), 1927, no. 3/4, p. 78. *Ibid.* (abridged), entitled *Uchitel'* (Teacher), in symposium: *A.D. Kastal'sky. Stat'i. Vospominaniya. Materialï.* (Articles. Reminiscences. Materials). Moscow, 1960, pp. 120-121. *Ibid.*, in the book: *Vospominaniya o Moskovskoy konservatorii* (Reminiscences of the Moscow Conservatoire). Moscow, 1966, pp. 406-407.

Glebof, I. [Asaf'yev, B.V.]: *Kastalsky and Russian Church Music. The Monthly Musical Record*, 1927, vol. LVII, pp. 228-229. Trans. by S.W. Pring. *Ibid.*, entitled *O khorovom stile Kastal'skogo* (Kastal'sky's choral style) in symposium: B. Asaf'yev: *O khorovom iskusstve* (On choral art), pp. 90-94.

Igor' Glebov [Asaf'yev, B.V.]: *Kastal'sky. (Vmesto nekrologa)* (Kastal'sky. (Instead of an obituary)). *Sovremennaya muzïka* (Contemporary Music), 1927, no. 19, pp. 233-235.

Igor' Glebov [Asaf'yev, B.V.]: *A.D. Kastal'sky ['Tryokh prekrasnïkh starikov...'* (Three grand old men)]. *Muzïka i revolyutsiya* (Music and Revolution), 1927, no. 1, pp. 9-10. *Ibid.*, entitled *A.D. Kastal'sky* in symposium: *A.D. Kastal'sky. Stat'i. Vospominaniya. Materialï* (Articles. Reminiscences. Materials), pp. 7-9. *Ibid.*, entitled *A.D. Kastal'sky* in symposium: B. Asaf'yev: *O khorovom iskusstve* (On choral art), pp. 101-103.

Lebedinsky, L.: *Kastal'sky* [Obituary]. *Muzïkal'noye obrazovaniye* (Musical Education), 1927, no. 1/2, p. 259.

R. N[ewmarch]: *Kastalsky, Alexander Dmitrievich. Grove's Dictionary of Music and Musicians*. Third edition, London, 1927, vol. 3, p. 6. *Ibid.*, fourth edition, London, 1940, vol. 3, p. 6.

Nikol'sky, A.: *Pamyati A.D. Kastal'skogo* (In memory of A.D. Kastal'sky). *Muzïka i revolyutsiya* (Music and Revolution), 1927, no. 1, pp. 7-9.

Nikol'sky, A.V.: *A.D. Kastal'sky kak kompozitor i kak issledovatel' narodno-russkoy pesni* (A.D. Kastal'sky as composer and researcher into Russian folksong). (Speech at the event at GIMN to mark the memory of the deceased, 28 March 1927), in *RUSAM*, vol. 1, pp. 317-322.

N-iy, A. [Nikol'sky A.V.]: *Publichnoye zasedaniye i kontsert GIMNa, posvyashchonnïye pamyati A.D. Kastal'skogo* (The public session and concert at GIMN dedicated to the memory of A.D. Kastal'sky). *Muzïkal'noye obrazovaniye* (Musical Education), 1927, no. 3, pp. 65-66.

Paskhalov, Vyach.: *A.D. Kastal'sky kak etnograf i reformator russkogo narodnogo stilya v muzïke* (A.D. Kastal'sky as ethnographer and reformer of the Russian folk style in music). *Muzïkal'noye obrazovaniye* (Musical Education), 1927, no. 3, pp. 57-62. *Ibid.*, (in extended form) entitled: *Vstrechi i vospominaniya* (Encounters and reminiscences), in symposium: *A.D. Kastal'sky. Stat'i. Vospominaniya. Materialï* (Articles. Reminiscences. Materials), pp. 19-26.

Trudï Aleksandra Dmitriyevicha Kastal'skogo (Works of Alexander Dmitriyevich Kastal'sky). *Muzïka i revolyutsiya* (Music and Revolution), 1927, no. 1, pp. 10-12. (Contains short list of compositions.)

Vecher Moskovskoy gosudarstvennoy konservatorii, posvyashchonnïy pamyati A.D. Kastal'skogo (An evening at the Moscow State Conservatoire dedicated to the memory of A.D. Kastal'sky). *Muzïkal'noye obrazovaniye* (Musical Education), 1927, no. 3, pp. 78-81.

1928

Belyaev, V.M.: *Igor Stravinsky's 'Les Noces': an Outline.* Trans. S.W. Pring. London, Oxford University Press, 1928, p. 37. (Compared to Kastalsky in treatment of folk material.)

1929

Belaiev, V.: *Kastalsky and his Russian Polyphony.* (Dated: Moscow, 10-24 January 1928.) *Music & Letters*, vol. 10, October 1929, pp. 378-390. Trans. by S.W. Pring. (Mainly a resumé of Kastalsky *'Osobennosti...'* (Peculiarities...).)

1930

Asaf'yev, B.: *Russkaya muzïka ot nachala XIX stoletiya* (Russian music from the beginning of the nineteenth century). Moscow, Leningrad, 1930. *Ibid.*, entitled: *Russkaya muzïka. XIX i nachalo XX veka* (Russian music of the nineteenth and early twentieth centuries). Ed. Ye. Orlova. Leningrad, 1968; second edition, Leningrad, 1979. *Ibid.*, in English: *Russian Music. From the Beginning of the Nineteenth Century.* Transl. A. Swan. Ann Arbor, Michigan, 1953. *Ibid.*, in German: *Die Musik in Russland (Vom 1800 bis zur Oktoberrevolution 1917).* Hrsg. und übs. von E. Kuhn, Berlin, 1998. An excerpt from this book devoted to Kastal'sky's choral style (*'Sil'naya khorovaya kul'tura...* (A powerful choral culture...')) entitled *Khorovoye tvorchestvo A.D. Kastal'skogo* (The choral compositions of A.D. Kastal'sky) appears in symposium: *A.D. Kastal'sky. Stat'i. Vospominaniya. Materialï* (Articles. Reminiscences. Materials), pp. 15-17.

Koval', M.V.: *Lenin v muzïke* (Lenin in music). *Proletarsky muzïkant* (Proletarian musician), 1930, no. 1, pp. 9-13.

1937

Aleksandrovsky, A.: *Pamyati A.D. Kastal'skogo. (K 10-letiyu so dnya smerti)* (In memory of A.D. Kastal'sky. (For the tenth anniversary of his death)). *SovM*, 1937, no. 3, pp. 93-94.

1943

Asaf'yev, B.: *Cherez proshloye k budushchemu. Iz ustnïkh predaniy i lichnïkh moikh vstrech-besed* (Through the past to the future. From oral traditions and my personal conversational encounters). *Sovetskaya muzïka* (Soviet music), symposium 1, Moscow, 1943, pp. 19-23. (Statements about Kastal'sky.)

1947

Bryusova, N.: *Massovaya muzïkal'no-prosvetitel'naya rabota v pervïye godï posle Oktyabrya. (Iz vospominaniy)* (Mass music-educational work in the first years after October. (From reminiscences)). *SovM*, 1947, no. 6, pp. 46-55.

1948

Belayev, V.M.: *A.D. Kastal'sky i yego rabota 'Osnovï narodnogo mnogogolosiya'* (A.D. Kastal'sky and his work 'The fundamentals of folk polyphony'). [Preface to Kastal'sky's work 'The fundamentals of folk polyphony']. Moscow, Leningrad, 1948, pp. 3-25.

Zhitomirsky, D.: *Iz proshlogo sovetskoy muzïki* (From the past of Soviet music). *Yezhegodnik Instituta istorii iskusstv* (Yearbook of the Institute for the History of the Arts), vol. II. Moscow, 1948, pp. 331-356. (Concerns Kastal'sky's work 'The fundamentals of Russian folk polyphony'.)

1949

T. Popova: *A.M. Listopadov. SovM*, 1949, no. 6, pp. 56-59. (Kastal'sky's use of recordings of folk polyphony by Listopadov, with fragments of a letter of 23 January 1913 from Kastal'sky, pp. 58-59; fragments of the letter are reproduced in *Vospominaniya o Rakhmaninove* (Reminiscences about Rakhmaninov), vol. 1, Moscow, 1967, pp. 501-503.)

Sergeyev, A.: *Rozhdeniye novogo* (The birth of the new). *SovM*, 1949, no. 11, pp. 48-52. (Reminiscences of his teacher.)

Zhitomirsky, D.: *Pesennoye i khorovoye tvorchestvo sovetskikh kompozitorov* (The songs and choral works of Soviet composers). First issue (1920s). Moscow, 1949, pp. 14-20. (Chapter about Kastal'sky.)

1951

Asaf'yev, B.: *O Kastal'skom.* [*'Alexander Dmitriyevich Kastal'sky – vïdayushchiysya master khorovogo pis'ma...'*] (About Kastal'sky. [Alexander Dmitriyevich Kastal'sky is an outstanding master of writing for choir]). *SovM*, 1951, no. 12, p. 35. (Article written in 1948 for a radio broadcast devoted to Kastal'sky's memory.)

Zhitomirsky, D.: *Idei A.D. Kastal'skogo* (The ideas of A.D. Kastal'sky). *SovM*, 1951, no. 1. *Ibid.*, extended and corrected, entitled *Idei i iskaniya A.D. Kastal'skogo* (The ideas and quests of A.D. Kastal'sky), in symposium: *A.D. Kastal'sky. Stat'i. Vospominaniya. Materialï* (Articles. Reminiscences. Materials), pp. 49-84.

1953

Lokshin, D.L.: *Vïdayushchiyesya russkiye khorï i ikh dirizhorï. (Kratkiye ocherki)* (Outstanding Russian choirs and their conductors. (Brief essays)). Moscow, 1953. Second edition published as *Zamechatel'nïye russkiye khorï i ikh dirizhorï. (Kratkiye ocherki).* (Remarkable Russian choirs and their conductors. (Brief essays)). Moscow, 1963, pp. 32-45. (About the history of the Moscow Synodal Choir.)

1954

M.D. C[alvocoressi]: *Kastalsky. Grove's Dictionary of Music and Musicians*, fifth edition, London, 1954, vol. 4, p. 708.

Keldïsh, Yu.: *Istoriya russkoy muzïki* (History of Russian music). Part 3, Moscow, 1954, pp. 473-480.

1955

Asaf'yev, B.: *Gogol' v muzïke* (Gogol' in music). Academician B.V. Asaf'yev: *Izbrannïye trudï* (Selected works), vol. 4, Moscow, 1955, pp. 154-156. (Two choruses by Kastal'sky on texts by Gogol' from the cycle *Pesni k Rodine* (Songs for the Motherland).)

Rakhmaninov, S.V.: *Pis'ma* (Letters). Comp. Z.A. Apetyan. Moscow, 1955, pp. 11, 389, 394, 398. *Ibid.*, second edition, vol. 2, Moscow, 1980, pp. 14-16, 18, 22-23. (Rakhmaninov's letters to Kastal'sky in relation to the writing of the Liturgy.)

1956

Arbatsky, Yu.: *Etyudï po istorii russkoy muzïki* (Studies in the history of Russian music). New York, 1956, chapter 3, p. 141.

Asaf'yev, B.V.: *O Kastal'skom* (About Kastal'sky). [*'17 dekabrya 1926 goda umer v Moskve...'* (On 17 December 1926 there died in Moscow...']. *SovM*, 1956, no. 12, pp. 37-39. *Ibid.*, in symposium: *A.D. Kastal'sky. Stat'i. Vospominaniya. Materialï* (Articles. Reminiscences. Materials), pp. 9-12. *Ibid.*, in symposium: B. Asaf'yev: *O khorovom iskusstve* (On choral art), pp. 87-90.

Istoriya russkoy sovetskoy muzïki (History of Soviet Russian music). Ed. A.D. Alekseyev and V.A. Vasina-Grossman. Vol. 1, Moscow, 1956, pp. 78ff.

1957

Asaf'yev, B.: *Ne zaklyucheniye, a prolog* (Not a conclusion – rather, a prologue) Academician B.V. Asaf'yev: *Izbrannïye trudï* (selected works), vol. 5, pp. 95-102. (Kastal'sky's 'Requiem for Fallen Brothers'.)

Gardner, Iogann von: *K 100-letiyu rozhdeniya A.D. Kastal'skogo* (For the centenary of A.D. Kastal'sky's birth). *Zhar-Ptitsa* (Firebird), San Francisco, March, 1957, pp. 17-20.

Lokshin, D.: *Khorovoye peniye v russkoy shkole* (Choral singing in the Russian school). Moscow, 1957. (Kastal'sky's views on the musical upbringing and training of children.)

Novozhilov, N.: *Pamyati A.D. Kastal'skogo* (In memory of A.D. Kastal'sky). *Pravoslavnaya mïsl'* (Orthodox Thought) [Czech Orthodox journal], no. 1, January-March, 1957.

Vospominaniya o Rakhmaninove (Reminiscences about Rakhmaninov). Comp. Z.A. Apetyan. Vol. 1, Moscow, 1957, p. 389; vol. 2, Moscow, 1957, p. 262. *Ibid.*, second edition, Moscow, 1961, vol. 1, pp. 405-406. *Ibid.*, third edition, Moscow, 1967, vol. 1, pp. 405-406. (Kastal'sky's 'Scenes of peasant merrymaking'.)

1958

Petrova, K.A.: *Kastalski. Die Musik in Geschichte und Gegenwart.* Kassel, 1958, vol. 7, cols. 732-734.

Swan, Alfred J.: *Russian liturgical music and its relation to twentieth-century ideals. Music & Letters*, vol. 39, July 1957, pp. 265-274.

1960

A.D. Kastal'sky. Stat'i. Vospominaniya. Materialï (A.D. Kastal'sky. Articles. Reminiscences. Materials). Comp., ed. D.V. Zhitomirsky. Moscow, 1960.
Materials first published in this symposium:

Asaf'yev, B.V.: *Kharakternïye osobennosti iskusstva Kastal'skogo* [*'Tvorchestvo Kastal'skogo, kak i kazhdogo bol'shogo mastera...'*] (Characteristic features of Kastal'sky's art ['The creative work of Kastal'sky, like that of every great master...']), pp. 13-15. *Ibid.*, entitled [*Kharakternïye osobennosti iskusstva Kastal'skogo* (Characteristic features of Kastal'sky's art)], in symposium: B.V. Asaf'yev: *O khorovom iskusstve* (On choral art), pp. 94-96.

Bortnikova, Ye.: *Fond A.D. Kastal'skogo v Gosudarstvennom tsentral'nom muzeye muzïkal'noy kul'turï imeni M. I. Glinki* (The archive of A.D. Kastal'sky in the State Central Museum of Musical Culture named after M.I. Glinka), pp. 279-280.

Kastal'skaya, N.: *Nemnogoye ob ottse* (A little about my father), pp. 99-114.

Kastal'sky, A.A.: *Tri zametki* (Three notes), pp. 115-119.

Lokshin, D.: *Muzïkal'no-pedagogicheskiye vzglyadï A.D. Kastal'skogo* (A.D. Kastal'sky's views about music education), pp. 85-98.

Lyubimov, A.: *Iz proshlogo* (From the past), pp. 124-129.

Preobrazhensky, A.: *A.D. Kastal'sky (materialï k biografii)* (A.D. Kastal'sky (materials for a biography)), pp. 27-48.

Smïslov, I.: *V rabochem klube* (At a workers' club), pp. 122-123.

1961

Popova, T., Tret'yakova, L.: *A.D. Kastal'sky i yego kniga 'Osobennosti narodno-russkoy muzïkal'noy sistemï'* (A.D. Kastal'sky and his book 'Features of the Russian folk musical system'). (Preface to the second edition of the book, Moscow, 1961, pp. 3-17.)

Sokhor, A.: *Sbornik o Kastal'skom* (Symposium about Kastal'sky). *SovM*, 1961, no. 7, pp. 140-141. (Review of symposium: *A.D. Kastal'sky. Stat'i. Vospominaniya. Materialï* (Articles. Reminiscences. Materials). Moscow, 1960.)

1965

Pariysky, L.N.: *Pamyati tserkovnogo kompozitora A.D. Kastal'skogo* (In memory of the church composer A.D. Kastal'sky). *Messager de l'Exarchat du Patriarche Russe en Europe Occidentale*, 1965, January-March, no. 49; completed in April-June, no. 50.

Aleksandrov, P.: *A.D. Kastal'sky. K stoletiyu so dnya rozhdeniya* (A.D. Kastal'sky. For the centenary of his birth). *Novoye russkoye slovo* (New Russian Word), 1965, 7 November.

1966

Moskovskaya konservatoriya (Moscow Conservatoire). 1866-1966. Ed. L.S. Ginzburg. Moscow, 1966, pp. 522-540. (About Kastal'sky in relation to the history of the Choir Faculty.)

1967

Swan, Alfred J.: *Notes on the Old Liturgical chant of the Russian church and the Russian folk song. Orthodox Life* (Jordanville, Holy Trinity monastery), July-August, 1967, vol. 4, no. 106, pp. 20-36. (Includes notes on Ossorguine's and Kastal'sky's harmonizations of *znamennïy* chant.)

1968

Beckwith, R.S. A.D. Kastal'skii (1856–1926) and the quest for a native Russian choral style. Cornell University, PhD., 1969.

1969

Malïy, Dm.: *U istokov muzïkal'noy leniniani* (At the sources of musical Leniniana). *SovM*, 1969, no.5, pp. 4-7.
Matskevich, I.S.: *A.D. Kastal'sky*. Moscow, 1969.

1970

Il'in,V.: *Pervïye khorï o Lenine* (The first choruses about Lenin). *SovM*, 1970, no. 3, pp. 9-12.
Istoriya muzïki narodov SSSR (History of the music of the peoples of the USSR). 1917–1932. Vol. 1. Moscow, 1970.

1972

Stepanova, S.R.: *Muzïkal'naya zhizn' Moskvï v pervïye godï posle Oktyabrya* (The musical life of Moscow in the first years after October). Moscow, 1972.
Neapolitansky, N.: A.D. Kastalsky. *Journal of the Moscow Patriarchate* (both English-language and Russian-language editions), 1972, no. 1, pp. 75-78.

1973

Swan, Alfred J.: *Russian Music and its sources in chant and folk-song*. London, 1973. Contains section on Kastal'sky.

1974

Dmitriyevskaya, K.N.: *Aleksandr Dmitriyevich Kastal'sky. Russkaya sovetskaya khorovaya muzïka* (Soviet Russian choral music). Moscow, 1974, pp. 7-45.
Tsïpin, G.M.: *Kastal'sky, Aleksandr Dmitriyevich. Muzïkal'naya entsiklopediya*, vol. 2, Moscow 1974, cols. 738-739.

1977

Rakhmanova, M.: *Aleksandr Kastal'sky i perspektivï yego idey* (Alexander Kastal'sky and the prospects for his ideas). *SovM*, 1977, no. 6, pp. 101-106.

1980

Asaf'yev, B.V.: [About Kastal'sky's choral style] [*'Smert' Kastal'skogo proshla sovsem nezamechennoy...'* ('Kastal'sky's death passed completely unnoticed...')], in symposium: B. Asaf'yev: *O khorovom iskusstve* (On choral art), pp. 90-94.

Barsova, Inna: *Kastal'sky, Alexandr Dmitriyevich. New Grove Dictionary of Music and Musicians*, London, 1980, vol. 9, pp. 822-823.

Brill, N.P.: *History of Russian Church Music, 988-1917*. Bloomington, Illinois. 1980.

Zatsepina, T.M.: *Traditsii natsional'noy pevcheskoy kul'turï v russkoy khorovoy muzïke (konets XIX – nachalo XX v.)* (The traditions of national church-music culture in Russian choral music (late 19th and early 20th centuries)). Dissertation, Leningrad Conservatoire, 1980.

1981

Vasil'yev, V.A.: *Dirizhorsko-khorovoye obrazovaniye v Rossii kontsa XIX – nachala XX v.* (The education of choir conductors in Russia in the late 19th and early 20th centuries). Dissertation, Leningrad, 1981.

1982

Gardner, I. A.: *Bogosluzhebnoye peniye Russkoy Pravoslavnoy Tserkvi. Istoriya* (The worship music of the Russian Orthodox Church. History). Vol. 2, Jordanville, N.Y., 1982, pp. 489-502. *Ibid.*, second edition. Republished Moskovskaya Dukhovnaya Akademiya (Moscow Theological Academy), Sergiyev Posad, 1998, pp. 521-535.

1984

Demchenko, A.I.: *Sovetskaya istoriko-revolyutsionnaya muzïka* (Soviet historical-revolutionary music). Dissertation, Leningrad Conservatoire, 1986.

Morosan, Vladimir: *Choral Performance in Pre-Revolutionary Russia*. Ann Arbor, Michigan, 1984, 1986.

Zatsepina, T.M.: *Osobennosti khorovogo stilya A.D. Kastal'skogo* (Characteristics of A.D. Kastal'sky's choral style). All-Russian festival *Nevskiye khorovïye assamblei* (Neva choral assemblies). *Materialï nauchno-prakticheskoy konferentsii 'Proshloye i nastoyashcheye russkoy khorovoy kul'turï'* (Materials of the scholarly-practical conference 'The past and present of Russian choral culture'). Leningrad, 18-24 May 1981. Moscow, 1984, pp. 154-155.

1985

Il'in, V.: *Ocherki istorii russkoy khorovoy kul'turï vtoroy polovinï XVII – nachala XX veka* (Essays in the history of Russian choral culture from the second half of the seventeenth to the twentieth century). Moscow, 1985.

1987

Zarubezhnaya pressa ob iskusstve Sinodal'nogo khora (k gastrol'noy poyezdke 1911 goda) (The foreign press on the art of the Synodal Choir (about the 1911 concert tour)), in *Pamyati N.M. Danilina. Pis'ma. Vospominaniya. Dokumentï* (In memory of N.M. Danilin. Letters, Reminiscences. Documents). Comp. A.A. Naumov. Moscow, 1987, pp. 24-49.

1989

Goldshtein, M.: *Kastal'sky [Kastálsky], Aleksandr Dmitriyevich.* In ed. Allan Ho and Dmitry Feofanov: *Bibliographical Dictionary of Russian/Soviet Composers.* Greenwood Press, 1989, p. 245.

1992

Gulyanitskaya, N.S.: *A.D. Kastal'sky: osvobozhdeniye tserkovnoy muzïki ot pravil i dogm obshcheyevropeyskoy sistemï* (A.D. Kastal'sky: setting church music free from the rules and dogmas of the common-European system). In her *Russkoye 'garmonicheskoye peniye'* (Russian 'harmonic singing'). Moscow, 1995, pp. 87-100.

Smirnov, A.P.: *Pamyati A.D. Kastal'skogo* (In memory of A.D. Kastal'sky). In symposium: *Naslediye. Muzïkal'nïye sobraniya 1992* (Heritage. Musical assemblies 1992). Moscow, 1992, pp. 69-73. *Ibid.*, in *RUSAM*, vol. 1, pp. 313-316.

1994

Traditsionnïye zhanrï pravoslavnogo pevcheskogo iskusstva v tvorchestve russkikh kompozitorov ot Glinki do Rakhmaninova. 1825-1917. Notografiya (Traditional genres of the Orthodox choral art in the work of Russian composers from Glinka to Rakhmaninov. 1825-1917. List of compositions). Ed. Ye.M. Levashov. Moscow, 1994. (List of Kastal'sky's sacred works, pp. 32-33.)

1995

Istoriya sovremennoy otechestvennoy muzïki (History of modern [Russian] music). Vol. 1, 1917-1941. Ed. M.Ye. Tarakanov. Moscow, 1995, pp. 75-76, 268-270.

1996

Plotnikova, N.Yu.: *Mnogogolosnïye formï obrabotki drevnikh rospevov v russkoy dukhovnoy muzïke XIX – nachala XX veka* (Polyphonic forms of treating ancient chants in Russian sacred music of the nineteenth and early twentieth centuries). Dissertation, Moscow Conservatoire, 1996, pp. 175-205.

Zvereva, S.G.: *Istoriya sozdaniya panikhidï Kastal'skogo 'Vechnaya pamyat' geroyam' (po arkhivnïm materialam)* (History of the creation of Kastal'sky's Memorial Service 'Eternal Memory to the Heroes' (using archival materials). *Nauka o kul'ture: itogi i perspektivï. Nauchno-informatsionnïy sbornik* (Scholarship about culture: results and prospects. Scholarly-information symposium). Issue no. 6. Moscow, 1996, pp. 74-76.

1997

Zvereva, S.G.: *K voprosu o 'neorusskom' stile v russkoy muzïke rubezha XIX-XX vekov* (The question of a 'new-Russian' style in Russian music of the turn of the nineteenth and twentieth centuries). *Vestnik Rossiyskogo gumanitarnogo nauchnogo fonda* (Herald of the Russian Humanities Research Fund). Moscow, 1997, no. 1, pp. 158-165.

Zvereva, S.G.: *A.D. Kastal'sky*, in *Istoriya russkoy muzïki v 10-ti tomakh* (History of Russian music in ten volumes), vol. 10a. Moscow, 1997, pp. 274-306.

1998

Russkaya dukhovnaya muzïka v dokumentakh i materialakh (Russian sacred music in documents and materials; *RUSAM*). Vol. 1: *Sinodal'nïy khor i uchilishche tserkovnogo peniya. Vospominaniya. Dnevniki. Pis'ma.* (The Synodal Choir and School of Church Music. Reminiscences. Diaries. Letters). Comp., ed. S.G. Zvereva, A.A. Naumov, M.P. Rakhmanova. Moscow, 1998.
Material about Kastal'sky first published in this symposium:
Zvereva, S.G.: *Aleksandr Dmitriyevich Kastal'sky*, pp. 221-228. (Preface to the publication of writings and letters by Kastal'sky.)
Nikol'sky, A.V.: *A.D. Kastal'sky kak kompozitor i kak issledovatel' narodno-russkoy pesni* (A.D. Kastal'sky as composer and researcher into Russian folksong), pp. 317-322. (Speech at the event at GIMN to mark the memory of the deceased, 28 March 1927.)
Smolensky, S.V.: *Sinodal'nïy khor i uchilishche tserkovnogo peniya (iul' 1889-may 1901)* (The Synodal Choir and School of Church Music (July 1889 – May 1901)), pp. 42-149. (Numerous references to Kastal'sky).

Sergeyev, A.A.: *Kak ya stal muzïkantom* (How I became a musician), pp. 431-435. (Chapters from reminiscences.)

Smirnov, A.K.: *Iz vospominaniy* (From reminiscences) (1893-1902), pp. 338, 348-350.

Smirnov, A.P.: *Vospominaniya o Sinodal'nom uchilishche i khore* (Reminiscences of the Synodal School and Choir), pp. 470-531. (Frequent references to Kastal'sky.)

Sokol'sky, N.N.: *Pis'ma k zhene 1911 goda* (Letters of 1911 to his wife), pp. 361-364, 367. (Relates to the Synodal Choir's foreign tours.)

Shumsky, S.A.: *Materialï dlya razrabotki temï 'Moskovskoye Sinodal'noye uchilishche i vozrozhdeniye natsional'noy dukhovnoy muzïki'* (Materials for developing the subject of the 'Moscow Synodal School and the revival of national sacred music'), pp. 615-629. (The Synodal Choir's interpretations of compositions by Kastal'sky.)

1999

Zvereva, S.G.: *Kastal'sky i Asaf'yev* (Kastal'sky and Asaf'yev), in *Keldïshevskiy sbornik* (Keldïsh Symposium). Moscow, 1999, pp. 221-231.

Zvereva, S.G.: *'Iskusstvo opredelyayetsya otnosheniyem k religii...'* ('Art is defined by its relationship to religion...'), in *Pyotr Suvchinsky i yego vremya* (Pyotr Suvchinsky and his time). Moscow, 1999, pp. 169-177. (About the history of a letter from Kastal'sky to Suvchinsky.)

Zvereva, S.G.: *Aleksandr Kastal'sky: idei, tvorchestvo, sud'ba* (Aleksandr Kastal'sky: ideas, creative work, fate). Moscow, 1999.

Knigi (Books). [Review of S.G. Zvereva: *Aleksandr Kastal'sky* (Moscow 1999)]. *Muzïkal'noye obozreniye* (Musical review), 1999, no. 12, p. 19.

2000

Chernodubrovskaya, Ye.: *Muzïka Aleksandra Kastal'skogo: mezhdu proshlïm i budushchim* (The music of Aleksandr Kastal'sky: between the past and the future). *Russkaya mïsl'*, 2000, no. 4307, p. 19. (Concerns the book by S.G. Zvereva: *Aleksandr Kastal'sky*, Moscow, 1999.)

Edmunds, Neil: Aleksandr Kastalsky – a composer transformed. In his *The Soviet Proletarian Music Movement*. Bern, 2000, pp. 164-179.

Fortounatto, M.: *Liturgical work in Russia. Cathedral Newsletter* [of the Russian Orthodox Cathedral of the Dormition of the Mother of God and All Saints, London], February, 2000, no. 338, pp. 17-19. (Concerns the publication of sacred choral pieces by Kastal'sky.)

Zvereva, S.G.: *Dukhovnaya konservatoriya (Ob opïte sozdaniya vïsshego tserkovno-pevcheskogo uchilishcha)* ('A conservatoire for sacred music' (About the attempt to establish a higher church-music school)). *Moskovskaya regentsko-pevcheskaya seminariya. 1998-1999. Sbornik statey, vospominaniy, arkhivnïkh dokumentov* (Moscow seminary for church choirmasters and church singers. 1998-1999. A collection of articles, reminiscences, archival documents). Moscow, 2000, pp. 35-61.

Zvereva, S.G.: *Muzïkal'nïy monument Pervoy mirovoy voyne. ('Bratskoye pominoveniye' A.D. Kastal'skogo)* (A musical monument to the First World War. (A.D. Kastal'sky's 'Requiem for Fallen Brothers'). *Rossiya-Germaniya. Kul'turnïye svyazi, iskusstvo, literatura v pervoy polovine XX veka* (Russia-Germany. Cultural links, art, literature in the first half of the twentieth century). Moscow, 2000, pp. 424-439.

Zvereva, S.G.: *Neizvestnïy Asaf'yev* (The unknown Asaf'yev). *Pamyatniki kul'turï. Novïye otkrïtiya. Yezhegodnik za 1998 god* (Monuments of culture. New discoveries. Yearbook for 1998). Moscow, 2000, pp. 187-198.

Zvereva, S.G.: *Zhanr istoriko-etnograficheskogo deystva v muzïke A.D. Kastal'skogo* (The genre of the historical-ethnographic play in the music of A.D. Kastal'sky), in symposium: *Gimnologiya* (Hymnology), issue no. 1, book 2. *Uchonïye zapiski Nauchnogo tsentra russkoy tserkovnoy muzïki im. Protoiyereya Dimitriya Razumovskogo* (Scholarly transactions of the Research Centre for Russian Church Music named after Archpriest Dimitry Razumovsky). Moscow, 2000, pp. 572-578.

2001

Zvereva, S.: *Kastal'sky, Aleksandr Dmitriyevich. New Grove Dictionary of Music and Musicians,* second edition., London, 2001, vol. 13, p. 403.

Zvereva, S.: *Alexander Kastal'sky: 'A Russian Requiem'. American Choral Journal*, vol. 42, December, 2001, pp. 27-36.

2002

Sponsel, Katharina: *Altes Erbe in neuen Formen – Das kirchenmusikalische Werk Aleksandr Kastal'skijs.* Berlin, Verlag Ernst Kuhn, 2002.

Russkaya dukhovnaya muzïka v dokumentakh i materialakh (Russian sacred music in documents and materials; *RUSAM*). Vol. 2, book 1: *Sinodal'nïy khor i uchilishche tserkovnogo peniya. Issledovaniya. Dokumentï. Periodika* (The Synodal Choir and School of Church Music. Researches. Documents. Periodicals)). Comp., ed.: S.G. Zvereva, A.A. Naumov, M.P. Rakhmanova. Moscow, 2002. (Research into the Synodal Choir and School of Church Music; archival documents; materials connected with the Synodal Choir's contribution to worship.)

Russkaya dukhovnaya muzïka v dokumentakh i materialakh (Russian sacred music in documents and materials; *RUSAM*). Vol. 3: *Tserkovnoye peniye poreformennoy Rossii v osmïslenii sovremennikov* (Church music in reform-era Russia as interpreted by contemporaries). Comp., ed.: S.G. Zvereva, A.A. xNaumov, M.P. Rakhmanova. Moscow, 2002.

Russkaya dukhovnaya muzïka v dokumentakh i materialakh (Russian sacred music in documents and materials; *RUSAM*). Vol. 4: Stepan Vasil'yevich

Smolensky: *Vospominaniya* (Reminiscences). Comp., ed.: N.I. Kabanova; ed.: M.P. Rakhmanova. Moscow, 2002.

Zvereva, S.: *Tserkovno-pevcheskiye traditsii Moskovskogo Kremlya: proshloye v nastoyashchem* (The church-music tradition of the Moscow Kremlin: the past in the present). *Trudï Moskovskoy Regentsko-pevcheskoy seminarii 2000-2001. Sbornik statey, vospominaniy, arkhivnïkh dokumentov* (Proceedings of the Moscow Seminary for Church Choirmasters and Singers, 2000-2001. Collection of articles, reminiscences and archival documents). Moscow, 2002, pp. 58-65.

The following volume is forthcoming:

Russkaya dukhovnaya muzïka v dokumentakh i materialakh (Russian sacred music in documents and materials; *RUSAM*). Vol. 2, book 2: *Sinodal'nïy khor i uchilishche tserkovnogo peniya. Issledovaniya. Dokumentï. Periodika* (The Synodal Choir and School of Church Music. Researches. Documents. Periodicals)). Comp., ed.: S.G. Zvereva, A.A. Naumov, M.P. Rakhmanova. Moscow, [2003]. (Concert programmes of the Synodal Choir; reviews and articles; syllabuses of courses at the Synodal School.)

Glossary of Terms

Archive of music manuscripts of the Synodal School (*Drevlekhranilishche pevcheskikh rukopisey Sinodal'nogo uchilishcha*) – the most important collection in the world of musical monuments of the Russian Orthodox Church, both monodic and homophonic. The collection was assembled at the Synodal School of Church Music from 1895 (its founder was S.V. Smolensky) until 1914. After the revolution, in 1922, it was transferred to the State History Museum, where it is preserved under the title 'the Synodal music collection' (*Sinodal'noye pevcheskoye sobraniye*); it comprises 1446 items.

Balalayka: a Russian plucked string instrument with a wooden triangular (or sometimes oval or hemispherical) shell, a long, slender sounding-board and three strings.

Bulgarian chant (*Bolgarskiy rospev*): one of the regional monodic chants of the Russian Orthodox Church, related to *znamenniy* chant. It emerged in church use in the mid-seventeenth century; it was written using both sign (*znamennaya* notation) and stave square notation. It entered the collection of chants in official use in the Synodal Church (see Synodal *Obikhod*) and has been preserved in that church's practice up to the present time mainly as the basis for polyphonic treatments. There are two kinds of Bulgarian chant: great chant (*bol'shoy rospev*), for feast days, and little chant (*maliy rospev*), for everyday use. Bulgarian chant conforms to the system of eight tones (*osmoglasiye*); it is characterized by symmetry of rhythm and repetitions of melodic lines.

Court chant (*Pridvorniy rospev/napev*): the collection of worship melodies formed in the practice of the imperial court churches up to the end of the eighteenth century, with the selection favouring shortened monophonic chants predominantly of south Russian origin.

Court Kapella (*Imperatorskaya pridvornaya pevcheskaya Kapella*): also known as the Imperial Court Singing Choir or the Imperial Court Chapel Choir: the body based in St Petersburg which sang wherever the court was worshipping; it also on occasion participated in concerts. It carried this official title from 1763 until 1917, though its origins lay in the sovereign's singing clerks (*gosudarevï pevchiye d'yaki*), founded in the fifteenth century, who moved to the new capital soon after its foundation in 1703. The choir's director acquired a right of censorship over the publication of music intended for use in the worship of the Orthodox Church throughout Russia; the latter power was relaxed in the early 1880s. During the 1830s classes to train child singers in music were established at the Kapella. In the 1880s, with the appointment of two famous Russian composers Balakirev and Rimsky-Korsakov to head the Kapella, the Music Classes (later known as Church Choirmasters' Classes) became one of the best music schools in Russia. The Kapella exists at present as the State Academic Kapella named after M.I. Glinka.

Chudov Choir: the choir of the Moscow Metropolitan, established in the mid-eighteenth century and named after the Chudov monastery in the Kremlin, where the residence of the Moscow primates was then. Right up to the second half of the nineteenth century, the Chudov Choir was considered the best in Moscow.

Clerk: see D'*yak*.

Demestvo, demestvenniy chant (*demestvenniy rospev*): a stylistic variety of Russian church chant included among the most widely spread and used at the most solemn and festive services. *Demestvenniy* chant emerged in the mid-fifteenth century and was initially notated in *znamennaya* notation. In the second half of the sixteenth century *demestvennaya* notation was devised. *Demestvenniy* chant does not conform to *osmoglasiye* and has an independent melodic vocabulary at its disposal. Between the eighteenth and twentieth centuries it became widespread among Old Believers; it exists in the repertoire of the Synodal Church in harmonized form.

Dogmatikon (*dogmatik*): hymn in honour of the Mother of God, revealing the doctrine of the Lord's incarnation.

Domra: an ancient Russian plucked string instrument with a large hemispherical or oval shell and a long sounding-board. It went out of folk use by the nineteenth century, but was reconstructed at the end of that century and used in professional orchestras of Russian folk instruments.

D'yachek: see D'*yak*.

D'yak (clerk): shortened form of the word *d'yakon* (deacon). This abbreviated form emphasized the distinction between a deacon, who was authorized to carry out priestly functions, and a simple *d'yak*, who served as reader and singer. The term *d'yachek* may be interpreted in the same way – it is a diminutive form produced from *d'yakon*. Since clerks of the lowest rank had a variety of duties in a bishop's office and were obliged to be literate, the name *d'yak* was combined with the concept of an office-worker or official. As a result of this, in the Middle Ages *d'yak* became a term applied not only to a junior participant in worship but also to an official of a certain status (for instance, a clerk of the Boyars' Council (*dumnïy d'yak*). A similar situation may be observed in the western church as well: in France, for instance, the word *clerc* (that is, clerk) served to denote a scribe or office-worker.

Fita: 1) an extended melismatic turn of phrase introduced into Russian medieval monody with the aim of embellishing it; 2) a symbol found in Russian neumatic notation.

Glas, pl. *Glasï* (tone): the fundamental modal and melodic structural unit of *osmoglasiye*. Analogies may be found in west European (*modus*), Armenian and other national varieties of medieval monody. There are several interpretations of *glas*: 1) *glas* as a modal scale of defined structure with prevailing and final tones; 2) *glas* as the totality of *popevki*.

Greek chant (*Grecheskiy rospev*): a regional variety of monodic chant, of Greek origin, used in the Russian Orthodox Church. It was used from the mid-seventeenth century in *znamennaya* and stave notations. Greek chant entered the collection of chants of the Synodal Church (cf. Synodal *Obikhod*) and has been used there in harmonized form until the present. Greek chant conforms to the system of *osmoglasiye*; characteristic of it are laconic melody, symmetrical rhythm, repetition of melodic lines and a modal tendency.

Gudok: the most ancient Russian bowed instrument with a pear-shaped wooden form, a long sounding-board and three strings. A bow, shaped like a bow, is drawn across the strings, with the instrument held on the knees.

Gusli: the most ancient Russian plucked string instrument of the harp type.

Heirmos (*irmos*) a genre in Byzantine and Russian hymn-writing. In the early Christian church an heirmos was a stanza combining an Old Testament song with New Testament hymns. From the eighth century to the present an heirmos is the first hymn in each of the nine songs of the kanon. The heirmos conforms to the system of *osmoglasiye*; the heirmos is linked in subject matter to the Old Testament.

Holy Synod (*recte* 'Most Holy Synod' – *Svyateyshiy Sinod*): The Most Holy Synod was the supreme state institution responsible for the affairs of the Russian Orthodox Church, founded in 1721 from the former Collegium (Ministry) for Religious Matters. The Synod occupied itself with all matters concerning the Church, from the interpretation of doctrine and fighting heresy to any questions of management, including the transfer of clergy and church employees, etc. The Synod was headed by a senior official appointed by the tsar and known as the *Ober-Prokuror*. In 1917 the post was renamed Minister for Religious Affairs.

'Hook' notation (*kryukovaya notatsiya, kryuki, znamyona*): see *znamennaya notatsiya*.

Ikos: see Kontakion.

Imperial Court Singing Choir: see Court Kapella.

Irmos: see Heirmos.

Itinerants (*Peredvizhniki*): group of Russian artists who in 1870 formed the Association for Travelling Exhibitions (*Tovarishchestvo peredvizhnïkh vïstavok*) in order to show and popularize Russian art widely. Breaking with academicism, the Itinerants proclaimed new forms of artistic language for that time, portraying real life with a maximum of verisimilitude and subtle psychology. The group included such famous artists as Kramskoy, Repin, Surikov, Polenov, Levitan and Shishkin.

Kanon: a genre in Byzantine and Russian church music. It represents a cycle of 9 hymns (sometimes 4, 3 or 2): the first stanza of every hymn is the heirmos, while the subsequent ones are troparia. In the Russian church only the heirmos of the kanon is sung, with the troparia being read. The kanon conforms to the system of *osmoglasiye*.

Kanonarkh: a singer or reader who announces in chant the tone (*glas*) and the opening text of a hymn before it is sung by the choir.

Kant: a species of homophonic song for domestic use whose content can be either secular or sacred (Psalms) which spread through Russia, the Ukraine and Belorussia in the seventeenth and eighteenth centuries. It is linked with the spread of syllabic poetry. The kant is typified by a three-part texture with parallel movement between the upper parts and a bass which provides a harmonic foundation.

Kapella: see Court Kapella.

Kathisma: a reading in church from the Book of Psalms.

Kievan chant (*Kiyevskiy rospev*): a regional variant of the monodic chant of the Russian Orthodox Church. It was disseminated in that church after the union of the Ukraine with Russia in 1653. Examples of Kievan chant entered the Synodal *Obikhod*, and served as the basis for polyphonic elaboration by composers. Kievan chant conforms to the system of *osmoglasiye*. Unlike the *znamenniy* chant to which it is related, in Kievan chant one often encounters repetitions of individual words and phrases from the text.

Kliros: 1) church choir; 2) the place in the church building where the choir stands.

Kontakion (*kondak*), pl. kontakia (*kondaki*): a genre in Byzantine and Russian hymn-writing. The basis of the kontakion lies in multi-stanza poems which include monologues and dialogues of their heroes. All the stanzas were united by a common metre, except for the first which was later given the name kontakion, while the subsequent ones were known as ikos. In present-day practice, for every event celebrated only the first stanza (kontakion) and one of the ikos have remained in use.

Litso, pl. *litsa*: a melodic turn of phrase in a tone (*glas*) in *znamenniy* chant, recorded by a short inscription (a 'secretly reserved' one) (unlike the *popevka* which are reflected in neumatic notation on the principle of 'for every sound a symbol').

Maliy (little) chant (*maliy rospev*): a short version of *znamenniy* chant, which appeared at the turn of the fifteenth and sixteenth centuries.

'Mighty Handful' (*moguchaya kuchka*): a creative partnership of Russian composers formed at the end of the 1850s and the beginning of the 1860s. The group is also known as the 'Balakirev circle', the 'New Russian Music School', and the 'Five'. Its members were Mily Balakirev (the head of the circle), Alexander Borodin, César Cui, Modest Musorgsky and Nikolay Rimsky-Korsakov. The ideas of the music critic Vladimir Stasov inspired the 'Mighty handful'. Their ambition was to create a national tendency in Russian music, and also to make it known.

Menaion (Mineya): a book for worship, containing the hymns for the yearly cycle (that is, for every day of the church year).

Monastery harmonization (*monastïr skaya garmonizatsiya*): a way of harmonizing monophonic medieval chants or later melodies (*napevi*) which arose spontaneously in monasteries of the Synodal Church. It was also applied in the sacred compositions of professional composers, e.g., Tchaikovsky and Rimsky-Korsakov. Monastery harmonization exists in several variants; the basic one involves the chant being used in the uppermost part; the second part sings in thirds with the first; the lowest (the fourth part) creates a harmonic foundation; the third part fills out the chords to form harmony in four parts.

Most Holy Synod: see Holy Synod.

Napev, pl. *napevï* (melody): monophonic church chants of late origin (eighteenth and nineteenth centuries) – for example, Serbian, 'Tikhvin', 'Simonov', 'for the ravaging of Moscow', etc., which arose in the practice of the Synodal Church. Unlike medieval chants, which conformed to the modal system and were composed in the medieval *Obikhod* scale, late melodies, emerging during the supremacy of homophonic harmony, are distinguished by a tonal tendency and exist predominantly in harmonized form.

Narkompros (stump-compound derived from *Narodnïy Komissariat prosveshcheniya*, 'People's Commissariat for Education'): an organ of the Bol'shevik government established in 1917 and fulfilling the functions of a Ministry of Education, into which it was converted in 1946.

Narodnik: someone with an interest in the customs and culture of the Russian peasants who tries to promote the betterment of the people's position and the preservation of their traditions. The term is applicable to writers, poets, artists and composers who poeticize the life of the people.

New Direction (*Novoye napravleniye*): a movement among composers of Russian sacred music at the end of the nineteenth century and the first two decades of the twentieth century for a renewal of musical language based on national traditions.

Ober-Prokuror: see Holy Synod.

Obikhod: 1) the whole complex of hymns for worship (both texts and melodies) used in the services of the Russian Orthodox Church; 2) the music book of the Russian Orthodox Church, containing the hymns of the All-Night Vigil and the Liturgy. See also Synodal *Obikhod*.

Octoechos (*Oktoikh*): a book for worship, containing the variable hymns using tones of the weekly cycle (see *osmoglasiye*), performed at Vespers and Matins.

Old Believers (*Staroobryadtsï, Staroobryadchestvo*): Orthodox Christians who could not accept the church reforms carried out in Russia in the second half of the seventeenth century. The Church Council of 1666-1667 condemned the adherents of the old rituals (Old Believers) as heretics and resolved to punish those who would not submit to the reforms. Until 1906 the Old Believers were a persecuted religious minority. In 1800 a section of the Old Believers transferred to the jurisdiction of the Synodal Church, forming the *Yedinoveriye* (Community of Faith) Church, which maintained the old traditions. The Old Believers are divided into a number of currents, persuasions and groups.

Osenini: the old Russian celebration on the occasion of bidding summer farewell and greeting autumn.

Osmoglasiye (literally *vos'miglasiye*: system of eight tones): the modal system used in Byzantine and Russian church hymn-writing, related to the Gregorian church modes. It is an entity made up of eight groups of hymns (texts and melodies) – tones (*glasi*). Hymns in one tone (*glas*) were sung over one week, after which they were replaced by hymns in the next tone in the sequence. The eight-week cycle of hymns from the first to the eighth tones formed the so-called pillar (*stolp*), which was repeated over the course of the entire church year.

Partesnoye mnogogolosiye: a style found in Russian, Ukrainian and Belorussian polyphonic choral music of the Baroque era (second half of the seventeenth century and the first half of the eighteenth century), based on the west European system of harmony and counterpoint.

***Podgolosok* polyphony** (*podgolosochnaya polifoniya*): a kind of polyphony characteristic of Russian, Ukrainian and Belorussian folk music and of professional compositions, including sacred ones, modelled on folklore. It belongs to the heterophonic type of polyphony. The musical fabric is formed from the fundamental voice and *podgoloski* (plural form) accompanying it, which are themselves variants of the basic melody. The supremacy of the linear principle determines the relatively free use of dissonances, notwithstanding the predominance of consonances.

Podoben: a model sticheron, to whose melody were set the texts of unnotated hymns from the Sticherarion with the equivalent text construction.

Popevka: a melodic turn of phrase typical of a particular tone in the medieval chants of the Russian Orthodox Church. In the Middle Ages a *popevka* was notated using an unchanging neumatic inscription peculiar to it alone, employing between three and seven symbols.

Proletkul't (stump-compound derived from *Proletarskaya kul'tura,* 'Proletarian culture'): a community cultural-educational organization (1917-1932) which had numerous branches throughout Russia which set itself the goal of educating the people and creating a new Proletarian culture. *Proletkul't* carried out a great amount of work to eliminate illiteracy, organizing people's universities, workers' clubs and studios (for drama, music, the fine arts and so on). It was marked by its large-scale character: hundreds and thousands of workers and peasants united around *Proletkul't*. With the hardening of party policy in 1925, it metamorphosed into an adjunct of the political system and a conduit of Party ideology.

***Putevoy* chant** (*putevoy rospev*): along with *znamenniy* chant and *demestvenniy* chant, one of the most widespread stylistic forms of Russian monophonic chants. It arose in the last quarter of the fifteenth century and was initially written down using *znamennaya* notation; by the 1580s an independent *putevaya* notation had been formed. It is distinguished by its very extended and triumphal character and abundance of intra-syllabic melodic decoration. Conforms to the system of *osmoglasiye*.

Radonitsa: the day for remembering the departed in the cemetery; occurs in the week which begins on the Sunday after Easter (Thomas' week).

***Razdel'norechiye* (*khomoniya*)**: consists in pronouncing additional vowels between consonants and after a final consonant while singing. When this device is used, the endings of verbs in the plural and the past tense acquire the suffix 'khomo' – for example, *sogreshikhomo*, *bezzakonovakhomo*; hence the origin of the name *khomoniya*. *Khomoniya* became widespread from the end of the fifteenth century. The Church Council of 1666-1667 condemned the practice and resolved to correct the texts and melodies in the worship books. This reform was also accepted by some Old Believers, though others have retained *razdel'norechiye* down to the present.

Rusalii: pagan folk spring games (dances, songs, masquerades and games) symbolizing the rising in spring and celebrating the renewal of life of the storm and rain spirits.

Sakellariy, or *klyuchar'* (sacristan): the priest in charge of a church's sacristy.

Samoglasen: a melodic model for hymns of the Octoechos. See also *podoben*.

Schism (*raskol*): the break-up of the single Orthodox Church into supporters and opponents of the reforms carried through by Patriarch Nikon between 1653 and 1656 with the aim of bringing Russian Orthodoxy closer to the eastern autocephalous churches. See also Old Believers.

Semik: an old Russian festival, linked with the cult of the dead and the spring agricultural rites. Took place on the seventh Thursday after Easter.

Serbian melody (*Serbskiy napev*): see *napev*.

Skomorokh: in the Russian Middle Ages, an itinerant actor who could also be a singer, an instrumentalist, a dancer, an acrobat, a magician, an animal trainer and a puppeteer. *Skomorokhi* were also employed at the courts of aristocrats.

Sopel' (*dudka*): the most ancient musical instrument of the eastern Slavs. A kind of longitudinal flute.

Stave square notation (*notolineynaya kvadratnaya notatsiya*): appeared in the worship-music books of the predominant Russian Orthodox Church in the second half of the seventeenth century and gradually supplanted staveless medieval notations. Inscriptions in this notation are square in shape and set out in the alto clef on a five-line stave; they are similar to west European notations of the sixteenth and seventeenth centuries. Books with monophonic chants laid out in stave square notation are in use in the Synodal Church up to the present day.

Sticheron (*stikhira*), pl. stichera (*stikhiri*): one of the basic genres of Byzantine and Russian church hymn-writing; a hymn comprising several lines. As a rule, stichera form cycles, which narrate the event being celebrated or tell the story of a saint. They conform to the system of *osmoglasiye*. Stichera are divided into several types depending on their place in the service, whether they are combined with other hymns, and their contents.

Stichera on '*Gospodi vozzvakh*' (Lord, I call): stichera performed at great Vespers after Psalm 114 ('Lord, I call').

Strict style of harmony: a manner of harmonizing ancient Russian church chants in the natural mode first used in the second half of the 1850s by Glinka and cultivated later by a number of church composers. Experiments of this kind in harmonizing monody were conducted under the banner 'ancient melody calls for ancient harmony' and proclaimed the rejection of the system of European tonality.

Strochnoye mnogogolosiye: an early form of Russian polyphony of heterophonic type which arose in the practice of the Russian Orthodox Church during the sixteenth century. Its flowering occurred in the second half of the seventeenth century; in the eighteenth century it was supplanted by *partesnoye mnogogolosiye*. A complete *strochnaya* score consists of four voices: *niz*, *put'*, *verkh* and *demestvo*, each of which performs a single-part chant. In the performance the voices cross over one another, giving rise to dissonant chords.

Supervisory Council (*Nablyudatel'nïy Sovet*) attached to the Moscow Synodal School of Church Music: established in 1886, in the course of the reforms of the Synodal School, to be an agency facilitating the development of the School and the Synodal Choir. The Council was made up of many eminent secular and church musicians as well as researchers into church music and church choirmasters. At the end of the nineteenth century the Council's functions were extended significantly: it had to carry out the censorship of sacred compositions, exercise authority over the activities of Moscow church choirs, encourage the development of research in the field of ancient church music, etc. The Council was abolished in 1918.

Svirel': the generic name for a group of Russian and Belorussian folk instruments of flute type.

Synod: see Holy Synod.

Synodal Church: the title of the Russian Orthodox Church after the abolition of the patriarchate and the establishment of the Most Holy Synod in 1721. The predominant Orthodox jurisdiction within the territory of Russia.

Synodal *Obikhod* (*Sinodal'nïy Obikhod*): the collection of medieval chants of the Russian Orthodox Church set out in its four fundamental music books (*Obikhod*, *Oktoikh*, *Irmologiy* and *Prazdniki*) and published in stave square notation by the Moscow Synodal Printing Works in 1772. This collection was created with the aim of preserving the inheritance of Russian church music and was the work of many specialists and supporters of church music.

Troparion (*tropar'*), pl. troparia (*tropari*): a genre of Byzantine and Russian hymn-writing; a short hymn of a single stanza in honour of a saint or an event being celebrated.

Yarilin den' (Yarilo's day): an ancient Russian festival (spring or summer) in honour of the Slav god of fertility, Yarilo.

Yekten'ya (Litany): a series of petitions, pronounced by the priest or deacon, to which the choir replies '*Gospodi, pomiluy*' ('Lord, have mercy'), '*Poday, Gospodi*' ('Grant it, O Lord') or '*Tebe Gospodi*' ('To Thee, O Lord'). The following basic kinds of Litany should be distinguished: the Great (*velikaya yekten'ya*) or Litany of Peace (*mirnaya yekten'ya*), which contains approximately ten petitions; the Short Litany (*malaya yekten'ya*), consisting of three petitions; the Augmented Litany (*sugubaya yekten'ya*) where the choir's petition '*Gospodi pomiluy*' is sung three times on each occasion; the Litany of Supplication (*prositel'naya yekten'ya*) which includes the choir's petition '*Poday, Gospodi*'.

Zadostoynik: a hymn in honour of the Mother of God, sung at the Liturgy instead of *Dostoyno yest'* ('It is meet') at the 12 greatest festivals of the Orthodox calendar and several others.

***Znamennaya* notation** (*znamennaya notatsiya*): a lineless ideographic form of notation of church hymns of the Russian Orthodox Church of the ancient period (tenth to fourteenth centuries) and the medieval period (fifteenth to seventeenth centuries), and also of the Old Believers. Palaeo-Byzantine ('Coislin') notation served as the source of *znamennaya* notation. *Znamennaya* notation can be deciphered from the mid-seventeenth century, when marks (*pometi*) indicating the pitch of the signs (*znamyona*) were introduced into it. In the last quarter of the seventeenth century, after the church reforms, *znamennaya* notation, along with other forms of neumatic notation, was gradually ousted by stave square notation. It has been preserved until our time by Old Believers.

***Znamennïy* chant** (*znamennïy rospev*): a basic stylistic form of Russian medieval church monody, which arose in Rus' in the first centuries of her Christianity and has been maintained in the practice of the Orthodox Church right up until our day. The melody of *znamennïy* chant conforms to the system of *osmoglasiye*, and is distinguished by the smoothness and balance of its wave-like contours. Several different types developed over the course of history can be discerned: *stolpovoy*, *bol'shoy* (great) and *malïy* (little). In the sixteenth and seventeenth centuries within the context of *znamennïy* chant there appear 'authors'' chants (for instance, by Fyodor Krest'yanin or Ivan Lukoshko), and 'local' chants (*Troitskiye* (Trinity), *Solovetskiye* (from the Solovetsky monastery), etc.). During the final quarter of the seventeenth century *znamennïy* chant, along with other varieties of church monody (see *grecheskiy, bolgarskiy, demestvennïy, kiyevskiy* and *putevoy* chants), within the bosom of the official church (see Synodal Church) began to be notated using stave square notation (q.v.); using *znamennaya notatsiya, znamennïy* chant has been preserved until our time by the Old Believers. Hymns in *znamennïy* chant comprised the main corpus in the church music of the Synodal Church and lie at the root of its repertoire.

Music Examples

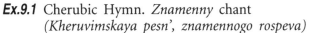

Ex.9.1 Cherubic Hymn. *Znamenny* chant
(Kheruvimskaya pesn', znamennogo rospeva)

Alliluiya, alliluiya, alliluiya, alliluiya, alliluiya, alliluiya, alliluiya.

Ex.9.2 'Open to us the doors of compassion'
('*Miloserdiya dveri otverzi nam*')

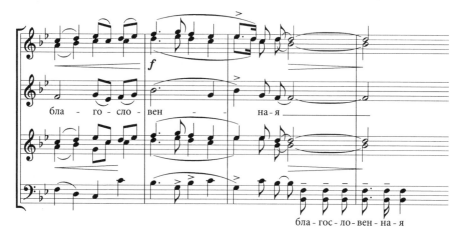

Open to us the doors of compassion, O blessed [Mother of God]

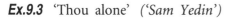

Ex.9.3 'Thou alone' ('Sam Yedin')

Thou alone art immortal,
Thoy alone art immortal, who hast created and fashioned man.

Ex.9.4 'The Lord is God' and Troparia for Matins of Great Saturday
('*Bog Gospod' i tropari v Velikuyu Subbotu na utreni*)

When thou, O immortal life, didst go down to death,
Then didst thou slay hell, slay hell

Ex.12.1 Seventeenth-century *strochnoye* chant
(Strochnoye penie XVII veka)

We hanged our harps upon the willows in the midst thereof. Alliluiya.

Ex.12.2 The Christians *(Khristiane)*

Картина богослужения в катакомбах. Священнослужитель запевает псалом, присутствующие повторяют за ним концы фраз.

A scene of worship in the catacombs. The clergyman sings the opening of a psalm, and those present repeat the ends of phrases after him.

I praise thee, Lord, with my whole heart.
With my whole heart I proclaim all thy wonders, all thy wonders.
I rejoice in thee, I sing of thy name, Most High.
I sing of thy name, Most High.

Ex.12.3 The Play of the Furnace *(Peshchnoye deystvo)*

Blessed be the Lord God of our fathers,
And may your name be praised and glorified forever

Ex.12.4 The first song of Klara *(Pervïy romans Klarï)*

From Goethe

С то - бо - ю мысль мо - я, го - рят - ли вол - ны мо - ря

в ог - не лу - чей,

I shall keep thinking about you,
even if the waves of the sea are aflame with rays of fire

Ex.12.5 Melodeclamation 'The Sphinx'
(*Melodeklamatsiya 'Sfinks'*)

Poem in Prose by Turgenev

[Reciter:] Stay, but I know those features... in them there is nothing Egyptian. White, low brow, prominent cheek-bones, nose short and straight, white teeth, curly beard, not large eyes, the head of hair with a parting...

Ex.13.1 'Bless the Lord, O my soul'. Greek chant
('Blagoslovi, dushe moya, Gospoda'. Grecheskogo rospeva)

Ex.13.1a

Bless the Lord, O my soul. Blessed art Thou, O Lord.
O Lord my God, Thou art very [great].

Ex.13.1b

Glory, glory to Thee, O Lord, who hast made all things,
who hast made all things!

Ex.13.2 'Let us praise the Virgin Mary'.
Dogmatikon in the first tone. *Znamenny* chant
(*'Vsemirnuyu slavu'. Dogmatik 1-go glasa. Znamennïy rospev*)

[Let us praise the Virgin Mary] – glory of all the world,
who begotten of man hast borne the Lord, the doorway to heaven we hymn,
O Virgin Mary, who, adornment of the faithful, is sung by the angelic hosts;

Ex.13.3 'From my youth'. Gradual antiphon in the fourth tone
('*Ot yunosti moyeya*'. *Stepennïy antifon 4-go glasa*)

From my youth up many passions have warred against me;

Ex.16.1 The Reading by a Clerk to the People of Moscow of the Epistle
from Patriarch Hermogen to the Tushino Traitors in 1609
(*Chteniye d'yakom lyudu moskovskomu poslaniya
patriarkha Germogena k tushinskim izmennikam v 1609 godu*)

Tenor solo: Listen, men!
Bass solo: I appeal to you, Orthodox Christians, for you have departed
from God, you have forgotten the precepts of our faith, you have transgressed
against the kissing of the cross and your vow to stand up for the Most Holy
Mother of God and the Muscovite state until death.

Ex.16.2 Verse about Russian Church Music
(Stikh o tserkovnom russkom penii)

The streams of song gathered together,
the streams of song, from distant lands

Ex.16.3 A Bazaar in Ancient Times in Rus'
(Torzhishche v starinu na Rusi)

The heights, the heights of heaven, the depths, the depths of Ocean-sea!

Ex.17.1 Requiem for Fallen Brothers. 'Requiem aeternam'
(Bratskoye pominovenie. 'Requiem aeternam')

Comrades! In memory of our brothers and dear ones,
heroes of the Great Union, fallen on the field of holy war,

Ex.18.1 The good thief
(Razboynika blagorazumnago)

O Lord, this very day hast thou vouchsafed the good thief paradise.
By the wood of the cross do thou enlighten me also and save me.

Ex.18.2 'I will pour out my petition'
('*Molitvu proliyu ko Gospodu*')

I will pour out my petition unto the Lord, and unto him will
I confide my grief. For my soul is filled with sorrow,
and my life hath drawn nigh unto Hell.

Ex.20.1 Scenes from Peasant Merrymaking in Rus'
(Kartinï narodnïkh prazdnovaniy na Rusi)

Not rushing   In the distance shepherds play their horns

Г л а ш а т а й: Подошел Егорьев день, пастух вышел за плетень.

Кто-то из волочебников: Э!.. Да ноне Юрьев день... Слышь - пастухи... Подыграй, что ли!..

Вдали время от времени раздается
мычание коров, блеяние овец.

mp   Easter carollers play

Г л а ш а т а й: Чу! рожок его поет, в поле стадо он зовет...

На широкую долинку   гонят   вербою скотинку,

Ex.20.2 To foreign brethren
(K zarubezhnïm brat'yam)

Brethren of all lands!

Brethren! The land of Russia, the granary of Europe, before abundant and so rich, is overtaken by a dreadful foe: King Hunger, Hunger!

отощалую от голода, обнищалую от холода. Гонят бабы да девчата,

гонят малые ребята, гонят стары старики, деревенски мужики.

Herald: As St George's day approached, the shepherd went beyond the confines of his own fence.

One of the Easter Carollers: Hey! Today's St George's day...

Listen - shepherds. Play!

Cows mooing and sheep bleating can be heard in the distance from time to time.

Herald: Hark! His horn sings, he's calling the flock into the field...

They're chasing the livestock with willows into the wide valley, emaciated with hunger, impoverished by the cold. They're being chased by women and girls, chased by little children, chased by old men, men from the country.

Index of Names

medievalist-musicologist, composer; professor at the Moscow Conservatoire, teacher at the Synodal School (1895—1910) and member of the Supervisory Council (1899—1916) 23, 37, 49, 103, 129, 139

Michelangelo, Buonarotti (1475—1564) – sculptor, painter, architect, poet 36

Mikhail – see *Kastal'sky, Mikhail Ivanovich*

Minin, Kuz'ma Minich (?—1616) – one of the organizers of a popular militia at the time of the Polish-Lithuanian intervention in the early 17th century 183

Mironositsky, Porfiry Petrovich (1867—after 1934) – church choirmaster and class singing teacher in St Petersburg; editor of the journal *Narodnoye obrazovaniye* (The Education of the People), member of the Education Committee attached to the Holy Synod 126

Monet, Claude (1840—1926) – painter 132

Mott, John Raleigh (1865—1955) – American religious and community figure, winner of the Nobel Prize (1946) 149, 170, 214

Mozart, Wolfgang Amadeus (1756—1791) – composer 32, 47, 50, 128, 132, 165

Musorgsky, Modest Petrovich (1839—1881) – composer 60, 70, 95, 97, 152, 169, 206, 229

Muzïchesku (Muzïchenko), Gavriil Vakulovich (1847—1903) – composer, choral conductor 131

Myaskovsky, Nikolay Yakovlevich (1881—1950) – composer, music critic; professor at the Moscow Conservatoire 227

Napravnik, Eduard Frantsevich (1839—1916) – conductor at the Mariinsky Theatre (from 1863), composer 144

Natalia (daughter of A.D. Kastal'sky) – see *Kastal'skaya, Nataliya Aleksandrovna*

Natalia (wife of A.D. Kastal'sky) – see *Kastal'skaya, Nataliya Lavrent'yevna*

Nechayev, Pyotr Ivanovich (1842—1905) – religious writer, editor of the St Petersburg newspaper *Sovremennost'* (The Present Day); inspector, member of the Education Committee attached to the Holy Synod 53

Nekrasov, Nikolay Aleksandrovich (1821—1877/78) – poet 210

Nesterov, Mikhail Vasil'yevich (1862—1942) – painter 36

Nezhdanova, Antonina Vasil'yevna (1873—1950) – singer (soprano), soloist at the Bol'shoy Theatre 228

Nicholas I (1796—1855) – Russian emperor (from 1825) 20, 37

Nicholas II (1868—1918) – Russian emperor (from 1894—1917); Russian saint 28, 68, 151, 201

Nikisch, Arthur (1855—1922) – conductor

Nikolay or Nikolya – see *Kastal'sky, Nikolay Dmitriyevich*

Nikolay Fyodorovich – see *Findeyzen, Nikolay Fyodorovich*

Nikolov, Anastas Nikolayevich (1876—1924) – church choirmaster in St Petersburg and Sofia; studied at the Synodal School 153-154

Nikol'sky, Aleksandr Vasil'yevich (1874—1943) – composer, music critic, choral figure; professor at the Moscow Conservatoire (1928—1943), teacher at the Synodal School (1915—1918), member of the Supervisory Council (1914—1918) 23, 53, 56, 89-92, 124, 187, 191, 219

Nikon (Minov) (1605-1681) – Russian Patriarch from 1652 to 1658

Noskov, Dmitry Grigor'yevich (born 1880s) – graduated from the Court Kapella (1904), composer of sacred works, assistant teacher of church music at the Court Kapella (1906—1913) 135

Obolensky, Nikolay Nikolayevich (1861—1933) – prince, senator, commander of the Moscow Military District (1917) 182

choirmaster in Moscow, author of
methodological textbooks on choral
singing 187

Zatayevich, Aleksandr Viktorovich
(1869—1936) – music ethnographer;
adviser on special projects in the
office of the Governor-General of
Warsaw, music reviewer of the
newspaper *Varshavskiy dnevnik*
(Warsaw Diary) (1904—1915) 145,

154, 157, 169, 215-218, 226
Ziloti – see *Siloti, Aleksandr Il'ich*
Zimin, Sergey Ivanovich (1875—1942)
– patron, founder and owner of an
opera theatre in Moscow (1904—
1924) 106, 160, 171, 173, 218
Zinov'yev, Vasily Nikolayevich (1872—
1925) – priest, choirmaster of the
archbishop's choir in Yaroslavl'
(1906—1917); composer of sacred
music and teacher of singing 213